Photographing the Unseen World

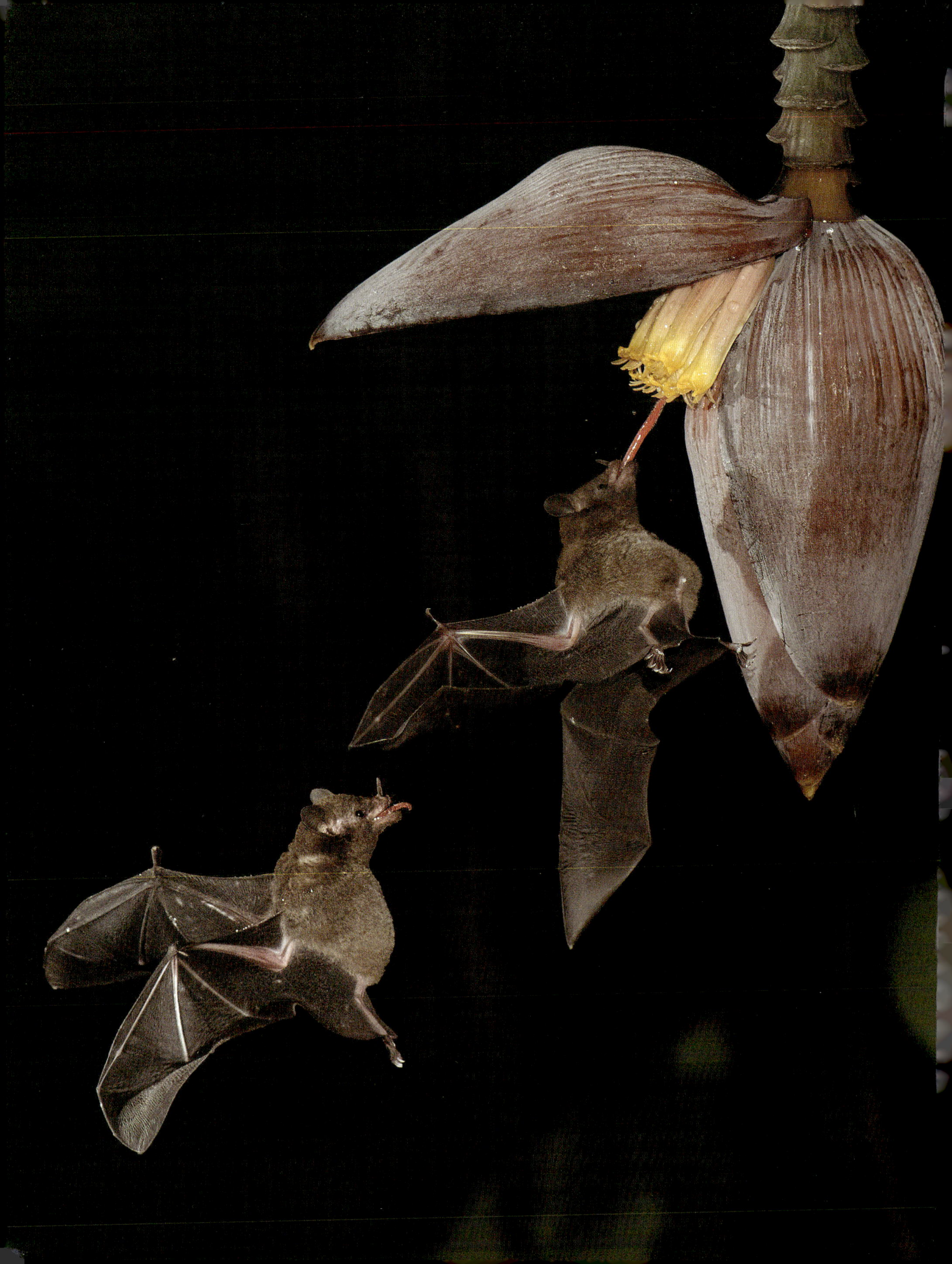

Photographing the Unseen World

Art and Techniques

Adrian Davies

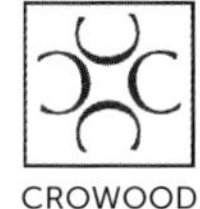

CROWOOD

First published in 2020 by
The Crowood Press Ltd
Ramsbury, Marlborough
Wiltshire SN8 2HR

enquiries@crowood.com
www.crowood.com

British Library Cataloguing-in-Publication Data
A catalogue record for this book is available from the British Library.

ISBN 978 1 78500 703 3

.

Acknowledgements
A book like this, covering a wide range of subject matter would not have been possible without the help of numerous friends and colleagues, for help, advice and occasional modelling! Andrea Blum, Bjorn Rorslett, and various members of the ultravioletphotography.com forum; Stephen Bleksley; Paul Buff Inc.; Matt Cass; Lucie Cash, Royal Mail; Paul Colley; Dr Jonathan Crowther; Hannah Davies (and 'Jack'); Janice Davies; Adam Davies, Maidenhead Aquatics; Robin Davies; Bryony Davies; Miles Herbert, Captive Light Photography; Kat Jack; Yealand Kalfayan; Nicola Musgrave BSc (Hons) MSc., Eurofins Forensic Services; Phred Petersen, RMIT University; Paul Reynolds, Sigma Imaging (UK); Martin Sanders; Hugh Turvey Hon FRPS, FRSA; Paul Wilson; Michael Robbs

Graphic design and typesetting by Peggy & Co. Design
Printed and bound in India by Replika Press Pvt Ltd

CONTENTS

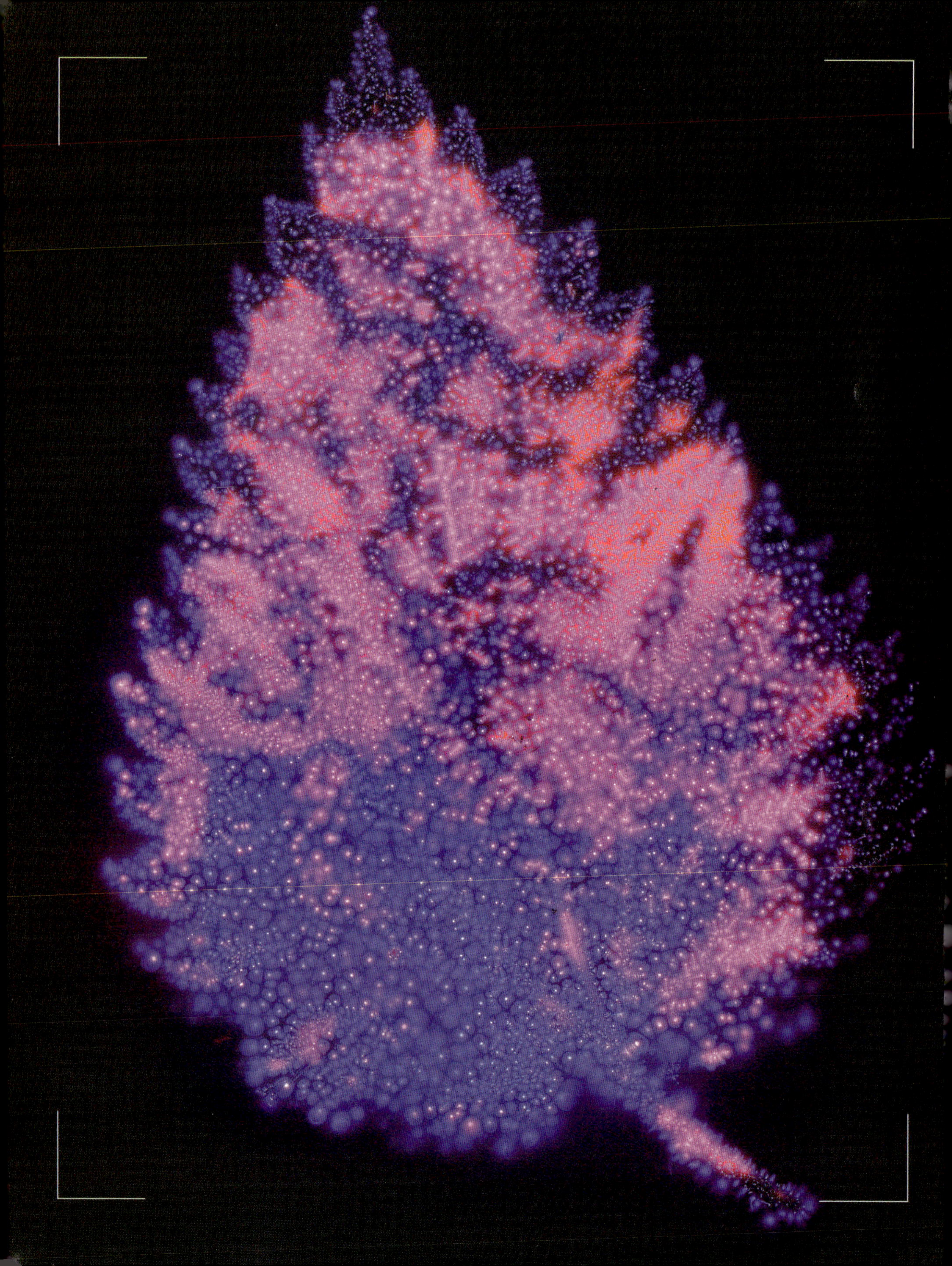

Chapter 1

Introduction

From its earliest beginnings, photography has been used to help visualize the unseen – events that are either too slow or too fast for the human eye to perceive, to record subjects that are visible only in areas of the spectrum outside the human range of sensitivity, or record detail that is too small for the human eye to see. There are, and have been, many imaging techniques for visualizing the invisible, including X-ray and gamma-ray imaging, various medical scanning techniques such as MRI and CAT scans, Kirlian photography, schlieren photography, electron and light microscopy, thermal imaging and various forms of satellite imaging, though most of these techniques are unavailable to most readers, being either too dangerous, too expensive or requiring unattainable pieces of equipment.

This book is concerned with those techniques that anyone with a good knowledge of photography can achieve with minimal outlay. It will look at ultraviolet (UV) and infrared (IR) photography, high speed and time-lapse photography, close-up, macro and photography with the aid of a microscope, and photography using polarized light and other related techniques. Some of the applications will utilize two or more of the techniques in combination, and do not fit into neat categories.

The very act of viewing a subject through a magnifying glass can reveal previously unseen details within a subject, and the higher the power of the magnifying glass, or microscope, the more detail will be revealed. In particular, 3D electron microscopy not only reveals otherwise invisible detail, but also produces, at times, stunningly beautiful images. Electron microscopes are very expensive, and well outside the scope of this book, but a brief discussion of light microscopy will be given in Chapter 8.

X-ray images of everyday subjects often reveal beautiful and startling details, such as the carnivorous pitcher plants shown here, alongside UV images of the same plant.

Schlieren photography is another technique used by scientists, and restricted to laboratory use, but capable of revealing heat and pressure patterns around suitable subjects such as the heat emitted from the soldering iron shown here. The cover image for John Martin's *Solid Air* album, from 1973, was a schlieren image of the heat emitted from a hand.

Kirlian photography (see Fig. 1.1) is another visualization technique, used to capture the phenomenon of electrical coronal discharges (often referred to as the aura around a subject). It is named after Semyon Kirlian, who, in 1939, accidentally discovered that if an object is placed on a photographic plate that is connected to a high-voltage source, it produces an image. It became popular in the 1980s, and various claims for the technique were made with regard to it being able to predict illness or other issues, or reveal the natural aura around a subject. There is little evidence for these claims, and the technique has largely fallen out of use.

◀ **Fig. 1.1**
Kirlian image of stinging nettle (*Urtica dioica*) leaf. The leaf was placed on a sheet of 5 × 4" transparency film in a dark room, which itself was placed on a metal sheet. A high voltage electrical current was passed through the metal sheet, resulting in a Kirlian image.
Home made Kirlian imaging device. 5" × 4" Fujichrome film. Exposure approx. 30 seconds.

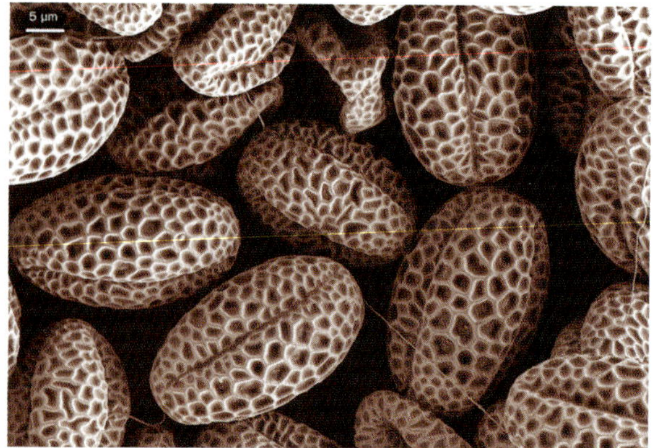

▲ **Fig. 1.2**
Image of lilac *(Syringa sp.)* pollen at a magnification of ×3,000, using a scanning electron microscope.
  Authors: Yapryntsev, A.D; Baranchikov, A.E; Ivanov, V.K. This file is licensed under the Creative Commons Attribution 4.0 International license.

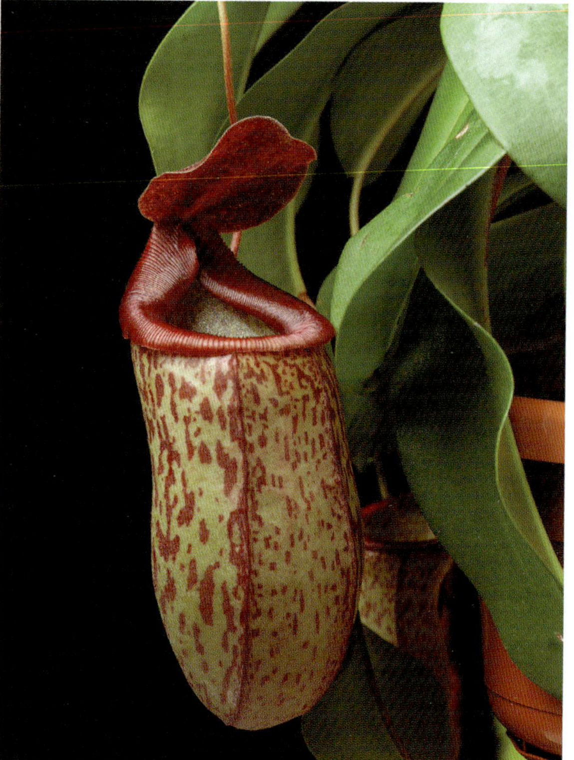

▲ **Fig. 1.3**
Several different imaging techniques were used to illustrate different aspects of a carnivorous plant (*Nepenthes* spp.), resulting in very different images and differing information about the subject in Figs 1.3 to 1.6.Conventional image of *Nepenthes spathulata* × *(copelandii* × *truncata)* shot with visible light.

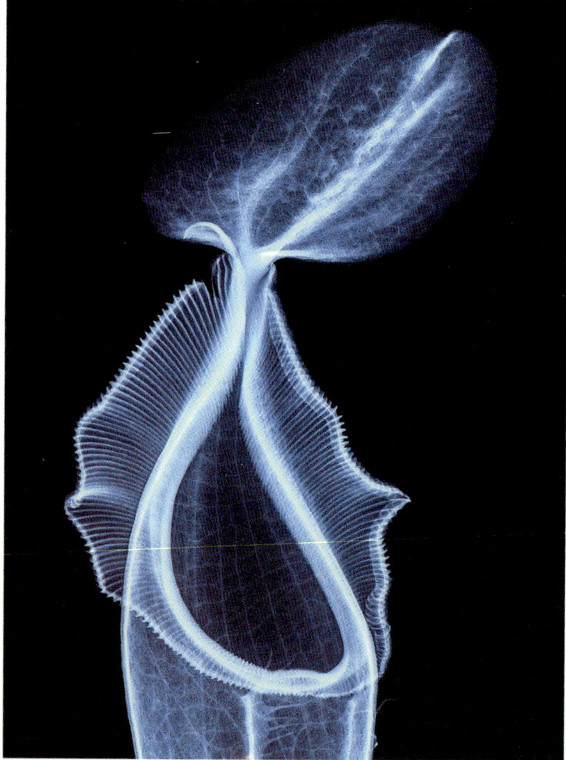

▲ **Fig. 1.4**
X-ray image of carnivorous pitcher plant (*Nepenthes ventricosa* × *talangensis*) yielding a truly beautiful image, showing remarkable clarity and detail. Unfortunately, the equipment required is not available to most people.
  Image copyright Hugh Turvey, Hon FRPS, FRSA.

UV photography, in particular, is nowadays helping us get an idea of how other animals see the world. As early as 1864, Hermann Vogel, a German chemist, photographed a woman using a photographic plate that at that time was only sensitive to UV and blue light, using a simple, uncoated lens that transmitted good quantities of UV. The processed image showed several black spots on the woman's face, invisible in normal daylight. A few days later the woman was diagnosed with smallpox. The significance of this UV reflectance image was not realized for another forty years or so.

Today, UV photography is used by forensic scientists for detecting trace evidence, by art historians examining works of art, and by botanists and entomologists investigating the hidden

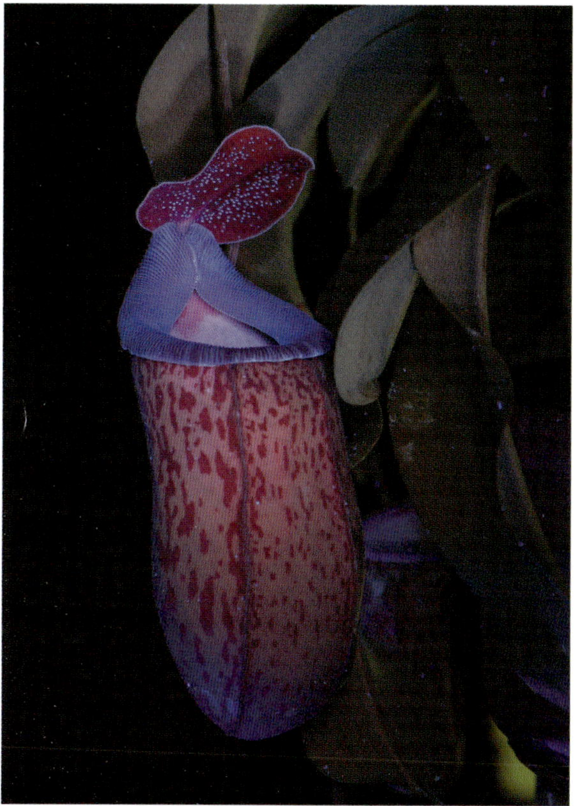

▲ **Fig. 1.5**
UV fluorescence image shot with UV light, showing fluorescent rim (peristome) possibly acting as an attractant to prey.

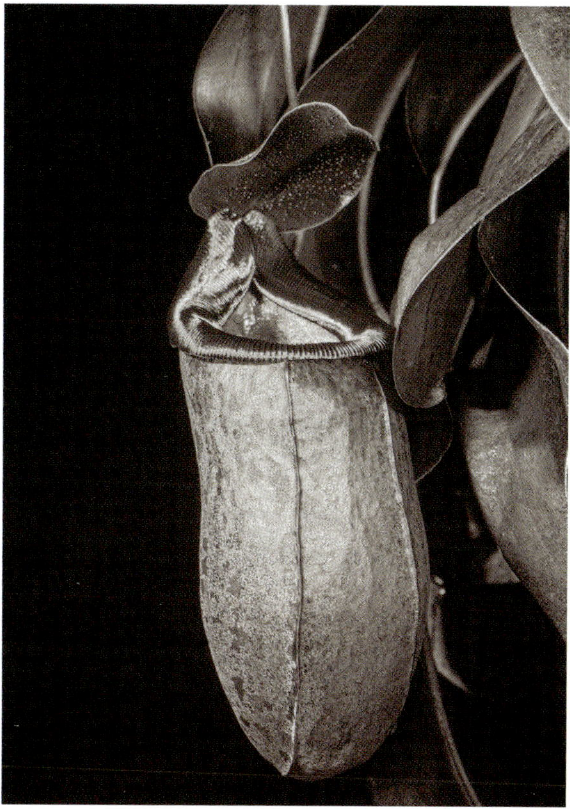

▲ **Fig. 1.6**
UV reflectance image of pitcher showing how visible light patterns disappear, and how nectar absorbs UV to become more apparent to potential prey.

patterns on flowers, invisible to us, but visible to insect pollinators.

IR photography, also, has a long photographic history, for penetrating haze in landscapes, camouflage detection, visualizing subcutaneous veins, revealing alterations to paintings, and helping diagnose plant diseases for example. It has enjoyed a great resurgence in recent years, with the ease of getting cameras converted to record IR.

▶ **Fig. 1.7**
Schlieren image of otherwise invisible heat waves rising from a soldering iron. Schlieren photography involves focusing a collimated beam of light to a point. If a knife edge is positioned precisely at that point, then the slightest disturbance in the medium will divert the rays of light to produce changes in brightness. It is used infrequently nowadays but was used to show changes in fluid density and refractive index of a substance in glass for example.
Author: Ian Smith. This file is licensed under the Creative Commons Attribution 3.0 Unported license.

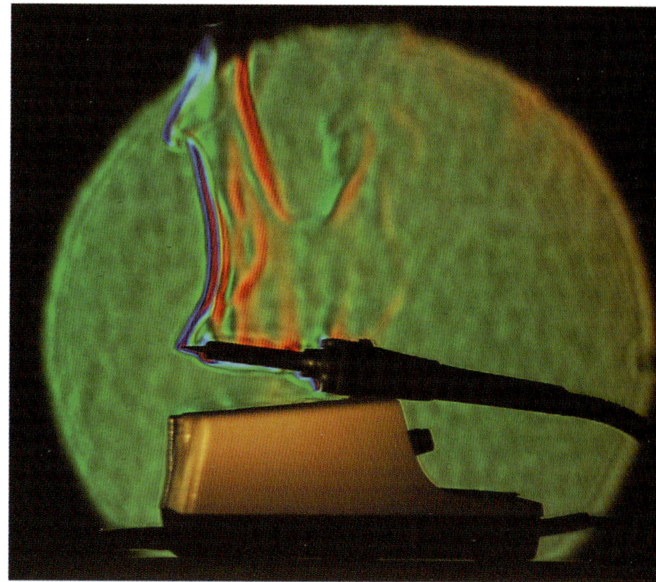

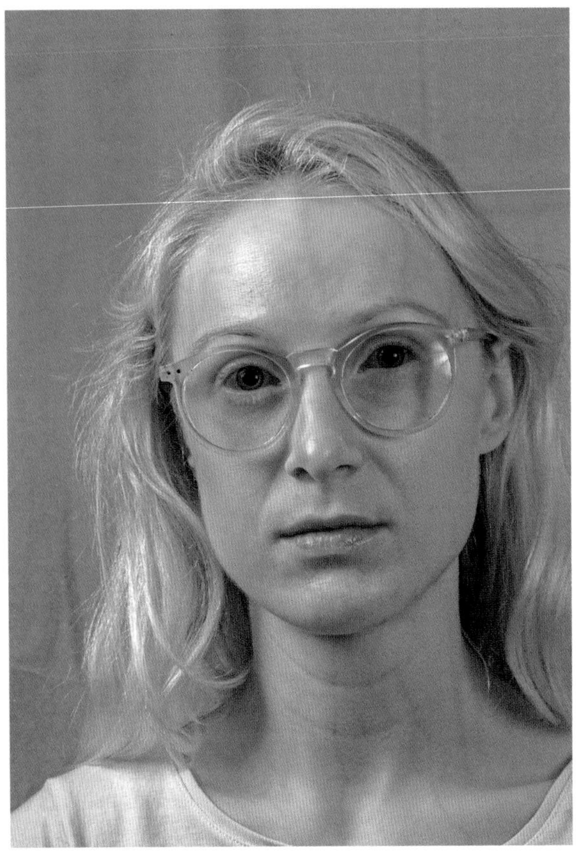

⬥ Fig. 1.8
Infrared (IR) image (850nm) of female model wearing plastic tinted sunglasses. The plastic becomes transparent in IR. Note too the veins in the neck and forehead revealed by the IR.

In 1872, the English photographer Eadweard Muybridge undertook photographic studies of animals in motion. These were carried out primarily for a commission from the ex-governor of California, Leland Stanford, who had a wager with a friend that horses had all four legs off the ground at the same time when running and trotting. By using from twelve to twenty-four cameras triggered with tripwires, Muybridge produced some of the first studies of animals in motion, and also helped prove that horses did indeed have all four legs off the ground at the same time, though not in the rocking horse attitude so often depicted in contemporary paintings! Muybridge rigged up a primitive projection system, and showed the images in quick succession, an early form of animation, giving the impression of movement. He produced a book entitled *Animal Locomotion* in 1887 that to this day remains one of the most comprehensive studies of animal motion of its type.

Taking this type of photography one stage further is time-lapse imaging, where a subject is photographed over a long period of hours, months or even years, and the result condensed into a short time to show precisely how plants grow or glaciers move down a hill for example.

One of the great pioneers of high speed photography was Harold E. Edgerton, who was a graduate student at the Massachusetts Institute of Technology in the 1930s. He was working on the reaction of electric motors to various loads. He was experimenting with arc rectifiers that, when close enough to the rotating motor, created a stroboscopic effect. Edgerton went on to develop the stroboscopic light and short duration electronic flashgun. He produced some, now iconic, high speed and stroboscopic images of milk splashes, sporting events such as golf swings, and light bulbs being smashed by bullets. In the 1950s he was hired by the US government to photograph atomic explosions, a feat that required a shutter speed of one-hundred-millionth of a second and requiring him to solve numerous technical difficulties.

The high-speed image of a milk drop splash shown in Fig. 1.10 was shot as an homage to Edgerton's famous image of a milk drop splash, shot after a huge amount of research in 1936, with relatively primitive equipment, and using single sheets of film, with a flash exposure 1/10,000th second.

Natural history photography has always made great use of high-speed flash, in particular, to photograph birds in flight. The British photographer Eric Hosking, working in the 1940s and 1950s produced some extraordinary images of owls, nightjars and other species in the field, using primitive and potentially highly dangerous electronic flash equipment.

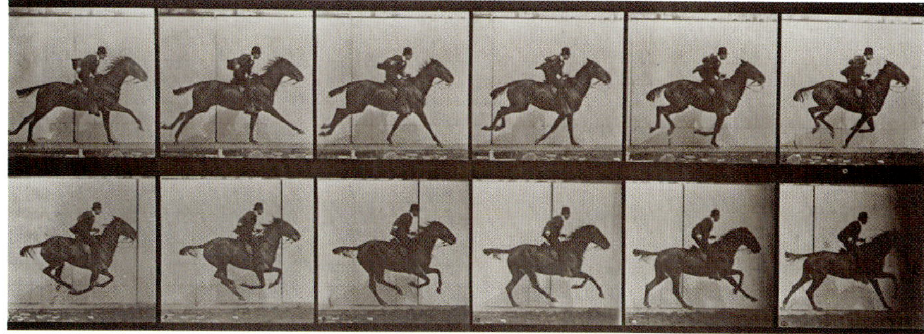

▶ **Fig. 1.9**
Sequence of horse galloping (*Daisy*). Eadweard Muybridge, c. 1880. Twelve cameras were triggered by trip wires to show the movement of the horse. This, and images like it, proved for the first time that horses had all four legs off the ground at the same time.
Source: Creative Commons.

One of the greatest challenges for nature photographers was the photography of smaller subjects such as insects in flight, which was taken up by Stephen Dalton in the 1980s. He developed a powerful short-duration electronic flash system together with a highly sensitive light-beam triggering system and high-speed camera shutter to photograph insects in free flight for the first time. He went on to take high-speed photographs of birds, amphibians, bats and other animals in extraordinary detail.

Today, it is possible to buy such pieces of equipment off the shelf, and its use is limited only by one's imagination.

Many of the techniques described in this book can be carried out with conventional cameras, lenses and flashguns, generally only requiring the ability to alter shutter speed and aperture manually. You will often be using the camera in manual mode, setting shutter speed and aperture rather than using the camera's automatic settings. However, most of the techniques are not necessarily straightforward, and much of the work will require ingenuity, improvisation, re-purposing of equipment, and a good working knowledge of photographic techniques and equipment to solve specific problems. In many cases, logistics becomes the most important part of the image-making process, getting the right subject in front of the camera at the right time.

It is very important to consider the purpose of the images. Are you a scientist wanting to gather data from the images, in that case you will probably need to shoot comparative control images, or

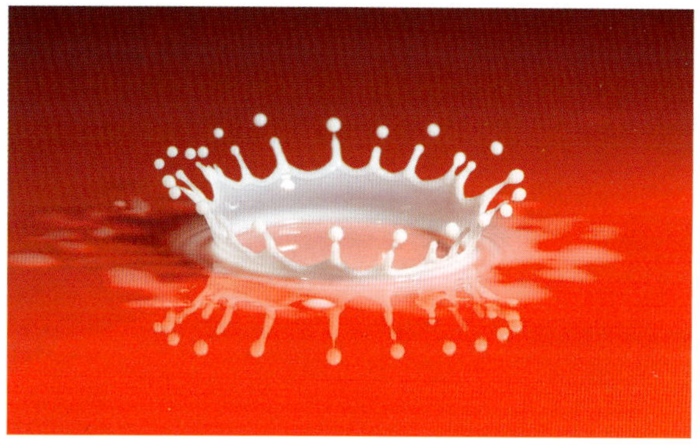

▲ **Fig. 1.10**
High-speed image of a milk drop striking a surface. This was shot in 2019, using readily available cameras and flashguns. Harold Edgerton's famous version was shot on a camera, taking single sheets of film and potentially lethal short-duration flash equipment.

include a scale for example, or are you primarily a photographer looking for new, challenging subjects with a pictorial emphasis? Some of the techniques described in the book, such as UV reflectance photography, are little used today, and one of the aims of the book is to re-kindle an interest in these areas. There is great scope for citizen scientists to discover new subjects and techniques during their photographic journey.

Photography is one of the few subjects where science and art come together to produce images, and some of the most beautiful and striking photographic images are those shot with some of the techniques in this book.

Note: Throughout the book, the terms IR and UV light will be used, even though it is strictly more technically correct to use the terms UV and IR radiation.

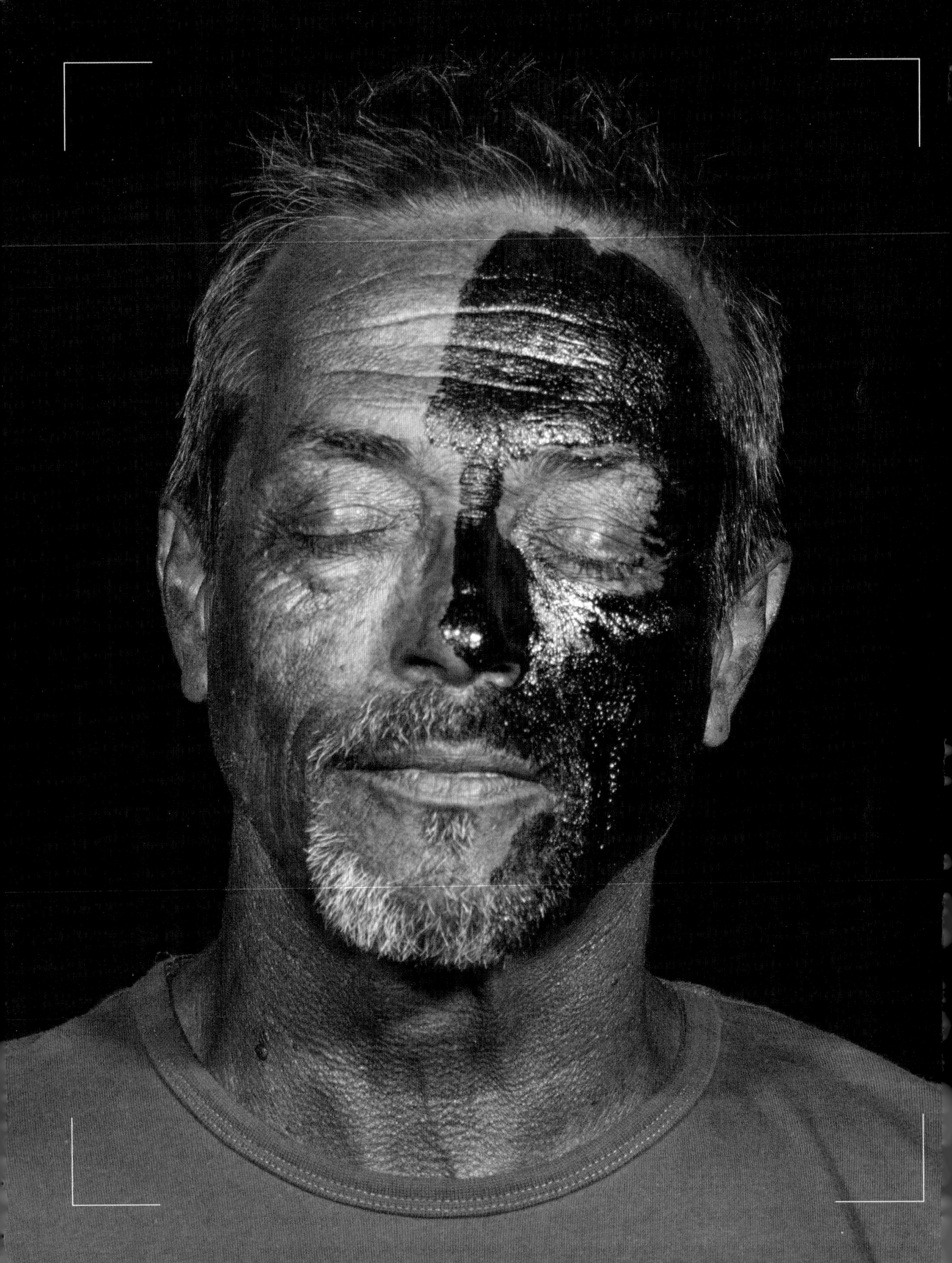

Chapter 2

The Electromagnetic Spectrum, Camera Conversions and Filters

In order to undertake UV and/or IR photography, you will need a digital camera that has been converted to make it record UV and/or IR wavelengths. It is sometimes possible to shoot UV and IR with unmodified cameras and appropriate filters, which we will discuss later. In order to fully understand the principles of UV and IR invisible light photography, and be able to make informed decisions as to what type of camera conversion you will need for your specific needs, it is useful to have a good working knowledge of the electromagnetic spectrum, and how the light that we see (visible light) is just one relatively small region of a very large spectrum of electromagnetic wavelengths that can be recorded by different types of imaging system. Different specialist filters and lenses will also be required, and these are discussed at the end of the chapter.

THE ELECTROMAGNETIC SPECTRUM

When a beam of sunlight passes through a prism it is split into its component parts. We see the classic rainbow of colours, from red through yellow and green to blue and violet. Many of us will have learned a mnemonic in school to help remember the order of colours e.g. Richard Of York Gave Battle In Vain (red, orange, yellow, green, blue, indigo, violet). This spectrum is continuous, with the colours gradually merging into each other rather than fitting into neat discreet boxes. It is often quoted that the colour (or hue) green, for example has a wavelength of 550 nanometres (nm), but this is not a precise figure, and green wavelengths will in fact cover a range of wavelengths.

Outside this visible (to the human eye) spectrum, however, are a whole host of other forms of electro-magnetic radiation. Beyond the red wavelengths are IR and heat (an old-style tungsten light bulb emits around 10 per cent visible light, and 90 per cent IR and heat, obviously highly inefficient as a light source), followed by increasingly long wavelength radio waves. At the other end of the spectrum, beyond the violet wavelengths, are UV, divided into three distinct regions (UVA from 400–320nm, UVB from 320–290nm, and UVC 290–100nm), followed by X-rays and gamma rays, both used in medical diagnostic imaging for example. In general, shorter wavelengths have higher energy than longer wavelengths, making them potentially dangerous in certain circumstances.

UVC is a very damaging type of UV but is filtered out by the ozone layer in the atmosphere. It is used as a biocide, for killing off microbes in various environments such as swimming pools and food processing plants.

UVB is highly dangerous but cannot penetrate superficial skin layers. It is responsible for delayed tanning and burning, enhances skin ageing and promotes the development of skin cancers such as melanomas.

◀ **Fig. 2.1**
UV reflected light portrait showing the application of sunscreen to one half of the face. Note how some areas have been missed and may become vulnerable to sun damage.
Nikon D300 full spectrum converted camera with 105mm El-NIKKOR lens and Baader U filter. Two full-spectrum converted Metz 45 CT1 flashguns.

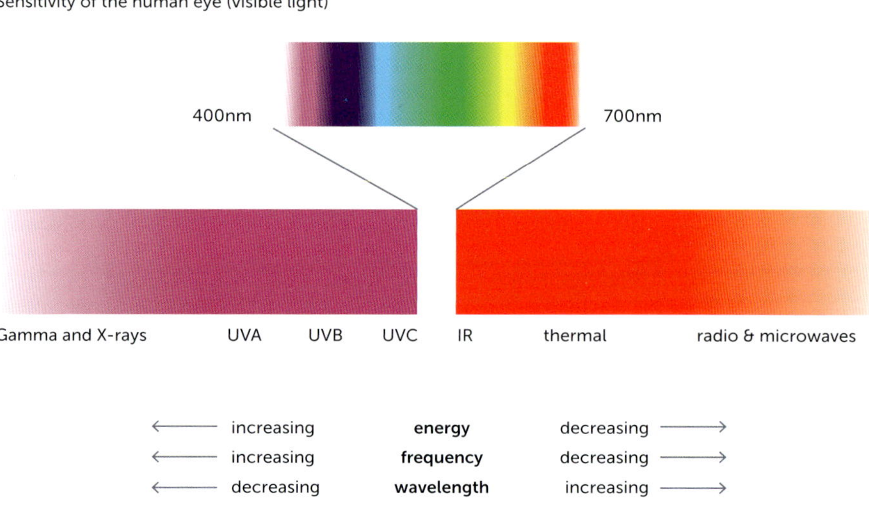

▶ **Fig. 2.2**
The electromagnetic spectrum, showing visible light, and positions of UV and IR wavelengths, arranged according to frequency, energy and wavelength.

UVA is responsible for the immediate tanning of the skin, contributing also to skin ageing and wrinkles.

UV of course causes sun tanning and sunburn, and it is becoming increasingly apparent that we should protect our skin with the correct application of sunscreen. There is also some evidence that IR radiation can cause skin damage, and several sunscreens are now available to protect against that as well. Photography and video are being used increasingly by manufacturers of sunscreens to show the effect of applying sunscreen incorrectly (*see* Fig. 2.1).

It is worth noting at this stage that many insects, birds and other animals can see UV wavelengths, and a few animals can see IR, and even detect heat patterns, usually from their prey.

The various areas of the electromagnetic spectrum have specific wavelengths, the length of which is described in metres or fractions of a metre. The visible light that the human eye can see ranges from around 400 nanometres (nm) for violet, to around 700 nm (red). Green is usually described as being in the region of 550nm. One nanometre is equivalent to one billionth of a metre ($10-9$ m). Radio waves can stretch to 1500 metres in length and beyond, while X-rays extend down to 0.01 to 10 nm for example, so the range of scale of the electromagnetic spectrum is vast.

THERMAL IMAGING

Heat is a major part of the electromagnetic spectrum beyond the IR, and specialist thermal cameras are available for recording the heat emitted by a subject. Converted digital cameras are not capable of recording heat. Thermal imaging cameras have a range of industrial uses, by the electrical utilities industry for example, when investigating early fire detection, as well as by fire fighters looking for any hot spots remaining after a fire has been extinguished. Various thermal imaging devices are now available, including some that attach to smartphones, such as the FLIR ONE®.

HUMAN VISION

Most humans can see the colours of the spectrum, from violet through to red. The cone shaped colour sensitive cells on the retina, (cones) are sensitive to red, green and blue light, and the human brain simulates all other colours from these three receptors. This is known as trichromatic colour vision. Some people are colour blind meaning that they have less sensitivity to some colours, often blue. Other people, very rarely, are known to have extra receptors in their eyes (giving them tetrachromatic vision) enabling them to see a wider range of colours than others. There is good evidence too that some people who have had cataract operations are able to see subjects illuminated only by UV light of around 365nm.

The human eye cannot see wavelengths longer than around 750nm, due to the light sensitive chemical called rhodopsin, which is the basis for most animal vision. The chemical reaction needed to produce a signal on the retina has an energy requirement that is higher than the energy emitted by radiation longer than 750nm.

It is also the case that we do not all see the same object as the same colour. A few years ago an image of a blue and black dress went viral on social media when many people claimed it to be white and gold rather than blue and black!

Other animal species have different colour vision to us. As might be imagined, the subject is highly complex, and only generalizations are possible here, but honeybees (*Apis mellifera*), for example, have trichromatic colour vision, with sensitivity to UV, blue and green, while butterflies generally have tetrachromatic vision, seeing further into the red end of the spectrum (some species of the swallowtail butterfly can see wavelengths from around 300–700nm), while many birds are also sensitive to UV. Dogs and horses are known to be dichromatic seeing mainly blue and yellow (though some may see UV), while bats are not thought to perceive colour, though some nectar feeding species may have some UV sensitivity.

It is possible, by using a suitable combination of filters, to simulate animal vision, and this will be covered further in Chapter 3.

Some snakes, such as pit vipers, can detect IR and also heat, which enables them to detect warm-blooded prey.

THE PENETRATING ABILITY OF UV AND IR

One of the most interesting facets of UV and IR photography is their ability to penetrate certain substances, to reveal hidden detail beneath the surface. IR, for example, penetrates 1–3mm into the surface of skin revealing invisible blood vessels, and also can show underpainting when photographing artworks. Some plastics are effectively transparent to IR, such as the sunglasses shown in Fig. 1.8. UV can penetrate water, depending on the turbidity and amount of organic substances in the water. These various characteristics are used by forensic and museum photographers, for example.

BASIC COLOUR THEORY

As we have seen, the human trichromatic system uses red, green and blue sensitive cells on the retina to produce all other colours. When dealing with light, when red, green and blue wavelengths

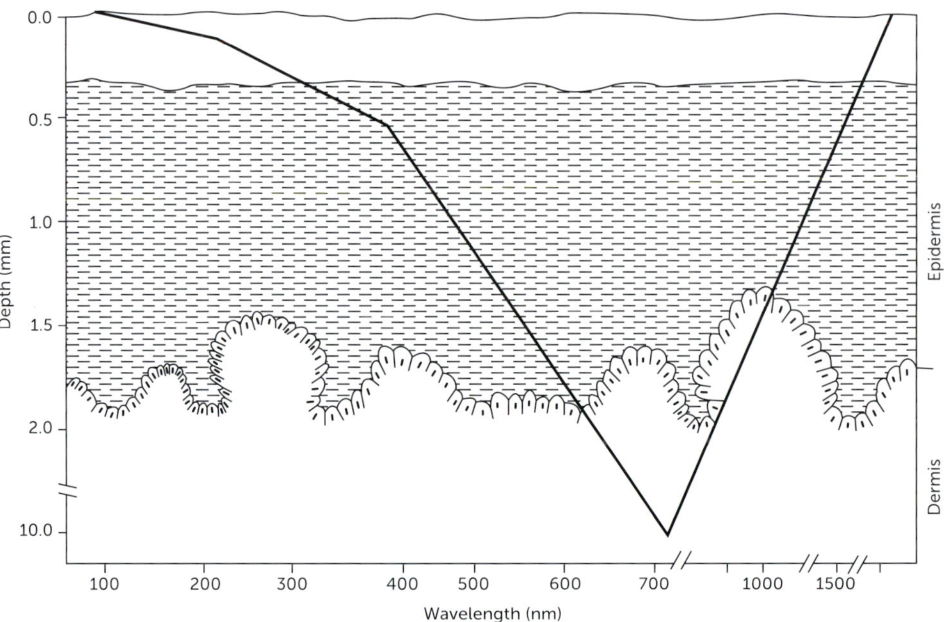

▶ **Fig. 2.3**
Approximate penetration of different wavelengths into human skin.

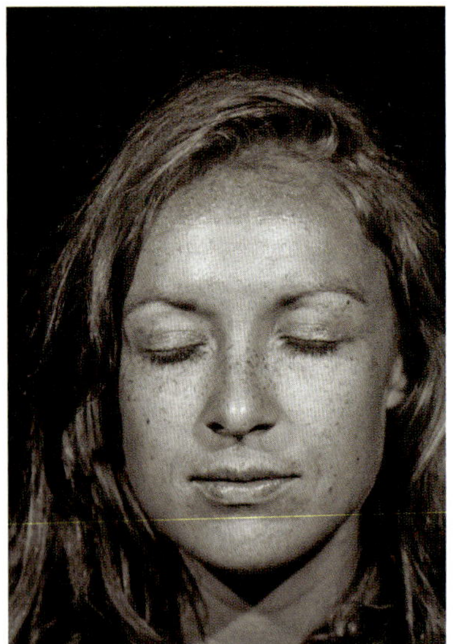
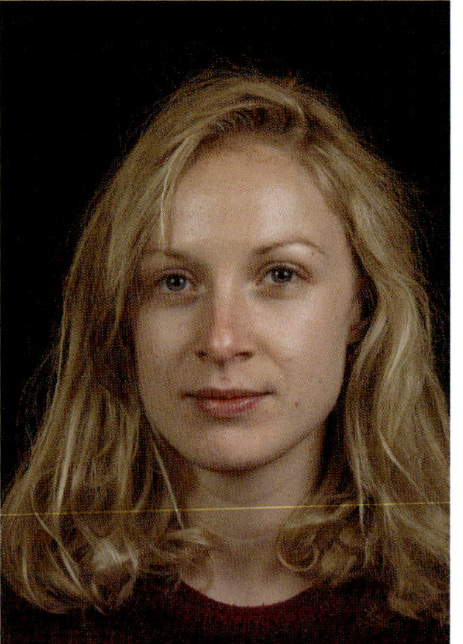
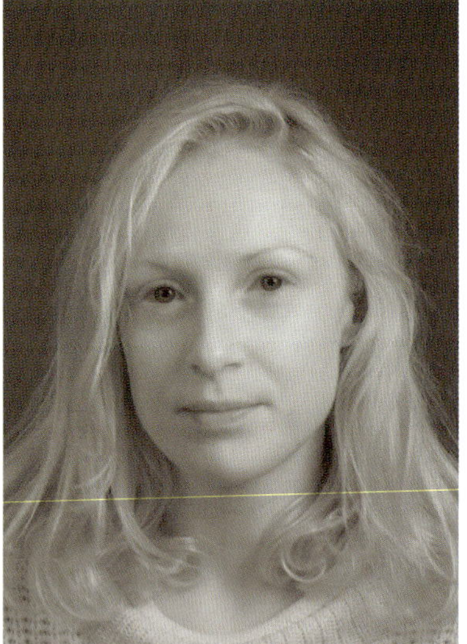

▲ **Fig. 2.4, 2.5, 2.6**
Portrait in reflected UV (365nm), visible and IR (850nm) light, showing different renditions of the skin in different wavelengths.

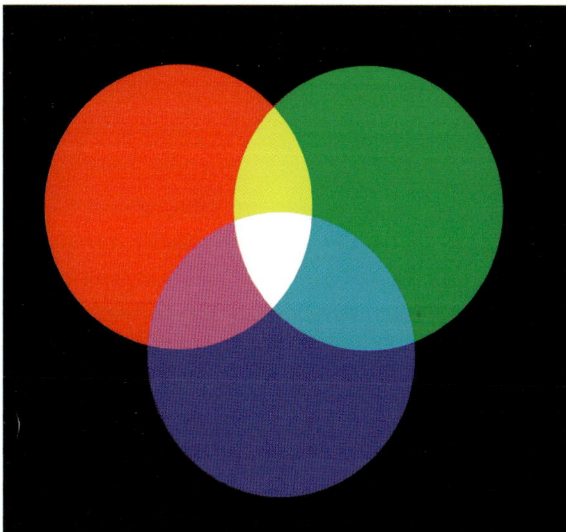

▲ **Fig. 2.7**
When mixed in equal proportions, the three primary colours of light red, green and blue make white light.

DESCRIBING COLOUR

Describing colour is surprisingly difficult – there are many versions of white for example. The generally accepted method is to use the HSL model: Hue, Saturation and Lightness. The hue is the name of the colour (e.g. blue); saturation is the intensity of the hue – a highly saturated or pastel shade, i.e. how much white is mixed with the pure colour; and lightness is the brightness of the colour.

In Adobe® Photoshop and other image-processing programs there is a Color Picker dialog box. Here, it is easy to move the cursor around the screen and see the values for hue, saturation and lightness (Photoshop® uses B for brightness).

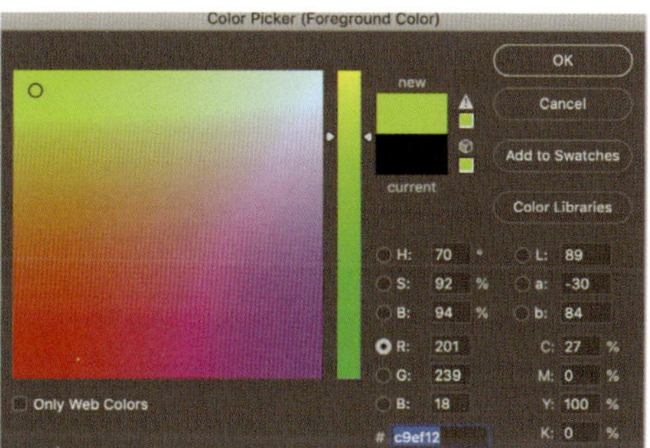

▲ **Fig. 2.8**
The ColorPicker in Photoshop®, showing the various ways the yellow colour can be described.

are combined in equal proportions, white light is created. Varying the relative amounts of red, green and blue produces different colour sensations such as orange or purple. In terms of light, red, green and blue are known as the primary colours (artists use red, blue and yellow as their primary colours when mixing paint).

If the three primary colours of light are projected in equal proportions so that they overlap, white light is created in the centre. Where only two of the primary colours overlap, this is white light minus a primary.

Thus white light = R + G + B

White light minus red = B + G = cyan (cyan is the opposite or complementary colour to red). If an image is too red, for example, you should add cyan to it to neutralize it.

W − R = G + B = Cyan
(cyan and red are complementary)
W − B = R + G = Yellow
(yellow and blue are complementary)
W − G = R + B = Magenta
(green and magenta are complementary)

CAMERA CONVERSIONS

Images are recorded by digital cameras (including those on smartphones) through the use of a light sensitive imaging sensor – usually a CCD (charge-coupled device) or CMOS (complementary metal-oxide semiconductor) type – situated in the focal plane of the camera. These devices contain a grid (matrix or array) of light sensitive photo diodes called picture elements, or pixels. The light falling onto an individual pixel creates an electrical current, in proportion to the amount of light. The values from the pixels are converted into a stream of digital data by an ADC (analogue to digital converter) in the camera. To record colour, the pixels are covered with transparent RGB (red, green or blue) filters, so that incoming light is effectively measured in terms of its red, green and blue content. Human colour vision is not equally sensitive to the various colours (it is more sensitive to green light than red or blue), and this is reflected in the colour pattern of the sensor in the camera. The pattern of the filters overlying the pixels on the sensor is very specific, there being two green filtered pixels for every red and blue one. This mosaic pattern is known as a Bayer array, and is designed to match the sensitivity of the human eye as closely as possible.

The imaging sensor is sensitive not only to visible light but also to UV (to around 320nm) and IR (to around 1100nm). Because the majority of photographers want to photograph in normal visible light without the effects of UV and IR as well, manufacturers filter out the UV and IR by placing one or more filters over the imaging sensor at the time of manufacture. This filter varies from one brand to another but is often called a hot mirror filter and is often incorporated with another called an anti-aliasing filter, designed to help prevent aliasing (or moiré), when photographing regular patterns with a regular pattern of pixels. This filter can be removed, to enable the camera to record UV and IR wavelengths.

When choosing which camera to convert, it will be best to have one that is capable of shutter and aperture priority settings, as well as fully manual settings. One that has a PC flash synchronization socket will also be useful, though this is not essential if it has a hot shoe. A Live view facility would also be useful, as discussed later. Digital SLRs, mirrorless cameras and compact type fixed lens cameras can all be converted, though a camera with interchangeable lenses will obviously be most flexible for a range of uses.

In order to convert a digital camera to record UV and/or IR, the UV and IR absorbing filter needs to be removed. It is possible to do this yourself, and there are many tutorials on YouTube and other internet sites telling you how to do it. However, it is not for the faint-hearted. The sensor is very delicate, and the most expensive element of the camera, and must be handled with extreme care. Not only will you require the right tools, but also a dust and static free environment in which to carry out the operation, together with having a good knowledge of the cameras being converted. Some Nikon models for example, have an internal IR shutter monitor that will contaminate images in a converted camera in which the internal UV/IR blocking filter has been removed.

SIGMA CAMERAS

While the vast majority of digital cameras on the market use CCD or CMOS imaging sensors, one manufacturer, Sigma, use a different system. It uses an imaging sensor called a Foveon X3 sensor. Rather than the mosaic structure of a Bayer array sensor, the Foveon sensor captures colour vertically, recording hue, saturation and brightness for each pixel, making use of the fact that silicon absorbs red, green and blue light at different depths. Uniquely, Sigma's interchangeable lens cameras such as the sd Quattro series have a user removable dust protector filter, which incorporates a hot mirror type IR blocking filter. Removing this filter enables the camera to record IR images, as well as UV reflectance images, when used with appropriate lenses and filters over the lens.

The camera was tested and found to have good sensitivity to both UV and IR wavelengths. You will need various adapters such as those shown in the image. For UV reflectance imaging, a Sigma to M42 thread was coupled with an M42 to Nikon adapter to enable a Nikon mounted El-NIKKOR enlarger lens to be used. For IR imaging you can use the normal Sigma lenses, and place appropriate filters over the front of them. The dust protector and filter should be replaced for conventional photography.

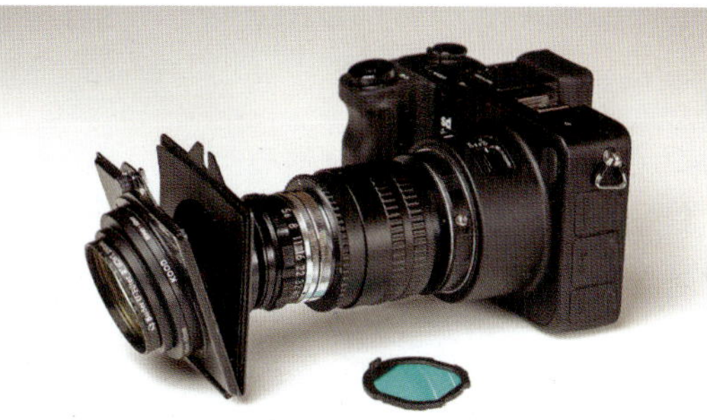

▲ **Fig. 2.9**
A Sigma sd Quattro camera with dust protector (hot mirror filter) removed, effectively converting it to full-spectrum sensitivity. Shown here with 80mm El-NIKKOR enlarging lens and Baader U filter for UV reflected photography.

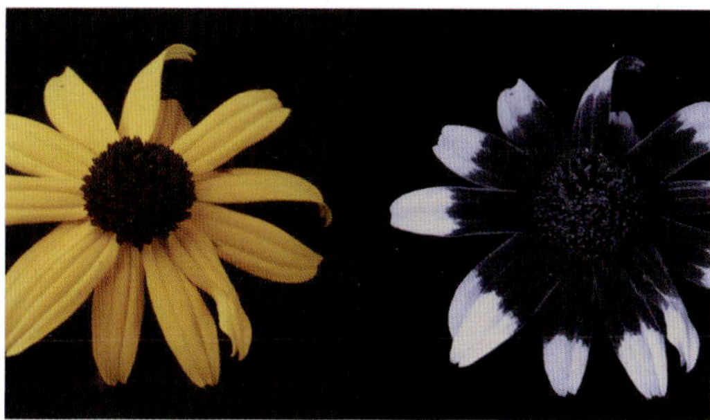

▲ **Fig. 2.10**
Flower (*Rudbeckia* sp.) in visible and UV reflected light with Sigma sd Quattro camera.

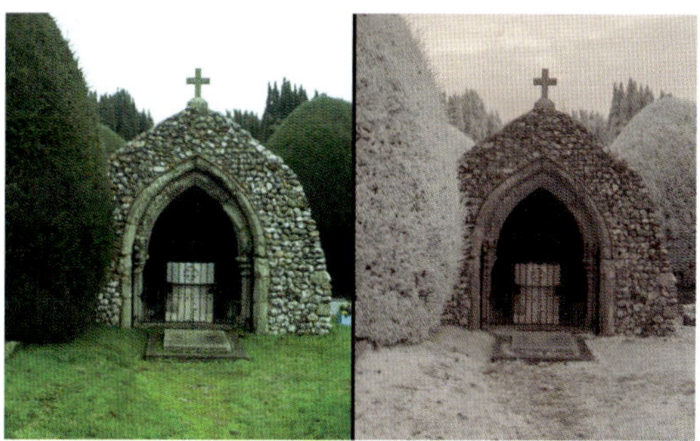

▲ **Fig. 2.11**
Churchyard tomb in visible and IR, with Sigma sd Quattro camera.

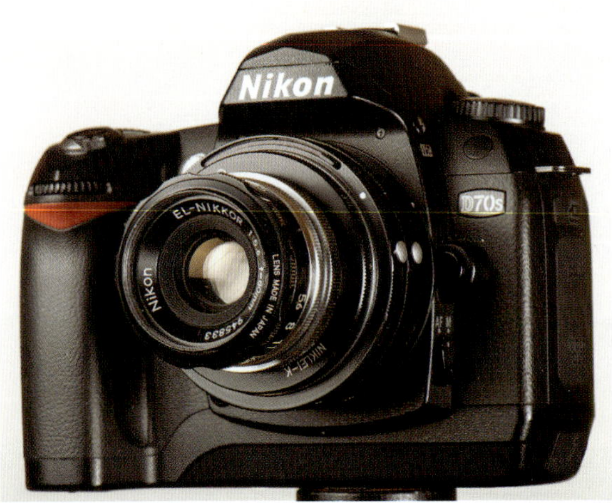

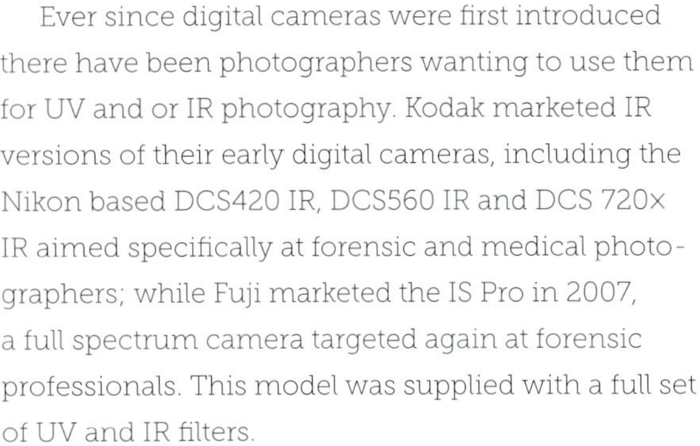

▲ **Fig. 2.12**
The Nikon D70 camera is capable of producing good UV and IR results without modification. Here it is shown with an 80mm El-NIKKOR lens and extension tubes to enable focusing.

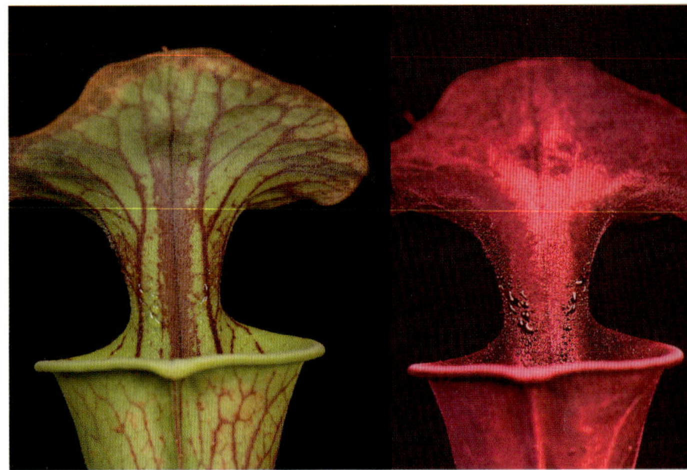

▲ **Fig. 2.13**
Images from the unmodified D70, of a carnivorous pitcher plant (*Sarracenia flava*) showing how UV makes the veining pattern invisible, but instead makes the UV absorbing liquid nectar droplets very dark. Nikon D70 with 80mm El-NIKKOR lens and Baader U filter.

Ever since digital cameras were first introduced there have been photographers wanting to use them for UV and or IR photography. Kodak marketed IR versions of their early digital cameras, including the Nikon based DCS420 IR, DCS560 IR and DCS 720x IR aimed specifically at forensic and medical photographers; while Fuji marketed the IS Pro in 2007, a full spectrum camera targeted again at forensic professionals. This model was supplied with a full set of UV and IR filters.

A couple of early DSLR models with CCD sensors, such as the Nikon D40x and D70, did record UV and IR well without any modification to the sensor, presumably because the filter fitted over the sensor was not very effective at blocking UV and IR. These models can often be found relatively cheaply on the used camera market and are a good starting point for those readers wanting to try out invisible radiation photography. Despite being only 6Mp, they can yield excellent results. They do not have a Live view facility.

SENSOR SIZE AND FOCAL LENGTH

One factor to consider when choosing which camera to convert is that of sensor size. There are various sensors in digital cameras, including full frame 35.9 × 24mm, APS-C 23.6 × 15.8mm and micro four thirds 21.6 × 17.3mm. They can contain different numbers of pixels, from a massive 45 million (a million pixels is 1 megapixel, Mp) to around 12Mp or so. In reality, a 12Mp sensor will give excellent results, good enough for a full-page reproduction in a book such as this one, or an A3 ink jet print. The main effect of different sensor size is the relationship with the focal length of the lens being used.

The focal length engraved on the lens barrel (for example 100mm) is strictly only valid when it is used with a full frame camera with a sensor of 24 × 36mm (the size of 35mm film). When the same lens is used on a camera with a smaller sensor, there will be a magnifying effect, (known as the crop factor) because the sensor is only seeing a smaller area of the image projected by the lens. An APS-C (Advanced Photo System type-C) sized sensor will have an approximate magnifying effect of ×1.5. The 80mm El-Nikkor lens, recommended later for UV reflected photography will effectively have an approximate focal length of 120mm when used with an APS-C sized sensor for example. A longer focal length lens will give a greater working distance from the camera to the subject, which may be useful when lighting small subjects with various lights, or photographing nervous insects, but may be too long for mid-range subjects such as portraits for example.

USING UNMODIFIED CAMERAS FOR IR

Although for most purposes best results will be obtained with a converted camera, it is possible to use an unmodified camera for IR, using an appropriate filter and a long exposure, probably in the region of five to ten seconds at f/5.6 at 400 ISO (discussed more fully in Chapter 6).

One test that you can easily perform to see if your camera can record IR images without conversion is to point it at a TV (or similar) remote control in a darkened room. If the camera has a Live view facility, turn this on and look at the screen while pressing the remote button. If you see a bright light on the screen then the camera has some sensitivity to IR. If it doesn't have a Live view facility, you will need to shoot an image of the remote in a darkened room. You will probably need to have the camera on a tripod to do this. Unfortunately there is not a similar test for UV sensitivity.

CAMERA CONVERSIONS

There are a number of companies specializing in camera conversions, and many are listed in the resources section at the end of the book. They can convert one of your own cameras or may offer a range of already converted cameras. Most types of digital camera can be converted – DSLR, bridge, mirrorless and compact, though an interchangeable lens camera will certainly offer most scope and flexibility.

There are three major options when converting a camera for recording UV and IR: UV only, IR only, and full spectrum (UV, visible and IR).

When the hot mirror filter is removed, it can be replaced with a UV only transmitting filter, an IR only transmitting filter (there is a range of options here, discussed more fully in Chapter 5), or a sheet of plain quartz glass allowing UV, IR and visible light (full spectrum) to reach the surface. It is worth thinking very carefully about the type of conversion you need, as they are expensive, and may limit the type of photography that you can carry out.

UV-ONLY CONVERSION

With this type of conversion, the hot mirror filter is replaced with a UV transmitting filter (usually transmitting around 365nm), which absorbs all visible light and IR. Depending on the conversion company used and your own requirements, specific wavelength UV filters can sometimes be fitted. No filter is required over the front of the lens (that needs to be capable of transmitting good quantities of UV), so the camera viewfinder can be used normally to compose and focus the image. The converted camera cannot be used for conventional visible light photography, or IR. This is generally an expensive conversion, due to the cost of the UV filter.

IR-ONLY CONVERSION

With this type of conversion, the hot mirror filter is replaced with an IR transmitting filter, which absorbs all visible light and UV. Depending on the conversion company used, specific wavelength IR filters can be fitted. No filter is required over the front of the lens (most lenses can be used for IR photography), so the viewfinder can be used normally to compose and focus the image, enabling it to be used for moving subjects. The converted camera cannot be used for conventional visible light photography or UV.

FULL SPECTRUM

This type of conversion replaces the hot mirror filter with a plain quartz glass filter transmitting UV, visible and IR wavelengths. Specific filters will then need to be placed over the front of the lens to transmit and absorb the required wavelengths. The converted camera can also be used to record normal visible light images by placing a hot mirror filter (such as the Kolari Vision Hot Mirror filter, or Schott S8612 filter) over the front of the lens, effectively converting it back to its original state. For many applications you will want to record normal visible light control images, for comparison with the invisible light images, and this conversion allows you to do that without changing the camera.

Focusing and composition through the camera viewfinder will usually not be possible when the UV or IR filter is placed over the lens, though some

WHITE BALANCING A VISIBLE LIGHT IMAGE

When using a converted camera for normal light images, using a hot mirror filter, you will probably need to white balance this image with a photographic 18 per cent grey card, or similar device, to achieve the correct colour. Shoot two images, one of which includes the grey card, which should receive the same lighting as the main subject. In the raw converter such as Adobe® Camera Raw, select the image with the grey card, then place the white balance tool on the card and click. This should neutralize it to grey. Now synchronize the two images (in the Filmstrip: **Select All > Sync Settings**) to apply the setting from the grey card image to the one without. It can also be used for multi-spectral imaging, discussed later in the book.

models with a Live view facility (particularly mirror-less models) will show an image, albeit probably very dim, on the rear LCD screen.

When converting the camera to full spectrum, the conversion company should calibrate the focusing for either UV or IR (they should ask you this at the time of conversion). When using the camera for visible light photography there may be a small but noticeable focus shift, and the images may not be pin sharp. It is worth testing for this and, if necessary, stopping the lens down to perhaps f/11 or f/16 if possible, to minimize the problem.

In this context, a full spectrum conversion means a camera that will record UV (to around 350nm), visible light, and IR (to around 1200nm) wavelengths. They will not record heat patterns.

Some of the advantages and disadvantages of each conversion type are shown in the table below.

MONOCHROME CONVERSION

Another, far less common and far more expensive type of UV conversion is a monochrome conversion, whereby the Bayer Colour Filter Array is removed from the front of the sensor, leaving just the unfiltered pixels. This is a very delicate process, only undertaken by a small number of companies. The result is a monochrome only image, unaffected by the Bayer array on the sensor. This type of conversion will yield sharper monochrome UV images as every pixel will contribute towards the final image.

	Advantages	Disadvantages
UV only conversion	• No need for expensive filters on front of lens • Use viewfinder as normal for focusing and composition • Use for moving subjects • No problem with focus shift	• Limited to the specific transmission characteristics of the internal filter fitted • Relatively expensive • Cannot be used for visible light control images • Cannot be used for multi-spectral photography
IR only conversion	• No need for filters on front of lens • Use viewfinder as normal for focusing and composition • Use for moving subjects • No problem with focus shift	• Limited to the specific transmission characteristics of the internal filter fitted (e.g. 720nm) • Cannot be used for visible light photography • Cannot be used for multi-spectral photography
Full spectrum conversion	• Very flexible – use for UV, IR and visible light photography • Can use wide range of different filters on front of lens • Can use for multi-spectral photography • Cost effective	• Use of viewfinder difficult or impossible • Possible problem with focus shift • Need various filters for front of lens • Generally not suitable for moving subjects

▲ **Advantages and Disadvantages of Camera Conversion Types.**

OTHER CAMERAS

Many of the conversion companies can now convert other types of camera such as GoPro action-type cameras, and cameras fitted to drones. Like the other conversions they can be full spectrum, UV only or IR only, and, in the case of drone cameras, a spectrum appropriate to NVDI work (normalized difference vegetation index), used in agriculture for the analysis of crops and other vegetation, often from drones.

RECOMMENDATION

If you know that you only want to do UV or IR photography (UV reflectance images of flowers, or IR landscapes, for example), then a single wavelength conversion will be the way forward, though, as we have seen, it may be limiting and inflexible.

A full spectrum conversion offers greatest flexibility at a reasonable cost and would be the type recommended for a beginner wanting to try both UV and IR photography.

FILTERS

In order to photograph in UV and/or IR with a full spectrum converted camera, you will need filters to selectively remove different wavelengths of light and transmit selected ones. The key word here is selectively. A filter, of any type, will selectively remove particles of a certain size (in oil or water, for example) or wavelengths of light, with photographic filters, for example. A green filter appears green because it selectively absorbs red and blue light and transmits just green wavelengths of light.

There are several different ways of describing the characteristics of a filter – unfortunately there is

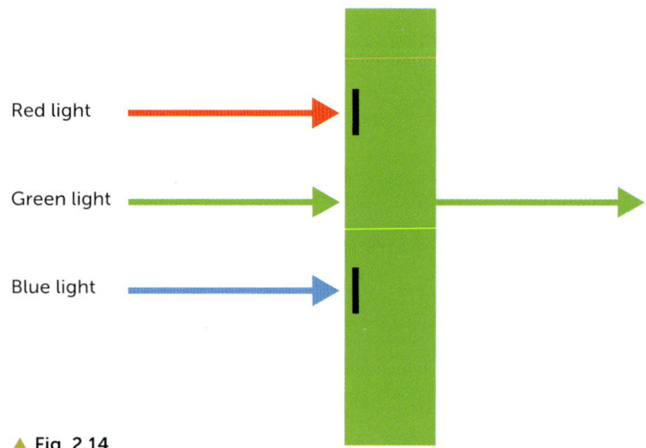

▲ **Fig. 2.14**
Light Filters: A green filter appears green because it absorbs red and blue wavelengths, and transmits green wavelengths

no universally used system, which leads to possible confusion.

Some are known by their colour (green, yellow), some by their main transmission wavelength, others by a trade name (e.g. Baader U, Hot Mirror) and others by a manufacturers code number (e.g. S8612).

Some modern filters are known by a specific number for example no. 12. This number is derived from the now defunct Wratten series of filters manufactured and distributed by Kodak. The companies Tiffen and Lee, for example, market a no. 12 deep-yellow filter, which was the recommended filter when using false colour IR film. A Wratten number reference table can be found online at www.liquisearch.com/wratten_number/reference_table.

Clip-in Filters

One type of filter manufactured by a few companies is a clip-in filter, which clips inside the camera, in front of the sensor, and behind the lens. More details are given in Chapter 4 on IR photography.

FOCUSING

Different wavelengths of light (and UV and IR) are brought to slightly different points of focus by a simple lens. Most modern lenses are specifically designed to bring red, green and blue light to a common point of focus, with apochromatic lenses, but do not do the same with UV and IR wavelengths.

If you have a full spectrum conversion, the conversion company can calibrate the camera to give the correct focus for either UV or IR. They should ask you which of the two regions you wish to have the calibration done for. If you choose UV, then it is possible (though not a certainty) that any IR images will be slightly soft. This can be corrected by using a small aperture if possible, or by shifting the focus ring in the correct direction. Old lenses designed for use with film cameras had an IR focus mark engraved on the lens barrel to help counter this problem – *see* Chapter 5.

It is possible to perform a simple test for this focus shift. You can either mount a ruler at 45 degrees, or buy an inexpensive focus shift calibration chart, and focus on the midpoint in visible light, with the camera mounted exactly horizontally above the ruler. Now shoot an image of the ruler in UV and/or IR and check the resulting image to see if the mid point is sharp, or if the point of sharp focus has shifted along the scale. If it has, re-adjust the focus by the amount shown, and shoot another image until the mid point is sharp. The focus shift will be in a different direction for UV than or IR. It is always worth stopping the lens down if possible to give more depth of field to cover the focus shift.

If you have a camera that has a Live view facility, it will be possible to see the UV and IR image on the rear screen, though the UV one in particular may be quite dark. It is useful to have a loupe, or magnifying glass, to see the image to help focusing. One particularly good one for the purpose is the Hoodman HoodLoupe, which fits almost exactly onto the rear screen of the camera, blocking out any extraneous light.

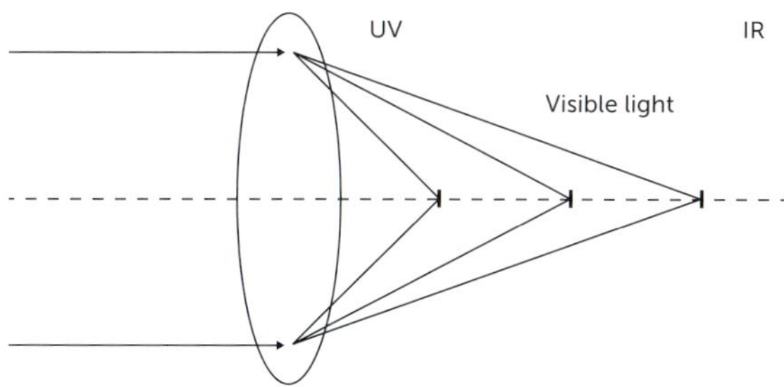

▲ **Fig.2.15**
Light of different wavelengths is brought to different points of focus by a simple lens.

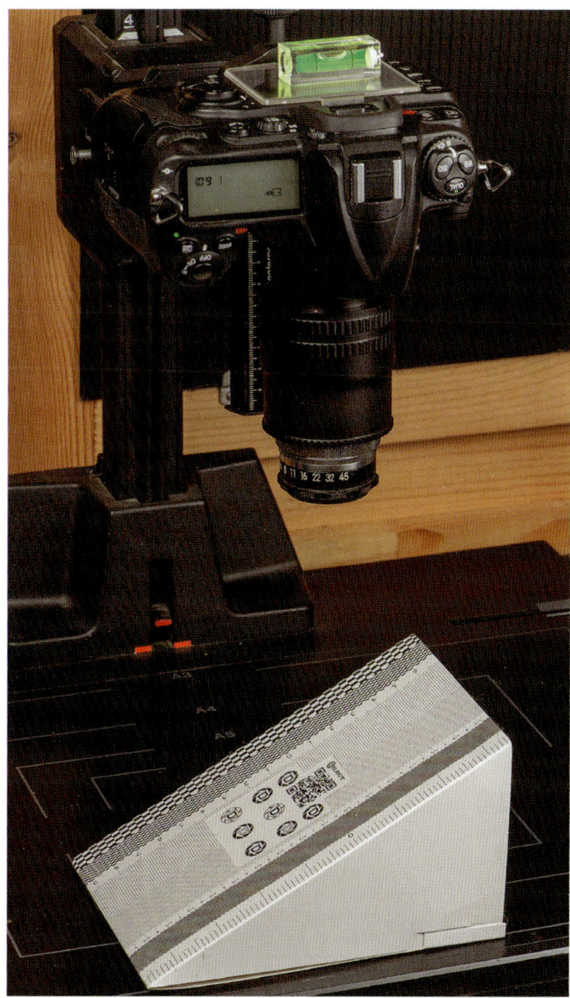

▲ **Fig. 2.16**
Lens/wavelength focus shift. The camera is pointed down towards the zero on the 45-degree scale of the focusing shift aid. Note the spirit level on top of the camera.

FILTER TERMINOLOGY

Some of the terms associated with light filters are listed below.

Absorption

The amount of light (or other electromagnetic radiation) lost through transformation to another form of energy whilst passing through a material such as glass.

Bandpass filter

A filter transmitting light, or UV or IR within a specific region of the electromagnetic spectrum.

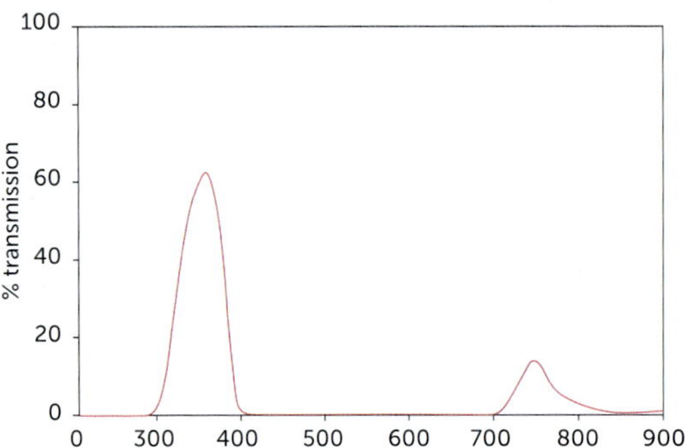

▲ **Fig. 2.17**
Typical filter transmission curve, for the now largely redundant Kodak 18A 'Wood's Glass' UV filter. Note the small but significant transmission in the IR, which would be recorded by a full spectrum converted camera.

They can transmit a very narrow range or wide range of wavelengths.

Bandwidth

This is the range of wavelengths transmitted by a filter.

Cut-off Filter

The wavelength where there is a transition from a region of high transmission to low transmission. This cut-off wavelength usually refers to the 5 per cent absolute transmission.

Cut-on Filter

The wavelength where there is a transition from a region of low transmission to high transmission, usually where the transmission increases to 50 per cent in a longpass filter. A Hoya R72 IR filter for example has a cut on wavelength of 720nm, so at 50 per cent maximum transmission, the corresponding wavelength for that particular filter is 720nm.

Not all manufacturers use the 50 per cent transmission (50%T) value to specify the cut-on wavelength. The wavelength at 0 per cent or 5 per cent is also sometimes used to denote the transition from a region of low transmission to an adjoining region of high spectral transmission. If the 0 per cent or 5 per cent figure is used, then the filter will always have a shorter wavelength than the 50 per cent value for longpass filters. For example, A Hoya R72 filter has a 5%T at 690nm (red) whilst at 50 per cent the value is 720nm. For IR photography in particular, the 0%T or 5%T value will give photographers a better understanding of how much visible red light will be transmitted through the filter.

Filter Factor

The amount of extra exposure required by a filter. For example, a neutral density (ND) filter with a density of 0.3 requires 1 extra stop.

Filter Thickness

When purchasing specialist filters for UV and IR photography, you may be given the option of different thickness – 1mm, 1.5mm or 2mm, for example. Generally, the intensity of transmitted light decreases exponentially with the thickness of the filter, although the wavelength of the transmitted light will practically remain the same. With longpass filters, the thickness will alter the cut-off wavelength as well as the per cent transmission.

CONTINUED

Longpass Filter
A filter which transmits wavelengths longer than the region absorbed, e.g. a filter blocks 400–700nm, and transmits IR wavelengths.

Optical Density
The amount of energy that can pass through an optical component.

Transmission
The percentage of light or invisible radiation transmitted by a filter. This will vary according to the wavelength, so transmission curves are produced by manufacturers, showing the percentage transmission at various wavelengths. This may be very narrow, transmitting a very limited range of wavelengths (e.g. the Baader U filter) or a broad range of wavelengths.

CONTROL IMAGES

It is likely that at some time (possibly all of the time) when shooting either UV or IR images that you will want to shoot a visible light control image alongside it to compare the two, particularly with subjects such as flowers where you are revealing previously unseen details. A visible light control image can be used to show the spectacular effects of UV fluorescence when the glowing image is compared with the original drab piece of rock, for example.

If you have a full spectrum conversion camera, this can be converted back to shoot visible light images by using a hot mirror filter over the lens, effectively replacing the filter that was removed from the front of the imaging sensor during the conversion process. Typical filters are the hot mirror filter marketed by Kolari Vision, and the Schott S8612 filter. These filters are a bluish colour and absorb much of the UV and IR wavelengths. Using one will enable you to shoot images in perfect registration – visible light and IR, for example, when producing digital simulations of false colour IR images.

It is important to achieve the correct colour of the control image, particularly if you have used non-standard lighting. We will address the issue of white balancing the UV and IR images in a later chapter, but a brief account of white balancing visible light images is given here.

It is always recommended to save your images as raw files to give maximum scope for post capture processing. There are various ways of white balancing images in modern cameras, either by using the camera's own in built white balance feature, or using a white balance tool such as a photographic grey card (it must be a true photographic 18 per cent grey card or similar), or a specialist device such as an X-Rite ColorChecker® Passport.

Different cameras will have different ways of setting a custom white balance (useful in particular when shooting IR images), but the basic principle is to place a neutral grey or white object under the lighting that will be used to take the final picture, and use the technique given in the camera manual to create a custom white balance (this will vary from one camera manufacturer to another).

The other method is to shoot two images of the subject, one of which includes the grey card or ColorChecker®. Make sure the chart receives the same lighting as the subject.

Open the two files in the raw converter and select the image with the color checker. Using the white balance tool, click on one of the grey patches. This will remove any colour from the patch and render it a neutral grey.

Under the Filmstrip tab, select all images, and then select Sync settings. Check that the colour balance setting is ticked. This will apply the settings from the grey card image to the image without it, giving its correct colour.

EXPOSURE MEASUREMENT

The exposure meter built in to a camera is designed to work with visible light, so when a camera is converted for UV, IR or full spectrum it may not perform perfectly. The only real answer is to do some tests to see how the meter performs, and whether you will need to apply a compensation factor to its readings.

Two facilities that are always worth using when assessing exposure are the highlights setting, and the histogram display.

Highlights

The highlights facility is a warning device that shows any overexposed highlight area, which will blink or flash repeatedly. This is particularly useful when photographing shiny flowers for example, where a highlight can easily become overexposed. Depending on the level and size of the highlight the issue may be solved by giving slightly less exposure, or perhaps diffusing the light source. Bear in mind that, if the flashing area in the image is pure white in the subject, then it should stay as white.

There is also a highlights (and shadows) facility on the histogram display in the Adobe® raw converter for example. Selecting the two arrows at the top of the screen will activate the facility. Any overexposed highlights will show as red in the image, any underexposed shadows will show as blue areas in the image.

Histograms

A histogram is a graphical representation of the tones within an image, mapped against a black (shadow) to white (highlight) scale on the horizontal axis. It is important to say right at the start that there is no such thing as a perfect histogram, either in terms of its shape or distribution of tones in the graph. This is because all images have different compositions of tones and colours. Images that need a pure white or black background will look very different than a typical landscape, for example.

The important areas of the histogram are the two ends, shadow and highlight. With a typical image, with no large black or white areas, the tones should sit within the two vertical axes, not falling off either end. Ideally, the graph should be weighted towards the highlight end of the graph, but without falling off the end.

The histogram on the camera is mirrored in image processing programs such as Photoshop® and Lightroom®, which display the Levels or Histogram dialog box.

The levels dialog box can be used to adjust the sliders at the base of the graph to alter highlights shadows and mid-tones.

RAW VS JPEG FILES

Most modern digital cameras give the option of saving images as raw files, JPEG or both. JPEG is a compression routine, applying a lossy compression algorithm to files to reduce the size of an image, enabling more images to be stored on a memory card. Huge savings can be obtained – one image from a 36Mp camera can be compressed to around 4Mb for example, depending on the level of compression. Different settings are available for different amounts of compression: fine, normal and basic, for example in the case of Nikon. Other manufacturers will use different terms. The process is remarkably good, and even at high compression settings there is virtually no loss in visual image quality (though, if the images are to be used for scientific analysis, it is best to use raw rather than JPEG, as some artefacts will occur as a result of the JPEG compression process). The main issue with JPEG files is that various other settings, set in the camera, such as white balance, are saved in the file, and cannot be undone.

Raw files are exactly that – raw image data without any compression, or settings for white balance and the like. Images have to be viewed in a raw converter, of which there are several programs such as Adobe Raw Converter®, Photo Ninja®, BreezeBrowser as well as those from the main camera manufacturers. It is important to realize that each manufacturer, and each model of camera from each manufacturer has a different raw file, so when a new model comes onto the market you will need to ensure your raw converter software can open it. Raw files are rather like exposed but undeveloped rolls of film. You have various choices as to how to process the film with regard to type of developer, timing and the like.

A digital raw file is similar. It needs to be viewed in a raw converter before it can be opened in Photoshop®, for example, and things like exposure and colour balance can be adjusted. Unlike film, the same raw file can be re-processed at a later date to give a different result. Raw processors can be very complex, with adjustments for lens corrections, conversion to monochrome, applying pre-made profiles and a host of other features, outside the scope of this book.

One particular use of relevance to many of the techniques in this book is when white balancing images. If you include a photographic grey card, or other white balancing device in your image, the white balance toll in the raw converter can be used to obtain the correct colour of the target. The settings used to do that can then be applied to an image without the card. As we will see later, particularly with UV reflected photography, the amount of adjustment required may be too much for many of the raw converters, and one program in particular, Photo Ninja®, is routinely used by UV photographers for this purpose.

One important thing to note when viewing images on the screen on the rear of the camera is that if you have shot raw files, the image displayed on the preview screen is a low-resolution JPEG version of the raw file. It will probably look rather different to the actual raw file, and should be treated with caution, particularly when viewing to check exposure, for example. It is always best to use the histogram option on the camera.

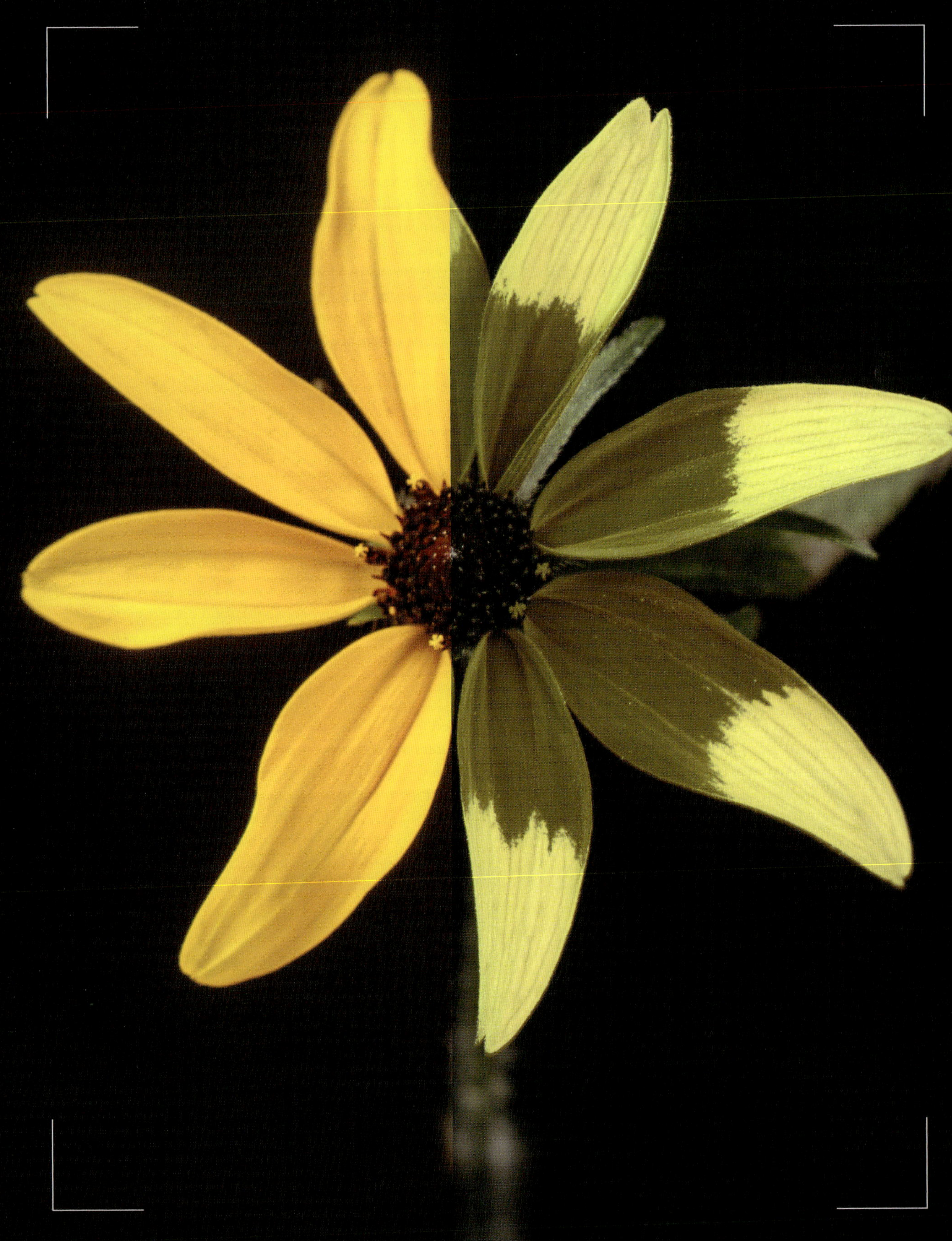

Chapter 3
Ultraviolet Reflectance Photography

As we have seen, when a mixture of electro-magnetic wavelengths fall upon a subject they can be absorbed and/or reflected. If the right combination of filters, lenses and light sources is used, with a UV sensitive camera, then we can record just the UV wavelengths that are reflected from a subject.

The technique is used by medical profes-sionals, forensic photographers, art conservators and scientists wanting to study insect vision, for example. Many flowers will show previously invis-ible patterns when seen in UV, visible only to their insect pollinators, and some insects such as various yellow butterfly species will appear differently in UV. The technique is also increasingly used by cosmet-ics companies to demonstrate the effectiveness of sunscreen and its correct application, often using real time UV sensitive video systems (see Fig. 2.1). Because the shorter wavelength UV is not absorbed into biological tissue, reflected UV can give a mark-edly improved rendition of surface detail of skin than visible or IR, and UV images can appear very sharp. Because UV barely penetrates skin, but is absorbed by melanin, portraits shot with UV tend to accentuate surface details such as freckles and enhance any uneven pigmentation. Much research has been carried out into whether UV photography can aid early detection of malignant melanomas, for example, though this seems to have declined in recent years. Early photographs from the 1800s, taken using the ambrotype, or wet collodion process, for example, show enhanced skin detail due to the high UV sensitivity of the plates used, and uncoated UV transmitting lenses.

UV reflectance photography is perhaps the Cinderella of all the techniques in this book, with relatively few photographers currently undertak-ing it, probably due to the challenge of finding the equipment required, and lack of knowledge of the technique and its applications. It is true that some of the necessary equipment can be relatively expen-sive, and hard to find, but the results are certainly worth the effort, and there is still much to learn about the technique and its results. Potential subjects include landscapes, art, portraits, flowers and insects.

THE UV REFLECTED IMAGING SYSTEM

Four main components are required of an imag-ing system in order to be able to record reflected UV wavelengths.

1   A camera with a sensor that is sensitive to, and capable of recording, UV wavelengths down to around 360nm.
2   A high-quality lens that transmits useful amounts of UV wavelengths down to around 360nm.
3   A filter that transmits only UV wavelengths and that absorbs all visible light and IR wavelengths.
4   A light source containing sufficient amounts of UV to enable practical and high-quality photography.

◀ Fig. 3.1
Brown-eyed Susan (*Rudbeckia triloba*) in visible and UV reflected light, revealing the 'UV signature' visible to some insects.

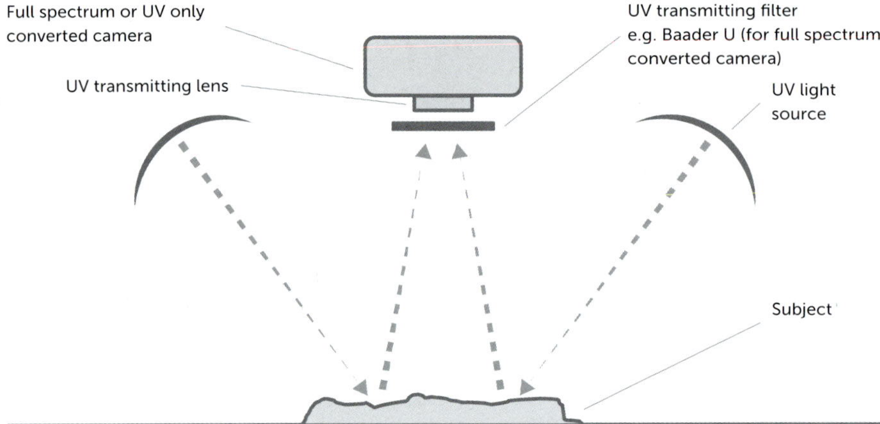

◄ **Fig. 3.2**
Basic UV reflectance photography, with converted camera (UV only or full spectrum), UV transmitting lens and filter, and appropriate light source.

The Camera

As discussed in Chapter 2, the CMOS or CCD sensor in digital cameras is inherently sensitive to UV but will require modification to make it either sensitive to UV only, or full spectrum, sensitive to UV, visible and IR wavelengths. To recap, a UV only converted camera has a UV transmitting filter fitted internally over the camera sensor, allowing full use of the camera viewfinder. A full spectrum converted camera will require the use of a UV transmitting filter over the front of the lens. As this filter is visually opaque, the camera viewfinder will be practically unusable (it may be possible to use the Live view facility, if your camera has one, though the image on the screen will probably be very dim).

It is worth noting that in the days of mono-chrome analogue photography, using silver-based film emulsions, the film was naturally highly sensitive to UV, and recorded UV images with no problem, though it still required a UV transmitting lens and suitable filter.

The Lens

Virtually all modern lenses are made from optical borosilicate glass which, like the crown glass used in windows, has very poor UV transmission, transmitting little below 350nm. In addition, most modern camera lenses have various coatings applied to them to prevent flare, and also to specifically absorb unwanted UV wavelengths. A lens to be used for UV reflectance photography must transmit useful quantities of UV and is ideally made from quartz or fluorite glass elements, though UV grade fused silica (UV glass) is also good, transmitting wavelengths down to around 195nm.

Over the years, several manufacturers have produced specialist UV lenses, constructed from quartz glass, aimed primarily at medical or forensic photographers. They were always expensive, being produced only in small quantities, and are now highly sought after by UV photographers today, commanding very high prices. Some historic examples are the Nikon 105mm UV-Nikkor, f/4.5, the Pentax Ultra-Achromatic Takumar 84mm f/4.5, and the Hasselblad 105mm f/4.3 UV-Sonnar.

The Nikon lens, although discontinued in 1990, is still made today by Rayfact, as the Nikon UV-105, 105mm f/4.5, available from Company Seven and other sources (see resources). It costs around £5000 at the time of writing, a substantial investment. Other currently available UV lenses are the Jenoptik CoastalOpt 105mm UV-vis lens, and CoastalOpt 60mm UV-VIS-IR lenses that have similar price tags.

Photographers on limited budgets wanting to carry out UV reflectance photography have tested various other types of lens, from enlargers, projectors, reprographic copy cameras and other devices, to see if any transmit sufficient UV for practical photography, and found that one type in particular, those designed for photographic enlargers, can work very well. In particular, Nikon enlarging lenses, known as El Nikkors, have been found to transmit good quantities of UV (down to around 360nm), and produce sharp, high-resolution images. When used for their original purpose, monochrome printing in a darkroom, enlarging lenses are designed specifically to expose photographic printing paper that was primarily sensitive to UV and blue light (and therefore could be safely used in the red safelights of a monochrome darkroom).

I recently carried out comparative tests between a 105mm UV Nikkor, and a 105mm El Nikkor enlarging lens from the same era and found remarkably little difference in the exposure required (the UV Nikkor is around half a stop faster than the El Nikkor with UV reflectance images) and with very similar properties in terms of sharpness. The El Nikkors lens has no focusing mechanism.

Although discontinued some years ago, it is possible to find used El Nikkors in camera shops and online auction sites relatively cheaply. The oldest ones are best for UV, with metal bodies and scalloped focusing rings. (These lenses are also renowned for giving superb results when used as close-up and macro lenses and are much sought

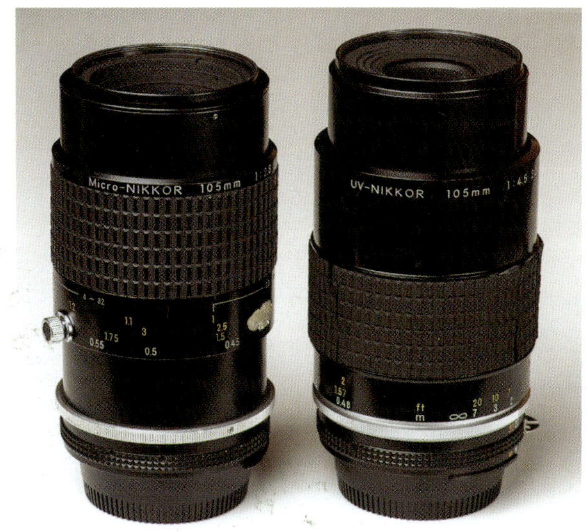

▲ **Fig. 3.3**
A special quartz glass 105mm UV-NIKKOR, compared to a 105mm micro-NIKKOR macro lens from the same era (1970s).

after by photographers for that purpose.) A range of focal lengths was produced, including 50mm, 63mm, 80mm, 105 and 135mm. Although Nikon did not publish transmission graphs, their brochures from the time stated that 'El NIKKOR lenses are corrected against chromatic aberrations, not only for visible light, but also for near UV rays, so that the image formed of the visible light exactly coincides with that of the UV ray, and focusing can be adjusted perfectly ....'

It goes on to say that 'Another important point is that a special type of glass is not used for making these lenses as such glasses are apt to absorb UV rays, resulting in the production of an enlarging lens with deficient brightness. In addition, an anti-reflection coating for the wavelength 400nm is applied to increase the transmission of UV rays. Thus, the lenses perform uniform spectral transmission covering the range from visible light to UV ray'.

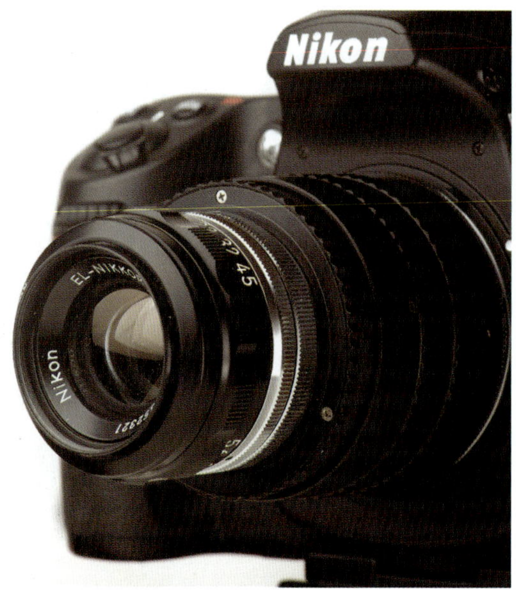

▲ **Fig. 3.4**
A full-spectrum converted Nikon D300 camera with El-NIKKOR 80mm lens mounted onto helicoid focusing extension tube.

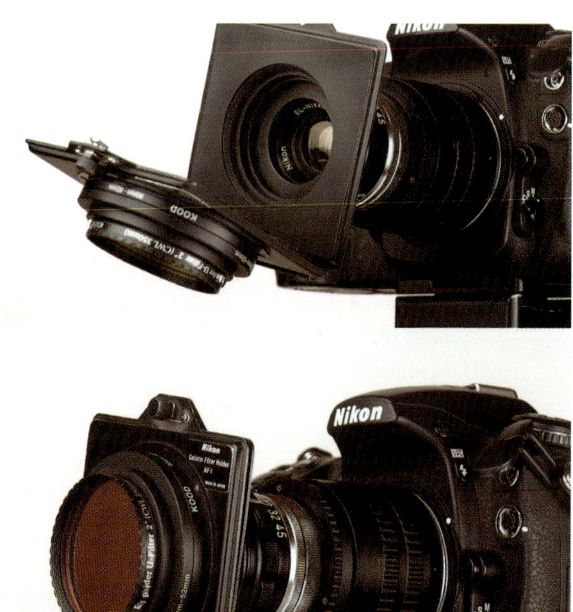

▲ **Fig. 3.5**
A full-spectrum converted Nikon D300 S with 105mm El-NIKKOR enlarging lens, mounted onto an extension tube with built-in helicoid focusing facility. A Nikon gelatin filter holder (AF-1) holds a 'Baader U' UV transmitting filter. This can be dropped down and raised quickly just before the exposure is made.

A Nikon technical brochure (NEX49) from 1970s gives the following spectral transmission figures for the El NIKKOR range of enlarging lenses:

50mm f/2.8 and f/4:   370–700nm
63mm f/3.5:   350–700nm
80mm f/4:   370–700nm
105mm f/4:   380–700nm

(Brochures from the 1980s give a more general figure of 380–700nm for later models of these lenses.)

All of the reflected UV images in this book were shot with either the 63, 80 or 105mm El Nikkor lenses on a full spectrum converted camera

When used on an enlarger, enlarging lenses are screwed into a bellows focusing system, and are not capable of being focused by themselves. This means that when they are used on a camera, they will need to be mounted on to extension bellows, fixed-length extension tubes, or, probably the most useful, an extension tube with built in helicoid focusing thread.

Most enlarging lenses have a 39mm Leica screw thread (the same as that found on early Leica range-finder cameras). This will require an adapter to fit onto the camera system being used (e.g. Leica M39 thread to Nikon bayonet).

You will need another adapter to enable the fitting of a filter onto the front of the lens. The 80mm El Nikkor has an unusual 34.5mm front thread for example.

Tip: While experimenting with UV photography you will undoubtedly acquire a variety of adapters and stepping rings for fixing various filters onto various lenses, sometimes in combination. These can, on occasion, become stuck or cross threaded, and a pair of cheap filter wrenches is a good investment for helping to uncouple filters or rings without damaging them.

One particularly useful refinement to the above set up is to mount the UV filter onto a drop-down filter holder, designed originally for holding delicate gelatin filters flat in front of the lens. Models such as the Nikon AF-1 are readily available second-hand. The AF-1 has a 62mm filter thread at the front and 52mm at the rear. By using this device, the image can be focused as normal, then the opaque UV filter quickly brought up in front of the lens in order for the exposure to be made. If you have purchased one of these filter holders, check that the foam rubber seal on the inside is intact. It is very important that the device is light-tight, with no visible light leakage around the edges of the holder.

Although the 63mm lens is generally reckoned to have the best UV transmission, from a purely photographic point of view the 80mm and 105mm lenses are probably the most practical focal lengths, giving a useful working distance from the subject, and allowing space for lights, reflectors and access to the subject.

OTHER LENSES

Many other, usually older uncoated lenses have been found to be useful for UV photography, often originating from Russia or East Germany, and several databases are available on websites such as ultravioletphotography.com, and photographyoftheinvisibleworld.blogspot.com. One type in particular that have found favour with UV photographers, trying to shoot UV landscapes, are old 35mm f/3.5 lenses, designed for SLR film cameras. These are usually of very simple construction and have been found generally to transmit good quantities of UV, though do not always give pin-sharp images. They are generally manual lenses, with no electronic linkage between the lens and camera body.

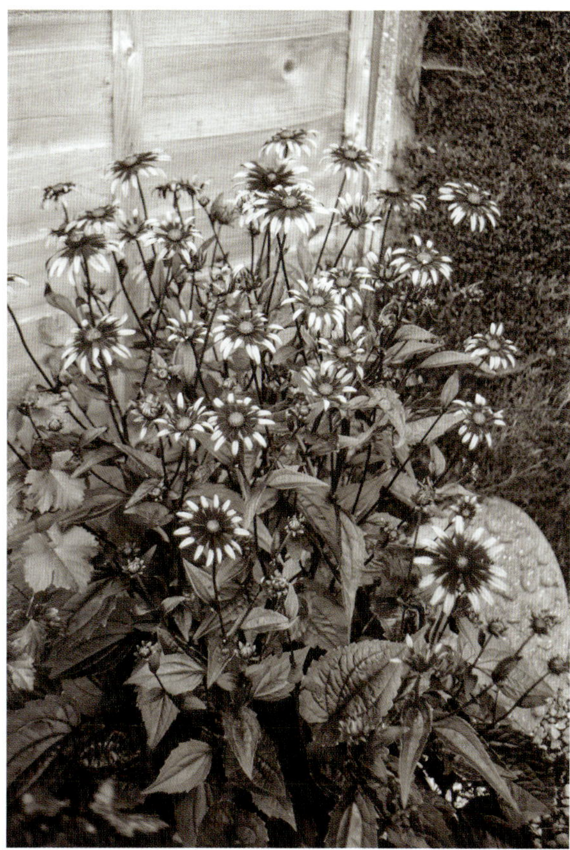

▲ **Fig. 3.6**
Image shot with full spectrum Nikon D800 full spectrum converted camera with Soligor 35mm f/3.5 manual focus lens from 1970's, and 'Baader U' UV transmitting filter. 1/4 second @ f/3.5, 800 ISO.

THE UV TRANSMITTING FILTER

UV reflected photography (and IR) was primarily developed by an American chemist in the 1930s, Robert Wood. He was a polymath, having interests in various areas of science. The title of his 1941 biography *Doctor Wood: Modern Wizard of the Laboratory. The Story of an American Small Boy Who Became the Most Daring and Original Experimental Physicist of Our Day—But Never Grew Up* gives an indication of his wide-ranging interests.

PINHOLES FOR UV

Long before photography was invented, people noticed that when light passed through a small hole, under certain circumstances an inverted image was projected onto the opposite side. Although never very sharp, images from pinholes have, and are still used by photographers. They have certain characteristics, including great depth of field.

Because there is no glass to hinder transmission, pinholes have good UV transmission, though the detail rendered will usually be very poor. Quality will be best for mid to long distance subjects rather than close-ups. Long exposures will be required too, often in the region of thirty seconds when used in normal daylight.

It is possible to make your own pinhole, and there are various tutorials on the internet showing how to do it. Manufacturers of scientific instruments also market pinholes of specific sizes for various applications. The image shown here was shot with a pinhole that had been cut with a laser into a Nikon body cap.

You will probably need to increase the ISO to achieve a reasonable shutter speed and find a way to hold the UV filter over the pinhole without any light leakage around the edges.

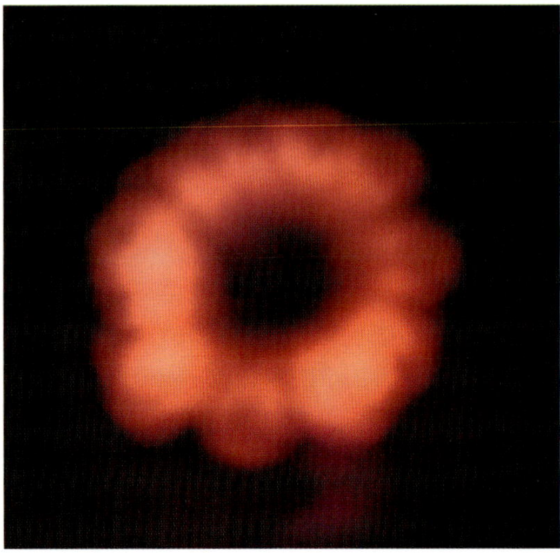

▲ **Fig. 3.7**
This image of a dandelion was shot with a commercially available pinhole, cut into the body cap of a Nikon camera, which was mounted directly onto the camera body. A Baader U UV transmitting filter was attached to the front. As can be seen, the resulting image lacks any definition and is virtually useless for recording reflected UV images. It is likely that a smaller pinhole would be sharper, but substantially more expensive, and would require far more light to give a good exposure.
Nikon D300 with pinhole. Baader U filter. 2 seconds, 400 ISO.

The first filter that was produced for UV reflected photography, named after him, was the Kodak Wood's Glass filter (Wratten no. 18A). This was a solid block of glass several millimetres thick, and visually opaque. It was a very good UV transmitting filter but had the disadvantage of transmitting a significant amount of IR wavelengths as well. This was not an issue when used with film, as normal panchromatic film was not sensitive to IR. However, with digital sensors being highly sensitive to IR, there was a considerable IR leakage that contaminated the images when used with a full spectrum converted camera. Today, there are several filters used by UV reflected photographers in particular the Baader U filter (often referred to as the Venus filter), the Andrea U MK II filter and the StraightEdgeU Gen3 UV Bandpass Filter. (Other possibilities include a stack of two filters, the Schott UG11, and S8612, for example.) These filters are quite expensive (around £250 at the time of writing) but produce excellent results. As can be seen from the graph (Fig. 3.8), the Baader U transmits in the UV mainly at around 360nm, with a very abrupt cut off at 400nm. Note that there is no IR leakage. The Baader U is designed primarily for use mounted inside a telescope (astronomers use it for viewing the UV absorbing clouds around the planet Venus), and has an unusual filter thread size (48mm) – so an adapter will be required to enable it to be fitted on to the front of the lens being used.

The Baader U filter is dichroic, i.e. it has a different colour on each side, yellow and magenta. Because it is designed to be used inside the eyepiece of a telescope, the threaded side would face the source of light, which is the opposite of how it would be when fitted to the front of a photographic lens. For this reason it is often recommended to reverse the filter in its mount, so that the magenta side (the dielectric coating) of the glass faces forward, probably as a precaution against internal flare from the highly reflective surface. This is easily achieved by carefully unscrewing the retaining ring that holds the filter in place in the mount, reversing the filter, and replacing the ring. Take care not to overtighten the ring which might alter the optical flatness of the filter. It is also always a good idea to use a lens hood on the front of the filter, to reduce the risk of flare.

THE LIGHT SOURCE

Several light sources contain UV, in varying amounts. Daylight, of course, contains UV (causing sunburn for example) but is very variable in terms of weather conditions and altitude. Other sources containing UV include electronic flash, lasers, fluorescent tubes and LEDs.

Various light sources containing different specific wavelengths of UV are available and are often used by forensic scientists and art conservators for example, for identifying specific substances, as well as philatelists who use it for detecting some phosphors on stamps. This discussion will concentrate on light sources emitting around 365nm (UVA). Shorter wavelength light sources are available, and these must be used with extreme caution.

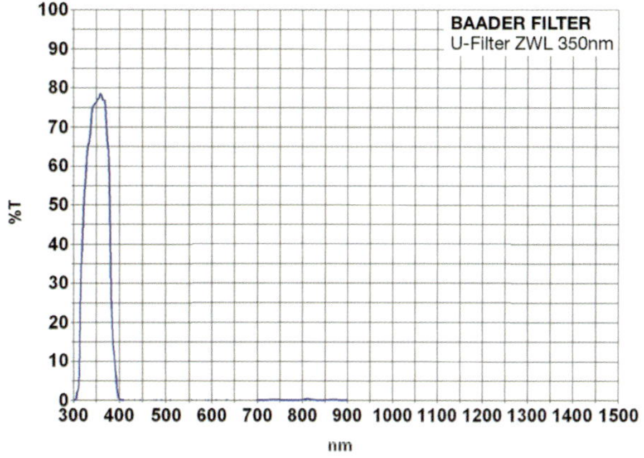

▲ **Fig. 3.8**
Transmission curve for Baader U UV filter. Note the peak transmission at around 365nm, and virtually complete lack of any IR wavelengths.

The best source by far for practical and consistent UV reflected photography is electronic flash. These units contain xenon flash tubes that are designed to emit good quantities of visible light, but also emit UV and IR wavelengths as well. Like the sensors in cameras and camera lenses, flashgun manufacturers filter out the unwanted UV wavelengths, either by coating the xenon tube with a yellowish filter or by placing a yellowish UV absorbing filter over the flash window. While it is sometimes possible to remove the coating from a flash tube it is far easier to use a model with an unfiltered tube, and to remove the UV absorbing plastic filter. Good examples of flashguns for reflected UV are the Mecablitz (Metz) 45 series (e.g. 45 CT1 or 45CL 4), the Vivitar 283 and 285 units, and the Canon Speedlight 199A, all of which can be found relatively cheaply on internet auction sites.

The plastic UV absorbing window needs to be removed. The Mecablitz guns have just four screws holding the flash head together. Discharge the flashgun and remove the batteries. Remove the screws (noting which holes have the longer screws) and lift off the top. The plastic UV filter can now be removed easily, and the top replaced. The Vivitar is more complicated, requiring more extensive dismantling of the unit. There are several YouTube tutorials on how to do this.

The batteries supplied originally with some of these units were of the NiCad type, which are now probably past their best, and you will need to use modern types such as Eneloop re-chargeable Lithium Ion (LiOn) types.

Safety note: If you will be using the modified flashgun/s for portraiture it is probably best to ask your model to shut their eyes or wear protective glasses during the shoot to minimize the amount of UV entering the eyes.

The spectral output graphs shown here are from two identical Metz 45 flashguns, one unmodified, the other with the UV absorbing filter removed from the front of the xenon tube. They show a distinct increase in the amount of UV output by the modified gun.

Safety note: Take extreme care when dismantling and modifying electronic flashguns. They contain capacitors that can, even after a long period of time, store large, potentially lethal amounts of electricity. Make sure the flashgun is fully discharged before attempting any modification and turned off. If you are in any way unsure of how to do this, get a qualified electrician to carry out the modification.

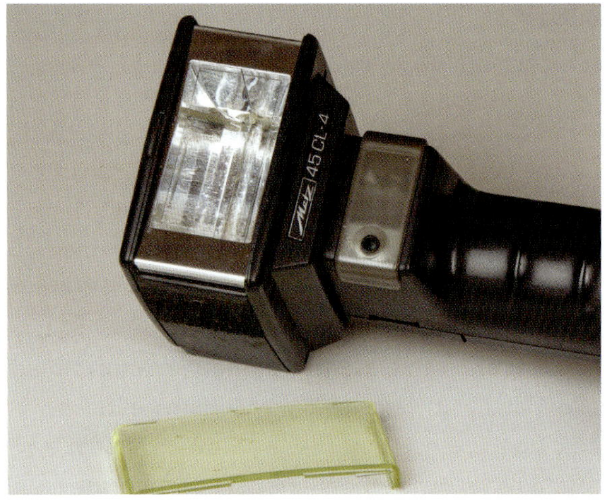

▲ **Fig. 3.9**
A Mecablitz 45 CL-4 flashgun, with the plastic UV absorbing window removed. Note the yellowish colour of the window. The light emitted contains good quantities of UV as well as visible light and IR.

HIGH VOLTAGE FLASHGUNS AND MODERN CAMERAS

There has been much discussion within the photographic community about using old style high voltage flashguns (such as the Vivitar 285HV) with modern digital cameras, with the concern that the trigger voltage of the flashgun could severely

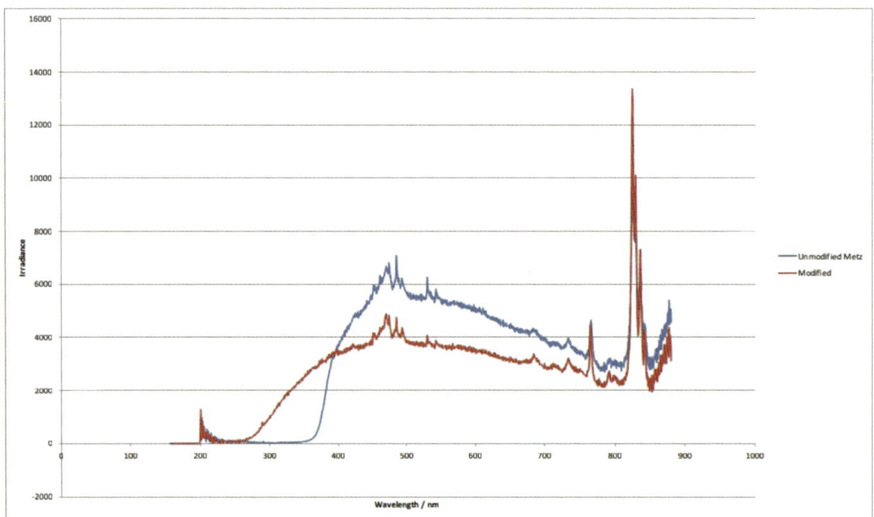

◀ **Fig. 3.10**
Spectral output curves for modified and unmodified Mecablitz flashguns show a significant increase in UV around 350–400nm.

damage the electronics of the modern camera. Some old flashguns could generate 300–400 volts to trigger the flash. There are various websites concerned with this issue and are well worth reading. One solution is to plug a slave cell into the flash and use the built-in on camera flash to trigger it or use a transmitter/receiver type trigger unit.

For indoor studio-based UV reflected photography you will almost certainly want to set the flash to give its maximum output, to enable a reasonable aperture to be used.

UV Flash

Some camera conversion companies offer a service to modify flashguns to make their output UV only. This is necessary when photographing subjects such as portraits, or plants in the field (or for UV fluorescence photography of moving subjects). A UV transmitting filter is fitted over the flash tube so that only UV is transmitted, and visible light and IR absorbed. It is possible to do this yourself, if you can find a suitable filter. The image shown in Chapter 4 is a Metz 45 CT1 flashgun with an old Wood's Glass (Kodak 18A) filter, cut in half, inserted in place of the UV absorbing filter. Although the filter emits some IR it was not found to be a major problem and could be filtered out with a suitable IR absorbing filter if necessary.

UV Reflectance in the Field

UV photography of plants and insects in their habitat is tricky, though not impossible. A system was built using two modified Metz Flashguns mounted onto a full spectrum camera. Because the camera viewfinder cannot be used, the camera must be mounted onto a tripod, and pre-focused on the subject. With a UV only camera it would be possible to use the viewfinder.

The images shown in Figs 3.11 and 3.12 were shot with daylight only, on a very still day.

STUDIO FLASH UNITS

Studio flash units are generally larger than speedlights, designed for illuminating large sets such as food or fashion shoots for example. Most units have either coated tubes, or glass UV absorbing domes over the tube to absorb UV. However, some older Bowens units, Bowens Gemini 500R and a Bowens Gemini 1500 Pro, had non-coated Bowens tubes, and have been found to be suitable for UVA reflected photography. They need to be connected to mains power or used with a transformer for location work.

Exposure

The sensor in a digital camera is not particularly sensitive to near UV wavelengths, thus generally requiring powerful light sources. Also, it is best, for quality reasons, to use the lowest ISO practicable, to keep digital noise to a minimum – this will exhibit itself as granularity in an image. Depending on which camera model has been converted, it might be worth designing your system to work with 400 ISO for example. If you are using daylight as the light source (for landscapes for example) the meter in the camera may give a false reading, and it will always be worth checking the histogram on the rear of the camera to ensure correct exposure.

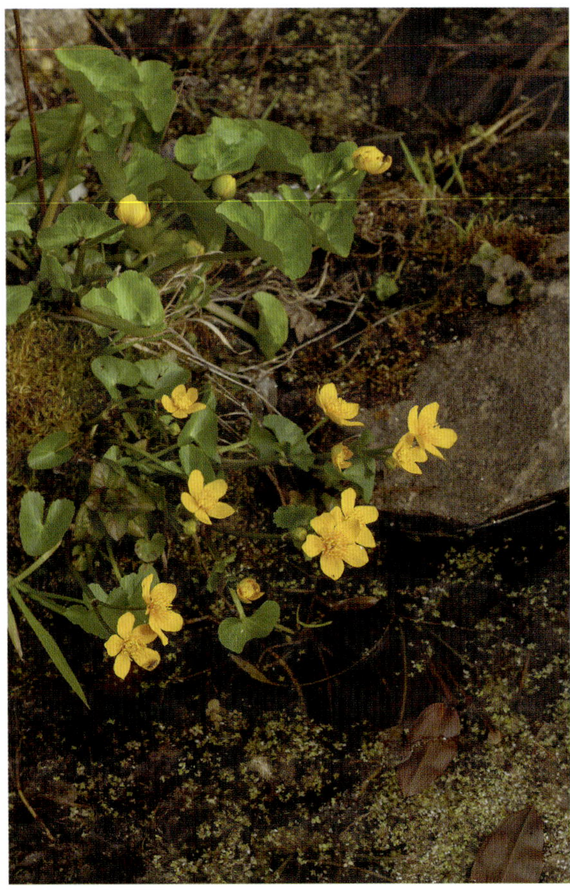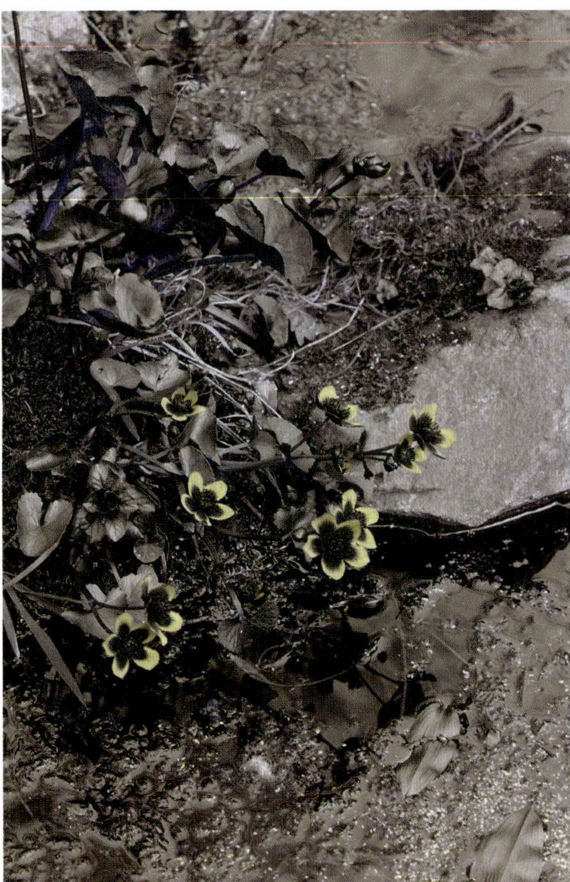

▲ **Fig. 3.11, 3.12**
Reflected UV on location. A still day was required for this 1 second daylight exposure of Marsh Marigolds (*Caltha palustris*) in a pond. The full spectrum converted camera had to be pre-focused before the filter was swung into place.
Nikon D300 full spectrum camera with 105mm El-NIKKOR lens, and 'Baader U' UV filter. 1 second @ f/8, 400 ISO.

THE STUDIO

As much UV reflected work will be carried out indoors, it is perhaps worth saying a few words about working in a studio environment generally, and some of the accessories that might be useful.

Backgrounds

If you want to achieve a black background, the best material by far is good quality black velvet. This can be quite hard to find nowadays. It is the only substance that will remain black if a small amount of light falls upon it. Black is, of course, an absence of light, so it is important to try and reduce the amount of light falling onto the background. You can use a piece of black card to block light from the light source and try to keep the subject as far away from the background as possible. You always seem to need more space than you might imagine, even for relatively small subjects.

Specimen Supports

If you are photographing rock specimens, for example, try placing them on top of a metal or glass column, which can support the specimen several inches from the surface of the background. Flat bottomed test tubes are very good for this if the specimen is large enough.

Flowers should be kept in narrow stemmed water-filled glass or plastic vases, and it is worth collecting a few of these for different sizes of specimen. To help position the plant, you can get lab jacks that are an adjustable platform to raise or lower the specimen. A rotating version is available. Cake icing turntables too make a good base for making precise rotations of a specimen.

Laboratory retort stands and clamps are very useful for holding specimens, reflectors, flashguns and other paraphernalia, as are the helping hand devices used by electricians to aid soldering. One particularly useful type of clamp is the reverse forceps that are squeezed to open rather than the bulldog clip type.

Safety

Take care with trailing cables in the studio, particularly when working in a darkened room. It may be worth wearing a head torch to help find camera controls and accessories without fumbling around in the dark.

Tethered Shooting

Because of the unpredictability of UV photography (and indeed many of the other techniques in the book), when working in a studio environment particularly, it might be worthwhile shooting in tethered mode, whereby the camera is linked directly to a computer via a cable, which will display the captured image instantly on the computer monitor when it is shot, enabling subtle changes to the setup to be made quickly. To do this you can either use the software supplied with some high-end cameras such as Nikon Capture or Canon EOS Utility, or software such as Adobe®'s Lightroom (**File > Tethered Capture**). To connect the camera you will need to use a suitable cable such as FireWire (IEEE1394), USB 2.0 or 3.0, (or a wireless connection

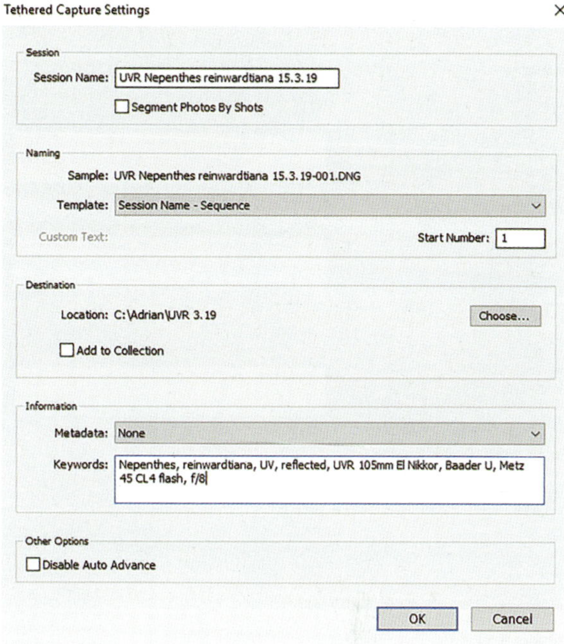

▲ Fig. 3.13
The Tethered Capture dialog box in Adobe® Lightroom. Note the folder into which the captured images will automatically be placed, and the keywords associated with the image.

with appropriate camera and software). This cable will need to be long enough to link the camera to the computer without getting in the way of other studio paraphernalia. Lightroom can be set up to add appropriate captions and keywords instantly to the image at the time of capture.

Tip

Because you will often be working with old, unconventional lenses and filters, which have no electrical connection to the camera, and will therefore not transmit metadata about the image set up to the software, it is always worth making a note of the equipment and exposures used at the time of capture. If you are not shooting in tethered mode this can be done in the File Info box (**File > File Info**) in Photoshop® or the Library facilities in Adobe® Lightroom. These keywords can be searched at a later date to help locate images using specific techniques, lenses or subjects.

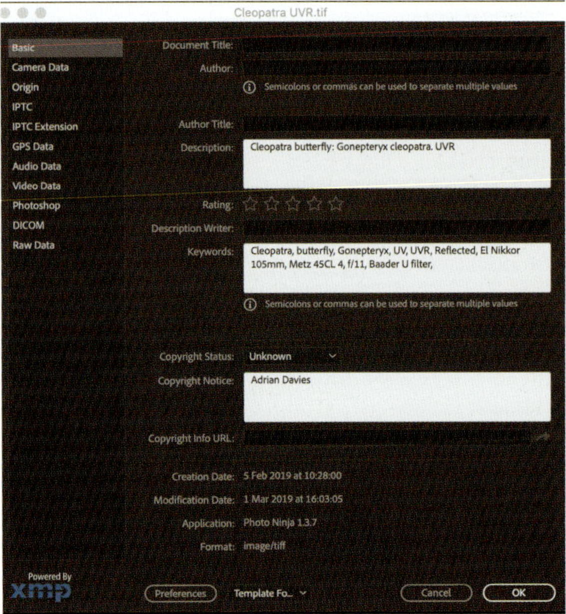

▲ **Fig. 3.14**
The File Info box in Adobe Photoshop®, showing image title, and keywords including a record of the lens, filter and lighting used.

WHITE BALANCING UV REFLECTED IMAGES

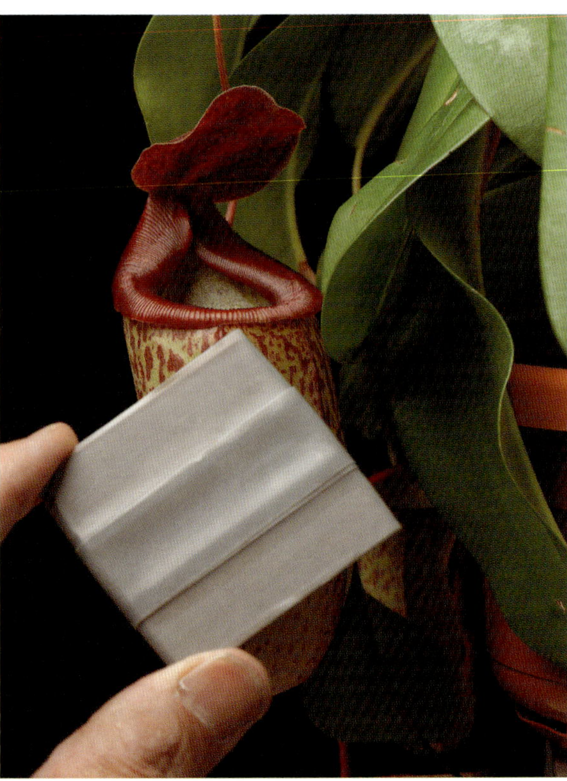

▲ **Fig. 3.15**
A home-made 'white balance' card for white balancing UV reflected images. It was made by wrapping grey PTFE tape around a small tile.

For a UV only record, a monochrome black and white image might seem to be the most appropriate presentation but, retaining some colour does lead to more aesthetically pleasing results. It may seem odd to try to white balance invisible UV images, but different models and makes of camera will have different characteristics when recording UV only images. To achieve some consistency, within different organizations, for example, or when sharing images on online forums, it is useful to have a way of achieving a standard white balance for this purpose.

With conventional visible light images, one method for white balancing images is to shoot two images, one including an 18 per cent photographic grey card or other white balancing device, positioned so that it receives the same light and exposure as the first image, and a second image without the card. In a raw converter, such as Adobe® Camera Raw®, open both images. Position the white balance dropper on the grey card and click. This will neutralize that area of the image to a neutral grey. Select both images (or more) and select synchronize. The adjustment settings from the grey card image will then be applied to the image without the grey card.

Normal photographic 18 per cent grey cards and other colour balancing charts do not perform the same way in UV as they do in visible light and are not suitable for white balancing UV images. After much experimentation, a target made from grey PTFE tape, wrapped around a 75mm square tile has been found to work well with UV images.

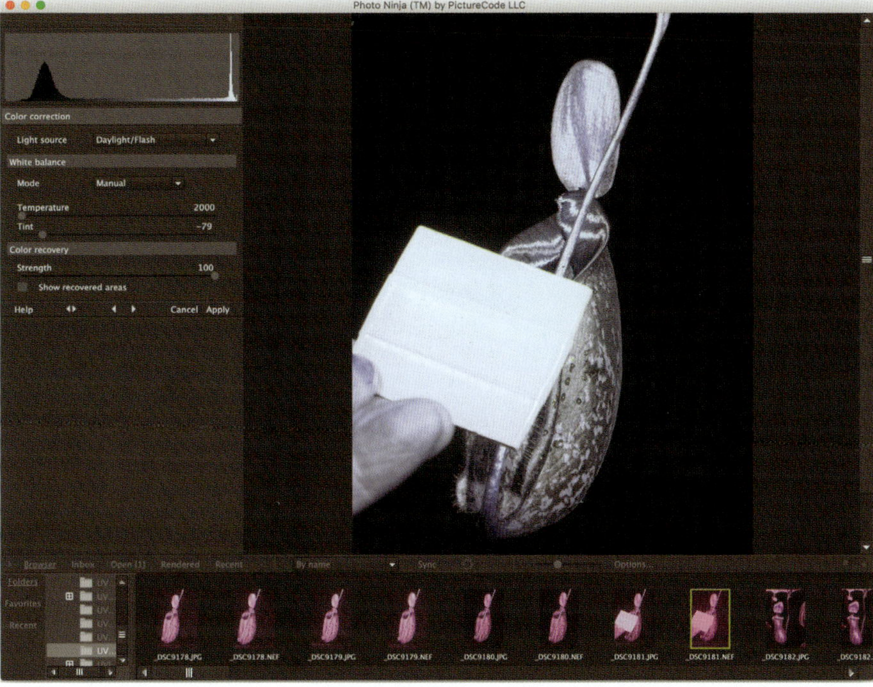

▶ Fig. 3.16
Screenshot of Photo Ninja® in Color correction mode, being used to white balance the home-made PTFE grey patch. The colour of the images straight out of the camera can be seen at the bottom of the screen.

The colour of the target in the recorded UV image will usually be a deep purple or magenta, a long way from neutral grey. Most raw converters such as Adobe® Camera Raw® and similar software are unable to white balance it correctly because it is so far away from grey. One raw converter in particular, Picture Code's Photo Ninja®, has been found to be capable of white balancing images that are significantly away from the grey tone required.

DIY UV Greyscale

It is possible to construct your own scale that works well with UV, using various ratios of magnesium oxide and carbon black powders mixed with laboratory grade liquid collodion (collodion with acetone solvent) at a ratio of 1 gram of mixture to 4ml of collodion. The following mixtures (by weight) have been used to construct a grey scale:

Step	Magnesium Oxide	Carbon Black
1	100	0
2	97	3
3	95	5
4	90	10
5	80	20
6	50	50
7	0	100

The mixtures can be painted onto the rear side of high-quality paper such as that used for inkjet printing.

Focus Stacking

With the various constraints of UV reflectance photography you will probably be working at fairly large apertures, f/5.6 or f/8, for much of the time to minimize noise within the image. This may not be sufficient to achieve adequate depth of field for your subject, particularly if it is quite small, such as a deep single bell-shaped flower. One technique, increasingly used by close-up and macro photographers,

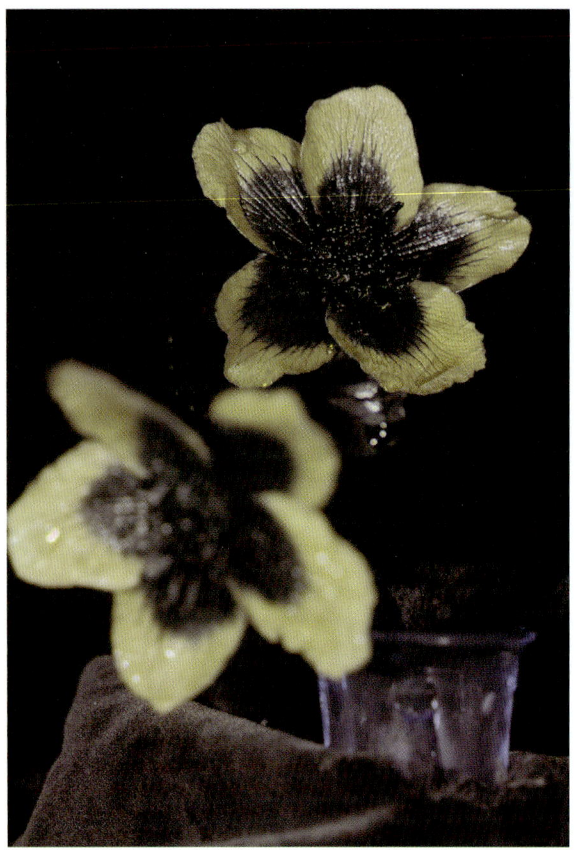

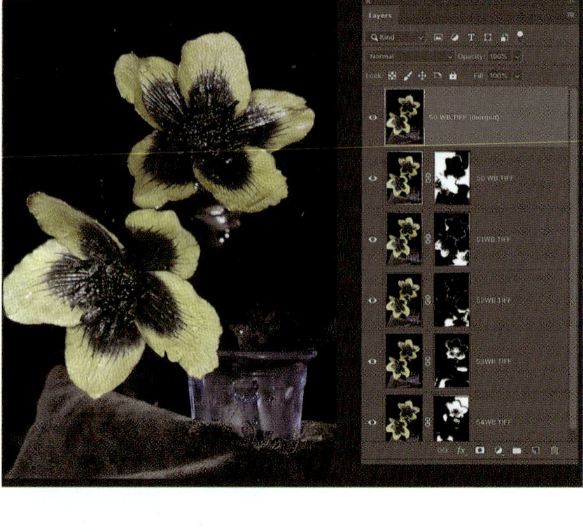

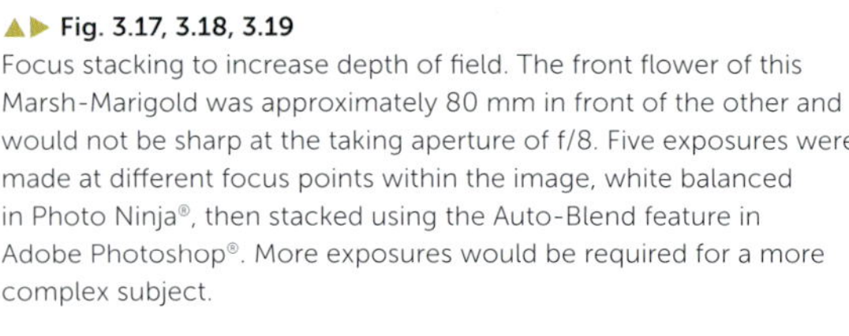

▲▶ Fig. 3.17, 3.18, 3.19

Focus stacking to increase depth of field. The front flower of this Marsh-Marigold was approximately 80 mm in front of the other and would not be sharp at the taking aperture of f/8. Five exposures were made at different focus points within the image, white balanced in Photo Ninja®, then stacked using the Auto-Blend feature in Adobe Photoshop®. More exposures would be required for a more complex subject.

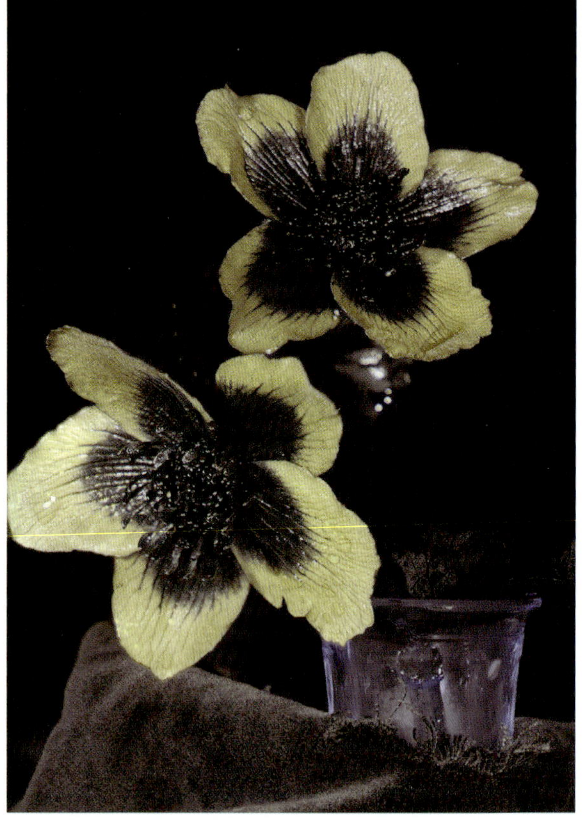

is focus stacking. This is where a number of images are shot of the same subject at different focus points and then blended together in an image processing program that performs the focus stacking operation. The technique is discussed in greater detail in Chapter 8. It does require practice and patience.

Carrying out focus stacking with reflected UV images brings its own problems, particularly if you are using a full-spectrum converted camera. In this case you may not be able to see the image through the viewfinder when the UV filter is in place, other than by removing it, re-focusing and replacing it for each shot, or by using a focusing rail with graduated scale. This is a good reason for using the drop-down filter system shown earlier. It is essential to do this without moving the camera. If using the CamRanger system, the image on the screen may be too dim when the UV filter is in place over the lens to enable the software to work. Meticulous attention to detail will be required.

APPLICATIONS

There are numerous applications of UV reflected photography, and probably many more still to be discovered.

Forensic Science

Forensic science is the application of scientific tests and other techniques during criminal investigation. Forensic scientists collect, preserve and analyse scientific evidence during the course of an investigation, of which photography plays a major role. Crime scenes and artefacts are photographed, often with a variety of techniques such as UV, IR or polarized light, often in combination, to detect the invisible signs left by criminals.

Medical

UV wavelengths do not penetrate skin (unlike IR that do) so UV tends to accentuate any surface markings such as freckles, moles, scars and the like.

Portraits

UV portraits are not flattering to the sitter, highlighting any surface details, though some photographers have experimented with it, including Cara Phillips who produced a folio called Ultraviolet Beauties. This was, however, shot with film rather than a digital camera. If you intend to try this, make sure to get your model to shut their eyes if you are using a full spectrum flash.

Botany

Many flowers (and other parts of plants) show marked differences when seen in reflected UV light, probably mainly acting as a guide to foraging insects looking for nectar. This is often referred to as the UV signature of the flower. It must be remembered that flowers do not exist to attract human eyes – they have evolved specific colours, patterns and scents to attract animals that will act as their pollinators. Good examples for UV reflected photography are Marsh Marigold (*Caltha palustris*), various types of Black-Eyed Susan (*Rudbeckia fulgida*), Beggarticks (*Bidens ferulifolia*), Yellow Iris (*Iris pseudacorus*), Evening Primroses (*Oenothera biennis*) and various Sunflowers (*Helianthius* spp.). In particular, the *Bidens* makes an excellent subject for experimentation when testing out new kit, and the flowers last a long time throughout the spring and summer. Several websites (some listed in the resources section) list those flowers that have been found to exhibit hidden markings, but there is still much scope for further research as UV reflected

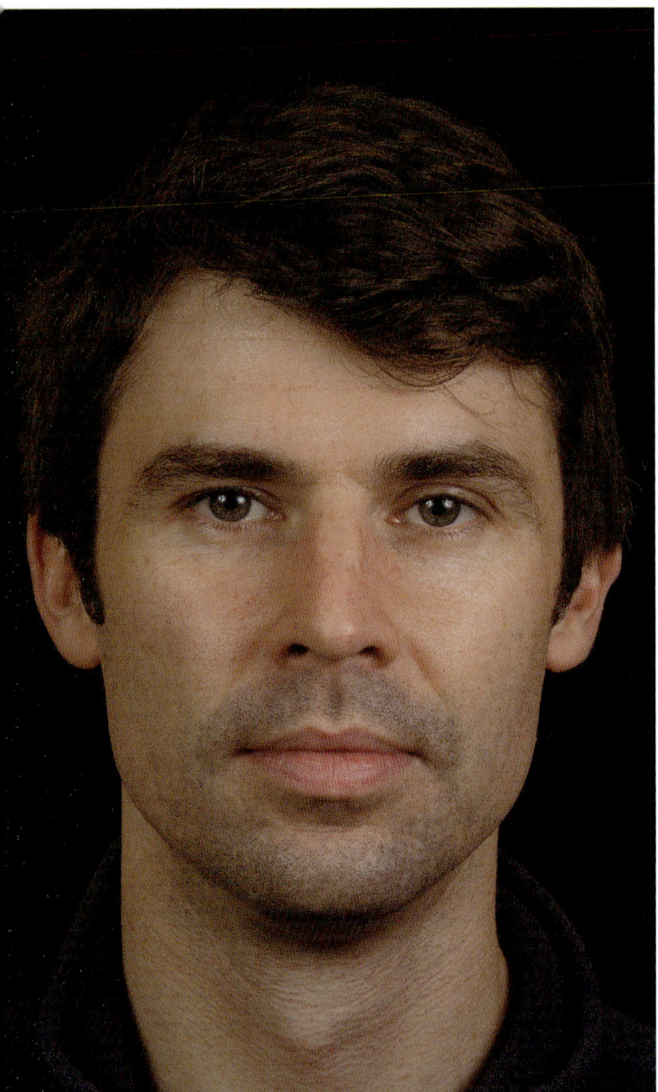 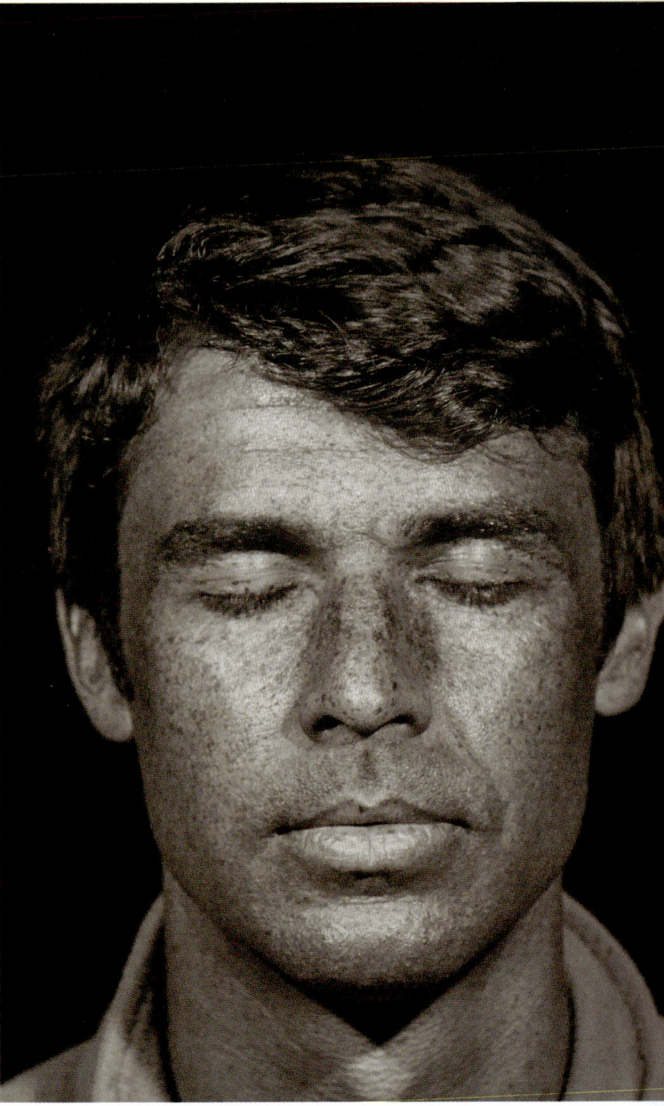

▲ **Fig. 3.20, 3.21**
UV reflected portrait. UV does not penetrate the surface of the skin, so tends to accentuate freckles and other skin markings. Note the double shadows under the chin, indicating that two lights of equal power were used to achieve an even lighting across the face.
   Nikon D300 with 80mm EL-NIKKOR lens, and 'Baader U' UV filter. Two Metz 45 CT1 full spectrum flashguns. 1/160th second @ f/8.

UV REFLECTED IMAGE OF FLOWER

The subject here is Marsh Marigold (*Caltha palustris*) flowers. The aim was to produce two images: a normal visible light image, and a UV reflected image for comparison, showing any hidden UV signature.

The flowers were cut from the plant growing in a garden pond, and the stems placed in a narrow vase containing water. This was placed around a third of a metre in front of a piece of black velvet.

Two studio electronic flashguns with diffusers were placed to light the subject for the visible light image.

For the UV reflected image two Metz 45 CL1 flashguns, converted for full spectrum by removing the plastic UV window over the flash tube were used. They were placed equidistant to the subject, and as close to it as practicable, with the aim of using the smallest possible aperture.

Note: When photographing subjects in reflected UV it is probably best to arrange for the lighting to be as even as possible, so that shadows do not obscure detail. There will probably be little scope for creative lighting!

The two sets of lights were put into position before the photography started, so that they would not need to be moved during the shoot, and thus risking disturbing the camera or flower.

The camera, a full-spectrum converted Nikon D300 with 105mm El Nikkor lens was set up on a solid tripod.

For the visible light control image, the lens was fitted with an S8612 Hot Mirror filter. The exposure was 1/160th @ f/11. Two exposures were made with the studio flash units, one with an X-Rite ColorChecker® Passport included within the frame, the other without. This would later be used to white balance the control image in Adobe® Camera Raw.

For the UV image, the Baader U filter was placed in the gelatin, filter holder over the lens, and brought into place after the image had been focused. The lead from the studio flash units was replaced by the synchronization lead for the Metz flash units, one of which was triggered by a slave cell. Again, two images were taken, one with the grey card made from grey PTFE, the other without. The UV exposure was 1/160th @ f/8 at 400ISO. The images were white balanced in Photo Ninja®.

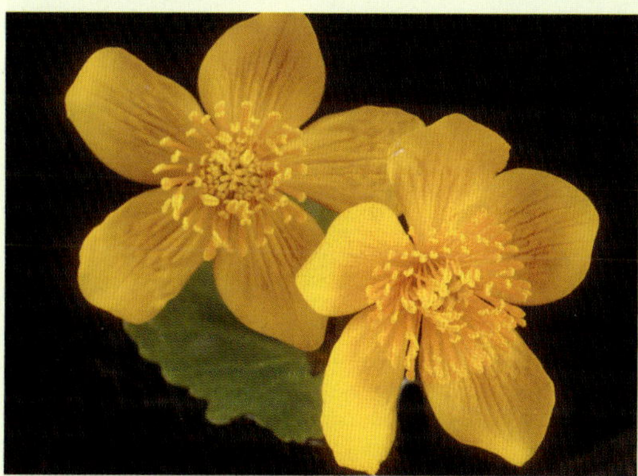

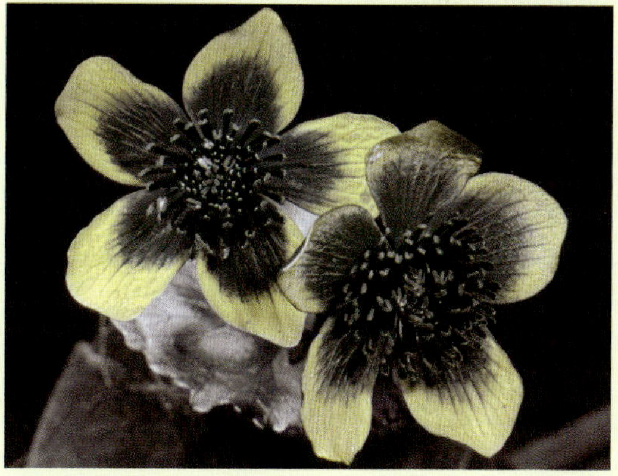

▲ **Fig. 3.22, 3.23**
Marsh Marigold (*Caltha palustris*) in visible light and reflected UV light. Nikon D300 with 80mm El-NIKKOR lens, and 'Baader U' UV filter.
    Two Metz 45 CT1 full spectrum flashguns. 1/160th second @ f/8, 400 ISO.

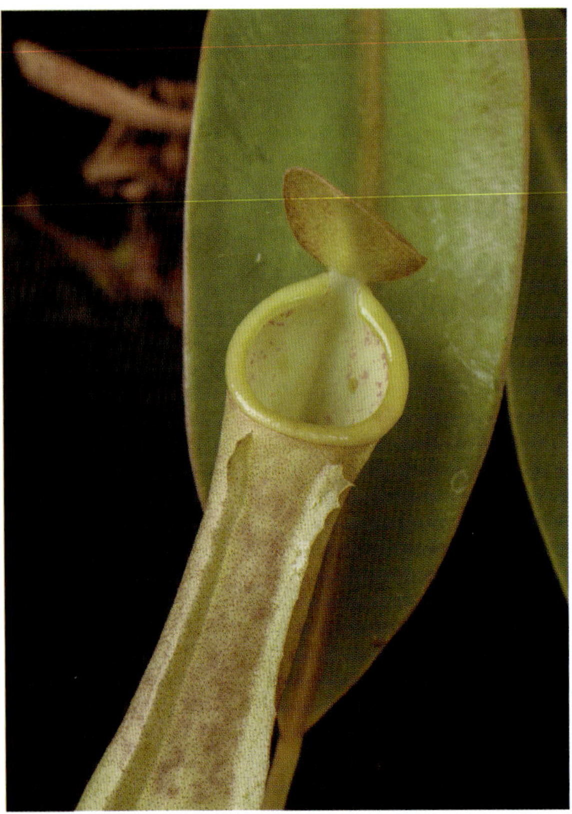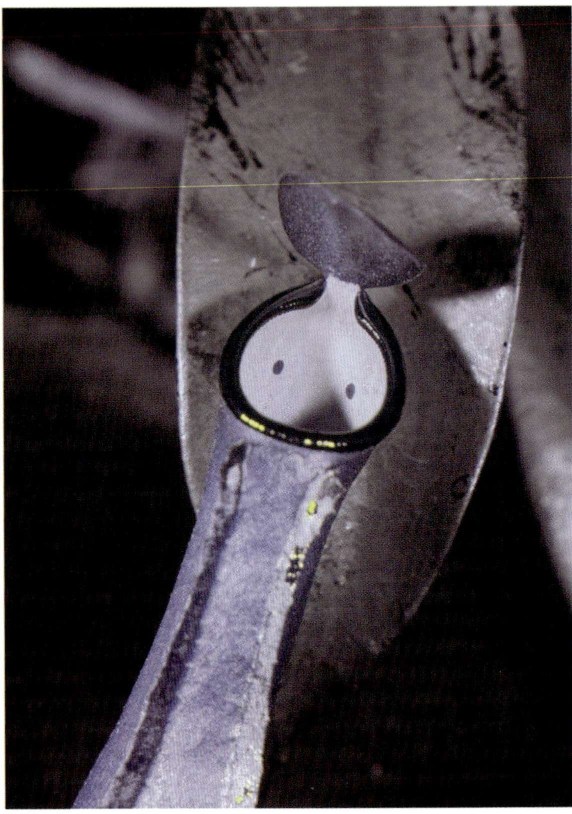

▲ **Fig. 3.24, 3.25**
This carnivorous pitcher plant (*Nepenthes reinwardtiana*) from Borneo is a fascinating plant in that the pitchers have two virtually invisible eye spots on the inner surface (a few specimens may have one or three spots). When photographed in reflected UV, the eye spots become very apparent. It is not known what purpose they serve, though they may be used to attract insects that can see reflected UV. This illustrates how much is still to be learned from UV photography.

Nikon D300S full spectrum camera with 105mm El-NIKKOR lens and Baader U filter. Two modified full spectrum Metz 45CL flashguns. 1/160th @ f/8. 400 ISO.

photography becomes more accessible.

The pitchers of many carnivorous plants, such as various *Sarracenia* and *Nepenthes* species, have also been found to be good subjects for UV reflected photography. Many have intricate veining inside the pitcher, which magically disappears when photographed in reflected UV. Instead, the previously barely visible drops of liquid absorb UV, and are recorded as a very dark, near black tone. It does beg the question: what is the purpose of the veining if potential prey do not see it?

Photography of plants in their habitat in daylight is possible, but difficult. Exposures will probably be quite long, requiring high ISO settings and wide apertures. Windless conditions will help. An example is shown here.

Insect Vision

When trying to illustrate how insects see the world, it must be remembered that they, like the human visual system, have complex multi chromatic visual systems.

Honey bees (*Apis mellifera*) for example, have been extensively studied over the years, and found to have a tri-chromatic visual system similar to human vision. However, unlike the human eye,

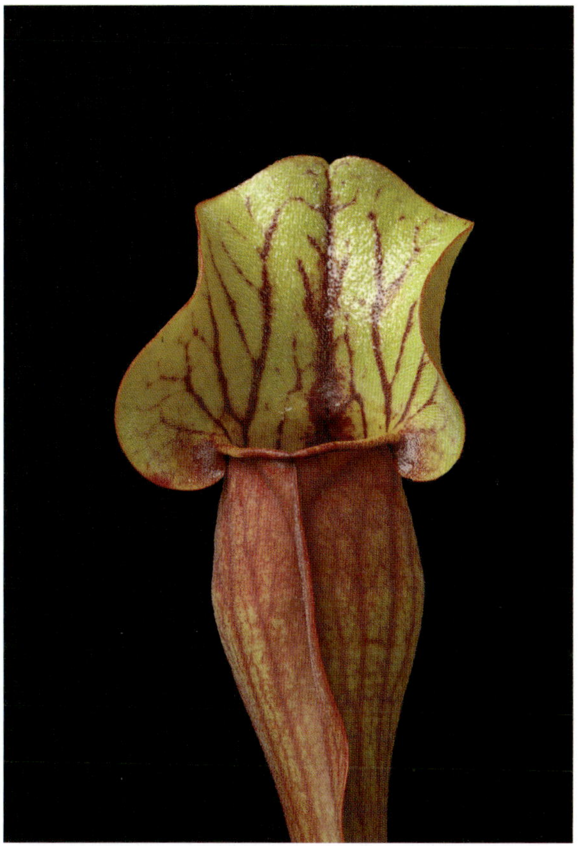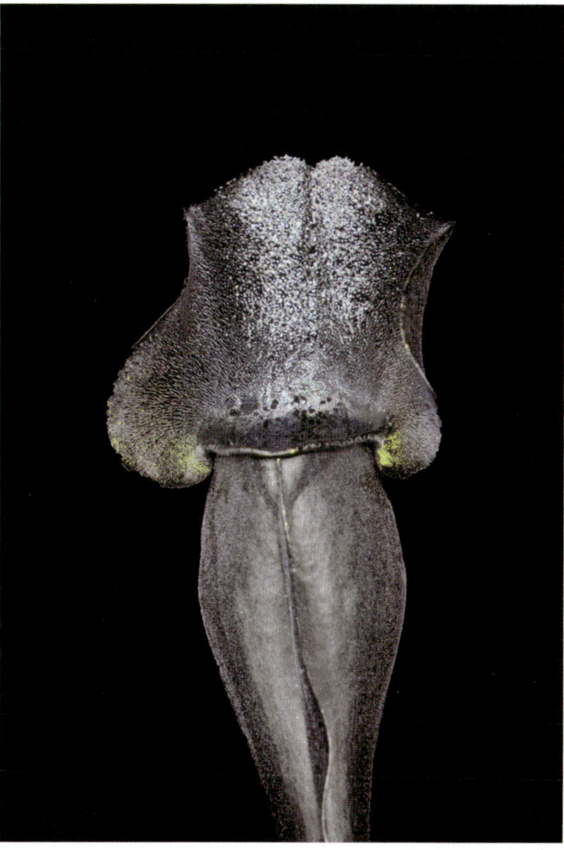

▲ **Fig. 3.26, 3.27**
The carnivorous pitcher plant (*Sarracenia purpurea* × *(catesbaei)*) in visible and UV reflected light. Note how the strong veining disappears in UV, and the UV absorbing insect attracting nectar shows as black blobs in the UV image.

Nikon D300S full spectrum camera with 105mm El-NIKKOR lens and 'Baader U' UV filter. Two modified full spectrum Metz 45CL flashguns. 1/160th @ f/8. 400 ISO.

sensitive to blue, green and red, the honey bee eye is sensitive to UV, blue and green. By using an appropriate combination of filters analogous to this sensitivity, it is possible to produce images that go some way to show how honey bees see their subjects.

A suitable filter combination for simulating the sensitivity of the honey bee is a Schott UG5 (transmitting UV, blue and green), and an S8612 hot mirror filter (absorbing red and IR wavelengths). Some photographers call this combination, or stack, a bee vision filter. Using this filter combination, shoot images with a full-spectrum converted flash, and use a PTFE grey card to establish a white balance.

Other insects and animals have also been extensively studied. Many butterflies for example have been found to have vision that extends further into the red end of the spectrum.

While it will never to be possible to say definitively that this is how an insect sees the world (some authors think that while bees can perceive UV, blue and green, these colours are not necessarily combined into one multi-coloured image), it does go some way to giving us a good insight into the visual world of insects.

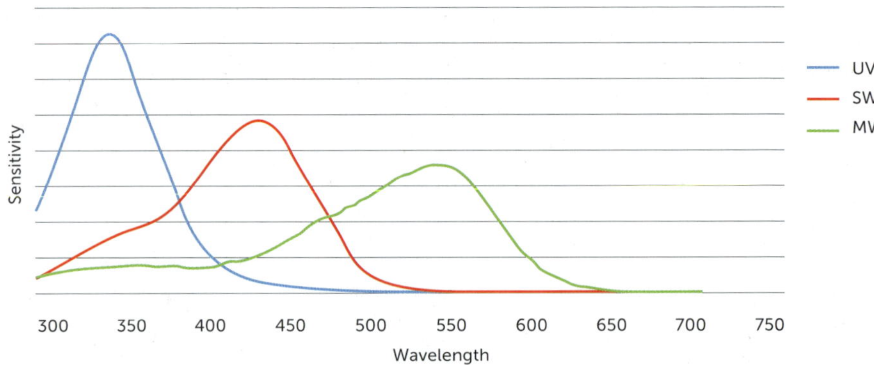

▶ Fig. 3.28
Spectral sensitivity of the honeybee. Like humans, honeybees have trichromatic vision, but have sensitivity to UV rather than red.

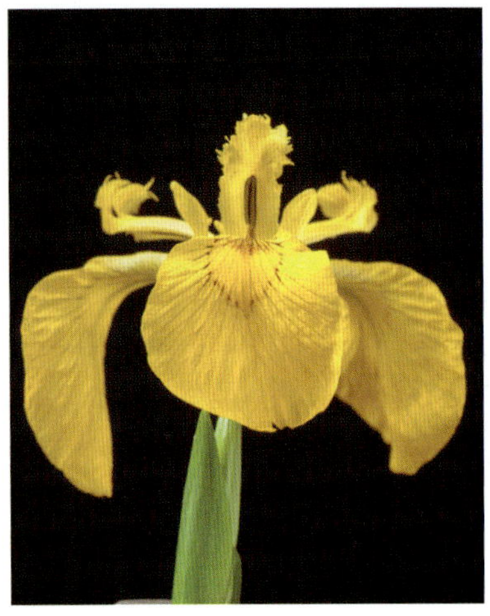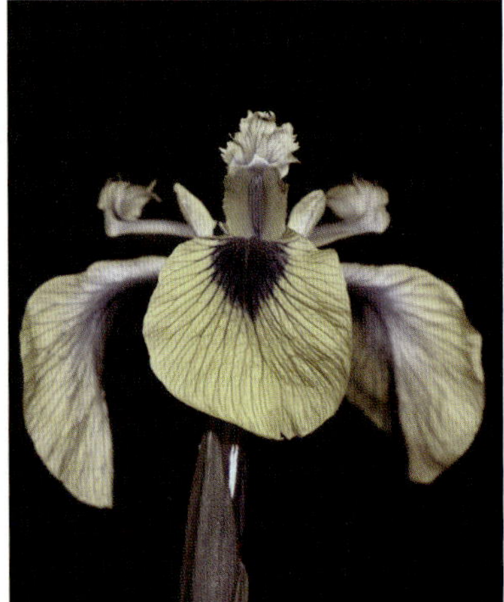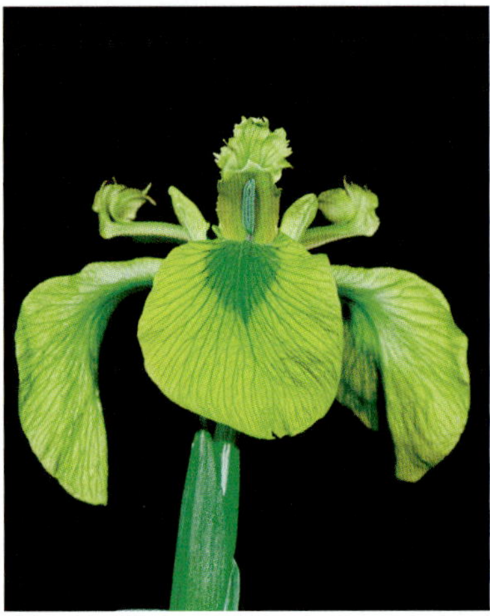

▲ Fig. 3.29, 3.30, 3.31
Yellow Iris (*Iris pseudacorus*) in visible light, UV only, and 'bee vision' using a combination of filters (Schott UG5 + S8612) to simulate bee vision. Nikon D300S full spectrum camera with 105mm El-NIKKOR lens.
  UV image: with 'Baader U' UV filter. 1/160th @ f/8. 400 ISO.
  'Bee vision' with Schott UG5 + S8612 filter combination 1/160th @ f/11. 400 ISO.
  Two modified full-spectrum Metz 45CL flashguns.

Zoology

As we saw in Chapter 1, the human eye is sensitive to wavelengths from 400–700nm, using three receptors on the retina, sensitive to red, green and blue light, giving trichromatic colour vision. There is good evidence that a few people, mainly female, have four receptors (for example the artist Concetta Antico) giving them tetrachromatic vision. There have also been studies to show that some people who have had cataract operations can see a test target in UV light of 365nm.

Many insects and other animals have receptors in their eyes making them sensitive to UV, and in some cases IR as well. Some snakes, beetles and vampire bats can also detect heat through the use of pit organs. Vampire bats (*Desmodus rotundus*) for example, looking for a warm blood meal, sense infrared radiation and heat using heat-sensitive pits on their faces, in the same way as boas, pythons and pit vipers do.

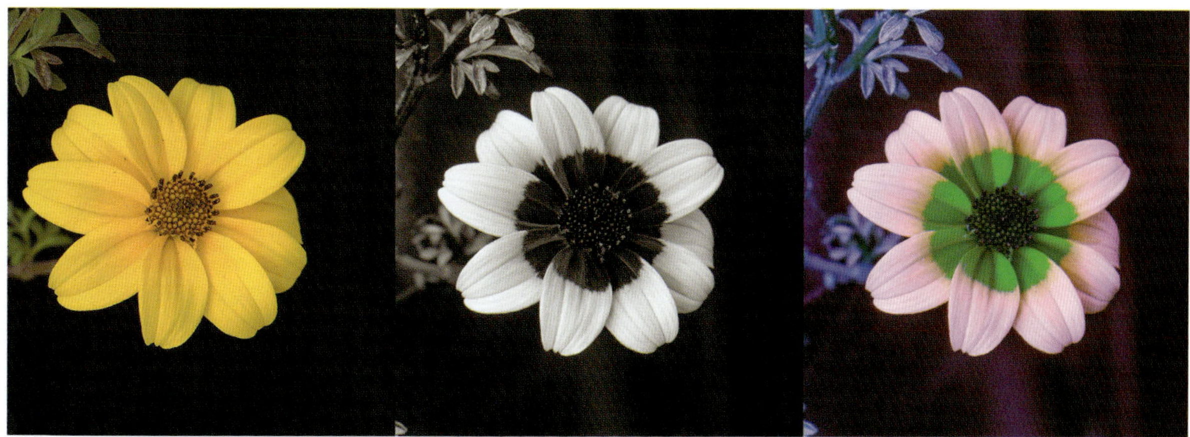

▲ **Fig. 3.32**
Beggarticks (*Bidens sp.*), a plant originally from Mexico, now frequently used in hanging basket arrangements, and a good subject for testing UV equipment, in visible light, UV only, and bee vision using a combination of filters (Schott UG5 + S8612) to simulate bee vision.
Nikon D300S full spectrum camera with 105mm El-NIKKOR lens.
    UV: with Baader U filter. 1/160th @ f/8. 400 ISO.
    Bee vision with Schott UG5 + S8612 filter combination 1/160th @ f/11. 400 ISO.
    Two modified full spectrum Metz 45CL flashguns.

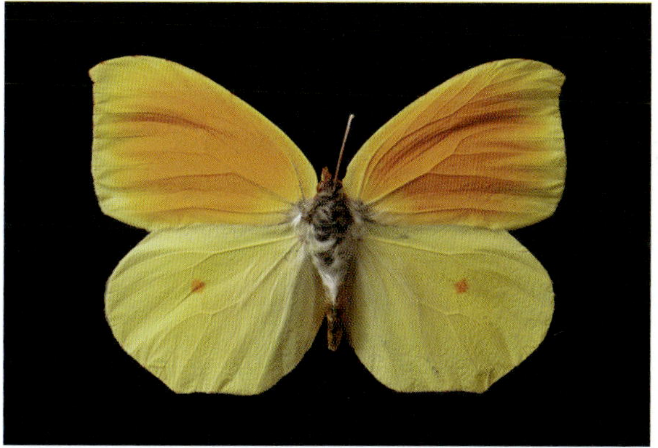 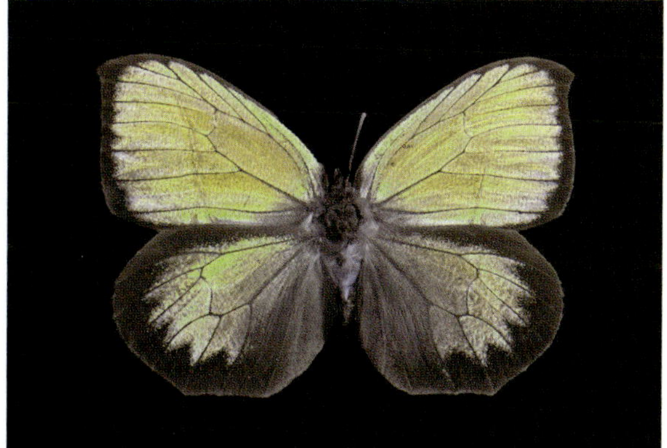

▲ **Fig. 3.33, 3.34**
Cleopatra Butterfly (*Gonepteryx cleopatra*) in visible and reflected UV light. The UV image was white balanced using a home-made grey target made from grey PTFE tape, and balanced in Photo Ninja®.

The animal group with the shortest wavelength sensitivity is the mantis shrimp (order Stomatopoda), which has UV sensitivity down to around 250nm, useful apparently when hunting prey underwater. In fact, mantis shrimps have been found to have twelve different colour receptors, the most of any animal so far studied.

► Fig. 3.35, 3.36
The tropical swallowtail butterfly (*Papilio aeneas)* in visible and reflected UV light. It is interesting that the bright patch on the wing, which can be seen in visible light almost disappears in UV.

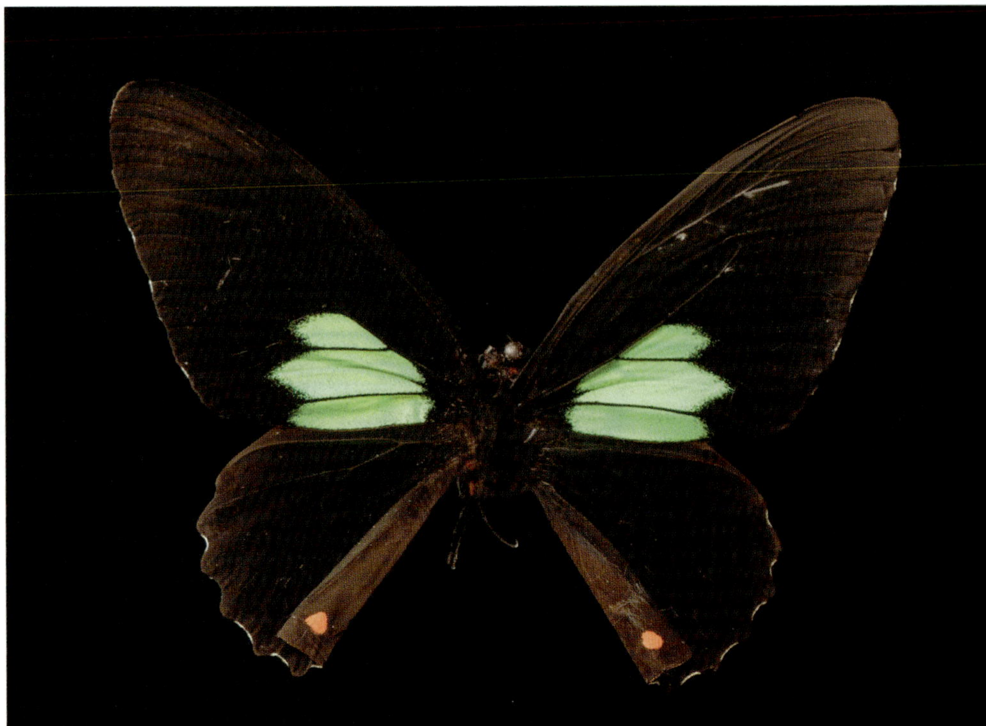

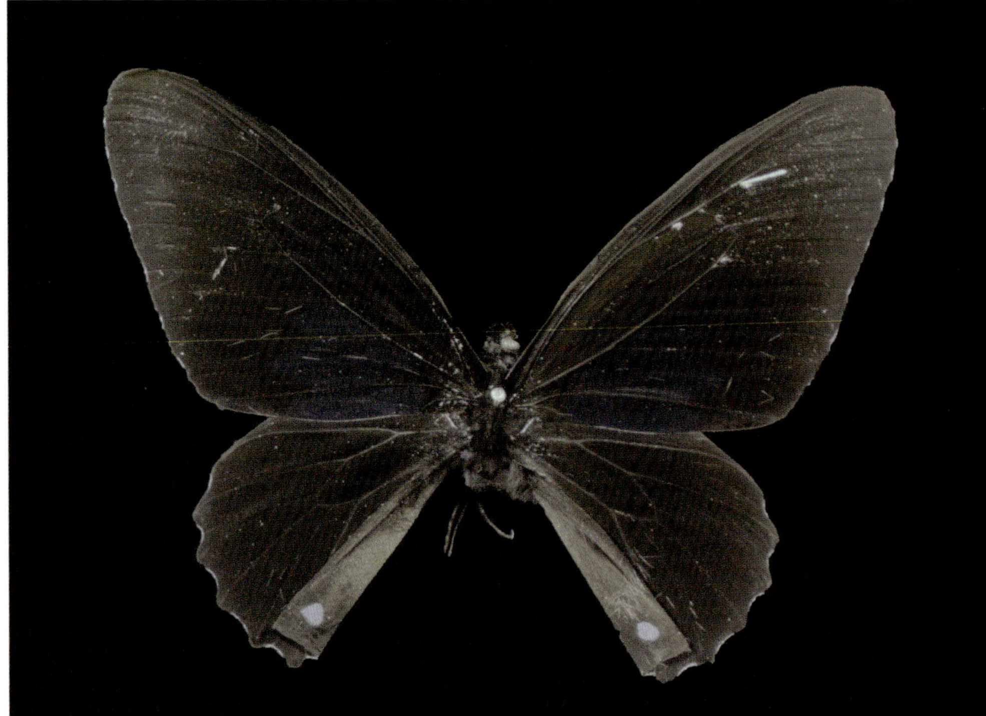

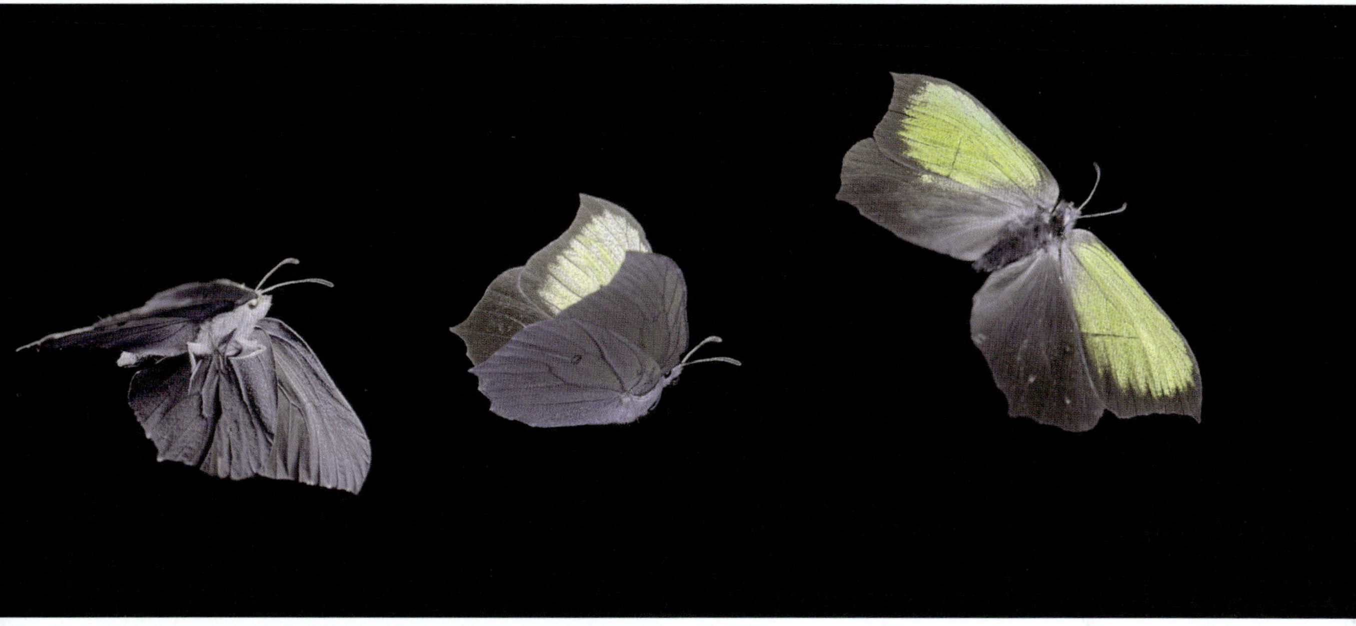

▲ Fig. 3.37

This composite image is an attempt to show why some butterflies, such as this male brimstone (*Gonepteryx rhamni*), have UV reflective areas on their wings, perhaps to attract a female when flying. The image is composed from three separate mounted specimens, each with their wings set in different positions.

The most commonly studied insect is the Honey Bee (*Apis mellifera*), which has been found to have trichromatic colour vision, but with sensitivity to UV (peaking at 353nm), blue (439nm) and green (540nm). By using a filter combination analogous to these figures it is possible to produce images that go some way to showing how a subject is perceived by the bee.

Some butterflies and birds and other animals can also see UV and are worthy of further study. Much research has been carried out by vision scientists over the last few years, trying to show how certain animals see flowers and other subjects. One particular piece of software, free to download, is micaToolbox, from www.empiricalimaging.com. It is an add-on for the open-source scientific imaging and analysis software NIH ImageJ and is capable of a huge range of sophisticated animal vision modelling and analysis tools. It does require calibrated images from a digital camera. There are extensive tutorials on how to do this on the Empirical Imaging website.

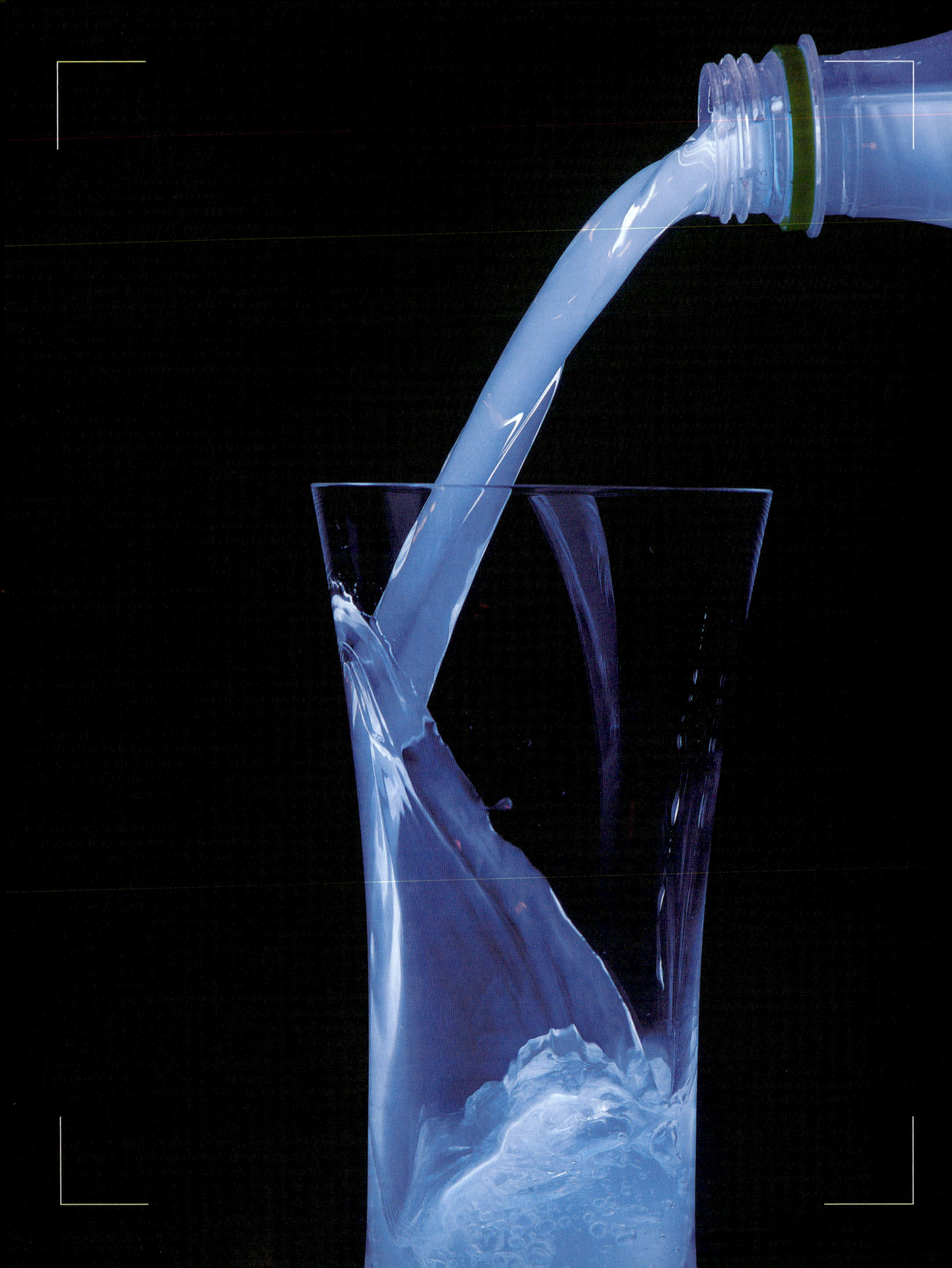

Chapter 4

Ultraviolet Fluorescence Photography

UV fluorescence photography is one of the easier techniques in the book, and certainly potentially capable of producing really exciting images. It can produce some beautiful, unexpected and informative images, and new discoveries and subjects are being found all the time and almost anywhere. UV fluorescence is used by mineralogists to help identify minerals, the fruit industry for finding mould, engineers for finding cracks in metals, by forensic scientists for detecting trace evidence, and by ecologists investigating how micro-plastics are ingested by plankton in the ocean. Palaeontologists are currently using UV fluorescence to gain information about the lives of mammoths from cut sections of their tusks.

The advent of high-powered, relatively cheap UV lights has led to the discovery, for example, of rare lichens in previously unrecorded areas (such as *Ochrolecia arborea*, which fluoresces a bright yellow colour), and on the island of St Helena, ecologists are using the technique to find new populations of the extremely rare and endemic Spiky Yellow Woodlouse (*Pseudolaureola atlantica*) that fluoresces brightly in UV.

In another case, a new type of rock was accidentally discovered in 2018. A gem and mineral dealer was scouring a beach on the edge of Lake Superior, Michigan with a UV torch, and found some highly fluorescent pebbles, which he named yooperlites (after the nickname Yoopers, given to people who live in Michigan's Upper Peninsula). The rocks have been studied by Michigan State and Saskatchewan Universities, who described them as 'syenite clasts containing fluorescent sodalite'.

Another new discovery in 2018 was the fact that the Pumpkin Toadlet (*Brachycephalus ephippium*), a species of frog resident in the Brazilian rainforest, has been found to have a skeleton that fluoresces in UV light. The entire skeleton has been found to fluoresce, but it is only apparent on parts of the body where bony plates sit underneath the thick skin. Another recent discovery is that the fur of flying squirrels fluoresces a pink colour in UV. One possible reason is that the fluorescence may help communication between animals, particularly in winter, when there is a high reflectance of UV from snow.

As spectacular as some of the fluorescent images are, particularly some of the plants, why some subjects fluoresce is a mystery, probably the result of a chemical accident.

UV fluorescence is a form of luminescence, where invisible radiation is converted into visible radiation of a longer wavelength through its interaction with the subject. In the case of UV fluorescence, invisible UV radiation is converted into visible light, which can be seen and photographed with normal cameras and lenses. The process is technically known as excitation. In the case of UV fluorescence, radiation of around 365nm in converted into visible wavelengths from 400–600nm for example. Forensic photographers and art conservators, for example, will often use very specific wavelengths for exciting certain substances such as blood or paint pigments.

◀ **Fig. 4.1**
Tonic water being poured into a glass, fluorescing in UV light. Tonic water contains quinine, which fluoresces in UV. Shot with short duration flash.

Nikon D300 with 105mm micro-Nkkor lens, two full spectrum UV modified Metz 45 CT1 flashes, duration approximately 1/10,000th second.

FLUORESCENCE

In order to understand the process of fluorescence, it is necessary to discuss briefly the structure of atoms. Atoms consist of a nucleus containing protons, surrounded by electrons. The electrons always orbit around the nucleus at their lowest energy state. When the atom absorbs energy, in the form of heat or light, the electrons are pushed into an excited state. When this energy is lost, as the electron returns to its lowest state, it is transformed into light of a longer wavelength. Not all wavelengths of energy can excite atoms.

From a photographic point of view, it is important to realize that atoms only absorb energy at certain specific values (wavelengths), with all other values not providing the excitation. Planck's theory states that an electron will only become excited to a higher level if a photon of light contains the appropriate energy to excite it to that level. In other words, molecules are selective in the wavelengths of light that they will absorb. This selectivity is determined by the electron energy levels that each element possesses.

Once excited into the higher state, the electron will quickly fall back to its original level, releasing energy and emitting the fluorescence. To ensure a continuous flow of energy from the atom, a continuous light (radiation) source is required. The fluorescence will disappear immediately on the removal of the excitation source.

The difference between the excitation wavelength and emitted wavelength is known as the Stokes shift.

FLUORESCENCE, LUMINESCENCE AND PHOSPHORESCENCE

There are several terms related to light emission and fluorescence, which can cause confusion, and it is worth clarifying them.

Luminescence

Luminescence is the visible light emitted from a subject as the result of a stimulus, such as excitation from a UV source, or chemical reaction. Different types include:

- bio-luminescence (as seen in glow worms, fireflies, some marine plankton and some fungi),
- chemi-luminescence, the result of a chemical reaction, as seen in Glow Sticks for example, and
- electro-luminescence, as exhibited with LED lighting.

Fluorescence

Fluorescence is the visible light emitted from a subject when illuminated, or excited with a shorter wavelength source such as UV. The emission ceases immediately following the removal of the excitation source. Another interesting form of fluorescence is IR fluorescence. This is where the subject is lit with visible light of a certain wavelength, usually cyan in the region of 480nm, and IR wavelengths are emitted. The wavelengths emitted are invisible, i.e. they are IR, so it is not known if the effect persists after the removal of the light source. This phenomenon should strictly be called IR luminescence. It is used primarily nowadays by art conservators looking at pigments.

Phosphorescence

In phosphorescence, the light emitted from the phosphors persists after the removal of the stimulus. It was used extensively in cathode ray tubes for television and other devices.

Fluorescence can be seen in everyday subjects, from Vaseline petroleum jelly, fluorescent marker pens, high visibility safety jackets to invisible markings on banknotes and passports. Every page on the UK passport has a different invisible bird or animal, which can be seen when viewed under a UV light source. Scientists use the principle for identifying both minerals and mould. The phenomenon is seen in night clubs (where longer wavelength lights are used, in the region of 390nm), where clothing may glow brightly under the near UV lights. The brightness of the fabric is caused by whiteners and residual washing powder. One way of finding scorpions in the desert or jungle at night is to scan an area with a UV torch. Scorpions fluoresce a bright blue colour. Many other invertebrates, including some millipedes and spiders, also fluoresce. Engineers make use of UV fluorescence for detecting otherwise invisible cracks by smearing metallic surfaces with fluorescent penetrating oil such as Zyglo®. If there are any cracks in the metal, these show up when the area is illuminated with UV light. The technique is known as non-invasive testing and is used extensively in the aircraft industry.

One particular type of glass, used for bowls and ornaments mainly during the art deco period of the 1920s and '30s was uranium glass, where a small amount of uranium oxide was added to the glass mixture. These glass pieces fluoresce a bright green colour when illuminated with UV light. Although considered completely safe, it is said that some pieces will register a tiny value on a highly sensitive Geiger counter. A well-verified story tells of a radiation technician working in a hospital, whose radiation monitoring badge kept getting fogged, despite no sign of any leakage at work. It was discovered by chance that she put the badge each night in a uranium glass bowl! The second world war saw an increase in the demand for uranium and manufacturing of the glass effectively ceased.

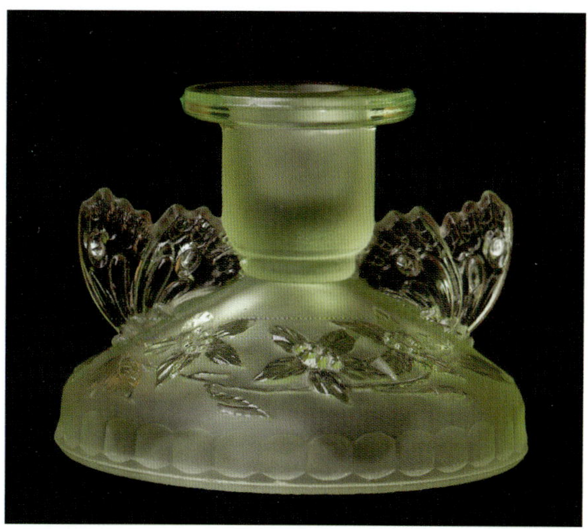

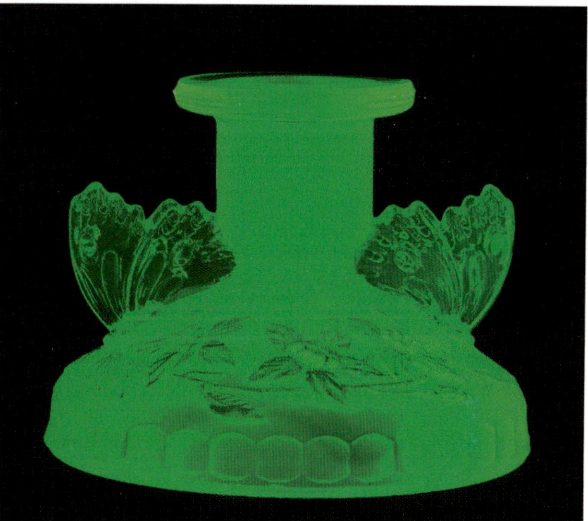

▲ **Fig. 4.2, 4.3**
An art deco piece of uranium glass from the 1920s, in visible light and fluorescing in UV. Soft diffused lighting was used to minimize specular highlights.

Nikon D800 with 105mm micro-NIKKOR lens. Light painted with single Convoy S2+ LED UV torch. UV exposure approximately 15 seconds @ f/16, 200 ISO.

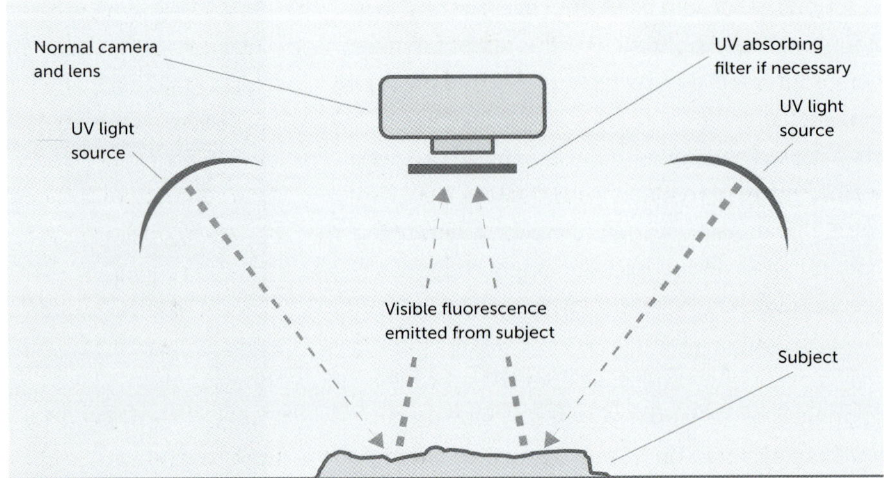

▶ **Fig. 4.4**
Basic set up for UV fluorescence photography carried out in a completely dark room.

PHOTOGRAPHY

Virtually any camera and lens can be used for fluorescence photography, provided that they have the capability for long exposures – you will often be using exposure times of ten or more seconds. A solid tripod and remote release together with a completely dark room will also be essential. Try to keep the aperture for the fluorescence image and visible light control image (if you shoot one) the same so that the depth of field of both images match. A low ISO, e.g. 200, will minimize the digital noise from the lengthy exposure.

Background choice is important. Many papers and fabrics will fluoresce themselves and could interfere with the fluorescence emitted by the subject. A good choice for subjects such as minerals is black velvet, which does not itself fluoresce and gives a good contrast within the image. Even with a solid black background, every speck of dust on the velvet or subject may fluoresce, so an amount of retouching may be needed afterwards. It is worth using a powerful blower brush on the subject before photography.

An alternative to black velvet is a black paint, such as Semple Black 3.0, from Culture Hustle, a boutique art materials supplier. This is reputedly one of the mattest and blackest paints on the market, and tests with UV lights show very little fluorescence. This would also make a good black background for some of the other techniques in the book.

LIGHT SOURCES FOR UV FLUORESCENCE

Various types of UV lamp are available, though most are expensive due to their specialist nature. Forensic photographers for example, use UV sources extensively, often of very specific wavelengths to make various fluids fluoresce (for which tuneable lasers are available), and mineralogists make use of powerful hand held UV sources to find and identify minerals in the field.

Laser (Light Amplification by Stimulated Emission of Radiation)

Various types of laser are used, primarily by forensic photographers requiring very specific UV (and other) wavelengths, to excite substances in trace evidence. Several models aimed at the forensic market are tuneable, in that they can be made to emit very specific wavelengths. They are specialist, expensive, and outside the scope of this book.

LEDs

LEDs (light emitting diodes) are tiny light bulbs that fit into an electrical circuit, and emit light when current flows through them. Unlike ordinary incandescent bulbs, they don't have a filament that will burn out, and they don't get especially hot. They are illuminated solely by the movement of electrons in a semiconductor material, and have a very long life, as long as a standard transistor. This effect is called electroluminescence. Various colours can be emitted, for example white, red, green and blue as well as UV and IR,

What is needed for most UV fluorescence photography is a small but powerful source, nowadays commonly available as LED torches. Although there are many such torches on the market, most are designed for checking banknotes or other documents, for example, and are generally not powerful enough for fluorescence photography. Two particularly good models for UV fluorescence photography are the MTE® 303, and the much cheaper but equally good Convoy S2+ UV. These both emit UV at around 365nm. Technically, they contain the Nichia 365 UV LED emitter, a very powerful UV source.

Most UV sources emit some visible light as well, which may affect the colour of the fluorescence image. One way of checking this is to illuminate, in a darkened room, a small piece of shiny metal such as a coin or ball bearing. Metal does not fluoresce, so should be invisible. Any hint of detail will indicate a visible light leakage. It is possible to get filters that remove most of this visible light, such as the Hoya U-340 filter, which is available in 20.2mm × 2mm size from UVIROptics, designed specifically to fit the Convoy S2+ torch (replacing the clear glass). The U-340 cuts below the 400nm point, thus allowing no blue or violet transmission at all.

You will need to unscrew the LED housing, and then unscrew the retaining ring holding the reflector and glass in place. You will need a pair of long-nosed pliers or perhaps a pair of scissors to do this. Replace the clear glass with the U-340 and re-assemble.

Other forms of LED lighting are available, emitting a wavelength of 365nm, such as the Lixada 7W 365nm LED light bulb. This has a plastic dome that can be removed by cutting it with a strong knife. Various models of outdoor security floodlight type lighting such as the YQL Outdoor UV Black Light, 10W UV LED Flood Light are also available, though these tend to emit longer wavelength UV from 385–415nm, probably too long for useful UV fluorescence photography. Both of these types are mains operated, so are restricted to indoor use.

Aquarium keepers use LED lighting with a variety of wavelengths including long wave UV of around 385nm upwards.

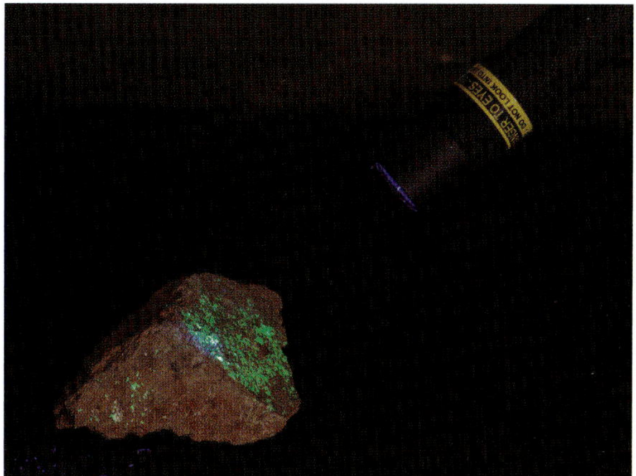

▲ **Fig. 4.5**
A Convoy S2+ LED UV torch, being used to produce UV fluorescence in a mineral specimen (willemite). Note the fluorescing dust on the velvet background.

PAINTING WITH LIGHT

The light emitted from a small UV torch is generally rather uneven, with a very definite hot spot and may not cover the specimen evenly. One way round this issue is to use a photographic technique called 'painting with light'. This is a technique used not just by UV photographers but also other studio photographers, when photographing large still life subjects for example. It requires a dark room (UV fluorescence photography needs a completely darkened room). The camera shutter is opened, and the subject painted with light, by moving the light source constantly throughout the exposure. Using this technique you can be certain of light reaching all areas of the subject, (or light can be concentrated onto one area or side if preferred). It may take a few tests to ensure an even coverage of the subject. You will need to ensure a shutter speed of at least ten- to twenty-seconds or more to give you enough time to cover the whole subject. You might need to hold the torch some distance away from the subject to achieve this exposure time. You can give more emphasis to the top of the subject, or other areas for example, and will probably need to do a few experimental shots to achieve the effect you are after. If you have a delicate subject, such as a flower, you may need to restrict your physical movement, and even hold your breath to prevent it moving during the exposure.

Try to use a relatively low ISO, such as 200, this will reduce the amount of digital noise in the image. Setting the camera to aperture priority mode should give a reasonably good exposure, though a level of exposure compensation may be required to prevent burned out highlights. It is worth checking the histogram, and also having the highlights flashing facility activated on the camera to check for over-exposed highlights.

Take great care when working and moving about in a dark room, and always have a normal light to hand. A head torch can be useful to help make camera adjustments and find pieces of kit without turning the room light on. It is worth putting a lanyard on the UV torch so that it can be hung around your neck, to save trying to find it in the dark.

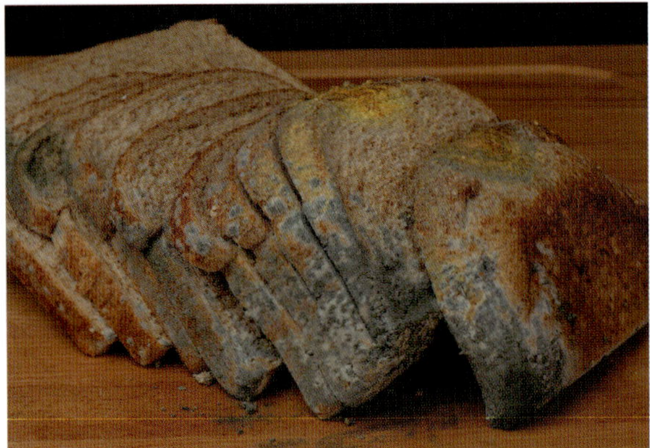
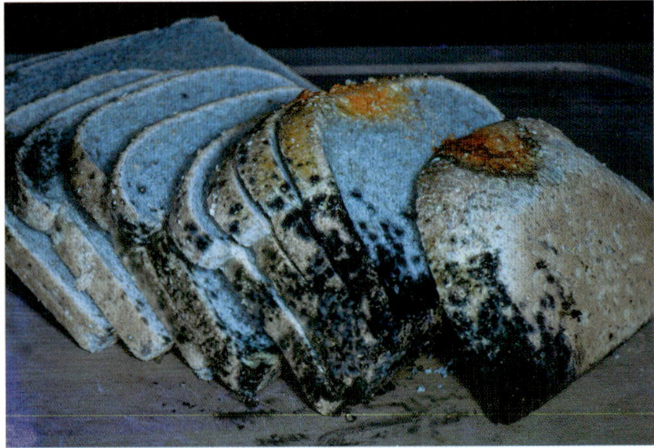

▲ **Fig. 4.6, 4.7**
This loaf of bread, covered in mould was light painted with a small Convoy torch during an exposure of approximately thirty seconds to ensure even coverage.

UV SAFETY

Take great care when using UV torches, in particular with your eyes, and never look directly at a UV source. Special UV safety glasses are available, and well-worth wearing if you are going to be doing a reasonable amount of this photography (ski goggles will also work). Get the wraparound type that will prevent the UV entering through the side. If you are photographing people with UV, always make sure they shut their eyes or wear protective glasses.

If you are using UV sources a lot it may also be worth covering areas of skin such as your arms with clothing. Although the risks are very small it is much better to be safe than sorry.

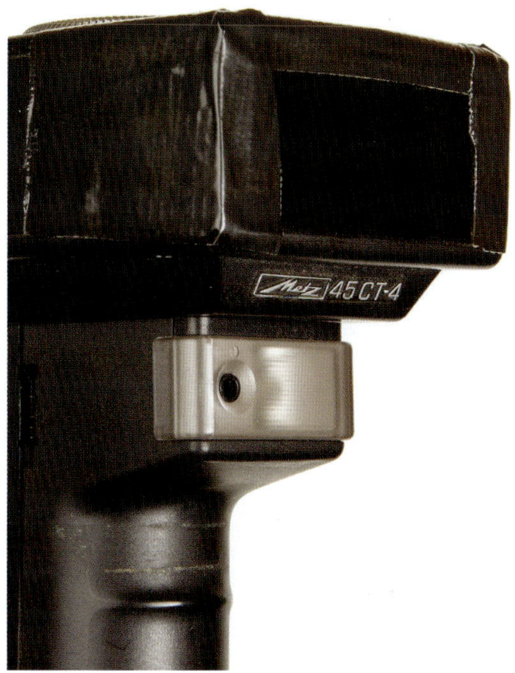

▲ **Fig. 4.8**
An old Metz 45CT-4 flashgun, with the UV absorbing filter removed, and replaced with an old Kodak 18A Wood's Glass filter.

UV Flash

For moving, non-static subjects such as live invertebrates or liquid, you will need to use a UV filtered flash source. Several of the camera conversion companies listed in the resources section sell them. It is possible to make your own if you can find a suitable UV filter such as a Wood's glass filter or similar, large enough to fit over the flash window. The one shown here is an old 75mm square Kodak 18A Wood's glass filter, which was carefully cut in half. By chance this fitted exactly into the aperture of a Metz 45CT1 flashgun. The UV absorbing filter will first need to be removed, as discussed in Chapter 3. The filter will need to be tightly taped with black tape to ensure that no visible light is emitted from the flash. Although this particular filter is well known for having a significant IR output, this will be no problem when used with a normal spectrum camera that is not sensitive to IR.

Note: Unless otherwise stated, all remaining UV fluorescence images in this chapter were shot with a Nikon D800 or D810 camera, 105mm micro-Nikkor lens, and light painted with a Convoy S2+ UV LED torch for around 15–20 seconds @ f/16, 200 ISO.

APPLICATIONS

As indicated in the introduction, UV fluorescence has a multitude of applications. A few are given below.

Minerals

Many mineral specimens fluoresce in UV, in particular fluorspar after which the mineral is named. Other good examples are Willemite, Hyalite and Calcite. Mineralogists use this property to help identify certain minerals, though the colour of the fluorescence may vary according to the precise source of the specimen. They often use large hand held UV lamps to find fluorescent minerals on the spoil heaps at the entrance to mines for example. Some minerals only fluoresce in short wave UV, of 254nm.

An excellent source of information for UV fluorescent minerals is: www.naturesrainbows.com

Some examples are shown here:

Mineral	Fluorescence Colour
Autunite	Yellow green
Calcite	Red, orange, sometimes blue or green depending on source of specimen
Fluorspar	Blue, yellow, green, red or white depending on source of specimen
Gypsum	Light green
Hyalite	Bright green
Wernerite	Golden yellow
Willemite	Intense green

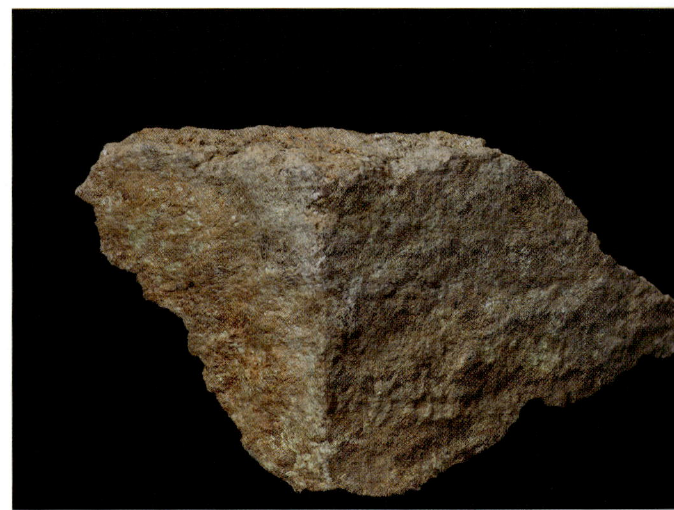

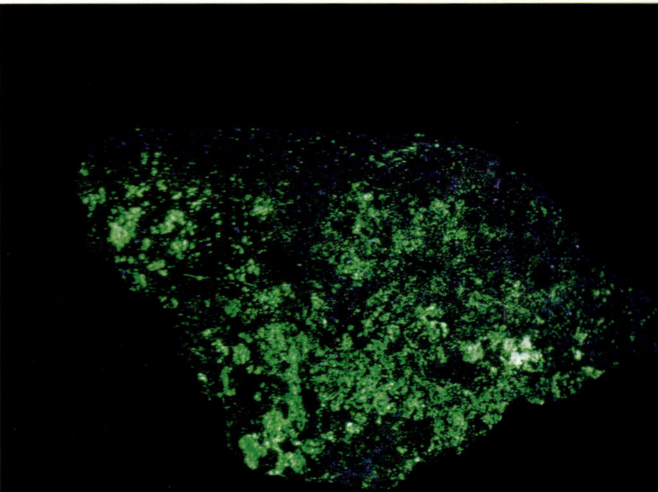

▲ **Fig. 4.9, 4.10**
The mineral willemite (Zn2SiO4) is highly fluorescent and makes a good subject for UV fluorescence photography.

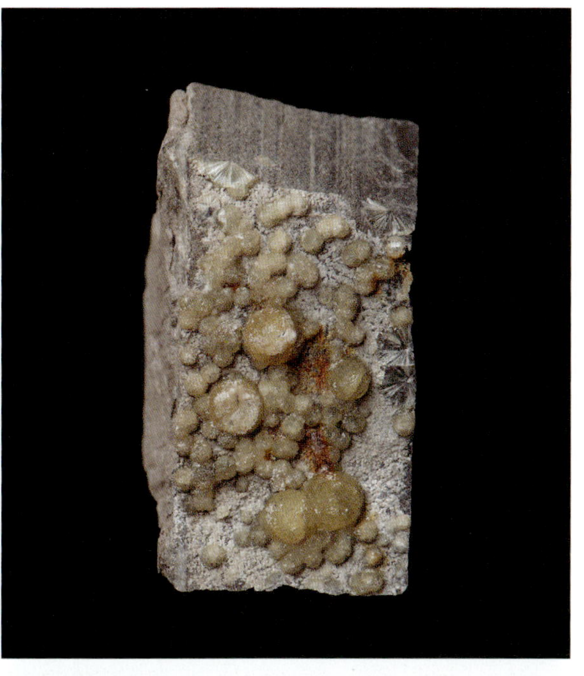

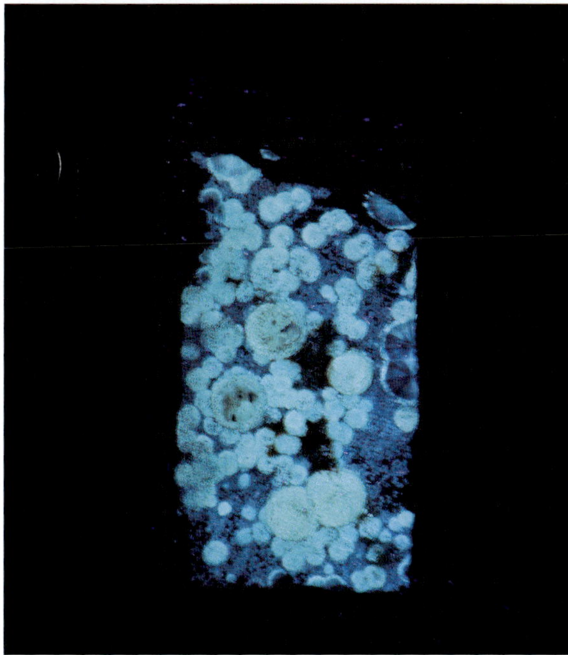

▲ **Fig. 4.11, 4.12**
Wavellite, a phosphate mineral.

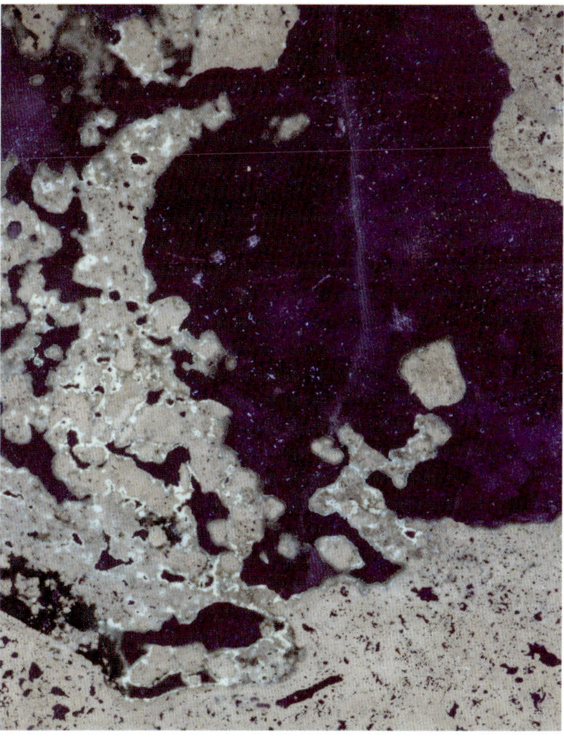

▲ **Fig. 4.13, 4.14**
Travertine, in this case a bathroom tile.

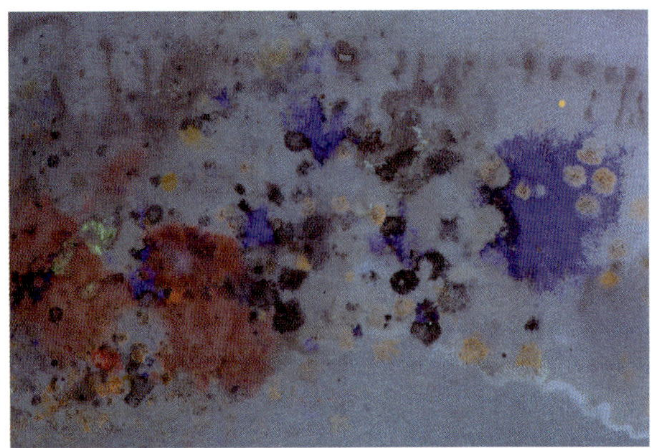

▲ Fig. 4.15, 4.16
Mould growing on a water damaged foam board. There are probably several different species revealed with the UV fluorescence.

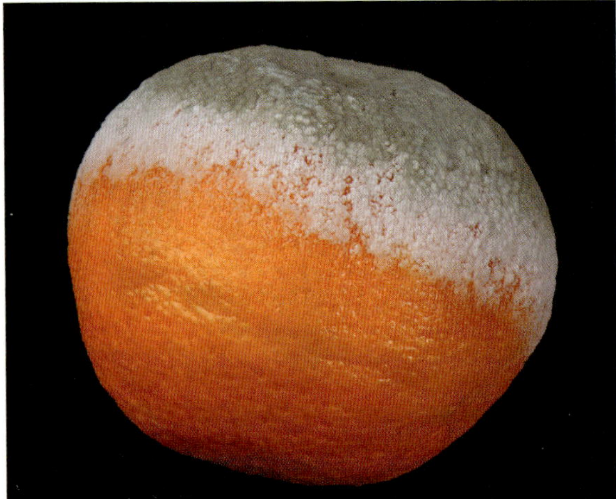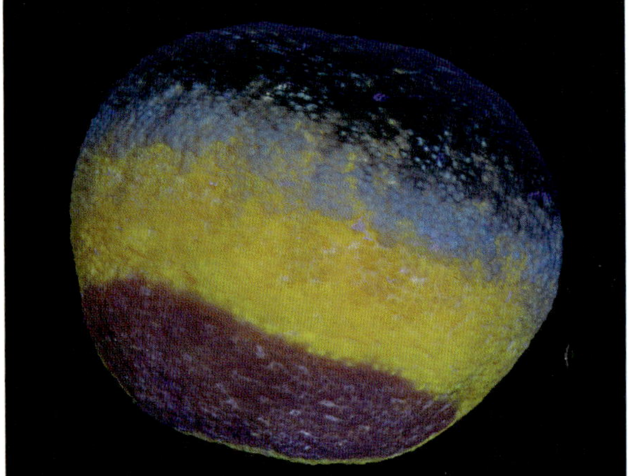

▲ Fig. 4.17, 4.18
Satsuma orange with mould.

Mould

Several species of mould fluoresce in UV light, and the citrus industry in the United States uses UV to detect mould on fruit. Other crops such as hay, grains, rice and the like also suffer from various moulds, which can be detected with UV. An examination of a well rotted compost heap at night with a UV torch can show a dazzling array of fluorescent colours.

The foam board shown here suffered from water damage, and when dried out a range of moulds appeared.

Satsuma oranges in particular often display a dazzling range of coloured moulds, probably the same species in different stages. If you find a suitable specimen it is worth keeping it, perhaps in a sealed plastic box, to see how the mould develops over a period of time. Wash your hands after handling mouldy fruit to prevent transferring spores from one fruit to another.

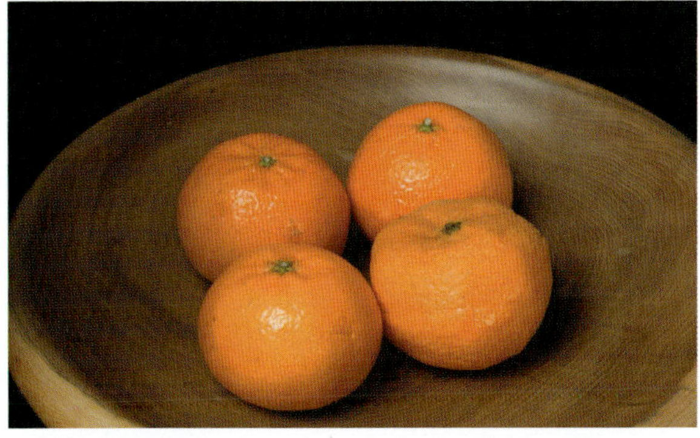 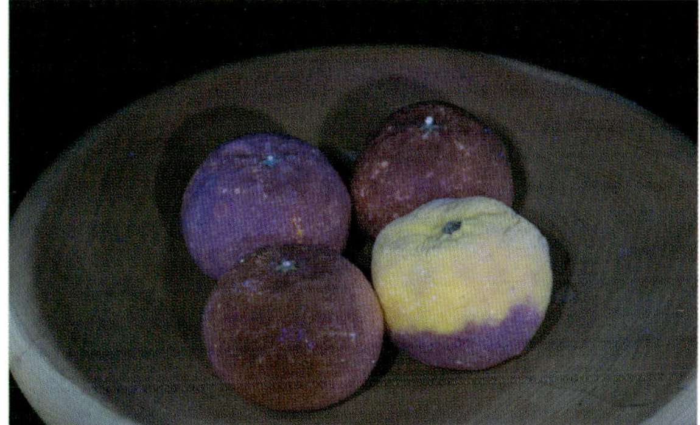

▲ **Fig. 4.19, 4.20**
Satsumas in bowl, one with mould, revealed with UV light.

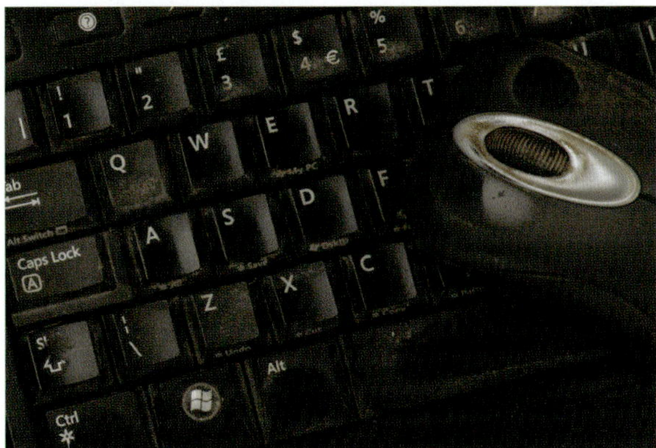 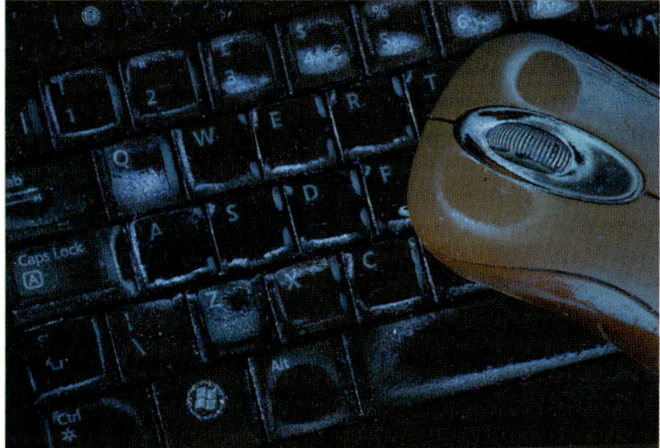

▲ **Fig. 4.21, 4.22**
Old computer keyboard and mouse in visible light, and fluorescing in UV light. Dirt and grease are shown fluorescing. Note the different materials used to construct the keyboard and mouse.

Computer keyboards and mice can become dirty with food particles, dirt and other germs, which are a potential health hazard. One commonly quoted statistic is that the average keyboard can be up to five times dirtier than the average toilet seat. The major culprits for this are people eating food at their desks and not washing their hands after using the toilet. In the former case, sticky fingers transfer sauces and edible particles onto and between the keys. It can be a very sobering experience seeing a computer keyboard and mouse fluoresce in a dark room!

When photographing mould (and many of the other subjects in the book) you will need to take opportunities when they arrive. If you find a good mouldy Satsuma it will quickly deteriorate so will need to be photographed quite quickly. Keeping it cool overnight will slow down the development of the mould. Remember to wash your hands thoroughly after handling it.

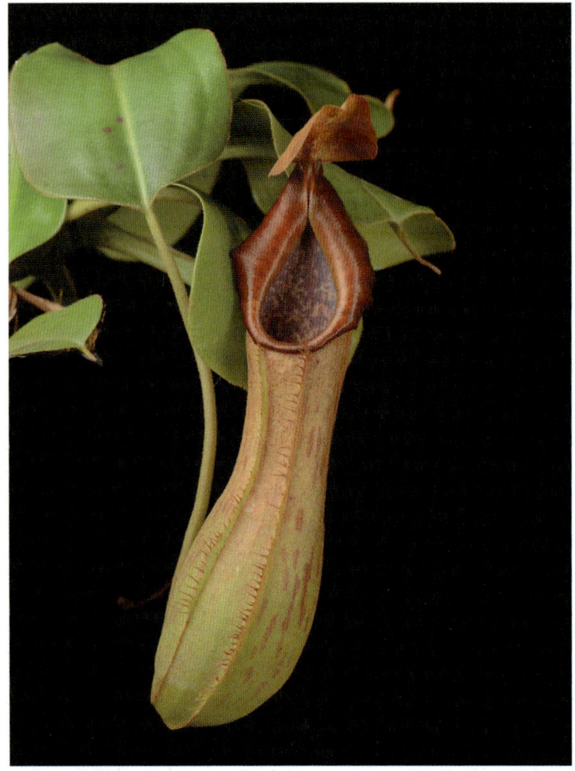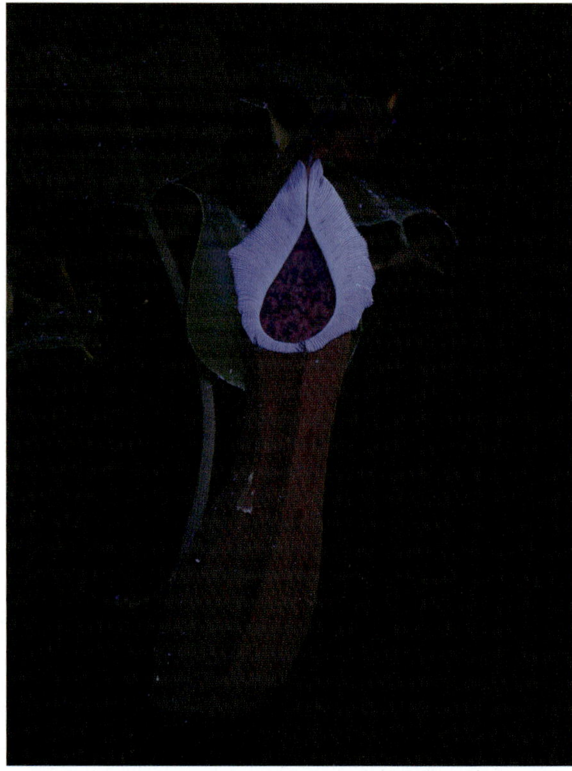

▲ **Fig. 4.23, 4.24**
Pitcher plant (*Nepenthes spathulata* × (*copelandii* × *truncata*)) in visible light and UV fluorescence. It has only recently been discovered that the rim around the pitcher (peristome) fluoresces in UV.

PLANTS, POLLEN, PINE RESIN, RED SEAWEED

Many plants, or part of plants, fluoresce in UV light. Chlorophyll fluoresces a bright red colour, for example.

One recently discovered fluorescent subject are carnivorous pitcher plants, such as the Tropical Monkey Cups (*Nepenthes spp.*) and north American *Sarracenia* species. The rim (peristome) of many pitchers has been found to fluoresce in UV light. The main reason would perhaps be that in a dark rainforest at night, lit only by moonlight (containing some UV), the pitchers are attracting their prey to the nectar secreting lid of the trap by having a bluish ring around the trap.

Many flowers too fluoresce brightly in UV, even if this is as a result of a chemical accident it is very visually interesting! Good examples are Gazanias, Coreopsis and Sunflowers. Like UV reflected images, it is often composite flowers such as Daisies that show the effects of UV fluorescence well.

Some pollen fluoresces, such as that of the Four O'Clock Flower, a plant from Mexico, whose pollen fluoresces brightly in UV, while the nectar from some plants fluoresces. Other good examples are the Pineapple Lily (*Eucomis bicolor*) that fluoresces a yellow colour, and Almond (*Prunus amygdalus*) that fluoresces a blue colour.

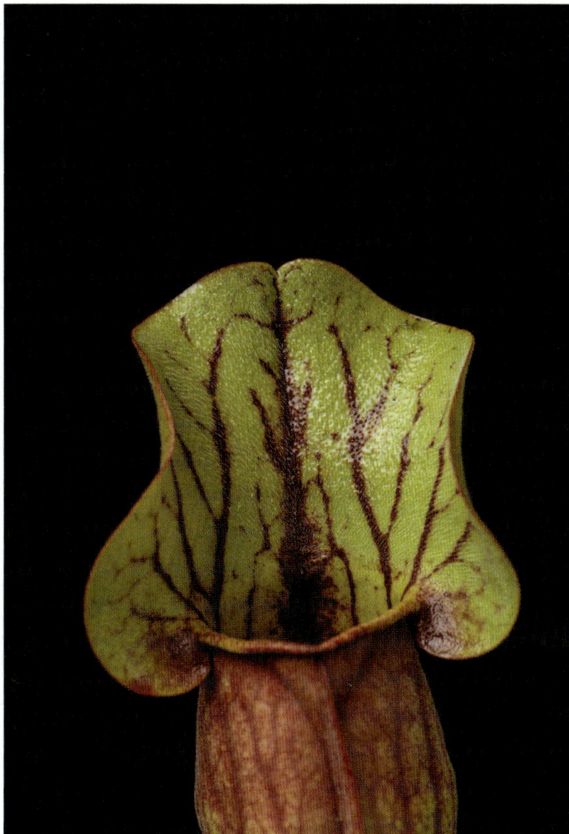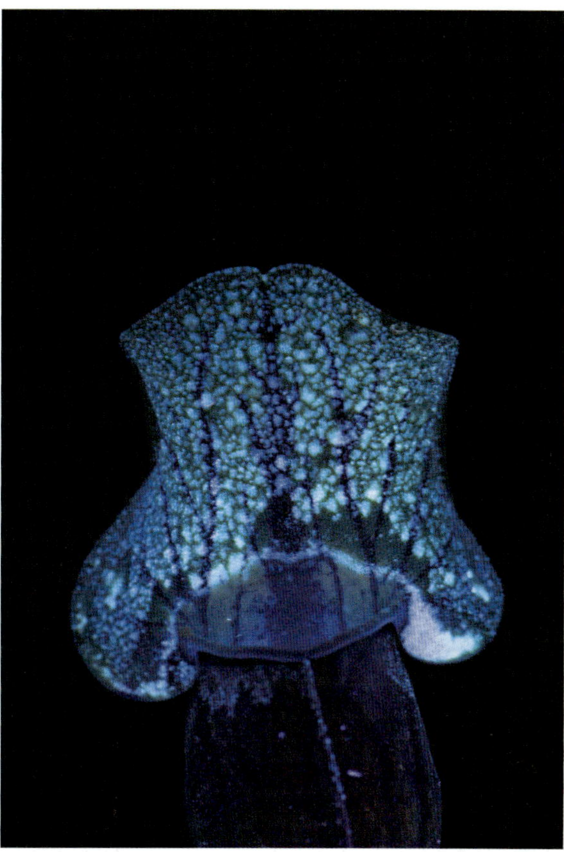

Another example of a plant product that fluoresces in UV is tonic water, which contains quinine, derived from the Cinchona Tree (*Cinchona officinalis*). Originally used as an anti-malarial drug, tonic water is of course now a major constituent of gin and tonic (the gin was originally added to make the tonic more palatable!). The fluorescence can sometimes be seen in daylight. If a glass of gin and tonic is placed in the sun, a faint blue colour can sometimes be seen. For the image shown at the beginning of chapter 4, tonic water was poured into a glass in a darkened room and exposed with the UV converted flash discussed earlier in the chapter, set to give its shortest duration.

A substance emanating from trees, particularly conifers, is resin, which has been found to have a distinct blue colour when fluorescing. One way (though not 100 per cent infallible) of distinguishing fossil resin (amber) from the many fakes on the market is to see if it fluoresces in UV. Genuine amber fluoresces a blue-green colour, while forgeries (usually plastic) do not fluoresce, or, if they do, it is a different colour.

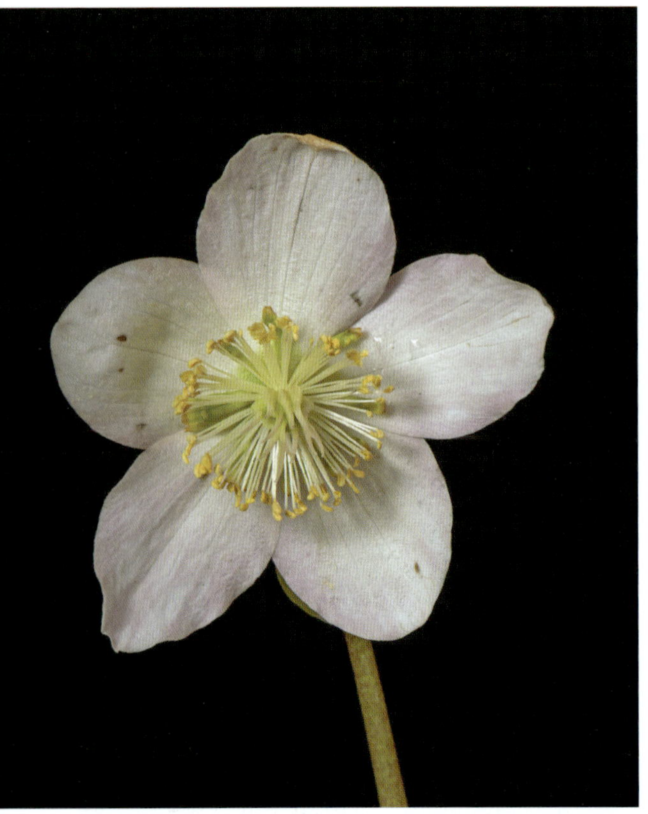

▲ **Fig. 4.27, 4.28**
The hellebore flower (*Helleborus niger)*, showing fluorescent pollen.

Lichens

Lichens are fascinating organisms, a mixture of fungus and alga growing in a symbiotic relationship. Lichens produce a variety of chemicals called rather imaginatively, lichen substances, probably having evolved to protect them against UV from intense sunlight. Some of these lichens show fluorescence when illuminated with UV light, in particular various *Cladonia* species. It can be a very rewarding and interesting experience to walk through a forest at night with a UV torch, to see which species fluoresce. On a recent trip to Costa Rica, the bark of some trees lit up like Christmas trees with fluorescent lichens when illuminated with a UV torch at night. Because most lichens are solid, growing on rocks or trees, they can be easily photographed in situ without fear of movement. You will obviously need to photograph them at night unless you build a box around them to exclude the ambient light.

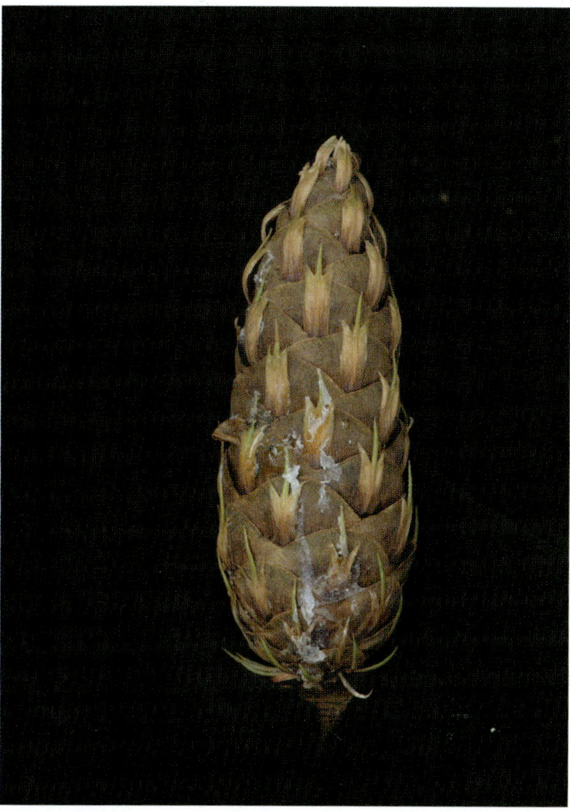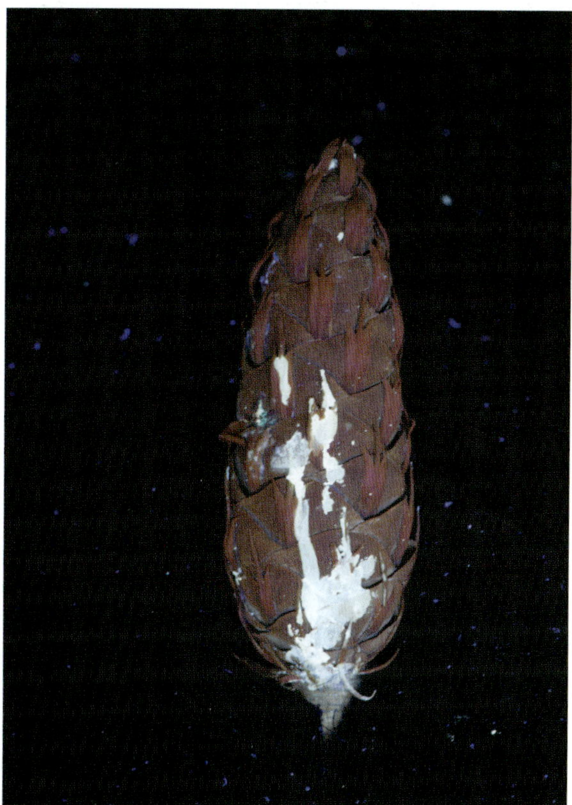

▲ Fig. 4.29, 4.30
Cone from fir tree (*Abies sp.*). Resin fluorescing.

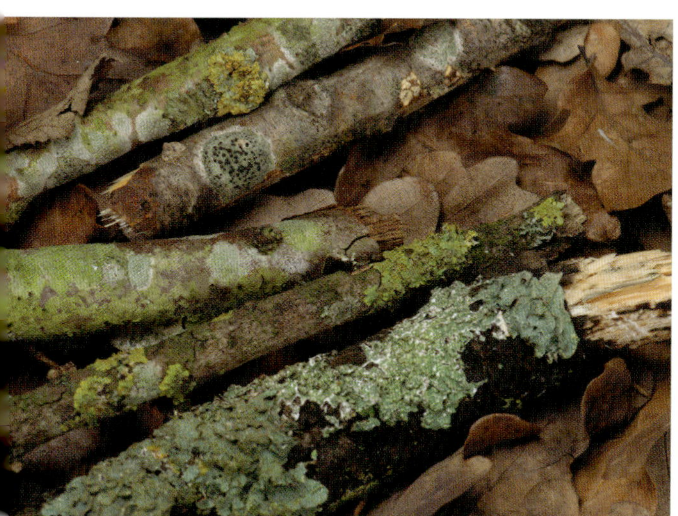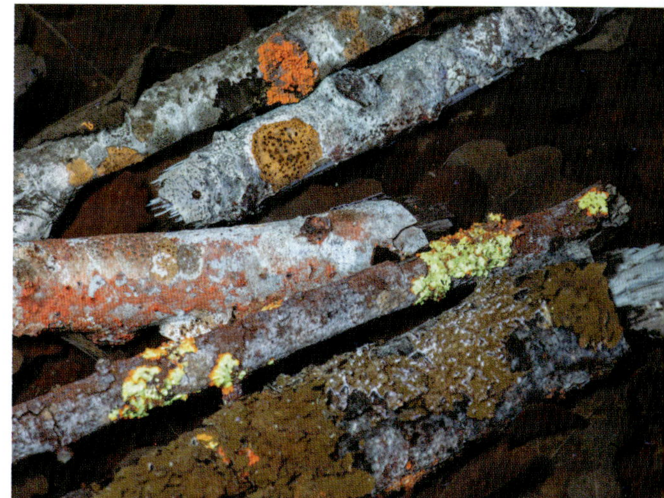

▲ Fig. 4.31, 4.32
A variety of lichens growing on tree branches, found on woodland floor in an ancient wood in the UK.

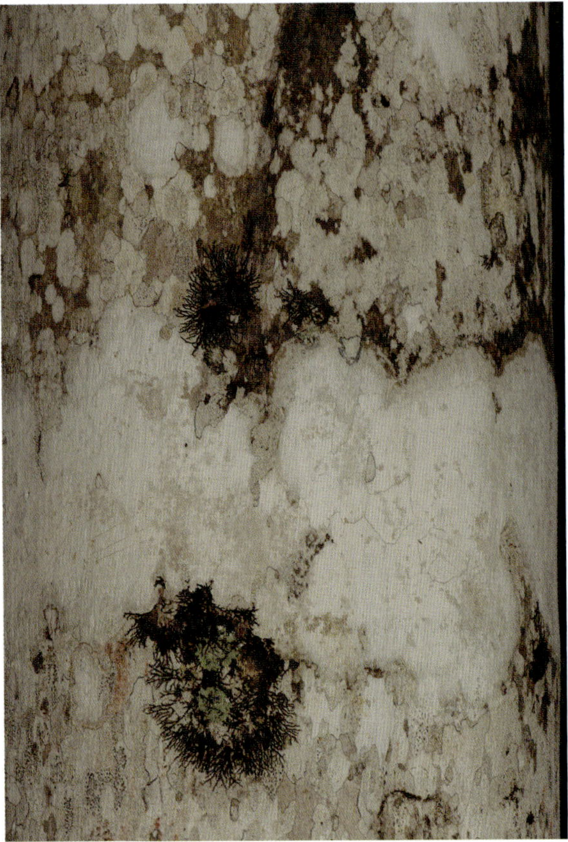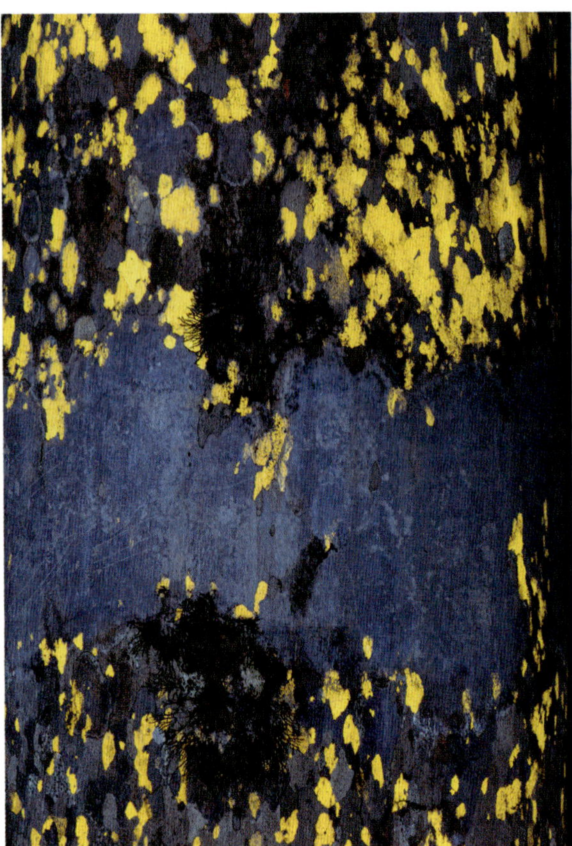

▲ **Fig. 4.33, 4.34**
The bark of a tree in a Costa Rican rainforest. Some of the lichens fluoresce brightly in UV.

Invertebrates

As already mentioned, several invertebrates fluoresce in UV light, including scorpions, some millipedes, spiders and stick insects for example. One way of finding scorpions at night for example is to use a UV torch to scan the ground or crevices. There is great scope here to find new fluorescent species.

The millipede shown here, a captive 10cm long giant pink-footed millipede, was very active during the photography session, constantly trying to climb out of its container. It needed the short duration from two UV converted flashguns to freeze its movement.

The set was a 25mm layer of fine compost, with a dried leaf from a tropical rainforest tree. The flashes were set up, exposures tested and lens pre-focused before the millipede was introduced into the set. It was placed on the leaf in its rolled-up position, from where it started to unroll quite quickly. The lights were turned off and the exposure made quickly before it moved off. Note the striped antennae in the fluorescent image.

There is an excellent folio of UV fluorescent images of invertebrates by Nicky Bay that show the diversity of subjects that fluoresce (*see* resource list).

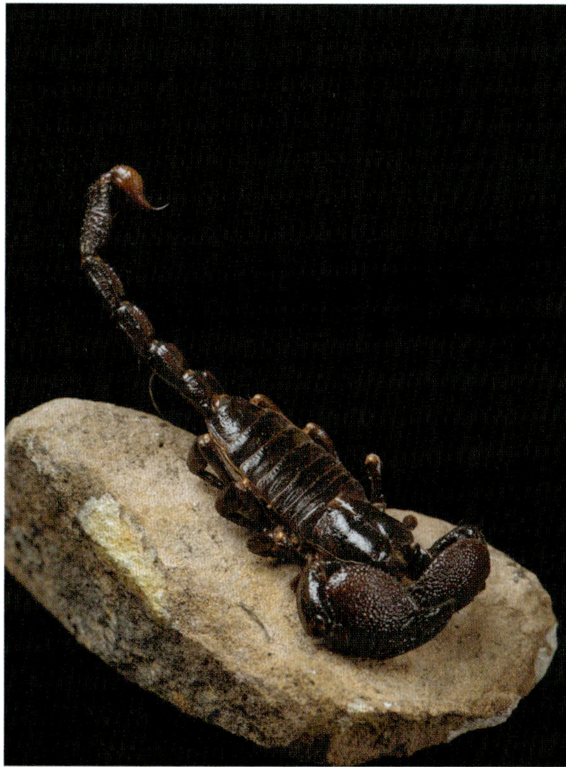
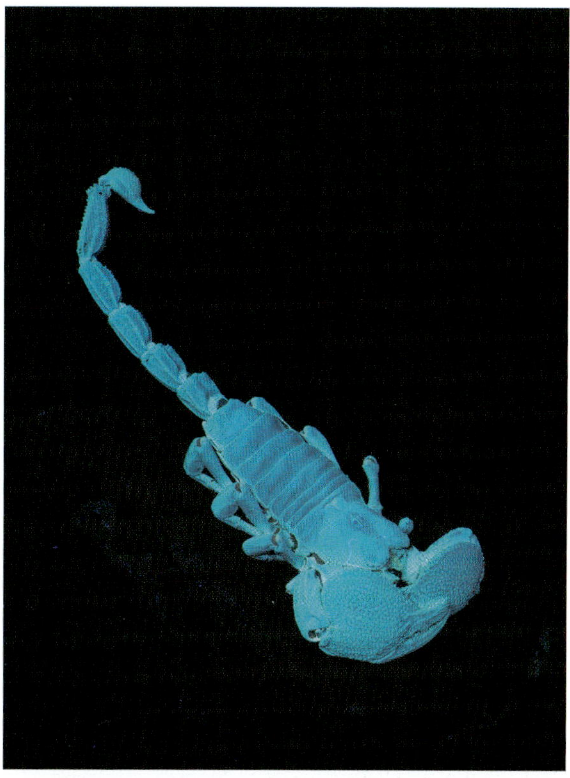

▲ **Fig. 4.35, 4.36**
Emperor Scorpion (*Pandinus imperator*) fluorescing in UV.

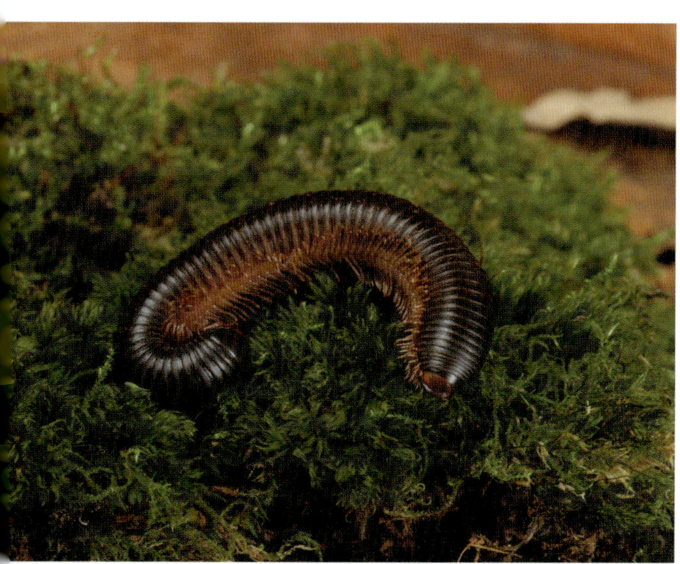
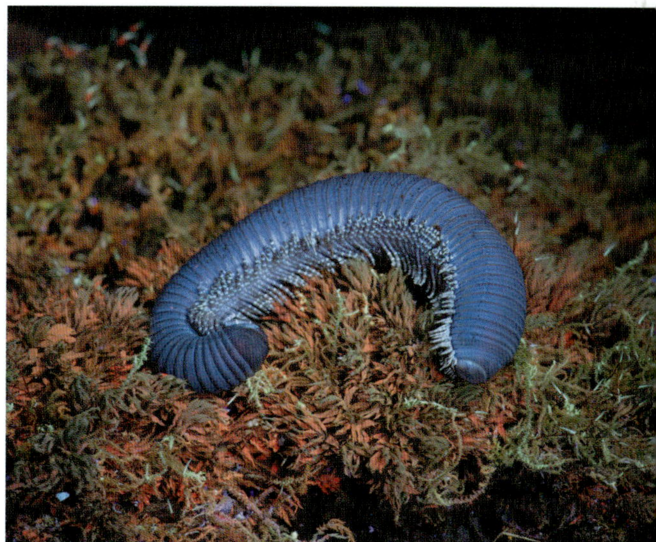

▲ **Fig. 4.37, 4.38**
Giant African Pink-Footed Millipede (*Archispirostreptus gigas*) in visible and UV fluorescence. Live specimen, using UV flash.

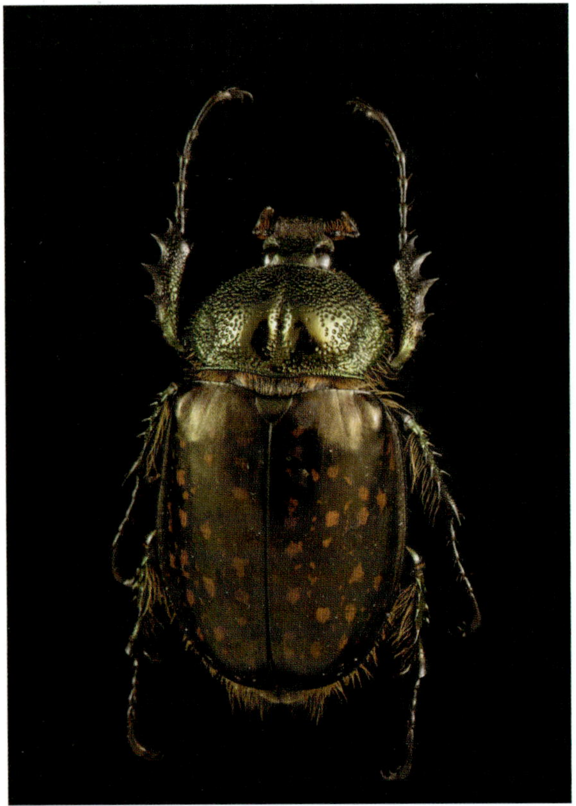

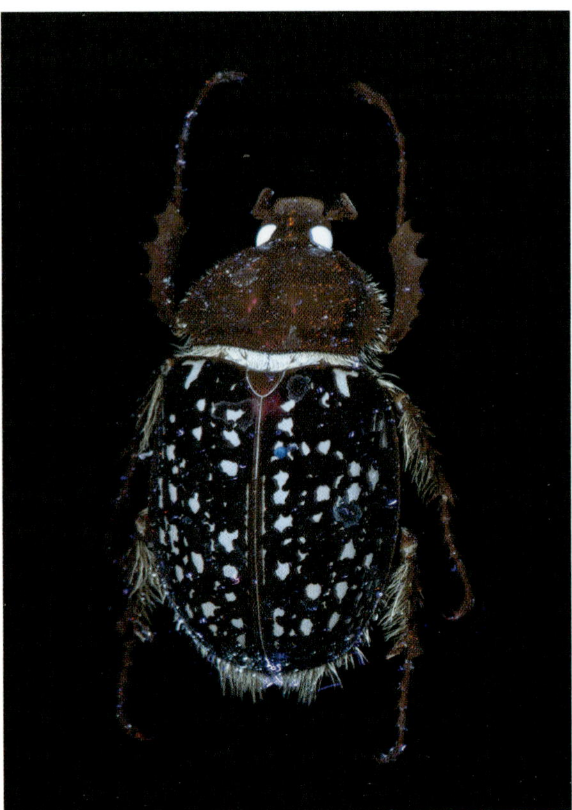

▲ **Fig. 4.39, 4.40**
Museum specimen of Long-Armed Beetle (*Cheirotonus sp.*) from Vietnam, fluorescing in UV.

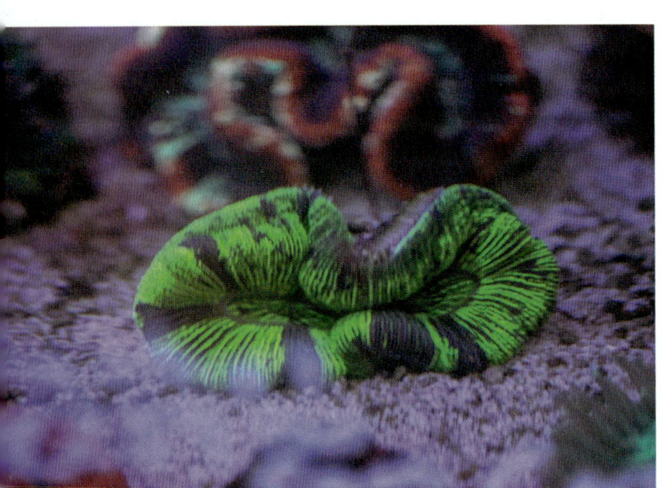

▲ **Fig. 4.41**
Open Brain Coral (*Trachyphyllia geoffroyi*), fluorescing in UV light of around 390–400nm. The image is slightly blurred due to the thick glass of the aquarium, the constantly moving water over the specimen, and relatively dim lighting.
   Image shot at 3,200 ISO.

Marine Life

It has recently been discovered that the Swell Shark (*Cephaloscyllium ventriosum*) and Chain Catsharks glow a bright green colour due to fluorescent proteins inside their skin that are excited by blue light (around 455nm) – the wavelength of visible light that is least absorbed as it travels through water. This biofluorescence (not the same as luminescence), is thought to be a form of communication to other swell sharks.

   Various underwater LED lights are available, such as the Underwater Kinetics Aqualite-S UV-395 Ultra Violet Dive Light. These units are usually either 395 or 455nm to simulate fluorescence and are safe to depths of 100 metres or so.

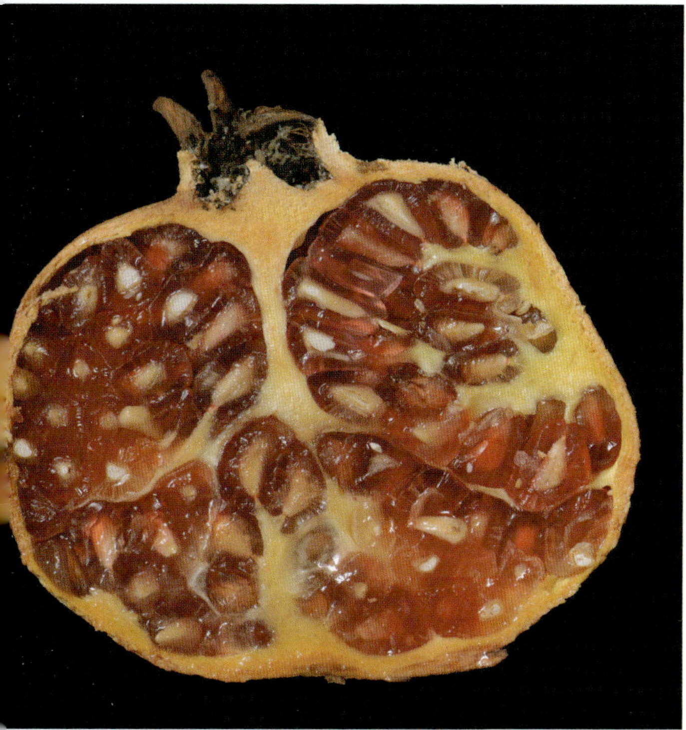
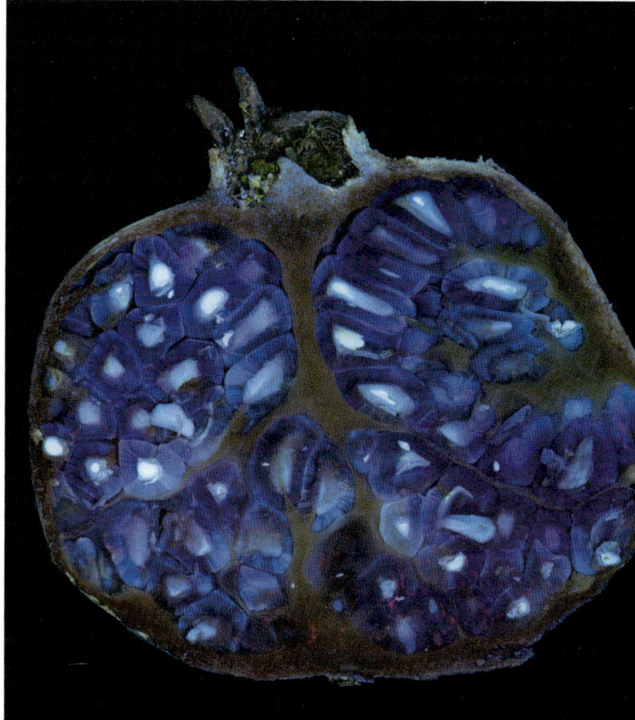

▲ **Fig. 4.42, 4.43**
Pomegranate (*Punica granatum*) fruit fluorescing in UV.

Many corals, sea anemones and other invertebrates (including their shells) fluoresce underwater. The Open Brain Coral (*Trachyphyllia geoffroyi*) shown here was photographed in a tropical marine aquarium in a shop, using long wave UV LED lighting.

One advantage of photographing fluorescence underwater is the lack of back scatter, where light from a flash or other source reflects back from the numerous particles in water and is seen in images as a host of bright spots. With fluorescence, light is emitted from the subject towards the camera, striking the rear side of the particles.

Fruit and Vegetables

Many fruits and vegetables fluoresce, particularly their interiors, including oranges, kiwi fruit, cucumbers and pomegranate. These can make attractive, impressive images, in particular enhancing the texture and detail of the internal structures.

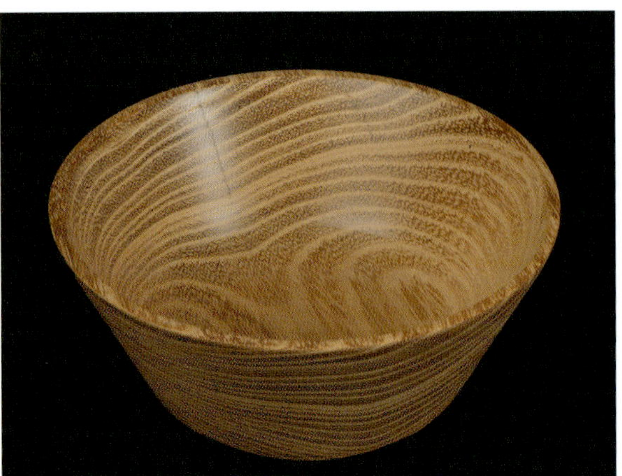 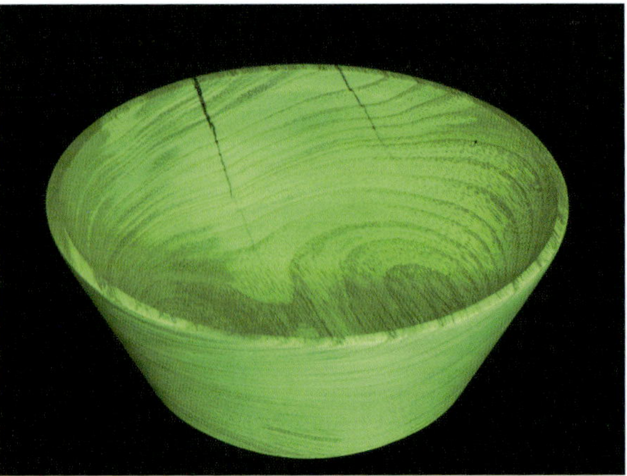

▲ **Fig. 4.44, 4.45**
Bowl turned from False Acacia, or Black Locust (*Robinia pseudoacacia*) wood. Note the filled cracks.

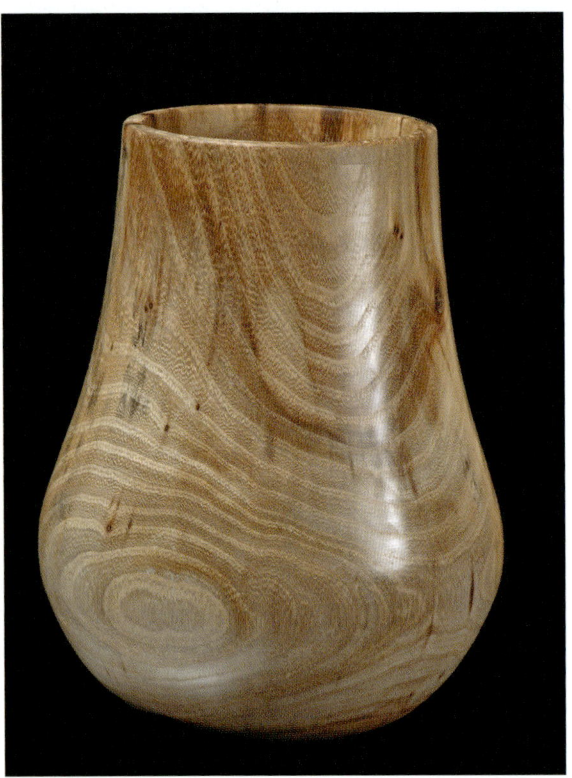 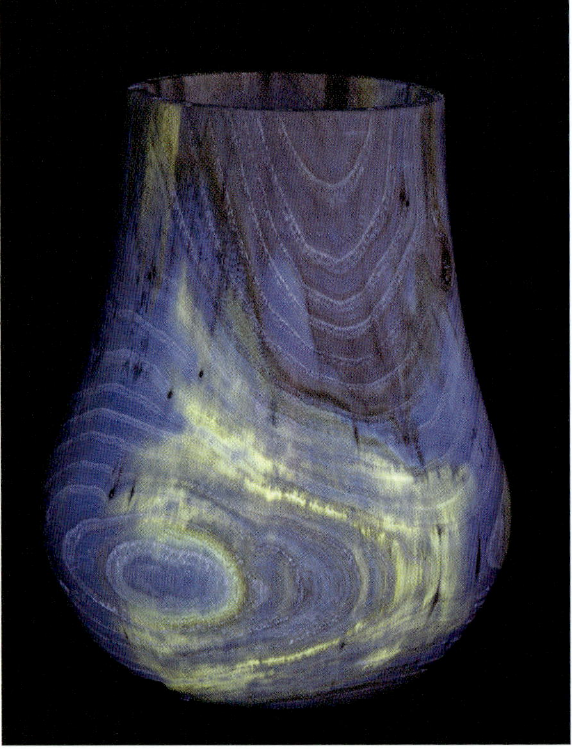

▲ **Fig. 4.46, 4.47**
Vase turned from Elm (*Ulmus procera*) wood. It is not known whether the yellow streaks in the fluorescence image are within the wood, or a by product of the turning process.

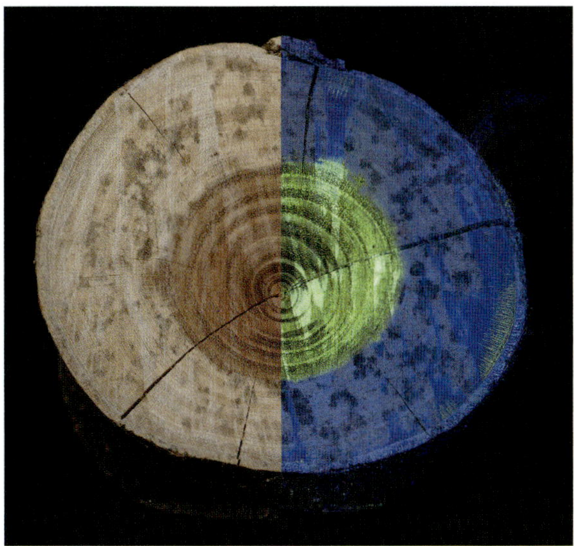

▲ Fig. 4.48
Cut section through Honey Locust (*Gleditsia triacanthos*) tree, showing fluorescent heartwood.

Wood

Various types of wood fluoresce, often in different colours. This characteristic is used by wood turners to help identify species that can be very similar in visible light. Sumac, for example fluoresces a green colour. Black Locust fluoresces a strong yellow-green colour while Mulberry, a visually very similar wood does not fluoresce. If the wood is infected with a fungus (spalted) this too may fluoresce.

Eggs

Many eggs fluoresce in UV. The phenomenon is due to a particular molecule found in egg shells called protoporphyrin IX (PPIX). The molecule is related to haemoglobin, the pigment that gives our blood (and that of chickens) its red colour. Interestingly, different eggs fluoresce different colours, and as shown here, duck, goose, quail and hen eggs have a different fluorescent colour.

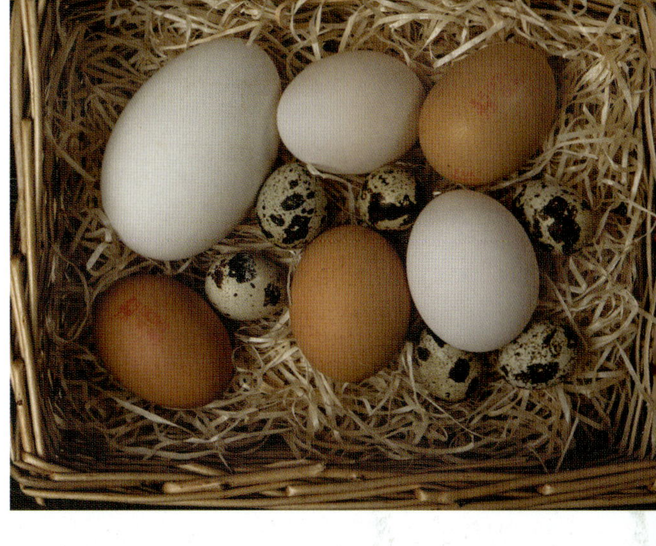

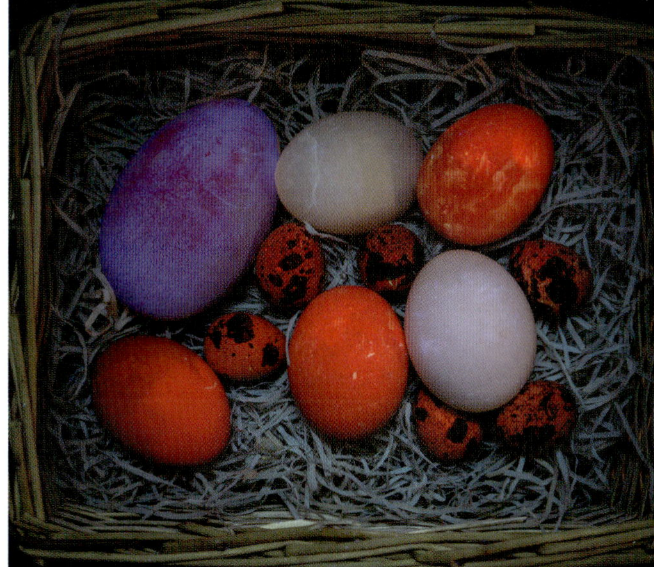

▲ Fig. 4.49, 4.50
Duck, goose, hen and quail eggs in visible and fluorescing in UV light.

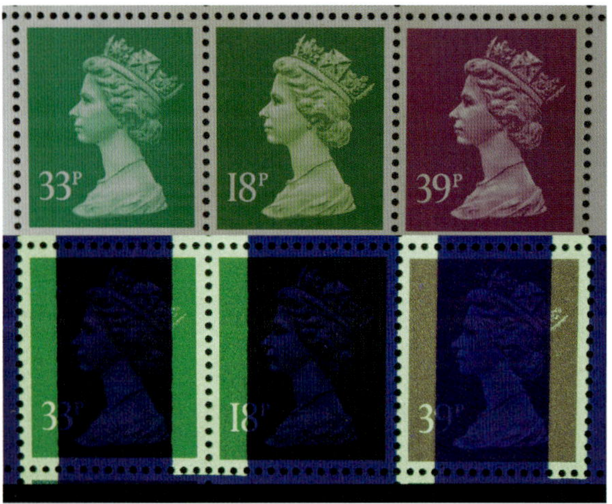

▲ **Fig. 4.51**
A strip of three Machin-style UK postage stamps, shot in UV light, showing fluorescing security bands. Note the different number of bands on the different denominations.
Stamp designs © Royal Mail Group Ltd.

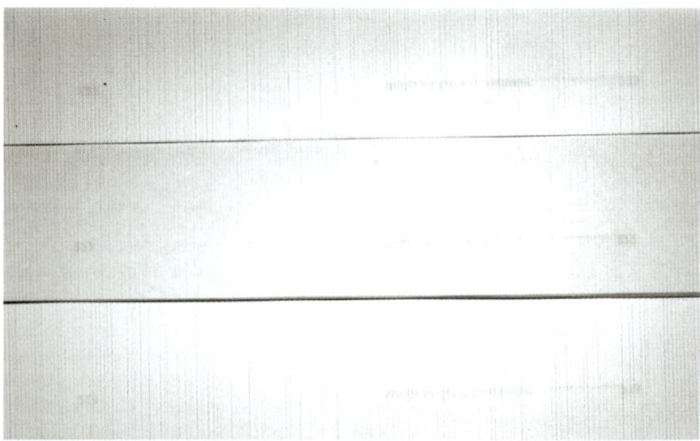

▲ **Fig. 4.52**
Three samples of copy paper, photographed with UV fluorescence, show very distinct bands which can be used by forensic scientists to help identify their source. The contrast has been increased here for reproduction purposes.

Security Markings

Many documents and other items such as stamps contain invisible markings that can be visualized with UV fluorescence. United Kingdom (and many other) bank notes reveal a hidden number when lit with UV light and since the early 1960s many United Kingdom stamps have had phosphor ink applied to the face. This is done to facilitate automatic postal sorting. The phosphor ink can be detected by the machines. However, the phosphor has no colour, and is not obvious to the naked eye, unless the stamp is held at a certain angle to the light. When lit with UV the phosphor band glows brightly. Stamp collectors make use of both long- and short-wave UV to visualize these phosphor bands, as well as forgery detection and paper type.

Photographing these documents is relatively easy. The camera needs to be parallel to the surface of the document (a copying stand is useful for doing this), and lighting must be even across the document, usually having two equally powered lights at 45 degrees to the document and equidistant from it. It is best to use a proper macro lens for this type of photography. They are usually specifically designed to have a flat field, i.e. they will give a rectangular image of a rectangular subject without any curvature of the lines. You may need to place weights on the corners of the document to hold it flat.

For the UV image if the subject is relatively small, such as a stamp, use the light painting technique with one UV torch, aiming for an exposure of several seconds to ensure even coverage.

Medical

One way of identifying ringworm (*Tinea capitis*) in patients and animals is to use UV. Many surgeries and veterinary practices still keep a Wood's glass lamp for the purpose.

Forensics

Forensic photographers have long used UF fluorescence techniques for detecting hidden signs and trace evidence such as the examination of documents and inks, fluids such as blood, gun shot residue and various other substances.

One technique recently developed by forensic scientists in the UK is to use UV fluorescence to effectively fingerprint a paper type. In a recent case, a multi-page contract was suspected of having been tampered with, and one of the pages replaced. Printer/copier paper has recently been found to have

Case Study

FLUORESCENT PITCHER PLANT

The main aim with this pair of images was to show a pitcher glowing in UV, together with a visible light record for comparison. The potted plant was placed on a rotating turntable (such as a small rotating cake stand) approximately 20cm in front of a black velvet background. A long plant stake was inserted into the pot and used to position the pitcher away from the pot and isolate it from the rest of the plant.

For the visible light record, two studio flash units were used, the main one from top left of the subject, the other close to the camera on the right-hand side. The main light was slightly more powerful than the second fill-in light. The camera was mounted on a solid tripod and was not moved during the two exposures.

For the UV fluorescence image the camera was set to the same aperture as the visible light record (f/16) and set to aperture priority mode. A remote release was used to avoid moving the camera during the long exposure. All lights were turned off in the room so that it was completely dark.

With the room dark, the shutter was opened, and the subject painted with a UV torch. Great care was taken not to make any air movements that would cause blurring of the image. Sometimes it may be necessary to hold your breath during an exposure. The final exposure was around thirty seconds.

Some post processing was necessary, both to lighten shadows in the UV image, and to retouch some dust spots on the background.

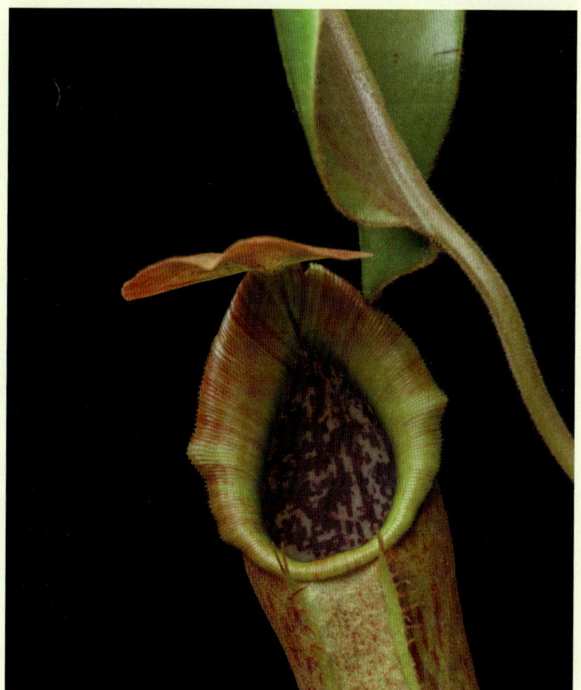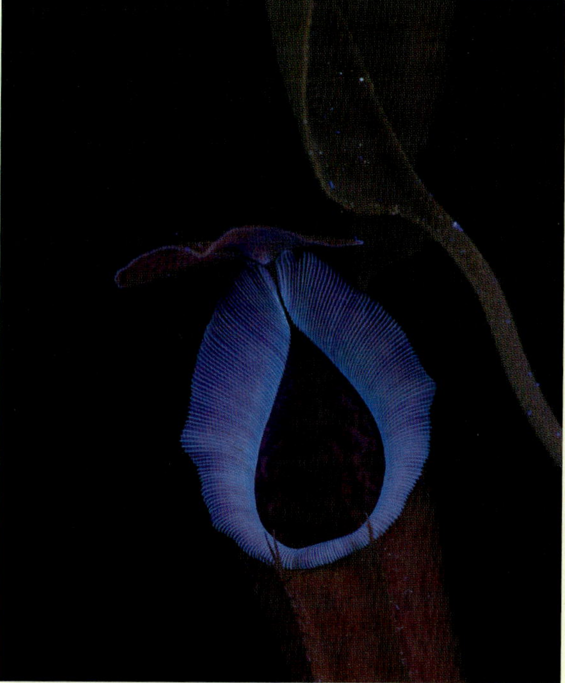

▲ Fig. 4.53, 4.54
The pitcher plant (*Nepenthes fusca* × *N. robcantleyi*) in visible and UV light. Note the fine detail in the peristome.

invisible distinctive line patterns, possibly caused by rollers during its manufacture. The pattern, rather like a bar code, can be made visible using UV light. These UV line patterns have been found to differ from one manufacturer to another, and even within the same batch of paper. Comparing pages from the main contract with the suspect page, showed that they had been printed on different paper types.

FLUORESCENT FACE PAINTS

Various face and body paints can be found that fluoresce in UV and can be used to produce highly distinctive images.

IR Fluorescence

Although not a UV technique, it is worth mentioning here, for the sake of completeness, that there is another form of fluorescence (more correctly called luminescence) in the IR end of the spectrum. A suitable subject is illuminated with visible light, usually cyan, in the region of 480nm (containing no IR), and emits longer wavelength energy in the IR, which is, of course, invisible to the human eye. Because it is invisible, it is not known if the emission persists once the light source is removed and should therefore strictly be called luminescence rather than fluorescence. This luminescence needs to be photographed in a completely dark room, with an IR only converted camera, or full-spectrum camera with an IR transmitting filter. The light source used is usually a pure cyan colour – several LED torches are available including a LedWave Wild Finder,

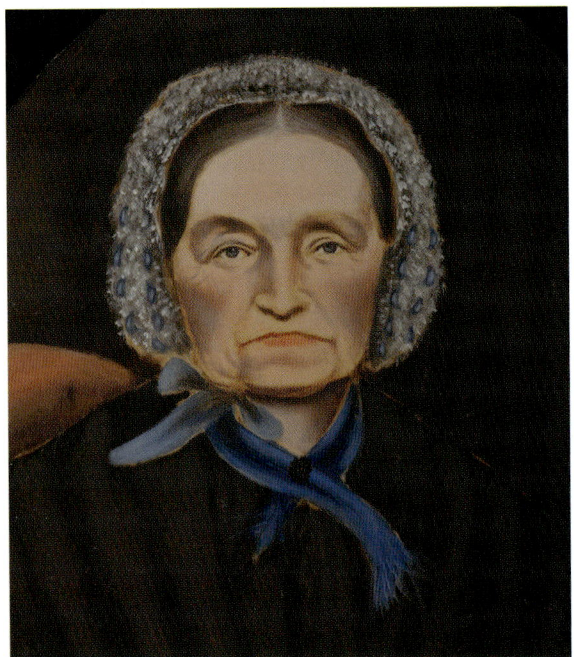
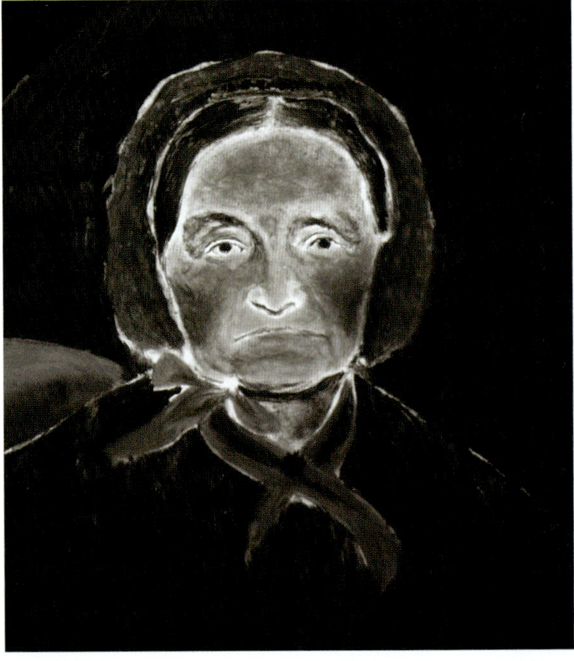

▲ **Fig. 4.55, 4.56**
This painting, dating back to the late 1800s shows various areas luminescing in IR, possibly showing the use of pigment rich in cadmium.
   Nikon D300 full spectrum converted camera with 105mm micro-NIKKOR, with 850nm IR filter. Light painted with Cyan LED torch. Shot in completely dark room. 30 seconds, @ f/5.6. 800 ISO.

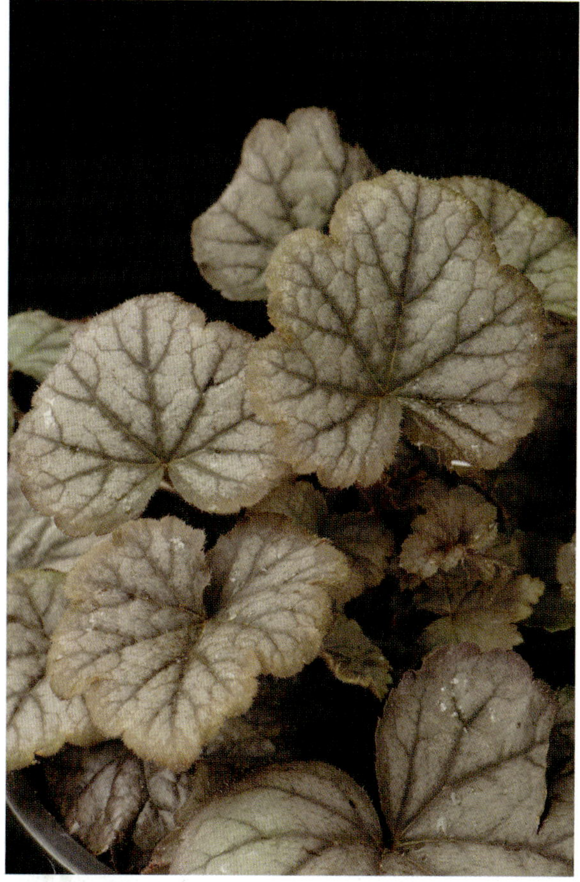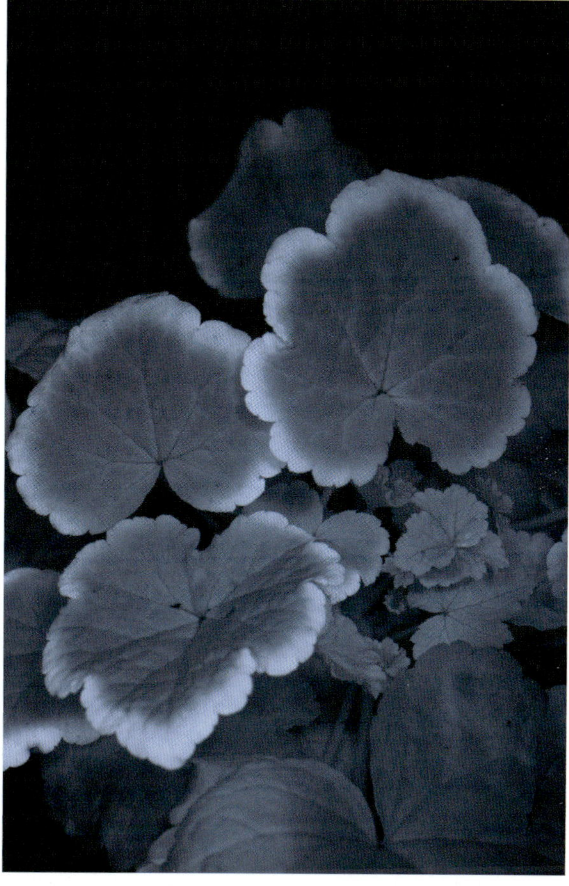

▲ **Fig. 4.57, 4.58**
Chlorophyll luminesces well in IR. This heucherella hybrid shows a distinct pattern on the leaf, virtually invisible in visible light.
　Nikon D300 full spectrum converted camera, with 105mm Series E Nikon lens, with 850nm IR filter. Light source: LightWave LED Cyan torch, 20 seconds @ f/11.

containing a Cyan LXML-PE01-0070-Luxeon Rebel SMT HIGH Power LED Emitter, emitting wavelengths from 490 to 520nm, peaking at 505nm, with no UV or IR emission.

The photographic technique is similar to that for UV fluorescence, arranging for an exposure of several seconds, during which the subject is painted with light. An IR transmitting filter will be needed over the lens if you are using a full spectrum camera – probably 850nm would be best.

The technique is used by art conservators, examining paint pigments that may exhibit the phenomenon (those containing cadmium show particularly strong IR luminescence).

Some minerals and fossils too, show IR luminescence, including the rare mineral Greenockite (Cadmium sulphide). Gallstones, containing bilirubin also exhibit IR luminescence. Chlorophyll also exhibits strong IR luminescence, and there has been research into whether the technique could be used to provide a method for the early detection of plant disease.

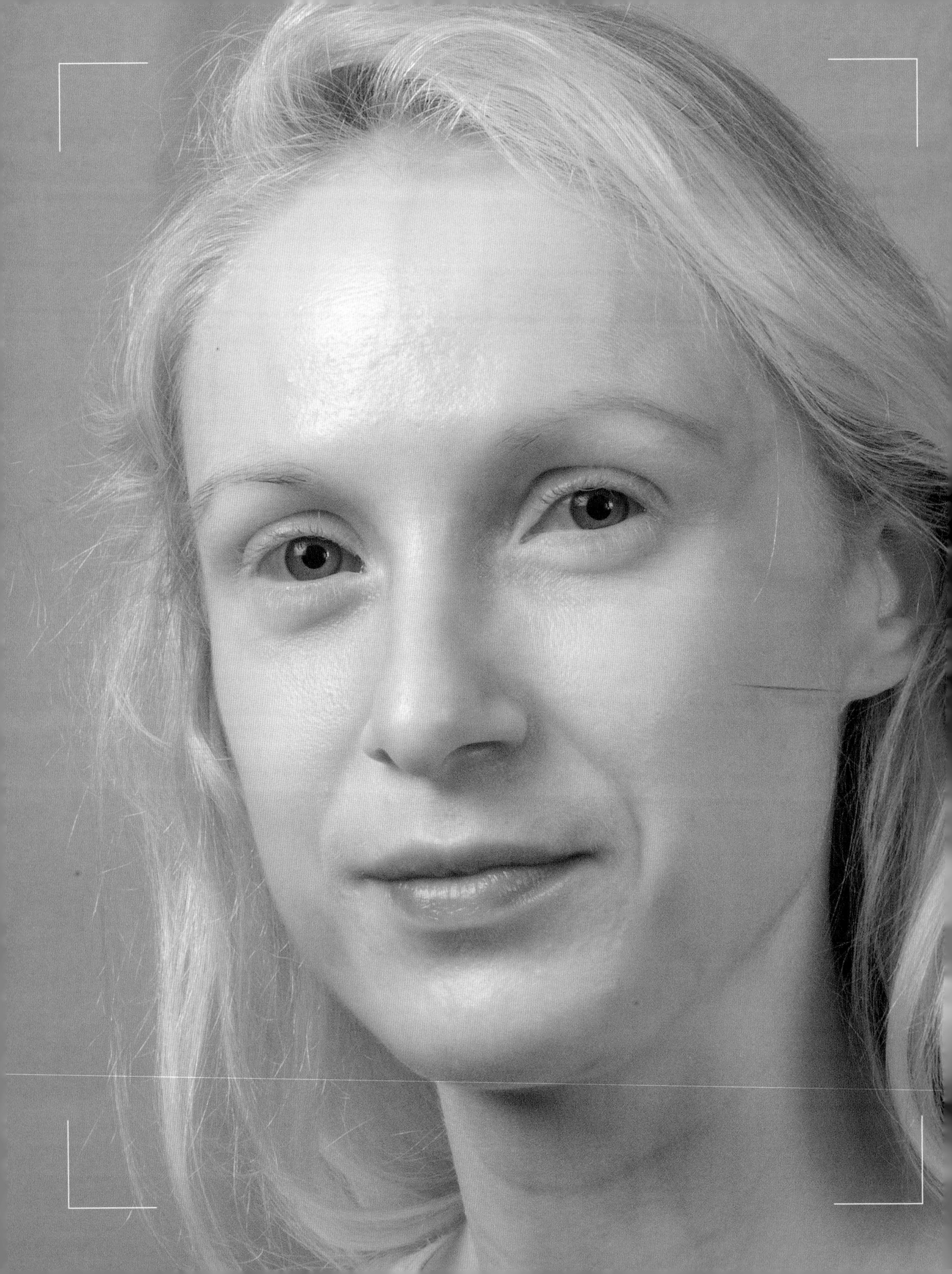

Chapter 5

Infrared Photography

Infrared photography has been popular for many years, particularly with landscape photographers but also with portrait photographers looking for something different in their images. Like UV imaging, the world looks very different in IR, often giving surreal, unworldly images. Infrared techniques are also used extensively in satellite imaging and various scientific, medical, forensic and security applications, as well as the technology used in the HotSpot application in cricket, to help decisions about whether the ball has touched the bat or not. An extraordinary high-speed IR image of bats in flight by Paul Colley won the British Wildlife Photography competition in 2018.

IR FILM PHOTOGRAPHY

Photographic film emulsions (analogue) are naturally sensitive to UV and visible light, but need to be sensitized to make them sensitive to IR. Several IR sensitive films used to be available (there were over thirty in the 1930s, from five different manufacturers), both in black and white, and also colour. These were impractical to use as they needed to be loaded into the camera, and also processed, in total darkness (not in plastic developing tanks). Some camera shutters leaked infrared, and so were useless for infrared photography, while other cameras, using leather bellows, needed to be shrouded in tin foil to make them IR-safe.

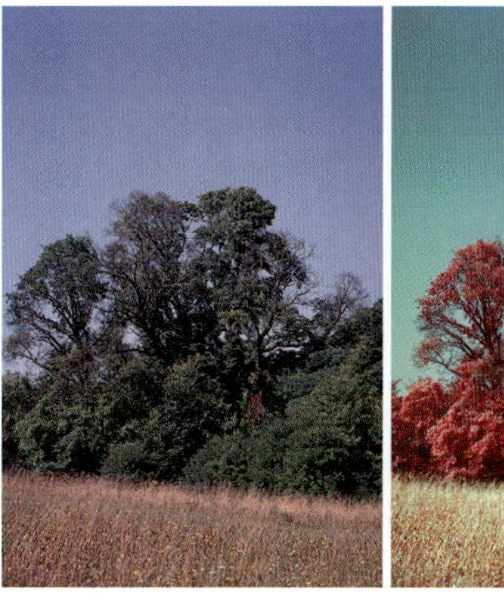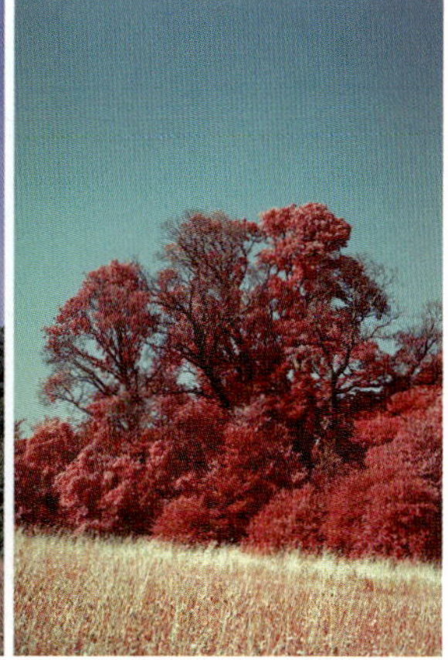

▲ **Fig. 5.2**
A pair of images shot in 1978 on 35mm Ektachrome film, and High Speed Infrared Ektachrome film, to see if the technique could detect Dutch Elm disease (it is not apparent in the image). The look of the IR version is now much copied by digital IR photographers.

Black and white IR films first became routinely available in the 1930s, though Robert Wood (of UV Wood's glass fame) had published IR images as early as 1911. One of the main characteristics of IR imaging is its ability to penetrate haze, which was utilized as early as 1930, when Captain A.W. Stevens of the US Air Force shot an image of Mount Shasta in California shrouded in mist from a plane at an altitude of 23,000 feet and a distance of 331 miles. Because of the mist the camera had to be orientated by compass. It was captioned the 'World Record Long-Distance Snapshot' and showed remarkably little haze on the mountain. Another famous image, made in 1935, was shot from a stratospheric balloon from a height of 72,000 feet, and showed the curvature of the earth and the division between the troposphere and stratosphere and the atmosphere.

◀ **Fig. 5.1**
A portrait shot in IR. Note the alabaster-like skin, and a hint of subcutaneous blood vessels. The model was asked to keep her eyes wide open to retain detail.

FALSE COLOUR IR FILM

Colour transparency, or slide film (such as Kodak Ektachrome or Fuji Velvia) for conventional photography is sensitive to red, green and blue light. During the development process, dyes of a complementary colour are added to each layer i.e. yellow dye is added to the blue layer, magenta dye is added to the green layer, and cyan dye is added to the red layer. When the final transparency is viewed, by shining light through the three coloured dyes (either by projection or on a light box), the correct colour is seen.

There were two varieties of IR colour film available at various times, processed in the E4 or E6 processes, though none is available now. Rolls of Kodak Ektachrome Professional Infrared EIR sometimes appear for very high prices on online auction sites. The film was sensitive to UV, blue, green, red and IR (all film emulsions are naturally sensitive to UV and blue wavelengths, and these wavelengths needed to be filtered out with a deep yellow filter over the lens – usually a Wratten number 12 or equivalent). During the processing, yellow dye was added to the green layer, magenta dye was added to the red layer, and cyan dye added to the IR layer. The final resulting colours were effectively shifted along the spectrum, and the

images known as False Colour IR. Healthy green foliage recorded as red, and red flowers as yellow for example. Diseased foliage, with a reduced chlorophyll content recorded as green or greenish blue, thus allowing botanists to potentially detect plant disease before it was visually apparent.

In effect, IR colour film had similar sensitivity to a full spectrum converted digital camera today i.e. UV, visible light and IR. By using the same filter as that used for the film, (a deep yellow filter e.g. Wratten no.12, Tiffen no.12 or Lee no. 12) the camera becomes effectively sensitive to green, red and IR, and images remarkably similar to the false colour IR film are possible (with some post capture processing), and recently, Kolari Vision has produced their IR Chrome filter, giving remarkably similar results to IR false colour film without the need for further processing. This is a multiple bandpass filter, which uses both visible and infrared wavelengths to blend different wavelengths to create the false colour effect.

The characteristics of false colour IR film can also be simulated digitally by shooting two images and combining them together. The technique will be discussed later in the chapter.

IR photography was later used by military organizations for detecting buildings that had been covered in camouflage netting for example.

Colour IR film became available in the 1940s and was again used for military applications, though it later became used by foresters for detecting diseased trees, and by creative artists for its highly distinctive, strange appearance. Kodak produced Aerochrome III, primarily designed for aerial, military or cartography purposes, in 120 film size until fairly recently.

The technique became commonly known as False Colour IR, due to how colours were shifted

along the spectrum. Several images, and album covers, from the 1960s and 70s used false colour IR images, including the iconic *Hot Rats* record sleeve by Frank Zappa.

Some black and white IR films are still available today, such as Rollei Infrared 35mm film, but are outside the scope of this book.

Today, digital IR photography is still being used extensively by landscape photographers, where a whole range of atmospheric effects can be achieved, either in black and white or varying amounts of colour. A whole host of colour variations can be produced, and it is worth experimenting to find a style that you like and suits your work. Portrait photographers and wedding photographers (mainly in the US) also use IR, as well as various technical applications in the fields of medicine, forensics and art conservation. It offers huge scope for creativity, with the potential for atmospheric images, or bizarre colour images. Automated camera traps or trail cameras are used extensively by biologists and film-makers for recording wildlife at night, and security systems make use of IR cameras and invisible IR lighting. Colour IR is still used in images produced by satellites, and drones when assessing crops for example, using a system called NVDI (Normalized Difference Vegetation Index). Orchards and other crops have been surveyed with IR, and problems such as nematode damage, and Phytophthora infestation can be identified.

IR CAMERA CONVERSIONS

We saw in Chapter 2 that there are several camera conversion options available for recording invis-ible UV and IR wavelengths: UV only, IR only, or full spectrum.

In the case of IR only conversions, there are several further options available when deciding which filter to fit in front of the sensor. Will you require colour for example, or just monochrome images? How far into the IR region of the spectrum will you want to penetrate? Again, this is where having a full spectrum conversion gives most flex-ibility as all of the IR filters are available to screw onto the front of the lens.

For an IR only conversion some of the options are listed below. Different conversion companies may give them different names.

550nm or 590nm. Known variously as Super Colour, Goldie or Golden Glow.

This filter transmits orange and red wavelengths as well as IR, producing a striking colour scheme, which can be further manipulated in post processing to produce other hues. Images shot with this filter can be very attractive without any post processing.

Enhanced Colour 665nm

This filter transmits red and IR wavelengths, produc-ing more subtle colours than the 590nm conversion.

Standard IR: 720nm

This filter transmits IR together with a small amount of visible red colour, producing IR images with a subtle hint of colour. This can be removed later if necessary in an image processing program. Gives slightly less contrast than an 830nm filter.

Deep Black and White: 830 or 850nm

This filter transmits only monochrome IR – this is probably the best choice for black and white only IR images.

NVDI: (Normalized Difference Vegetation Index)

The Normalized Difference Vegetation Index is a simple graphical indicator that can be used to analyse remote sensing measurements, typically, but not necessarily, from a satellite in space, and assess whether the area being observed contains live green vegetation or not. It is routinely used by farmers for example, using drones to capture the images, to assess the health of their crops.

Some companies offer other proprietary conver-sions, including 'super color' and 'hyper color', offering other transmission capabilities. It is worth looking at the websites of the companies listed in the resource list to help decide which conversion is best for you.

The same woodland scene shot with a variety of IR filters.

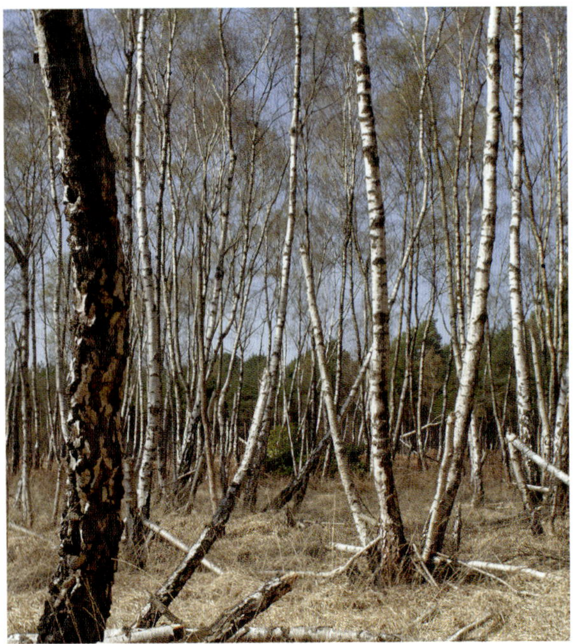

▲ **Fig. 5.3**
Birch woodland in normal visible light.

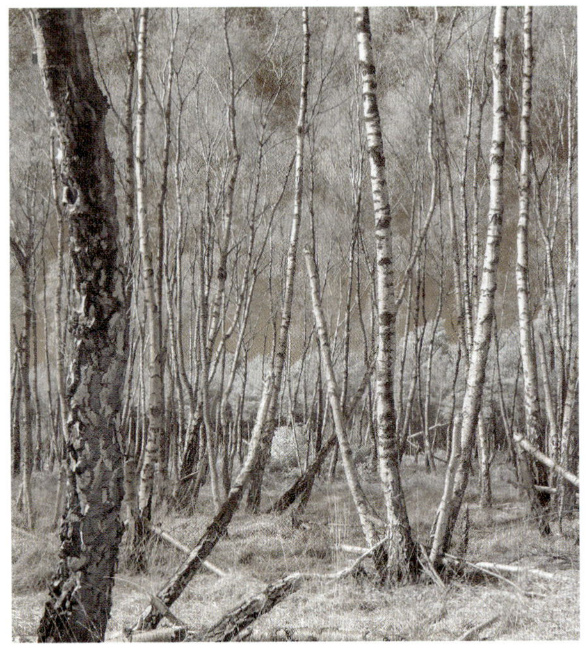

▲ **Fig. 5.4**
IR image shot with 720nm filter.

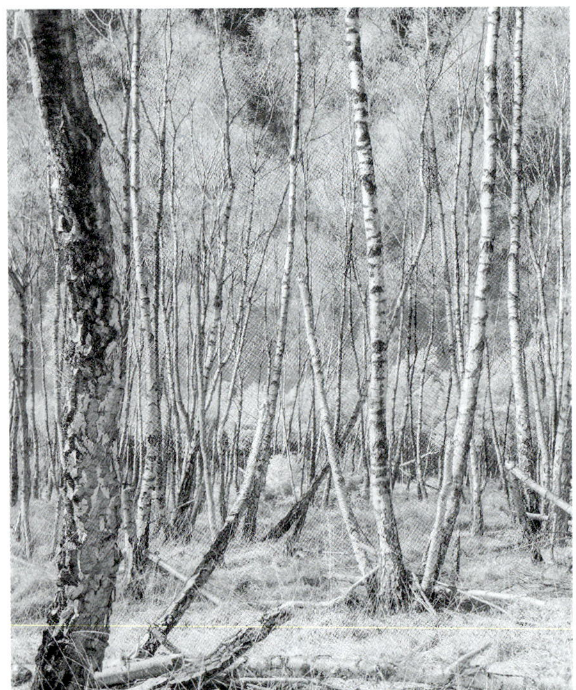

▲ **Fig. 5.5**
IR image shot with 850nm filter.

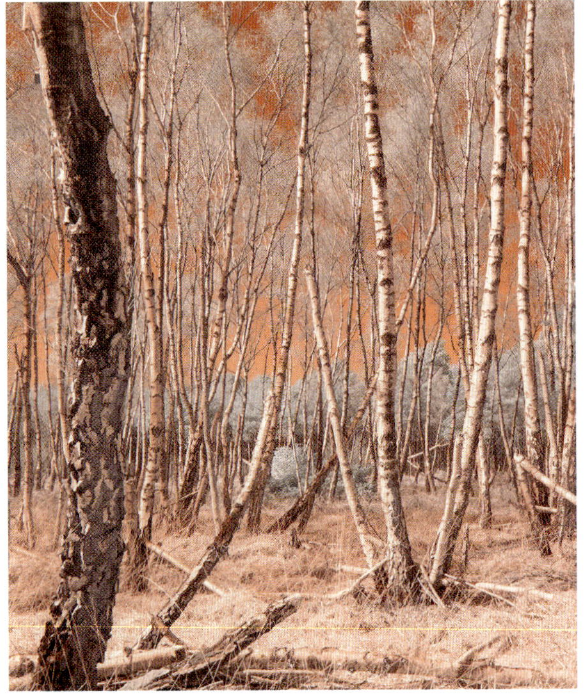

▲ **Fig. 5.6**
IR image shot with 'Goldie' filter transmitting orange and red
wavelengths as well as IUR, from around 550nm.

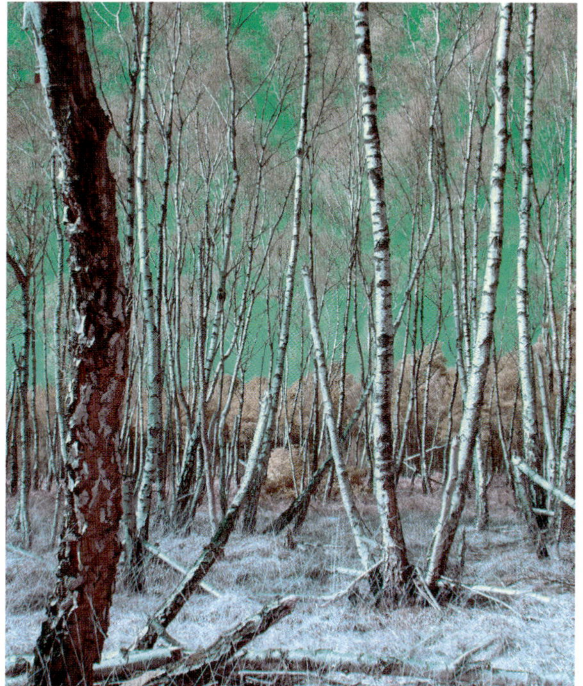

▲ **Fig. 5.7**
IR image with Goldie filter, channel swapped.

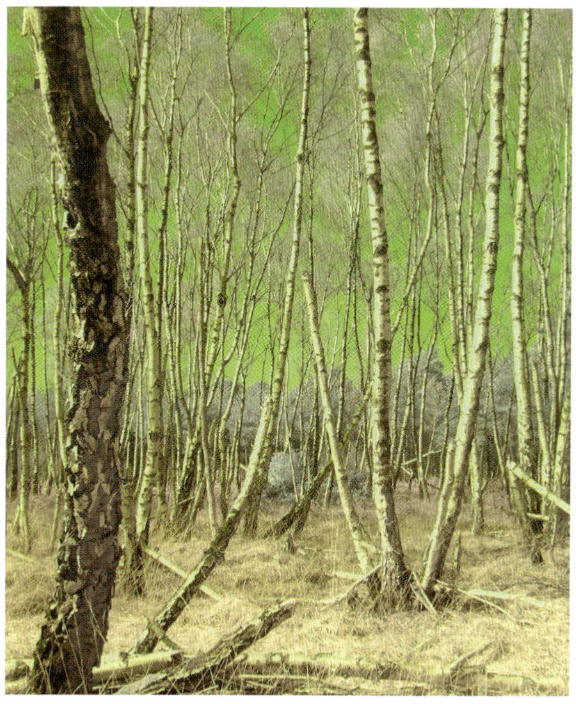

▲ **Fig. 5.8**
IR image with no. 12 yellow filter.

▲ **Fig. 5.9**
IR image with no. 12 yellow filter channel swapped.

IR PHOTOGRAPHY WITH UNMODIFIED CAMERAS

Although this chapter will concentrate on how to obtain the very best quality IR images with full spectrum and IR converted cameras, it is possible to use an unmodified camera to produce IR images. This is obviously a much cheaper option for those readers wanting to try out IR before taking the plunge and getting a camera modified. You will need to place an IR filter over the lens (e.g. Hoya R72, and Cokin P007 Infrared 720 (89B) Filter) this will considerably reduce the amount of light, possibly by as much as ten stops (there is still an IR absorbing filter over the sensor), so a long exposure will be required, probably in the region of several seconds at f/5.6 at 400 ISO. A tripod will be essential. Use the histogram to determine the correct exposure.

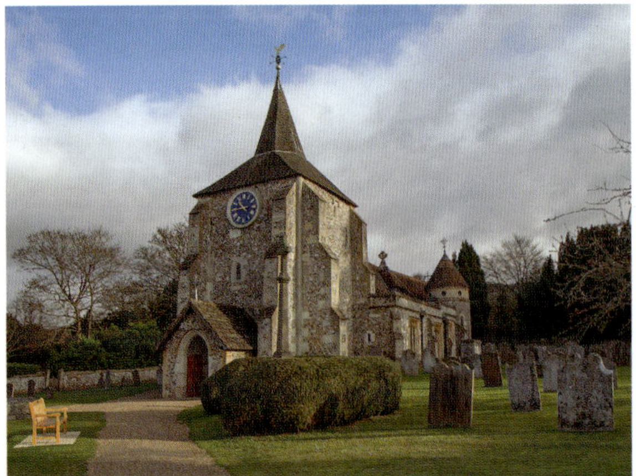

▲ **Fig. 5.10**
Using an unmodified camera for IR is possible, though will require a long exposure. Normal light version.

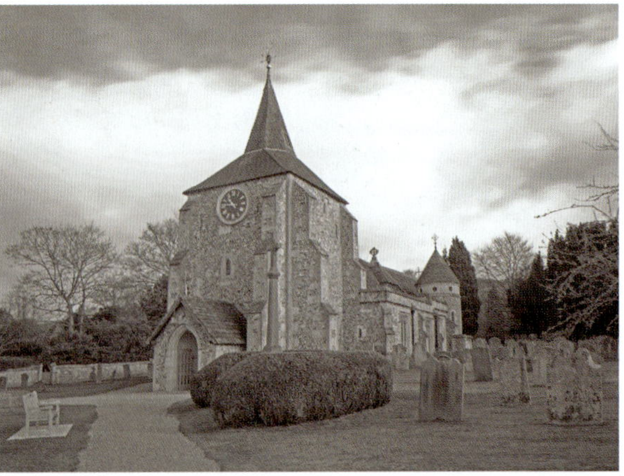

▲ **Fig. 5.11**
IR version with unmodified D800 camera and 850nm filter. The image required a 10 second exposure @ f/5.6 with 400 ISO. The original image was very red and has here been converted to black and white

The images straight from the camera will be a very strange colour, very orange and red. Make sure to shoot raw files so that they can be processed to a more acceptable colour, converted to black and white, or shoot in monochrome mode if your camera has one.

IR Filters

If you opt for a full spectrum conversion, then a range of IR filters is available, usually relatively cheaply,

For monochrome IR, it is possible to get specific IR filters that transmit 720, 760, 850 and 950nm transmission for example, as well as various colour filters such as a red Goldie (e.g. B & W 090), and yellow (e.g. Tiffen no. 12).

Several companies produce ranges of clip-in filters that clip inside the camera body over the sensor and behind the lens. Installing the filter will prevent the mirror on a DSLR moving up and down, so it will need to be locked up, either by a menu option in some camera models, or through the use of the Live view facility. This will not be a problem with mirrorless cameras.

SHARPNESS OF IR IMAGES

One factor perhaps to be taken into account with some broadband IR filters, compared with a single wavelength 720nm or 830nm filter is that of image sharpness. As each individual wavelength will focus at a very slightly different point, the wider the bandwidth you are looking at the softer the image might be. Images shot with a 590nm filter may be slightly softer than a 720 or 830nm for example. This would be worth experimentation.

LENSES FOR IR

Before starting to discuss the various techniques and subjects for IR photography, it is necessary to look at the issue of lenses, and which ones are best suited for IR.

While virtually all camera lenses transmit IR wavelengths, and can be successfully used for IR photography, there is a major issue of 'hot spotting' that occurs with some models. Hot spots show up as

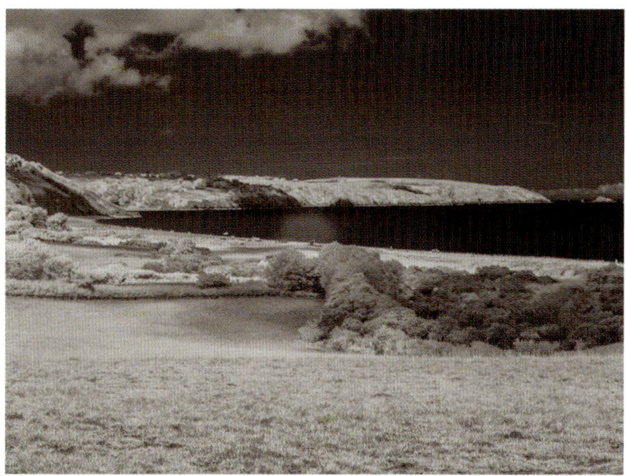

▲ **Fig. 5.12**
Hot spot in centre of image caused by a lens that was not suitable for IR photography (20mm NIKKOR lens).

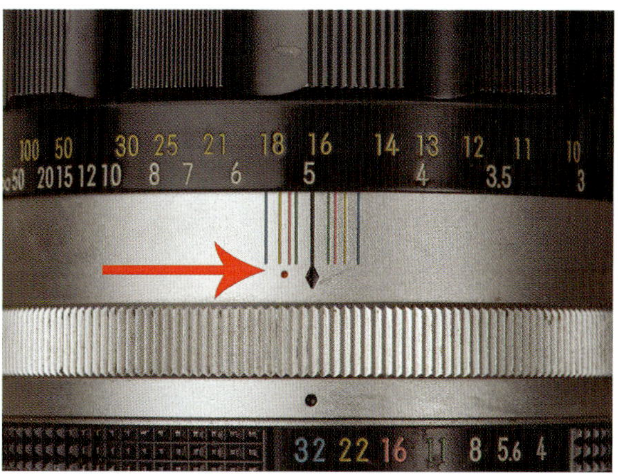

▲ **Fig. 5.13**
IR focusing spot (red dot to left of the main focus line) on an older style manual focus NIKKOR lens (200mm).

a circular area of higher density in the centre of the image. They can be difficult to remove afterwards in image processing programs, so are best avoided by choosing the right lens.

The main problem is that not all lenses exhibit hot spotting (even the same focal length from the same manufacturer), and it is highly unpredictable. It is not confined to prime lenses or zoom lenses, wide angle or telephoto, and may vary from one camera model to another. It is not clear why some lenses do this, and others not, and, in the end, only practical tests will show whether a particular lens is good for IR photography or not. Several databases are available on the internet, mainly on the websites of conversion companies, listing lenses that have been found to be suitable or not for IR photography. In the end, you will need to test the lenses that you wish to use and see if any of them exhibit hot spotting. As always, it is a good idea to use a lens hood with IR filters.

Focusing

As noted in Chapter 2, focusing may be an issue when shooting IR images and you may need to perform some tests to see if your converted camera is giving sharp images with IR. This can be done by placing a ruler with a millimetre scale at 45 degrees underneath the camera. Focus on the centre point in white light, then without changing the focus point, shoot an IR image. Examine the resulting image carefully to see if there has been a noticeable focus shift. If you have an IR only converted camera, the conversion company should have calibrated the focus for you at the time of conversion.

Older, manual focus lenses often had a small red infrared focus spot engraved on the lens barrel. If the lens was focused visually at a certain distance, this distance setting was placed alongside the red spot to ensure correct focusing when used for IR photography.

If your converted camera has a Live view facility you can use this to focus IR images. It is good to do this with some sort of magnifying loupe.

LIGHT SOURCES FOR IR PHOTOGRAPHY

Daylight contains a good quantity of IR and is of course essential for landscape photography. The amount of IR is unpredictable though, varying according to time of day, cloud cover and other weather conditions.

Electronic Flash

For smaller, studio-based work the best, most consistent source of IR is electronic flash. While UV is filtered out by the plastic window in front of the tube (which needs to be removed for UV work, *see* Chapter 3) this does not affect IR output, and so most electronic Flashguns emit good quantities of IR. If you want to use the flash for night time surveillance or wildlife photography, with no visible light emittance, then you can cover the flash window with a suitable IR filter such as a Cokin Infrared 720 (89B) A007 square filter that is 67mm square. Other acrylic 67mm IR filters are available through online auction sites. Make sure that you seal the edges with black tape to ensure that there is no visible light leakage around the edges. It may be possible to cut acrylic filters to the right size for your flashgun.

Incandescent and Halogen Lights

Incandescent (tungsten) lighting and quartz halogen lamps may produce sufficient IR for studio-based shooting but will get hot.

LED

Another light source that might be considered for small subjects are LEDs, found in various torches, similar to the one suggested for UV work. Various models are available, similar to those available for UV reflectance and fluorescence work. An IR LED is used in TV remote controls. LEDs generally output a single specific wavelength, for example 850nm, so you will need to check that the wavelength of the LED is higher than the IR filter being used on the camera. For example, a 780nm IR LED will work with a 720nm filter, but will not be visible using an 850nm filter. Advanced Camera Services in the UK sell a 36 LED array, which can be custom modified to either 850nm or 940nm for use with IR and full spectrum converted cameras. 850nm LEDs give off a dull, red, visible glow that does not seem to disturb wildlife, while the 940nm version has no visible output, which makes them an ideal light source for security surveillance work. Several of these units can be joined together to provide a larger more powerful light source.

White Balancing IR Images

The white balance facility on digital cameras is used to minimize colour casts that may result when you are using light sources with a particular colour. If you use tungsten-based lighting, for example, with a relatively low colour temperature (3200K) images may have a strong orange cast if shot with a daylight white balance setting. The auto white balance setting (AWB) adjusts for different coloured light sources reasonably well. However, when shooting IR, the AWB will not function properly, and images may be very red. It is possible on many cameras to set a custom white balance, specifically for the light source or filter being used.

Nikon cameras use the preset manual facility to record and recall white balance settings for shooting in mixed lighting conditions, or lighting that has a strong colour cast (such as IR). Other camera systems will use similar systems, but you will need to read the manual for specific models.

For Nikon cameras the following procedure can be used (though different models may vary somewhat).

Place a neutral grey or white object under the lighting that will be used to shoot the image.

1 Set white balance to the Pre (preset manual) setting.

2 Select the direct measurement mode.

3 Press and hold the WB (white balance) button until pre flashes on and off on the top LCD screen.

4 Aim the lens (with filter attached) at a photo-graphic 18 per cent grey card or grass (try to fill the frame with the grass or card) and take a shot.

5 If the custom white balance was successful, the word 'Good' will flash on the top LCD screen. (Nikon cameras are known to have problems when trying to set a custom white balance for IR, and the words 'No Gd' may appear).

Adobe® have a free to download piece of software called Adobe® DNG Profile Editor, which can be used to create a custom white balance profile for your own specific camera and conversion.

EXPOSURE

The TTL metering system in modern digital cameras is designed to give the correct exposure measurement in visible wavelengths, not IR, so may not always be accurate for IR images. As always, make sure to use the camera histogram to check exposures. Over time you will gain experience with how the camera meter copes with exposure measurement. The various lens filters, used with full spectrum cameras, will have different transmis-sion characteristics, which again experience will help with exposure. As a rough guide the following exposure compensation settings scan be used as a starting point for three typical IR filters:

720 nm: 0
850 nm: + 1 stop
950 nm: + 3 stops.

One word of caution – the preview image on the rear screen of the camera shows a JPEG version of the recorded raw image. The camera does render this much darker than the actual raw file with IR images, making the histogram a much better way of assessing exposure.

SUBJECTS FOR IR

The IR photographer has many choices when it comes to the range of subjects available. A wide range of images can be produced, from punchy, high contrast images to subtle low contrast monochrome images, while in colour pretty much anything goes. If you have a full spectrum converted camera, it is worth trying to shoot the same scene with a variety of IR filters, to see which one works best for you.

Landscape Photography

It is often said that in order to shoot good black and white IR landscapes you need a good blue sky with fluffy white clouds, and they certainly do give dramatic effects, but IR landscapes can be shot in any weather. The ability of IR to penetrate haze is worth exploring, as is its rendition of different foliage types. Results can be unpredictable and unexpected, and it is only by shooting lots of different types of subject in different weather conditions will you find out which subjects work best for you. Some will work best in black and white, others will look best with a hint of colour, and others with a more garish saturated colour. Different foliage colours, in autumn for example, are very often rendered the same grey tone in an IR image.

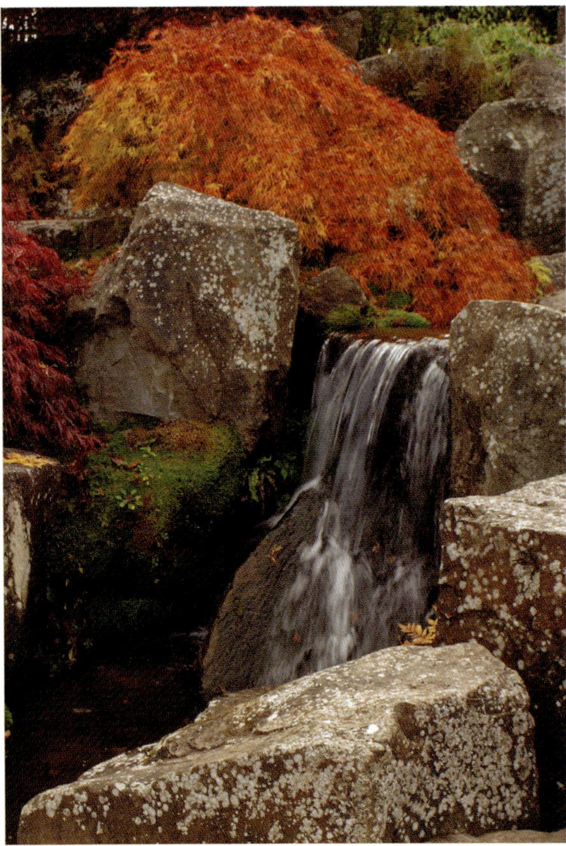
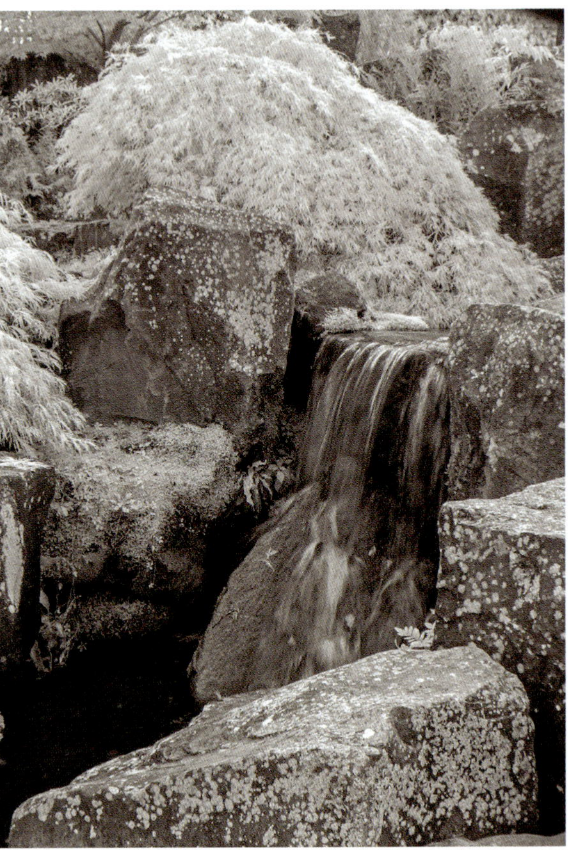

▲ Fig. 5.14, 5.15
A waterfall in a rock garden in a botanic garden in autumn. Note how the different coloured foliage is recorded as having a very similar tone in IR.
  Nikon D300 full spectrum converted, with Nikon 28mm f/2.8 lens. 850nm IR filter.

Haze Penetration

Haze can be thought of as a general loss of contrast in an image due to light being scattered by fine particles in the air. There are several forms of scattering that will affect whether IR penetrates the haze or not. Sunlight shining through the smoke of a bonfire often results in rays of light due to the sunlight being scattered by smoke particles in the air. Scattering will be dependent on the size of particles in the atmosphere.

Large particles in the atmosphere, such as raindrops, snow and ice crystals result in non-selective scattering, affecting all wavelengths of light, and IR photography will have no effect on haze penetration.

Another form of scattering called Mie scattering occurs with particles in the atmosphere that are approximately the same size as the wavelength being scattered. These particles are usually spherical and formed by dust, pollen and droplets of water vapour, producing fog, for example. Again, IR photography has no effect on these particles. Images shot in heavy fog are not usually enhanced by IR.

The type of scattering where IR photography has most effect is known as Rayleigh Scattering. The particles in the atmosphere are much smaller than the wavelength of light being scattered and are mainly formed by oxygen and nitrogen molecules. These molecules absorb light and re-emit it in a

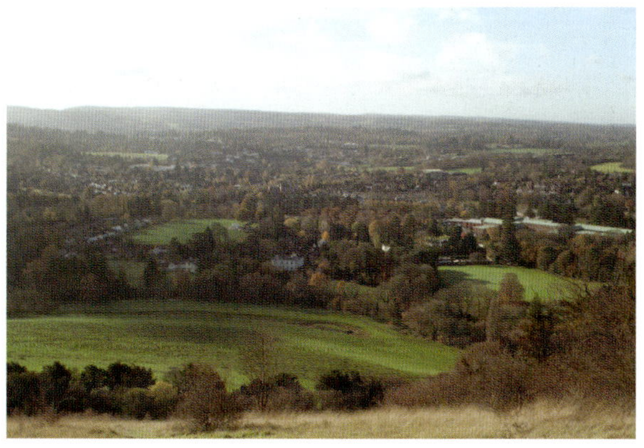

▲ **Fig. 5.16**
A view from Box Hill, Surrey, UK, towards the South Downs on a very hazy day.

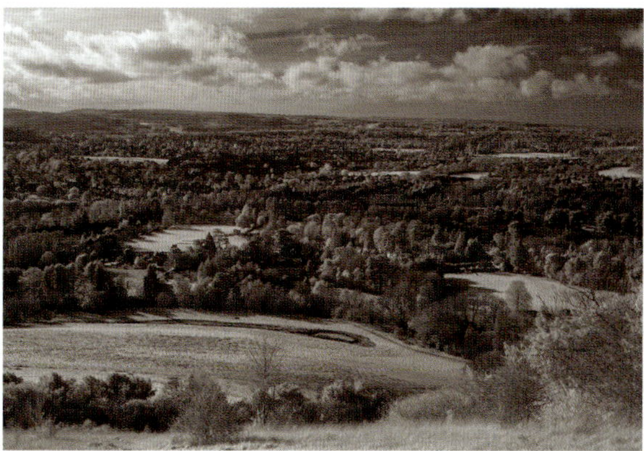

▲ **Fig. 5.17**
The same view shot with an IR 850nm filter penetrates the haze and greatly accentuates the clouds.
Nikon D300 full spectrum converted, with Nikon 28mm f/2.8 lens. 850nm filter.

random pattern, thus causing a scattering of light. Technically, the amount of Rayleigh scattering is inversely proportional to the fourth power of the wavelength. IR radiation of 800nm, for example, is scatted 1/16th as much as blue light at 400nm.

At ground level, all three types of scattering are present, and will affect the amount of haze. At higher altitudes (aerial photography for example) IR photography can have greater haze penetration benefits as there is generally less dust at these higher altitudes. Most scattering at high altitudes is of the Rayleigh type.

High Dynamic Range and IR

When shooting sunny high contrast scenes, digital cameras may not be capable of recording detail in both shadow and highlight areas in one exposure. It may be worth shooting a sequence of differently exposed images to be post processed as an HDR (High Dynamic Range) composite. This is where several images are shot of the same subject (usually three) at different exposures, covering the brightness range of the subject. The usual starting recommendation is to shoot one at the correct exposure, one 2 stops under, and one 2 stops overexposed. They need to be in perfect register, so a solid tripod will be

necessary. Some cameras have an auto-bracketing facility that may be useful here. To vary the exposure, use the shutter speed rather than the aperture control so that depth of field is the same in all three images. It is also best for solid, static subjects rather than ones that might move between the exposures.

The sequence needs to be loaded into a software program capable of processing HDR images. While Abobe® Photoshop, Elements and Lightroom can produce HDR images, there are perhaps better examples, such as PhotoMatix Pro.

Open the software and select the three images for processing. You will usually be given a dialogue box with various options, including remove ghosts, which will identify areas where the images haven't completely registered, and would produce ghost images around edges of subjects. Having selected OK, the main work area will be displayed giving a multitude of options for processing the composite including painterly, realistic, photographic, grunge and surreal! These can all be previewed before selecting Process. You can choose a very subtle process or something more garish.

Once you have an image you like, save it, when it can be opened in Photoshop® for further processing of colour and the like if required.

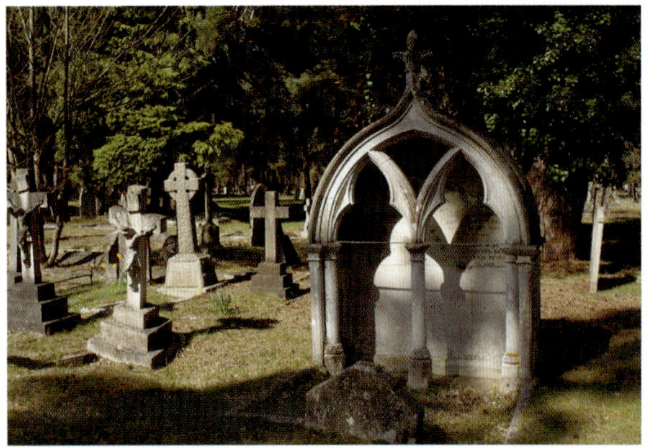

▲ Fig. 5.18
This high-contrast scene was shot on a very sunny day. Note the lack of detail, particularly in the shadow areas of the trees.

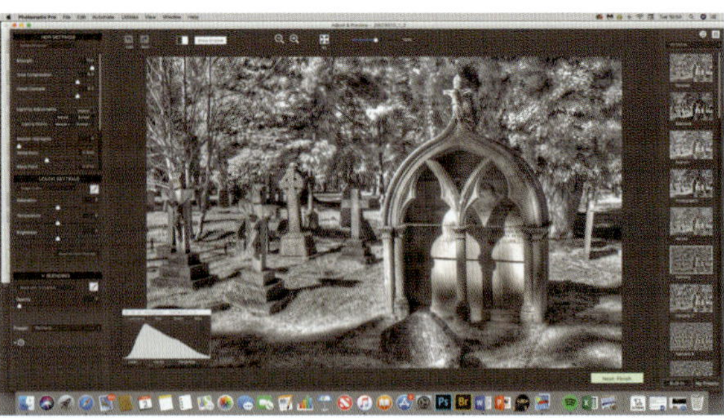

▲ Fig. 5.19
Three exposures were shot in IR with an 850nm filter, one at the correct exposure, one at 2 stops under, and one at 2 stops overexposed. The three images were loaded into PhotoMatix Pro HDR software and rendered using the Painterly mode.

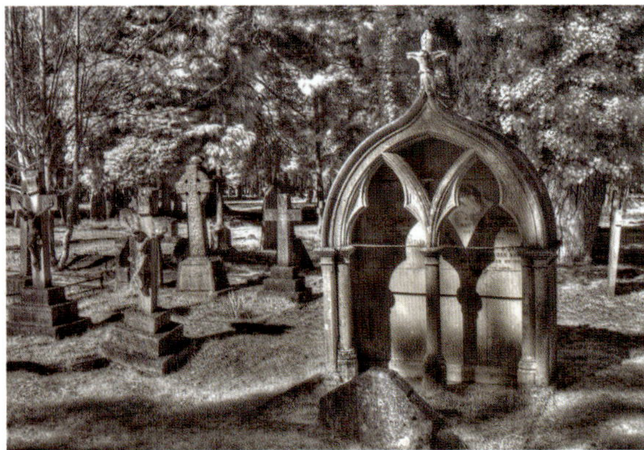

▲ Fig. 5.20
The final image shows detail in all areas of the scene, though may not be to everyone's taste.

A much-loved subject by IR photographers are churches and graveyards, where the effects can give rise to spooky ethereal images. The image shown here had a gaussian blur applied to it to create an ethereal look, as described later.

Channel Swapping

When shooting with IR and colour combined, with the 550nm Goldie filter for example, the image out of the camera will be predominantly an orange/red colour. While this may be quite attractive it is possible to apply a whole range of adjustments to the

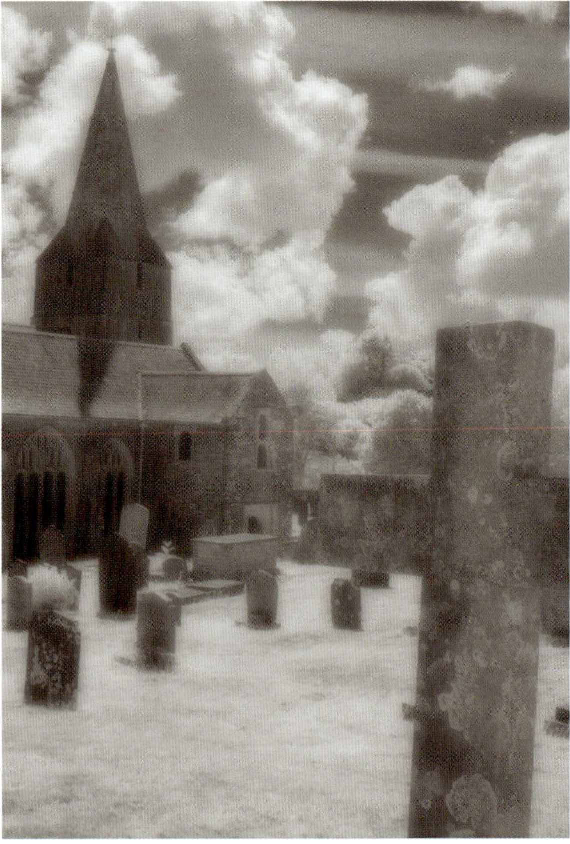

▲ Fig. 5.21
A churchyard image shot with a 720nm IR filter. It had a heavy Gaussian blur filter applied to it to create the rather ethereal feel.

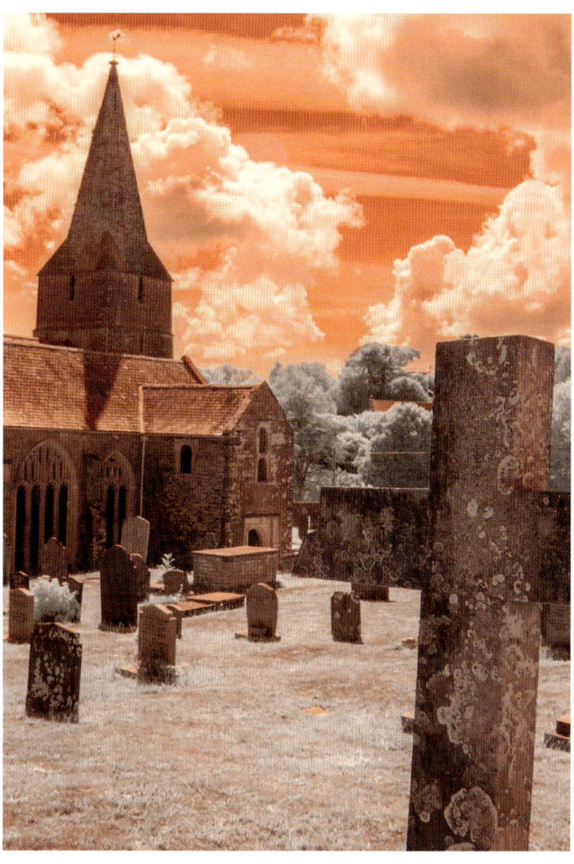
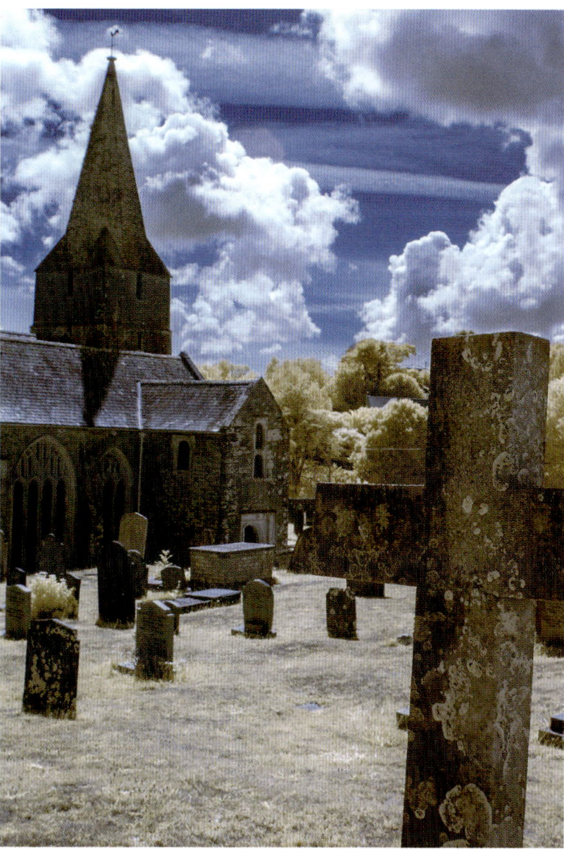

▲ **Fig. 5.22, 5.23**
Channel swapping. The original image was shot with a Goldie filter and gives a very orange/red image.
Channel swapping gives it a blue sky and false coloured foliage.

image in programs like Photoshop® and Lightroom® to give it a variety of different colour schemes. One commonly used technique, particularly with landscape images is to swap channels where the red and blue channels are swapped so that the sky will end up as blue in the final image, with warm-toned coloured foliage.

Most digital images are composed of three colour channels usually (but not always) red, green and blue, relating to the colours in the original scene. These channels can be seen in the Channels panel in Adobe Photoshop®. (You will need to select the Show Channels in Colour box in **Preferences > Interface**, to see them in colour.) The red channel is coloured red, the blue channel blue and the green channel green. It is possible however to re-colour the channels, making the red channel blue, for example.

You will need Adobe Photoshop® (or another program), which enables you to manipulate the different channels of the image, using a control called the Channel mixer. Open the required image in Adobe Photoshop® and open the Channel mixer dialog box (**Image > Adjustments > Channel mixer**).

With the output channel set to red, make the red channel 0 per cent, and the blue channel 100 per cent. Then switch to the output channel for blue, and make the red channel 100 per cent, and the blue channel 0 per cent. This should result in blue skies in a landscape image, with yellowish foliage. The results can be adjusted further using various other adjustment controls.

Photoshop Actions

The above sequence of operations can be recorded and saved as a Photoshop® action, which can be replayed over subsequent images.

Open the Actions panel (**Window > Actions**) and in the menu at top right go to **New Action**. Give the action a name (e.g. IR Channel Swap) then select the Record button. Now everything that you do to the image will be recorded, until you select the Stop button (the square button at the bottom of the

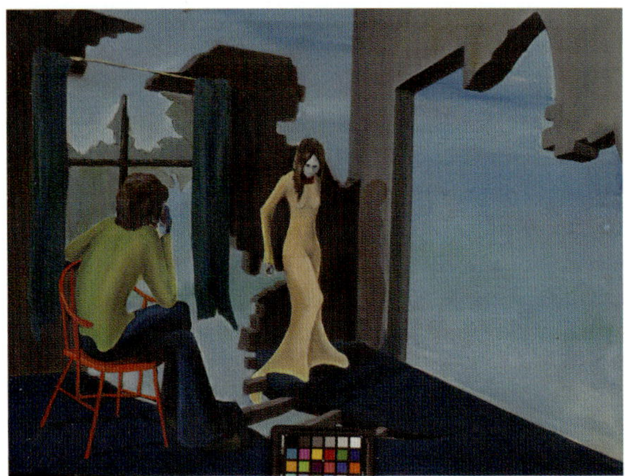

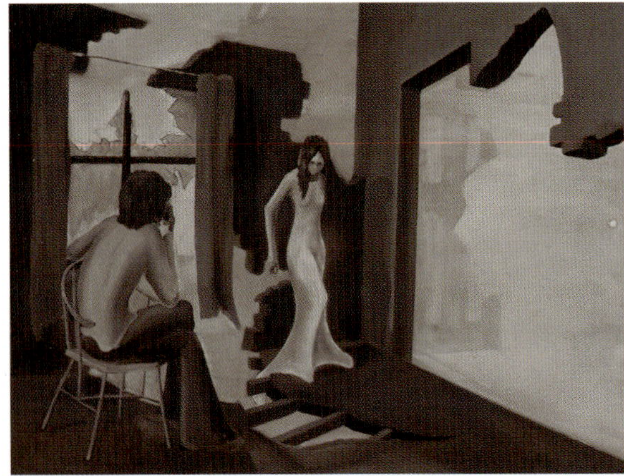

▲ **Fig. 5.24, 5.25**
A modern painting by artist Stephen Bleksley, in visible light and IR, using an 850nm IR filter. The IR image shows underlying details in the sky area which was painted over in the final version. Note the inclusion of a standard colour chart in the visible light image to help achieve the correct colour.

Nikon D300 full spectrum converted camera, with 105mm Series E Nikon lens, 850nm IR filter. Two Elinchrom® flash heads.

Actions panel). All of the operations in the Actions are listed, and can, to some extent, be edited.

When you open another image the action you created can be replayed by selecting the action required and selecting Play.

Several websites have various Photoshop® actions specifically for IR images, which can be downloaded. One example is the False Color Action Suite for Photoshop® from the camera conversion company Kolari Vision (*see* resource list), which is a set of five actions including: the standard channel swap, a channel swap that only keeps the blue colour, a 665 to 720nm action, a 590nm to 665nm action, and a 590 to 720nm action.

OTHER APPLICATIONS OF IR PHOTOGRAPHY

Art History

IR imaging has long been used by art historians and conservationists working with paintings and other art materials. Because of the ability of IR to penetrate surface layers such as varnish and paint, IR can show previous versions of paintings for example, or sketches underlying the paint.

Much of the work carried out on the Dead Sea Scrolls was carried out using IR techniques, revealing and enhancing the text on decaying parchment. Old documents known as palimpsests often have several layers of text overlain on top of each other, and again, IR imaging can reveal underlying information.

Dark brown spots on old books and documents, known as foxing, usually caused by mildew and other mould, can often be removed or minimized by using IR photography to aid the clarity of the document.

When photographing documents, paintings or other artwork it is important to hold the object as flat

CONTENTS.

CONTENTS.

▲ **Fig. 5.26, 5.27**

This page, from an 1883 edition of *The Royal Shakespeare*, shows severe foxing due, probably, to damp storage at some time. This was almost completely eliminated using an IR 850nm filter with a full-spectrum camera.
Nikon D300 full spectrum conversion with 50mm lens, and 850nm IR filter.

as possible, with the camera parallel to it, and illuminate it as evenly as possible, preferably with two equally powered lights equidistant from the subject. To check the evenness of the lighting you can place a vertical object such as a flat broad bottomed marker pen gently on the surface of the artwork and make an exposure. The shadows formed on either side of the pen should be even. It is useful to include colour and grey scales in the image, such as the X-Rite ColorChecker® Passport or Datacolor SpyderCHECKR® 24 – SCK200, 24 Color Patch and Grey Card, which can be used to help achieve correct colour balance and exposure.

Forensics

IR photography is used by forensic photographers in many ways, including night time surveillance, forgery detection, restoration of burnt documents, and the visualization of gunshot residue and blood.

In one well-documented case, a young girl was being routinely abused by her father but could not prove it. She set up a hidden IR camera and filmed the abuse. Although the perpetrator's face was not visible, the subcutaneous vein structure in his arm was revealed by the IR camera, and matched to his real arm. Unfortunately, he was acquitted on a technicality, but the potential for the technique is high.

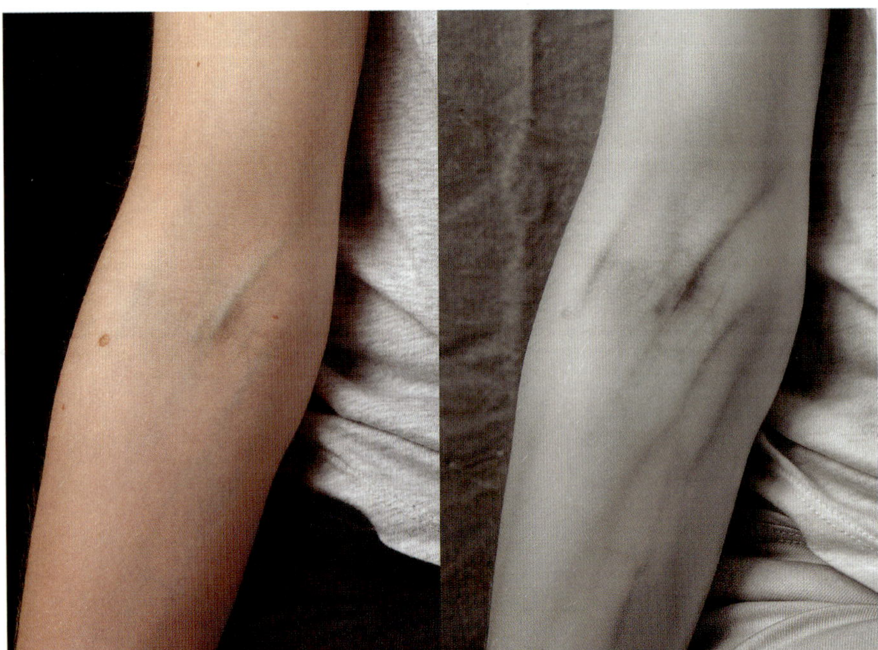

Although the techniques are not used as much now as they used to be, IR photography was a major tool in the detection of forged documents, where perhaps a different type of pen was used to modify a document from the original.

Medical

Because of its ability to penetrate the surface of skin by 2–3mm, IR can be used to visualize subcutaneous veins. A medical device, called Vein Viewer, is used by healthcare professionals to help find veins by projecting a real time image of the veins underneath the surface of a patient's skin. A lot of research was carried out in the 1960s and '70s into the use of IR (and UV) for the early diagnosis of skin cancers and other skin conditions. While the results were promising, the techniques were overtaken by other, better technologies.

Portrait Photography

Infrared wavelengths penetrate human skin to around 2–3mm, removing surface blemishes and wrinkles. and IR portraits have a very characteristic smooth alabaster like appearance, smoothing out all wrinkles and freckles. Sometimes veins, which absorb IR, can become distractingly apparent, and may need to be retouched if appropriate. Eyes too can be a problem, absorbing IR and often appearing very dark and menacing. Try to get your subject to keep their eyes wide open.

For portrait and other photography of moving subjects, an IR only conversion will be the best choice, allowing the use of the camera viewfinder.

If your sitter is wearing glasses they can give interesting effects, as shown here where the sunglasses become transparent in the IR record.

IR has a similar effect with some plant leaves. The succulent leaves shown here have lost all of their surface detail in IR.

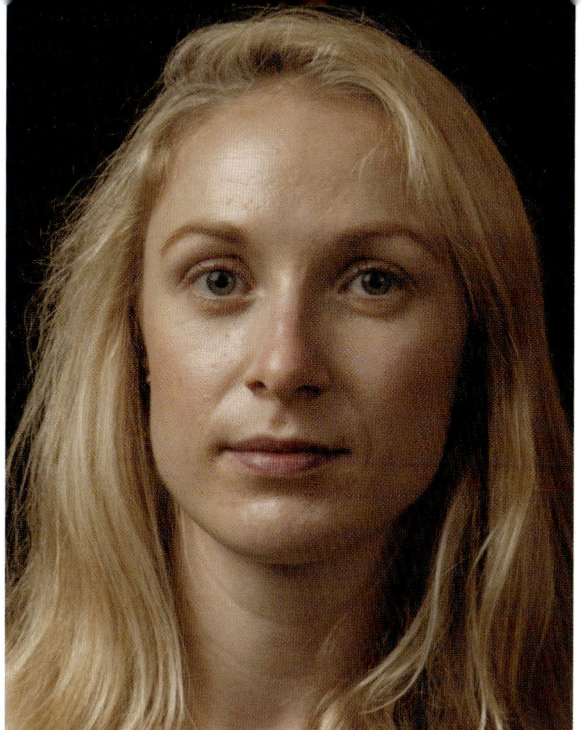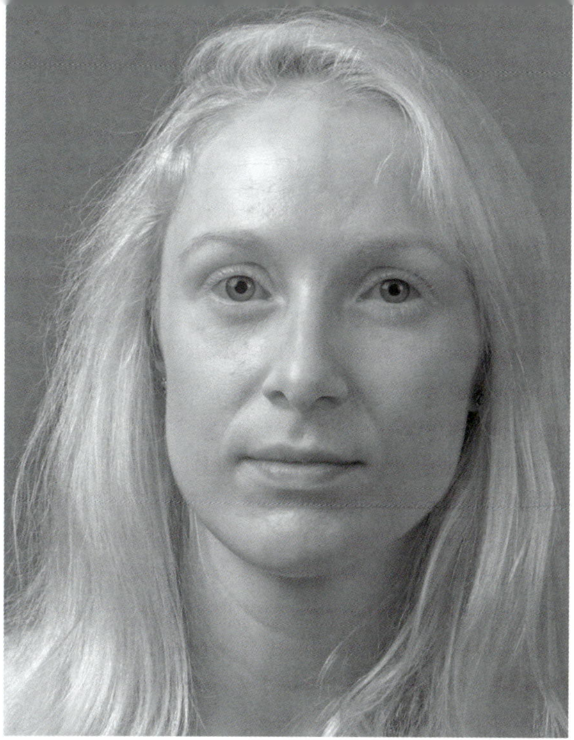

▲ Fig. 5.29, 5.30
An IR portrait removes all blemishes and wrinkles from the surface of skin, giving it an alabaster like appearance. Note too, how some veins have become visible.

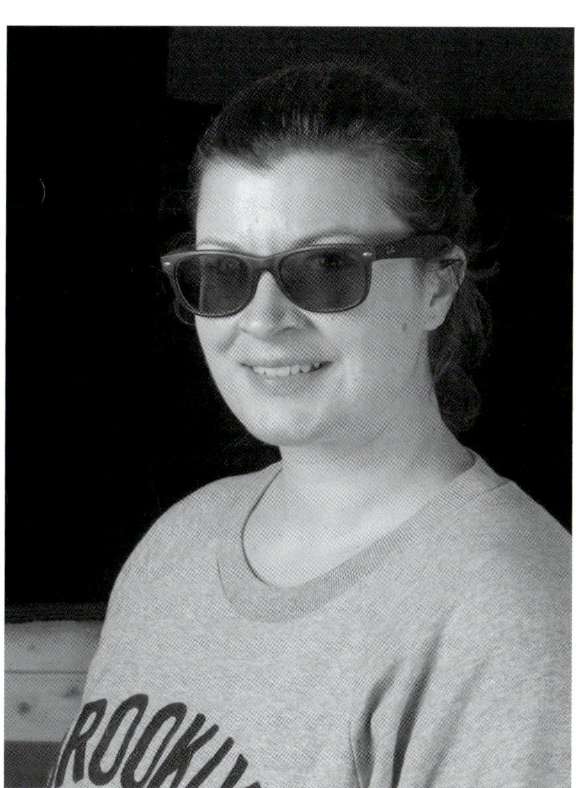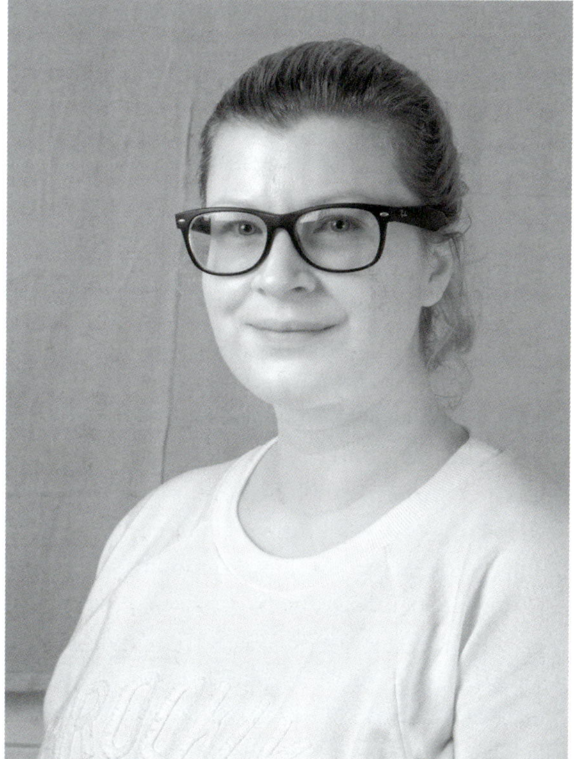

▲ Fig. 5.31, 5.32
In this case the IR makes the tinted sunglasses completely transparent. Note too, the lettering on the sweatshirt, which becomes virtually invisible in the IR record.

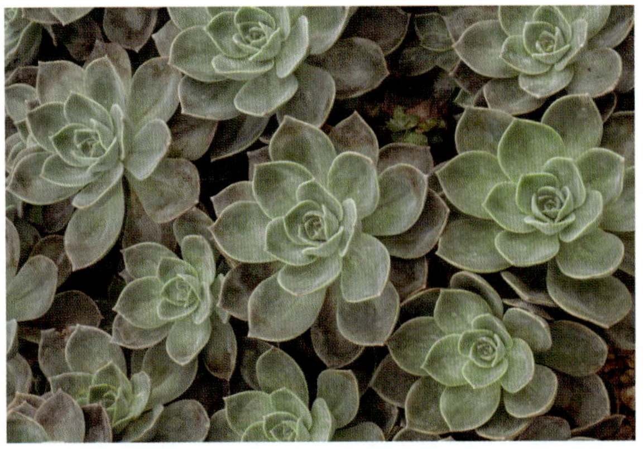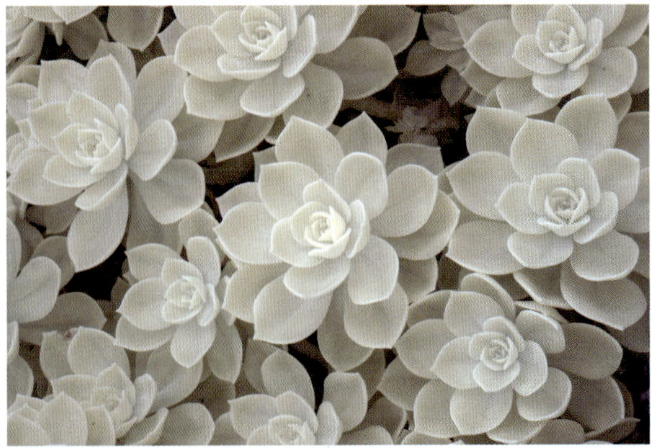

▲ **Fig. 5.33, 5.34**
A succulent plant in IR, giving a similar effect to an IR portrait, showing the almost complete loss of surface detail.
Nikon D300 full spectrum converted camera with 100mm Nikon lens. 850nm IR filter.

Wedding Photography

There are a number of photographers, primarily in the US, who specialize in IR wedding photography, for those couples looking for something different from conventional wedding pictures. One problem that the photographers found early on was with the suits worn by male guests. Black suits, made from different materials, may appear the same tone of black in visible light, but become a completely different tone when photographed in IR. Some photographers go so far as to issue guidelines to guests as to which particular suit to wear.

Trail Cameras

A trail camera (sometimes called a camera trap) is an automated camera that can, depending on the model, record still and video footage in IR or visible light. They are used by biologists for recording wild-life species, and are generally weatherproof, often being left in position for weeks or months at a time, and by photographers shooting images in remote areas. Many prize-winning images in natural history photographic competitions have been shot with trail cameras, and in 2019, the British photographer Will Burrard-Lucas photographed a black leopard in Kenya, the first authenticated images of the species in Africa in nearly a century.

Trail cameras can also be used as security cameras, triggered by intruders. Some can be set up to send images directly to a smartphone.

They are triggered by movement, detected by the PIR (passive infrared) sensor. Different models will have the capability of adjusting the detection area in terms of both distance and angle of view. Some models can monitor ambient temperature and adjust the sensitivity of the sensor according to the ambient temperature.

There has been a great increase in the use of automated camera traps over the last few years, for recording wildlife at night. They are usually an unconventional design, more akin to something out of a science fiction film. There are several different types producing IR images, full-colour images and video sequences. Many can be left in place for long periods of time. If you intend doing this, make sure you start with a fresh set of high-quality batteries, usually lithium-ion (Li-ion).

Many of the images of animals shot with trail cameras show significant eyeshine due to the fact that the IR flash is close to the lens axis. This means that the flash is reflected straight back into the lens from the rear of the eye. Foxes in particular, as well as several other mammals, have, in effect, a double

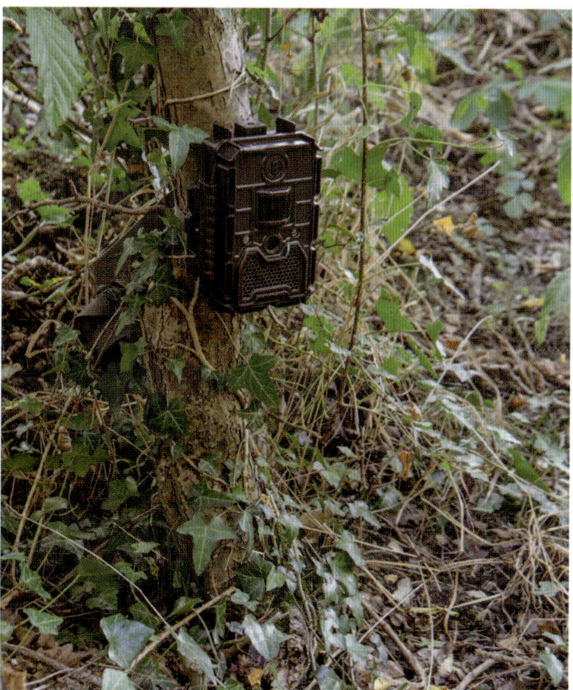

▲ Fig. 5.35
A typical trail camera, attached to a tree, overlooking a baited area for animals.

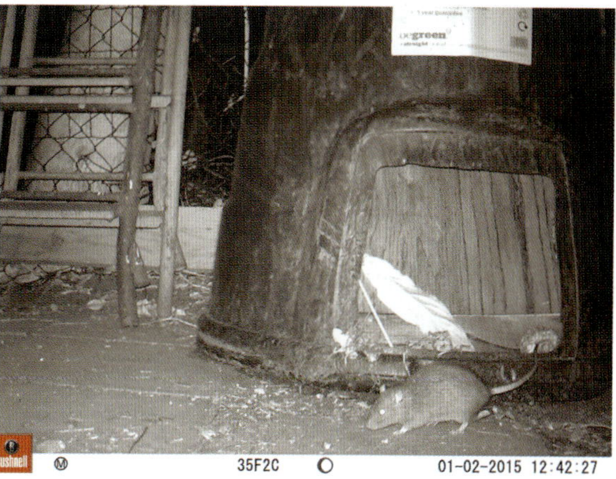

▲ Fig. 5.36
This image from a Bushnell Trophy Cam HD 12 Mp trail camera confirmed that rats were visiting a garden compost bin at night. Note the date, time, and temperature at the bottom of the image.

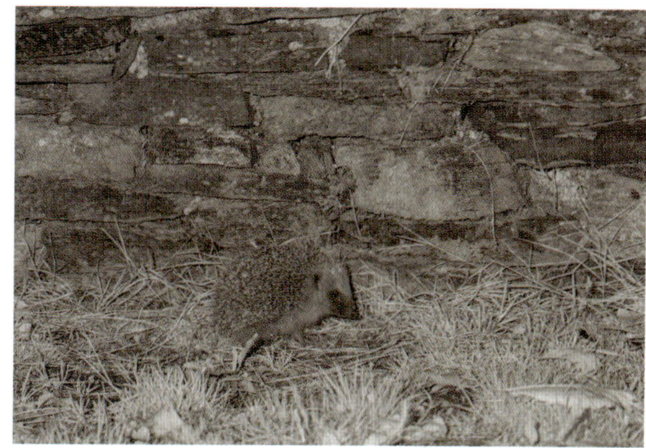

▲ Fig. 5.37
A Hedgehog (*Erinaceus europaeus*) shot with a remote-controlled IR camera and 720nm IR filtered flash.
 Nikon D300 full spectrum converted camera, with 105mm Series E Nikon lens, 720nm IR filter. Mecablitz 45CT1 flashgun with IR filter over flash head.

retina, known as the tapetum lucidum, which increases the eyeshine.

Most camera traps use relatively low-quality lenses and relatively low pixel counts, so image quality will never be the same as a conventional camera, but they may well be the only way of recording a particular species.

The cameras cannot be focused, so it may be worth keeping the camera a reasonable distance away from the area to be monitored (more than a metre) to help with depth of field.

Most trail cameras will imprint data regarding date, time and temperature at the bottom of the image, very useful for biologists using the camera for monitoring purposes.

Word of caution: If you are leaving the camera out for a period of time, make sure it is well hidden and/or secured in a locked box to deter thieves.

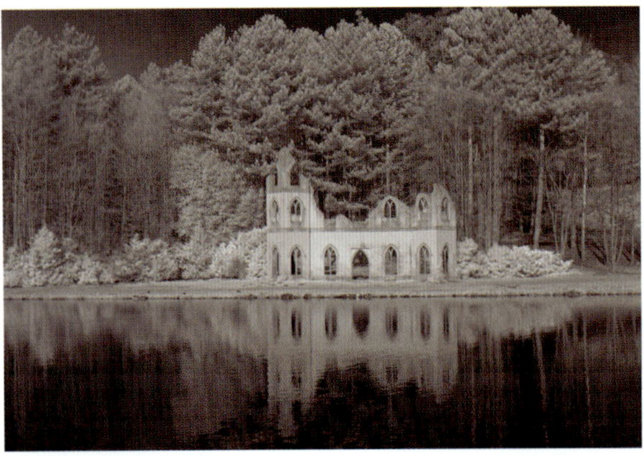

▲ **Fig. 5.38, 5.39**
A view of The Ruined Abbey grotto at Painshill Park in Surrey, UK, shot with an 850nm IR filter. The second image had a Gaussian blur applied to it (amount 20 pixels) to give a soft halo around detail edges. The amount of blurring is highly adjustable according to taste.

MONOCHROME IR PHOTOGRAPHY

One of the reasons for the distinctive feel of monochrome IR images when shooting film was that the film emulsion suffered from a phenomenon called halation, where edges within an image had a characteristic glow around them. Light would strike the rear layer of the film and bounce back into the film emulsion. Conventional film had an anti-halation layer built into it to prevent this for normal visible light photography, but it had no effect in IR photography.

The effect can be simulated digitally with the use of software filters such as Nik Software Glamour Glow, and Adobe® Photoshop's Diffuse Glow.

A good technique for producing a similar effect using Photoshop® is to make a duplicate of the image in Photoshop®'s Layers panel by dragging the small thumbnail to the 'create a new layer' icon at the bottom of the dialog box.

Next, apply a Gaussian blur filter to the duplicate image (**Filters > Blur > Gaussian blur**). You can experiment with the amount – try 30 pixels radius to start with. Now, slowly reduce the opacity of the duplicate image using the opacity slider so that the original starts to show through. There will be a glow effect in the image. This technique works really well with woodland images and other landscapes. Obviously you can vary the effect greatly.

When an image is downloaded from the camera it may have a pinkish or bluish tinge depending on the filter used. There are several methods in software programs for converting a colour image to black and white. Adobe® Lightroom, for example, has a number of presets including B&W high- and low-contrast and B&W landscape. More black and white presets are available from a number of sources for further choice.

In the Adobe® Camera Raw converter, clicking the B&W button in the Treatment menu will enable monochrome only editing. In Photoshop® itself there is the option for converting colour images to black and white (**Image > Adjustments > Black & White**), that again, gives complete control over the tonal balance of the image.

SIMULATING IR FALSE COLOUR FILM

As discussed earlier, false colour IR film had a very distinctive look, which is relatively easy to simulate using digital techniques. Various techniques have been used to try to simulate IR false colour film, and there is even a Flickr group devoted to simulating the Kodak EIR style.

The first method is to use a filter combination that effectively mimics the look of the false colour IR images produced by colour film. As mentioned earlier, Kolari Vision have recently introduced their IR Chrome filter, aimed at producing the same colours as IR False colour film.

Another method is to shoot two images and blend them together. It is a rather cumbersome technique but does mimic precisely how IR colour film recorded images and is well worth trying. It relies on having a full spectrum converted camera and shooting two images that need to be in pixel perfect alignment. The basic idea is to shoot a visible light image and a separate IR image with the same camera and lens. The green and red channels from the visible light image are combined with the IR image, with each channel coloured according to the colour scheme of the original IR film. The IR image will be coloured cyan, the red channel magenta, and the green channel yellow. You will need to use Photoshop® or similar image processing program, which has the ability to access and separate the channels within an image, as well as having a layers facility.

Technique

Set up the shot with a full spectrum converted camera, on a sturdy tripod. You will be shooting two images that will be later combined so precise alignment of the two images is essential. Use the same aperture for the two images, adjusting the exposure with the shutter speed.

Shoot the visible light image with a hot mirror filter over the lens. Examples are the Kolari Vision Hot Mirror filter, or the Schott S8612 filter. To help achieve the correct colour, shoot two images (raw files are best), one with a photographic 18 per cent grey card included within the image that can later be used to white balance the image in the raw converter software.

Without moving the camera, shoot the IR image with a 720, 760 or 850nm filter over the lens, to achieve a monochrome IR image.

Open both the visible light image and IR image in Photoshop, and, if necessary, use the levels control to achieve an acceptable exposure.

Open the channels and layers dialog boxes.

The IR image needs to be coloured cyan. Double click on the foreground colour panel at the bottom of the toolbox, which opens the Colour Picker. In the R, G, B boxes type a value of 0 in the Red box, and 255 in the B and G boxes. This will give a pure cyan colour. Select OK.

With the IR image active, go to **Edit > Fill > Foreground Colour** with the blending mode set to **SCREEN**. The image should now be a pale cyan colour.

Save this image with a descriptive name e.g. IR cyan image.

Make the RGB image active by clicking on it. In the channels dialog box go to the sub menu and select Split Channels. This will open three greyscale images, labelled as red, green and blue.

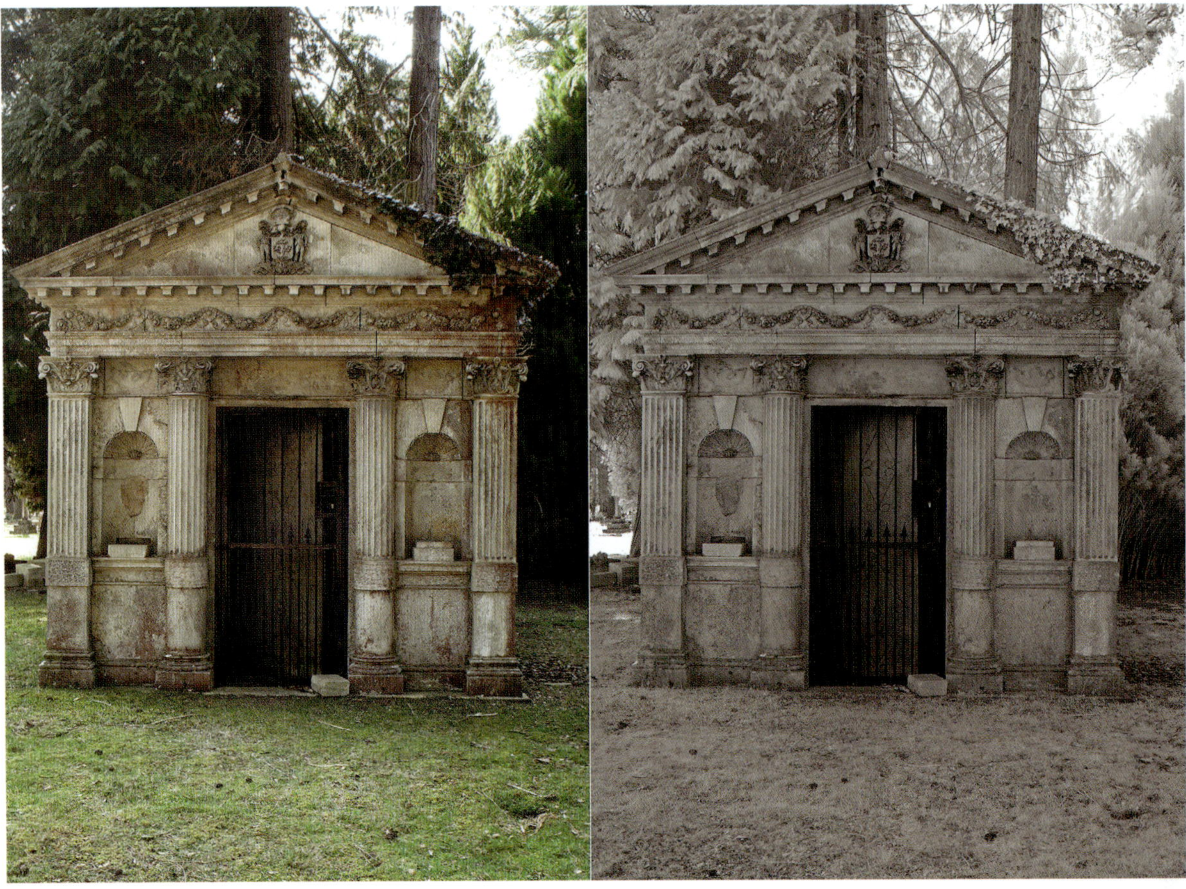

▲ **Fig. 5.40**
The original visible light and IR images of the tomb, (the IR shot with 850nm filter), shot with the same camera
and lens to ensure perfect registration.

Make the red channel active and convert it to RGB mode (**Image > Mode > RGB color**). In the foreground colour panel type in the figures: R: 255 and B: 255, similar to step 6. Click OK. Follow step 7 with the red image – it should appear magenta.

Repeat step 10 with the green channel image, using the figures: R: 255 and G: 255 so that the image appears yellow.

Make the red image active, go to **Select > All**, then **Edit > Copy**.

Make the cyan coloured IR image active and paste the red image on top of it. It will appear as layer one in the Layers panel. Select the option **MULTIPLY** in the blend mode drop down box.

Make the green image active, go to **Select > All**, then **Edit > Copy**, and past it into the image containing the IR and red images. Again, select the **MULTIPLY** option in the blend mode drop down box.

You should now have a three-colour image simulating how IR colour film would have recorded the scene. The saturation and vibrancy of the colours can be adjusted in Photoshop afterwards.

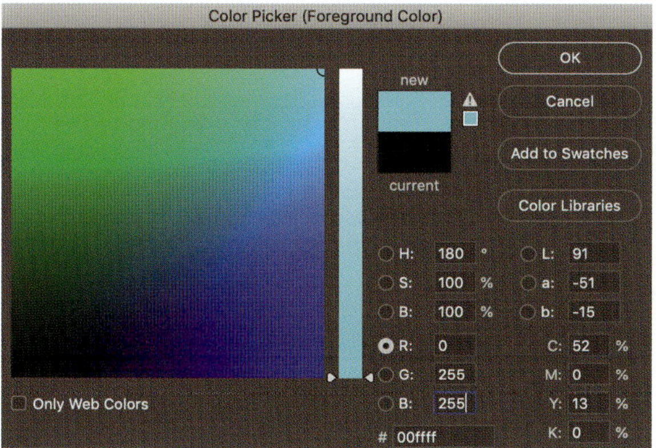

▲ **Fig. 5.42**
The red channel from the RGB image is coloured magenta, the green channel from the RGB image is coloured yellow, the three colour channels to be combined to make the final composite.

▲ **Fig. 5.41**
Photoshop® Color Picker, showing the cyan selection.

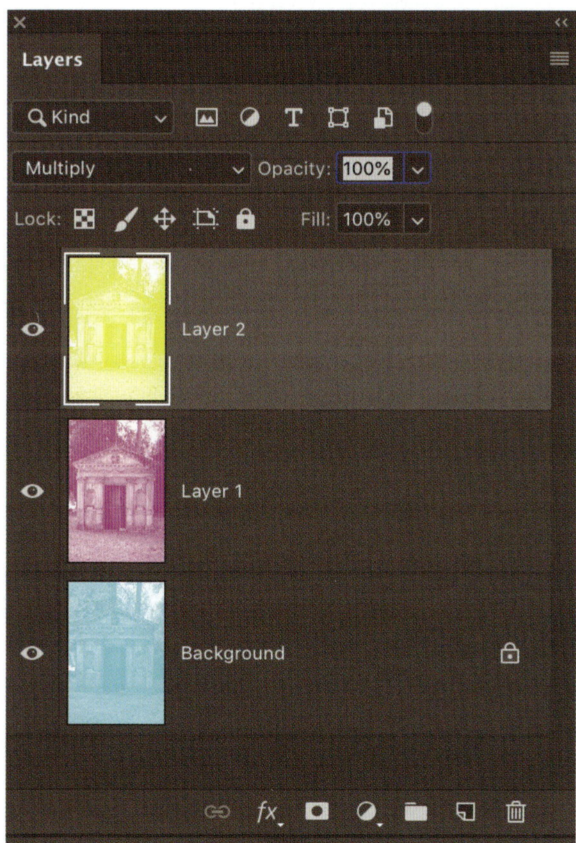

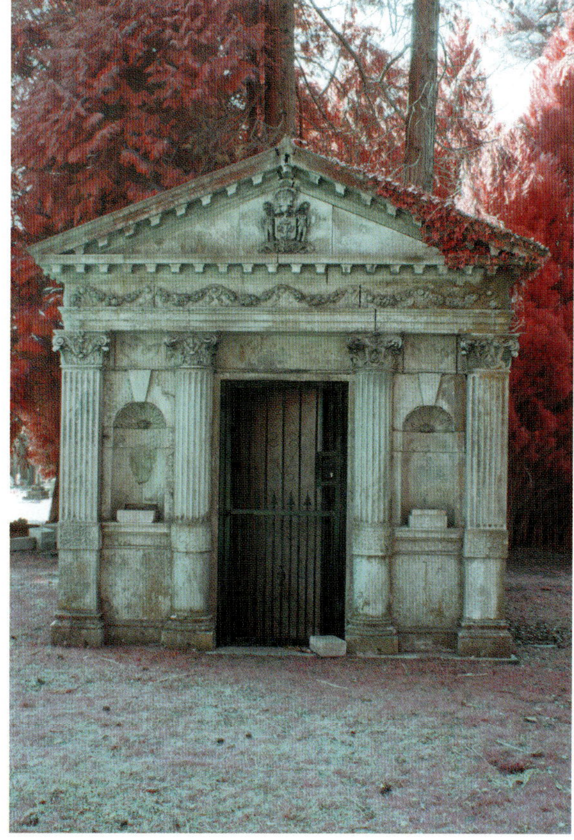

▲ **Fig. 5.43**
Photoshop® layers palette showing the three images to be combined.

▲ **Fig. 5.44**
The final composite, very similar to the effect given with false colour IR film.

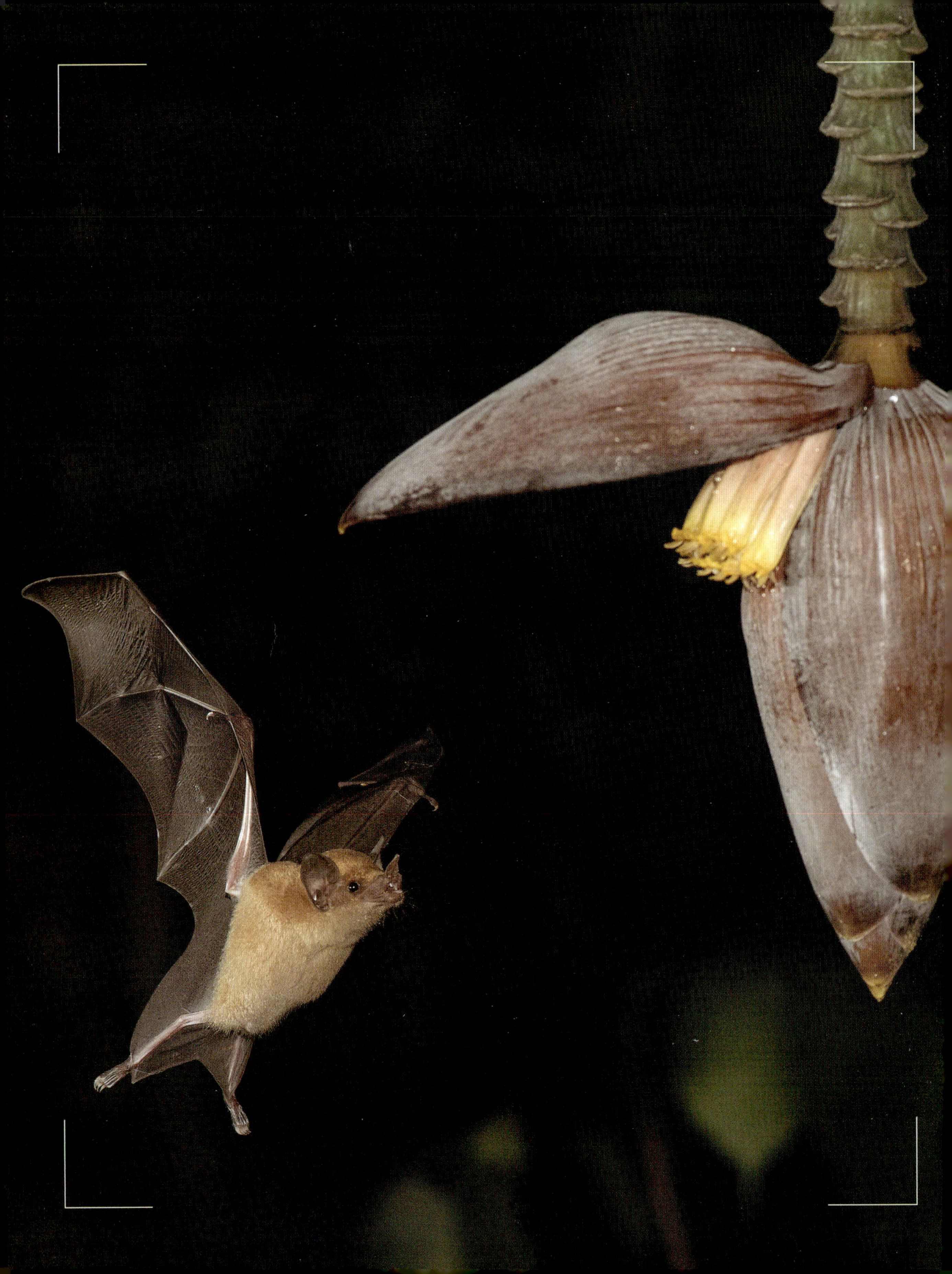

High Speed/Short Duration Photography

There are many moments in time (events) that happen too quickly for the human eye to perceive and require the use of a fast shutter speed or short duration flash to capture the event in the camera. We cannot see what happens when a balloon bursts, how a puffball fungus discharges its spores, or what a hummingbird's wings look like when hovering above a flower. While 1/100th of a second or so is a very short space of time in the conventional world, in photographic terms it is a relatively long period of time. Shutter speeds of 1/8000th second or less are now common in modern DSLR and mirrorless cameras, which also often have ISO ratings of up to 25,600 ISO, enabling these fast shutter speeds, with remarkably good quality, often in low light levels. Many modern electronic flashguns can have durations of 1/40,000th second or shorter in some cases (some specialist commercial units can have durations of less than one millionth of a second!).

High speed photography (sometimes referred to as short duration photography) has numerous applications, from forensic scientists investigating ballistics, car manufacturers looking at the impact of crashes, to biologists looking at the mechanics of insect or bird flight, or sports coaches analysing athletic technique for example. Recent advances in electronic technology means that camera manufacturers are now able to incorporate many useful features in the camera for freezing action, while several companies nowadays offer sophisticated triggering devices at reasonable prices

for photographing short duration events such as the impact of water drops, or balloons bursting, for example.

The main aim with high speed photography is to ensure that the camera shutter is fully open and, if used, the flash fires, at the time that the peak of the event is happening. In some cases, this can be done by eye, as in the case of the pollen and spore dispersal images shown here, or larger birds in flight for example. For other subjects, such as flying insects, balloons bursting, or bullets in flight, some form of electronic trigger system will invariably be required, where the subject itself triggers the camera and flash, by flying through a light beam, touching an electronic switch, or making a loud bang for example. As with much photography of unseen subjects, high speed photography will involve a great deal of planning, experimentation, improvisation, meticulous technique, and a good deal of luck. Just like the studio-based UV techniques discussed earlier, it may be worth shooting in tethered mode to enable instant viewing of the results on a large monitor, and to enable instant captioning of the images with the various equipment and settings used.

BASIC HIGH SPEED PHOTOGRAPHY

Many short duration events can be captured with a modern digital camera using a fast shutter speed and high ISO. Image quality with high ISO settings is now very much better than it used to be, with

◀ **Fig. 6.1**
Leaf-nosed bat (*Phyllostomidae sp.*) feeding from banana flower at night in Costa Rica.
   Nikon D810 camera with 70-300mm lens (at 200mm) three Nikon SB-900 flashes. 1/250th second @ f/11. 1000 ISO.

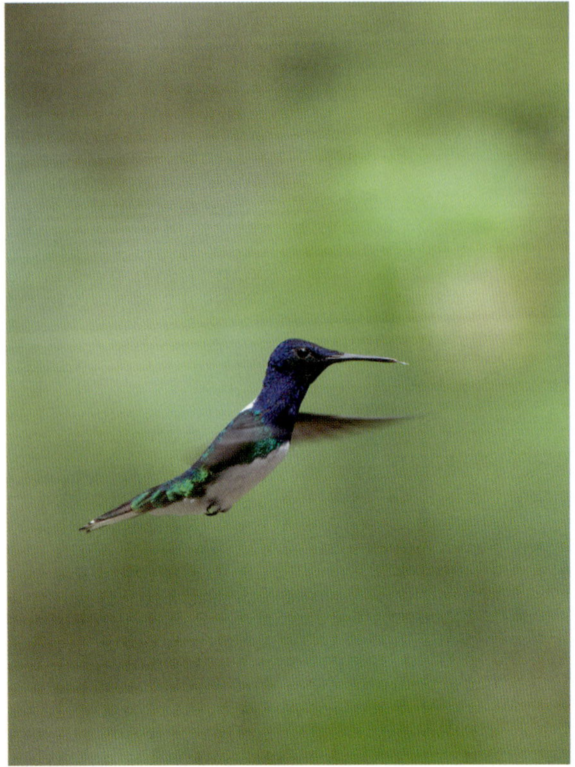

▲ Fig. 6.2
Male Blue-Chinned Sapphire Hummingbird (*Chlorestes notata*) photographed with daylight in Trinidad. Nikon D800 with 80–400mm lens (at 400mm) 1/1000th second @ f/5.6, 1600 ISO.

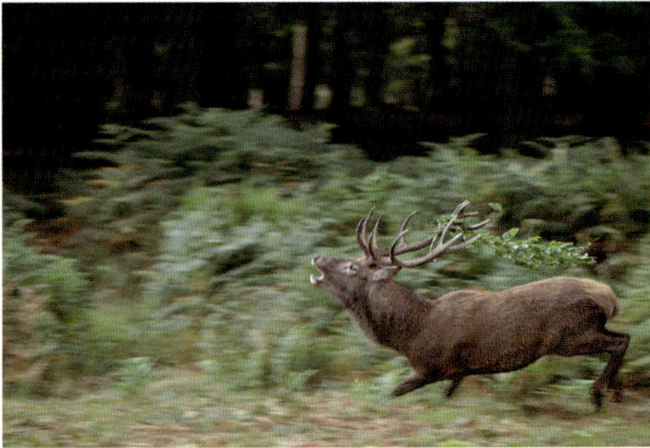

▲ Fig. 6.3
Red Deer Stag (*Cervus elaphus*) during the rutting season. This stag was running around frenziedly in front of females. The camera was panned to try to give an impression of his movement. Note that some areas of the fur are sharp, but the background appears as an overall blur.
 Nikon D800 with 80–400mm lens at 400mm. 1/80th second @ f/8. 200 ISO.

remarkably little digital noise even at settings up to 3,200 ISO or higher. In good light, this will allow shutter speeds in excess of 1/4000th or shorter, fast enough for most birds in flight, animals running and even larger insects such as dragonflies in flight.

Capturing birds in flight, running animals or racing horses for example requires good technique. Modern cameras with their sophisticated automatic focussing systems, fast shutter speeds and high ISO capabilities now allow us to photograph birds in flight like never before. Some mirrorless cameras even have the ability to capture an image before you actually fully press the shutter release button. Olympus call this Pro Capture for example. With this mode set and the shutter release button half-depressed, the camera starts recording images at up to 60 frames per second, but does not write them to the memory card, keeping the last fourteen images in a memory buffer. When the release button is fully depressed the camera starts recording images to the card, including the buffered fourteen.

Triggering Systems

There are many subjects that cannot be captured with a conventional technique and will need some form of trigger to fire either the camera or flash. There are several different types of triggering system available for high speed photography, including light beam, make/break trigger, vibration, movement, lightning and sound.

Various commercial electronic triggering systems are available, and anyone with a reasonable competence with electronics can find circuits on the internet for building their own. There are also some incredibly sophisticated systems that have been built, such as that shown at https://petapixel. com/2010/02/05/photo-grandpa-shoots-with-laser-rigs/ (more links are given in the resource list at the end of the book), which uses a cross beam system and high-speed shutter, all built into one portable device.

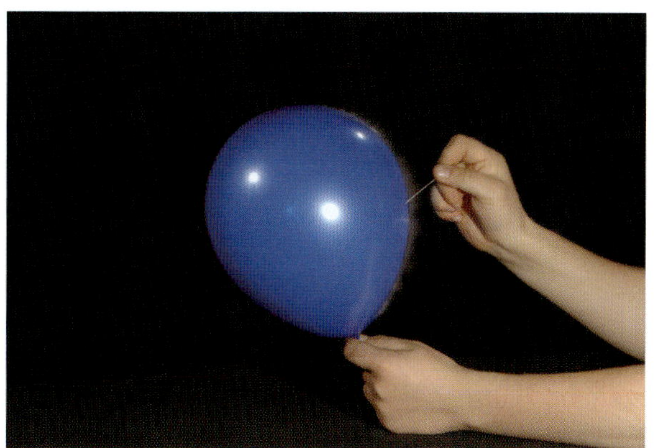

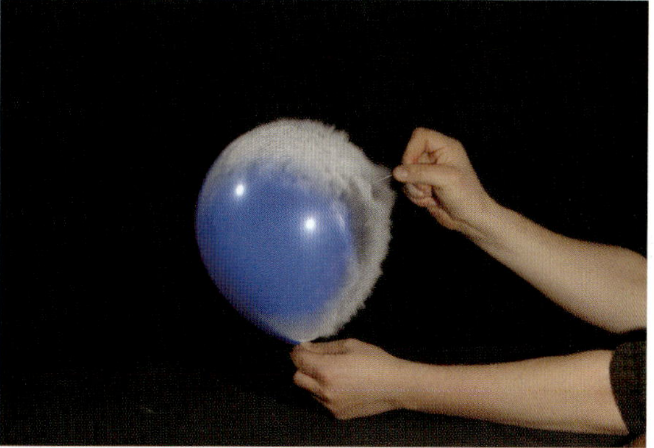

▲ Fig. 6.4
A balloon being burst, showing shock waves in flour added to the balloon.
  Nikon D800 with 70–300mm lens at 85mm. Two Nikon Speedlights at 1/16th power output (approximately 1/10,000th second) open flash technique, f/11.

Most of the commercially available devices have variable sensitivity settings, and an important variable delay setting, which will help determine precisely when the event is captured.

Triggering devices can fire the camera, or flash units. Firing the camera means releasing the shutter, which, if mechanical, such as a focal plane shutter, has a delay in opening which will need to be taken into account when setting up the shot. Triggering the flash units will probably involve working in a darkened room, with the shutter being opened before the event occurs.

Sound Activation

A sound trigger involves having a microphone close to the subject that will make a noise, such as a bullet or pellet being fired from a gun, a balloon bursting, or light bulb being smashed. If the microphone is connected to a trigger device that has a variable delay, then different stages in an event can be photographed by increasing or decreasing the delay setting. An alternative way of doing this is to increase or decrease the distance from the microphone to the subject. Sound travels at around 340 metres (1126 feet) per second in air.

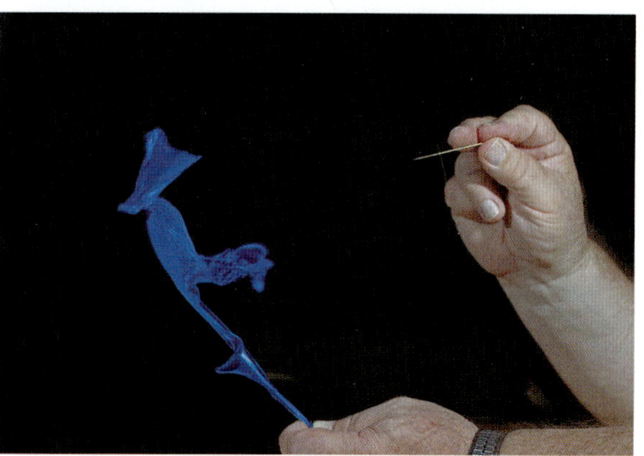

▲ Fig. 6.5, 6.6
Different stages in bursting of a balloon achieved by varying the distance of the microphone sensor to the balloon.

Moving the microphone 30 cm (1 foot) away from the subject will introduce a delay of approximately 1,000th second, a relatively long time in the case of a balloon collapsing after being burst. It is interesting, and often frustrating, that even when using the same delay setting, and the same type of balloon for example, that completely different images are often obtained with no changes to the set up.

The images shown here were shot using an open flash technique in a completely dark room. The shutter was opened on its B setting, but, being dark, no light entered the camera. The balloon was then burst with a pin, triggering the flashes, and the shutter then closed. The two flashes were set to

1/32nd output, giving an approximate duration of 1/20,000th second. This technique means that the shutter is not involved in the process, eliminating the inherent mechanical delay. It may be worth getting the person bursting the balloon to wear glasses to prevent pieces of flying balloon entering their eyes.

To enhance the image, a very small quantity of fine flour was placed into the balloon. When it burst, the shock waves could be clearly seen in the flour cloud.

Safety note: Take care when working in a dark room, particularly with pins and bursting balloons! Make sure you do not move around and have the light switch to hand. A head torch might be useful.

Make/Break Trigger

This type of trigger works when a connection is either made, by two electrical contacts being brought together, or broken, when two electrical contacts are separated. Such triggering systems are often used to capture animals in the field, where they may step onto a sprung pressure plate for example, making a contact when their weight makes the contacts touch.

A break trigger can be made by stringing a very thin wire across a pathway, which is pulled out from a suitable circuit when an animal passes through it, or when a bullet passes through it, for example.

Vibration Trigger

A vibration trigger operates when two contacts are temporarily brought together when the subject moves. Good examples are birds landing on a branch, with the trigger being attached to the branch. The circuitry may need to have a mechanism to prevent the camera or flash firing repeatedly if the vibration persists for a long period.

Light Beam

Similar to a door opening when you walk through a light beam, in this case the camera or flash is triggered when an insect, bird, animal or other suitable subject flies or passes through a light beam. The light beam can be a laser, which makes it highly directional, or another narrow light source focused with a lens onto the sensor. Alignment of the beam and sensor is obviously critical, and it may well be worth building some sort of rig that holds the light source and sensor firmly in relation to each other, without any movement. Take great care when aligning a laser beam that you do not look directly at it.

The main problem with this system is that if the beam is a metre long i.e. the light source is one metre from the sensor, then the camera will be triggered wherever the beam is broken, possibly out of the camera's field of view. To solve this problem it is possible to use a cross beam system, where two light beams cross at a point where the camera is focused. If only one of the beams is broken, nothing happens, it is only when the two beams are broken together that triggering occurs. This is technically known as an AND gate when used in the context of electronics, where the system is triggered when beam 1 and beam 2 are broken at the same time.

An alternative system, known as an OR gate, is where beam 1 or beam 2 are triggered, but not together. There are other variants of these systems.

If you are trying to photograph a small subject such as an insect in flight, it may miss the beam as it flies through due to its size. One way of increasing the chances of a small subject breaking the light beam is to direct the beam towards a mirror, which then reflects the beam back onto the sensor thus producing two beams. If you have mirrors on both sides, a wall of beams can be created, greatly increasing the chances of the system being triggered.

High-Speed Shutter

The mechanical focal plane shutter on a digital single lens reflex camera takes approximately 1/10th second, or 100 milliseconds (100 mS) to fully open. In that time, an insect, flying through a light beam at 5 metres per second would be around 50cm in front of the beam before the shutter was open and the flash triggered.

In order to obtain images of insects in free flight, a shutter with a much more rapid opening time is required. Photographers such as Stephen Dalton have devised and built their own, and one company, Cognisys, markets one called the High-Speed Shutter System, taking just 5.8 mS to open, though it is expensive at around £800 at the time of writing. To use it you need to lock open the camera shutter, and use the high-speed shutter, which is fitted to the front of the lens.

Lighting

Over the years various light sources have been used for high speed photography, including sparks, which were used to record projectiles in flight at Woolwich Arsenal as far back as 1860. The spark was produced by discharging a high voltage capacitor across a spark gap. The projectile was fired between the camera and spark, so that the final image was recorded as a silhouette. Durations of around one millionth of a second were possible with the spark, but photographic emulsions at the time were not always very good, so results were generally poor. The problem with short duration sparks was the extremely low level of illumination and the practicality of the system.

By far the best type of lighting for high speed photography is electronic flash, developed initially by Professor Harold Edgerton in the 1930s.

With electronic flash systems, the energy from a capacitor is discharged between two open electrodes, which are enclosed in a glass or quartz tube containing a rare gas usually Xenon (Krypton has also been used). This results in a much brighter light, but at a significantly longer discharge time. With electronic flash, speed and power are in direct conflict. Generally, you can have a short duration and low power, or high power with longer duration. Electronic flash units are now found in various devices such as smartphones and cameras, as well as large studio-based units.

Flashguns are available in a range of sizes and power, from large studio-based systems used for portrait and still life work, to smaller, portable, battery powered units, sometimes known as speedlights. Larger studio units are generally too slow for high speed photography. The duration of an Elinchrom BRZ500 flash head, a typical studio unit, for example, is 1/1558th second. This would be far too slow to capture an insect in flight, for example.

A typical speedlight, the Nikon SB5000, has a variable output from full power to 1/256th power, when the duration of the flash is 1/30820th second. The amount of light output diminishes with the shorter duration, and it will be necessary to carry out tests to find the optimum power/duration ratio for your purposes.

The following flash duration figures for the Nikon SB5000 speedlight are given in the instruction manual:

Power Output	Duration (seconds)
1/1	1/980th
1/2	1/1110th
1/4	1/2580th
1/8	1/5160th
1/16	1/8890th
1/32	1/13479th
1/64	1/18820th
1/128	1/24250th
1/256	1/30820th

One word of caution – it may not always be best to select the shortest possible duration. A completely frozen subject can look unnatural, and some blurring of wings or pollen may be a better option. Experimentation will be required.

ELECTRONIC FLASH DURATION

Specifying Duration

How flash duration is measured is worth discussing. When the flash tube is triggered, there is a rapid ionization period as the tube output rises to maximum brightness. This is followed by an exponential decline in tube current, voltage and light as the capacitors are discharged to zero. The standard engineering term for stating flash duration is t.5. This relates to the time it takes for 50 per cent of the total flash output to be dissipated. Whenever the term flash duration is quoted, it can be assumed to be the t.5 specification.

However, the t.5 specification doesn't adequately predict the actual motion freezing capability of a flash. There is a much longer trailing edge that continues to emit the remaining 50 per cent of the light. This causes considerably more motion blur than the t.5 value implies. In order to better compare flash duration specs to an equivalent shutter speed, the term t.1 was introduced by the photo industry. t.1 specifies the time it takes for 90 per cent of the total flash to be emitted. But even following the t.1 time, there is still light being emitted at sufficient intensity to cause some ghosting or motion trails in some circumstances.

IGBT Control of Flash Power

Currently, most low-power camera flashes (for example, Nikon Speedlights) employ IGBT (Insulated-Gate Bipolar Transistor) technology to control of flash power instead of variable voltage control. These are, essentially, very fast electronic switches. The technology is easily implemented in low power units, but only recently have IGBT devices become available with sufficient power handling capacity for use in higher powered studio flash, especially those offering fast flash durations, such as the Paul Buff Einstein™ unit.

In an IGBT flash unit, the voltage and current remain constant as power is reduced by abruptly shutting the tube off when the desired amount of light has been emitted. This results in flash durations that become shorter and shorter as power goes down, as well as the complete elimination of the exponential flash trail that is responsible for motion blur in non-IGBT flash units. Today, even relatively small flashguns can provide good quantities of light at short durations, particularly for small subjects.

One particular high-speed studio flash unit of interest is the Einstein™ from Paul Buff Inc. This has a flash duration of 1/588 sec. at full power, and 1/13,500 sec. at 1/256 power in its action mode. It is mains powered so could not be used in the field.

movement in a subject, such as the hummingbirds shown in this book.

Typical high-contrast subjects include weddings (white dress, black suits) and black and white birds such as puffins and penguins.

In the case of a wedding on a sunny day, a white dress may reflect 800 units (arbitrary number) of light, while a black suit may only reflect one unit (an 800:1 contrast range). It is beyond the capability of most digital cameras to record detail in both highlights and shadows. By using even a relatively weak flashgun, adding just one unit of light to the whole scene, the highlights now reflect 801 units and the shadows 2 units, a reduced contrast range now of

USING ELECTRONIC FLASH WITH DAYLIGHT

There are several ways that a flash can be used in conjunction with daylight, either to reduce contrast in a subject, or sometimes to show or enhance

400:1. It can be seen that the extra light has far more effect on the shadows rather than highlights, adding detail to them. This is known as fill-in flash.

When using flash with daylight, the shutter speed controls the amount of daylight that registers, while the aperture controls the amount of flash. When doing this, there is the chance that you will get a ghost image, where the main subject is sharp, and there is another image showing which registered after the flash had fired. In the case of the hummingbird images, the main body of the bird, which was relatively static, is frozen by the flash, while the wings are rendered as a blur by the extra daylight exposure. This may not be to everyone's taste. If you want to render the hummingbird totally sharp, you will need to completely override the daylight, and use several flashguns, some to light the bird, and others to light a probably false background.

Front- and Rear-Curtain Synchronization

One technique, when using electronic flash, of visualizing the movement of a subject is to use rear-curtain synchronization (sync), which is a setting in the flash modes menu on many cameras. This applies to those cameras with mechanical focal plane shutters (DSLRs, mirrorless). A focal plane shutter works by having two blinds that travel across the focal plane of the camera, just in front of the sensor. When set to a relatively fast shutter speed, when the shutter is fired, the first blind starts to travel across, and is quickly followed by the second blind, creating a narrow slit that travels across the focal plane. With longer shutter speeds, the second blind may not start to travel until the first one has reached the end, exposing the whole frame for a time.

In normal front-curtain sync, the flash fires when the first shutter blind opens, triggering the flash. A moving subject will be exposed with the flash at the start of the exposure, then, if there is sufficient ambient light, this will be recorded until the shutter

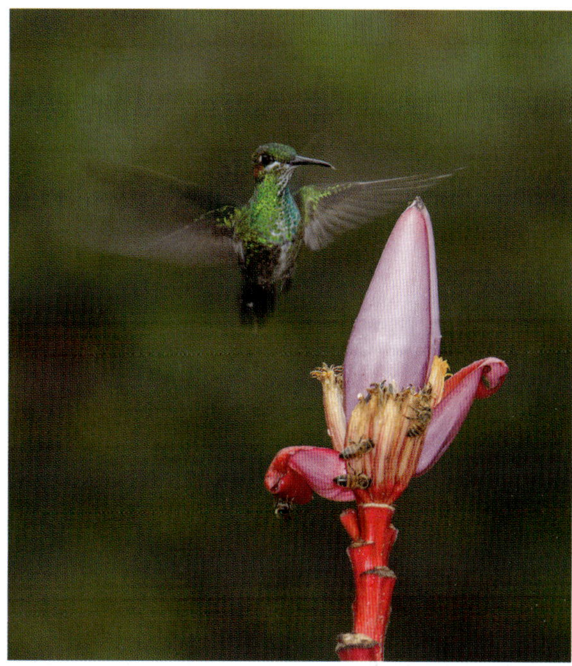

▲ **Fig. 6.7**
A Green-Crowned Brilliant Hummingbird (*Heliodoxa jacula*) shot with a mixture of daylight and flash. Because the bird is hovering in front of the flower the head is stationary and sharp. The wings are almost a total blur, due to the relatively slow shutter speed used (1/80th second), but give a good impression of the movement. Note the streaks of rain caught by the flash.
   Nikon D810 with 70–200mm lens and ×1.4 converter, Single SB-900 flash, 1/80th second @ f/9, 400 ISO.

has shut. This can cause ghost images in some scenes, and a streak or blur in front of a subject moving across the field of view.

With rear-curtain sync, the flash is triggered just before the shutter closes. The effect this has with a moving subject is to show the subject with the streak or blur following behind it, giving the impression of movement and direction. You will need to use a relatively long shutter speed, such as 1/30th or 1/15th second and have some ambient light to mix with the flash to achieve the blur trail. If the ambient light is not the same colour temperature as the flash, halogens for example, you may end up with a yellowish trail.

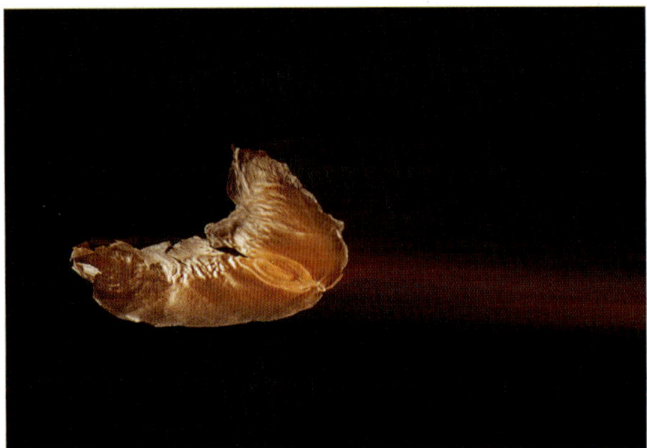

▲ Fig. 6.8

Seed of the Javan Cucumber (*Alsomitra macrocarpa*) from the rainforest of Borneo. These huge seeds (up to 13cm) do not spiral down like a sycamore, but instead glide down to the forest floor, often over a great distance. Their shape was copied as early as 1904 by the German aircraft designer Igo Etrich when designing a human glider, and by the flying wing stealth bomber. I set one up in the studio to demonstrate three ways of using flash.

Normal front curtain synchronization was used here. The blurring at the end of the flight is unnatural and fails to show the direction the seeds travel in.

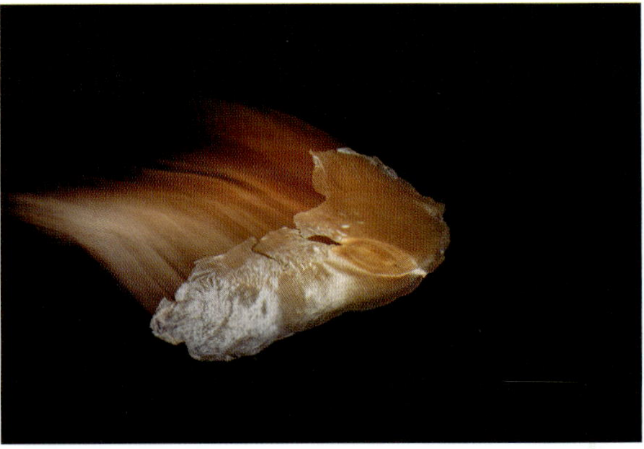

▲ Fig. 6.9

Rear curtain synchronization was used to try and show the flight of the seed. 1/2 second @ f/16. The blurring is in the correct position at the end of the image.

Using Multiple Units

Depending on the model of flashgun used, it may be possible to link multiple units wirelessly together to increase the amount of light output, as well as providing scope for different types of lighting such as backlighting. With Nikon Speedlights, for example, it is possible to set up one flash unit as the master, and other units as remotes, which are triggered virtually instantaneously by the master unit using IR. Make sure they are all set to the same output power so that the duration of the flashes is the same for each unit.

NEW TECHNOLOGY – LED LIGHTS

Light emitting diode (LED) technology has advanced in leaps and bounds over the last few years, being found everywhere from domestic lighting and car headlamps to lighting for video and stills photography.

Recently, several short-duration flash units have appeared, such as the Vela One™, consisting of nine chip-on-board LEDs. They use circuitry that drives the LEDs up to 20 times brighter than rated, without damaging them or overheating, emitting up to one million lumens. The units are capable of a range of durations, adjustable between 500 nanoseconds (1/2,000,000 sec) and 5µs (1/200,000 sec), around 100 times faster than a typical Xenon tube speed-light, and fast enough to freeze high-velocity bullets in mid-flight.

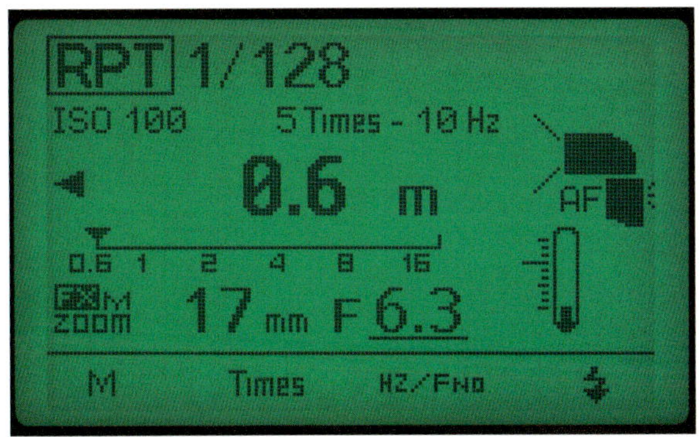

▲ **Fig. 6.10**
Rear screen of Nikon SB-900 flashgun in repeating mode, showing the setting for the flash to be fired five times at the frequency of 10 Hz.

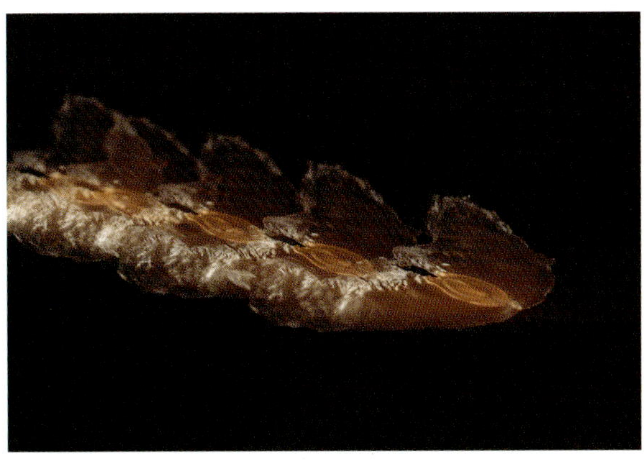

▲ **Fig. 6.11**
The repeating flash setting was used on a single Nikon SB-5000 flashgun, to produce a stroboscopic effect and to show the direction of flight. The repeat rate was set to 10 flashes per second.
All images: Nikon D810, 105mm micro NIKKOR lens, Studio, controlled conditions.

Stroboscopic Photography

Stroboscopic photography is where several images are exposed on the same frame through the use of a rapidly flashing light source. It is used for analysing sporting and dance movement for example, or bird flight, where the pattern of wing beats of a bird or insect can be seen. Like the electronic flash system, stroboscopic lighting was originally developed by Harold Edgerton in the 1930s.

Several modern flashguns have a stroboscopic facility – Nikon call theirs repeating flash mode, where the flash can be fired with a frequency of up to 100 times per second in certain circumstances. The total number of flashes on a frame will be dependent on the length of time that the shutter is open for. Settings on the flashgun will be the output (fraction of full power) and the frequency (the number of times per second that the flash fires), expressed in hertz. The total number of flashes fired at the elected output can also be set. The shutter speed needs to be sufficient for the number of flashes. With the shutter open for a long period, ambient light may become an issue, and you may want to work in a darkened room. Set the camera to manual exposure mode and do a few test exposures to determine the correct aperture.

SAFETY NOTE

Take care when using stroboscopic lighting in the presence of people prone to epilepsy. Photosensitive epilepsy (PSE) is where someone has seizures that are triggered by flashing or flickering lights, or patterns. Different people will be affected by lights flashing or flickering at different rates. Lights that flash or flicker between sixteen and twenty-five times a second are the most likely to trigger seizures, but some people are sensitive to rates as low as three or as high as sixty a second. If you are using the technique when other people are present it is worth warning them of the potential hazard.

SUBJECTS FOR HIGH SPEED PHOTOGRAPHY

Birds in Flight

Photographing birds in flight can be a fascinating, if often frustrating experience. Subjects can range from large birds such as kites, pelicans, and swans with slow leisurely wing beats, kestrels and terns

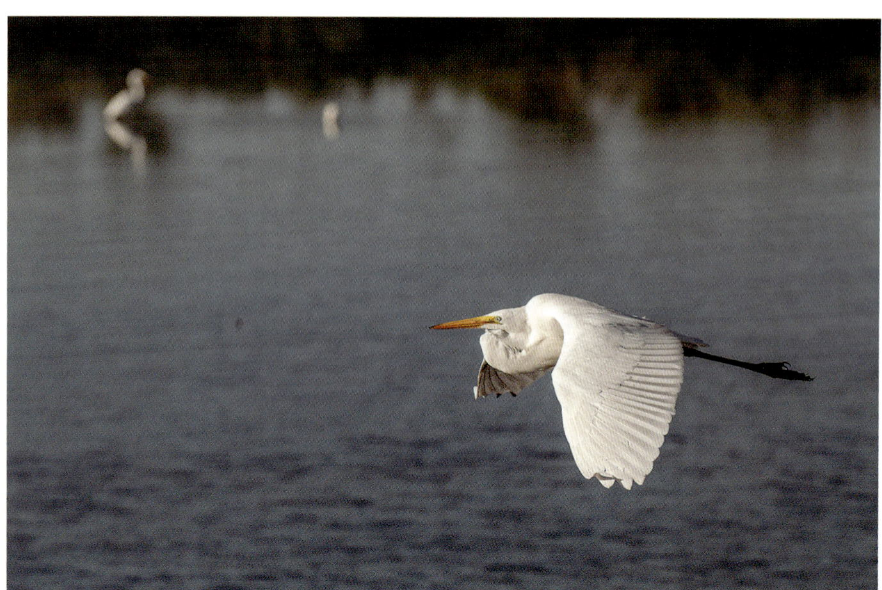

Great Egret (*Casmerodius albus*) in flight in the Florida Everglades. The camera was panned with the bird as it flew across the frame.

Nikon D300 with 70–200mm lens (at 200mm) 1/4000th second @ f/5.6, 400 ISO.

hovering, to hummingbirds with wing beats as fast as around twelve beats per second in the largest species, to over eighty in some of the smallest species. Techniques can range from photographing birds in free flight to hummingbirds hovering in front of flowers while sipping nectar.

Panning

This technique involves following the flight of the bird (or running animal or athlete) by panning the camera and releasing the shutter at an appropriate moment during the pan. Using this method it is possible to obtain sharp images of your subject at relatively long shutter speeds (e.g. 1/60th or 1/125th second), while rendering the background as a blur or streak. It requires some practice to perfect the technique. You can choose to hand hold the camera, providing maximum flexibility, and swivel your body to follow the action, or mount it on a tripod on a head that allows you to follow the flight easily. Particularly useful tripod heads for doing this are gimbal type heads such as the Wimberley head or Mongoose action head. These will hold the camera and lens (usually a long telephoto) on a gimbal type mount rendering the camera virtually

weightless, and capable of easy movement in all directions. Using the camera's continuous shooting mode will help get a larger percentage of good results. A typical high end DSLR can run at speeds up to twelve frames per second in the case of a Nikon D5 for example, while mirrorless models can shoot at up to sixty frames per second nowadays in electronic mode.

For this technique auto focusing will be extremely useful. Different camera manufacturers use different methods and terminology, but most systems nowadays have the ability to track the subject, keeping it in focus as you pan with it, or even as the subject flies towards you. Again, using the continuous shooting mode will greatly help.

Hummingbirds

Hummingbirds are small highly active birds found in central and south America. They are the only birds capable of flying backwards – indeed in any direction. Their wings beat very rapidly – from ten up to eighty beats per second in some species. They readily visit feeders or flowers sprayed with sugar water, so a camera can be set up and pre-focused on a particular spot. They will hover, while feeding,

Two Green-Crowned Brilliant Hummingbirds (*Heliodoxa jacula*) feeding at a banana flower. The one on the right is braking, in order to land, so the wings are beating relatively slowly, and are nearly frozen, whilst the left bird is hovering, beating it's wings rapidly.
   Nikon D810 with 70–200mm lens (at 200mm) 1/125th second @ f/6.3, 200 ISO Single Nikon SB-900 flash.

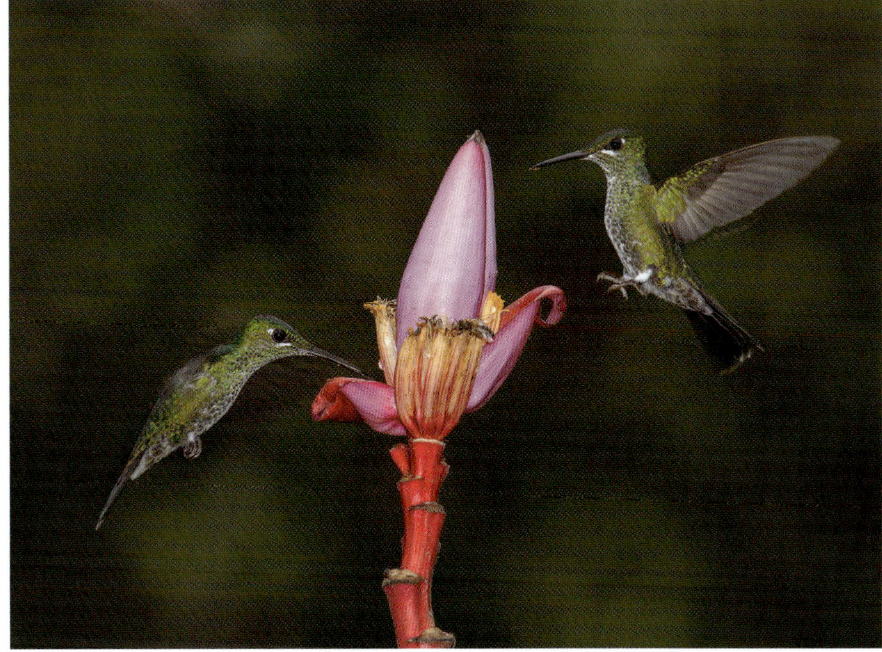

with the body and head remaining motionless with the wings keeping them in place. There are several different approaches, daylight only, daylight with flash, or flash only. Daylight images are of course limited by the light available – usually good in areas which hummingbirds frequent. Every image will be different, depending on the attitude of the bird and whether it is hovering, coming in to land or taking off. The image shown here was shot at 1/1000th second, at 800 ISO. While the body and head of the bird are static, and therefore sharp, the wings are almost invisible. The other images were shot with a combination of daylight and flash, rendering the wings as a blur, but conveying a sense of movement.

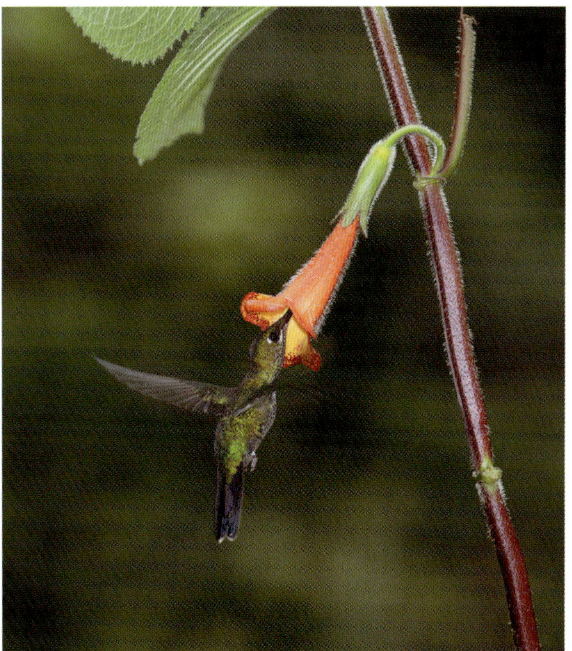

▲ Fig. 6.14
Green-Crowned Brilliant Hummingbird feeding at a flower. The nearly frozen wings, together with the ghost images of the wings give a wonderful impression of movement.
   Nikon D810 with 70–200mm lens (at 200mm) 1/125th second @ f/6.3, 200 ISO Single Nikon SB-900 flash.

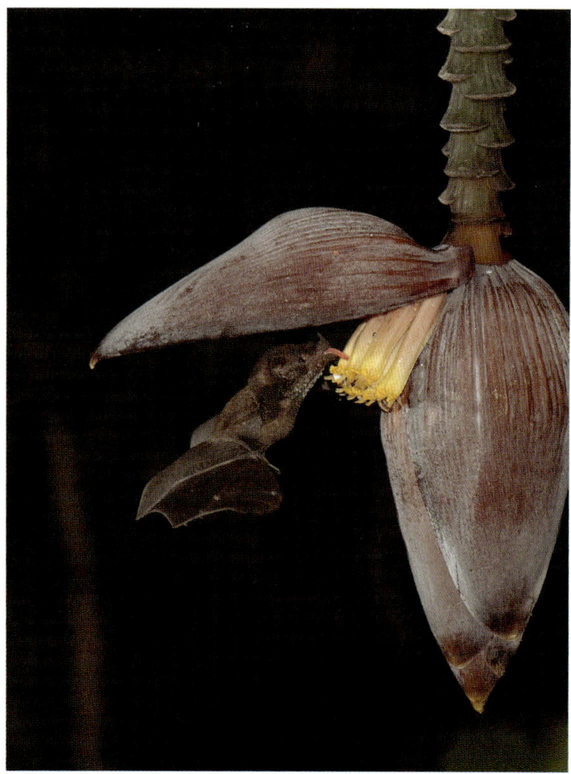

▲ Fig. 6.15
Leaf-Nosed Bat (*Phyllostomidae sp.*) approaching a banana flower.
Note the extended tongue and pollen on the chin.
   Nikon D810 camera with 70-300mm lens (at 200mm) three Nikon
SB-900 flashes. 1/250th second @ f/11. 1000 ISO.

Bats

Photographing bats in flight at night is normally
very difficult, requiring light beam or other triggers, and short duration flash units. In the UK,
due to the alarming decline in bat numbers, and
possible disturbance, a licence is required from
Natural England before any photography of bats can
be undertaken.

   The image shown here of a leaf-nosed bat was
shot in the middle of a rainforest in Costa Rica,
at a feeding station specially set up for nectar
feeding species. Feeders, similar to those used for
hummingbirds, are hung regularly in the same
place, and are visited by several species of plant

feeding bats. For the photography, the feeders were
temporarily replaced by banana flowers that were
sprayed with the same sugar water as used in the
feeders. One Nikon flash was placed behind the
flower, to backlight the bat, while two were used at
the front. They were linked by the Nikon wireless
communication system. Working after dark, the ISO
needed to be raised to 1000 ISO to enable the setting
of 1/16th power for the flashes, giving a duration of
around 1/10,000th second. Several dozen images
were shot in order to get a few sharp ones!

Amphibians and Reptiles

Good subjects for high speed photography are
frogs jumping, and animals such as chameleons
catching prey with their long sticky tongues. Their
actions are often unpredictable, and they will not
always perform to command, or jump in the right
direction. You will need time and patience and a
well-designed set for this type of work, as well as
respect for the welfare of the subject.

   For the chameleon image shown here, the
specimen was placed on a sturdy piece of wood
by a qualified handler. All lighting and other
photographic issues such as exposure were tested
before it was put into position. The session started
by using a light beam trigger, with the light beam (a
laser pen) positioned just in front of the chameleon's
head. A live cricket was placed on a twig just out of
camera view. The chameleon did extend its tongue
to catch the cricket several times but missed the
light beam on most occasions. The projectile tongue
can extend to over 20cm, and is held coiled within
the mouth, and can be shot out with a sudden rush
of blood. In some species the tongue can hit the
prey at 20km per hour. The tip is very sticky to grab
prey items.

   An alternative method was tried, without any
form of triggering at all. Instead, when it looked as
though the animal was just about to shoot out its
tongue (this was very obvious), the shutter on the

▶ **Fig. 6.16, 6.17, 6.18**
Panther Chameleon (*Furcifer pardalis*) catching locust. In the first image, the tongue can be seen starting to emerge from the mouth, giving a good indication that the animal is about to strike.

Nikon D800 with 105mm and ×1.4 converter. Three Nikon SB-900 flashes, 1/32nd power. 1/160th @ f/16. 400 ISO.

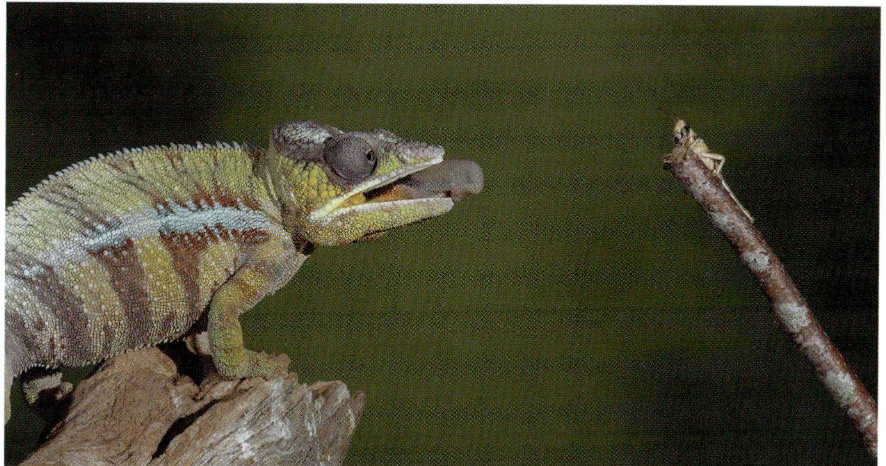

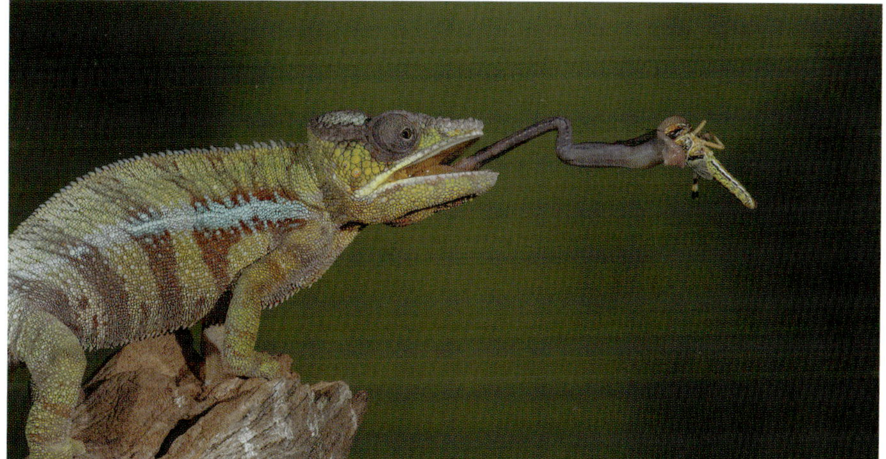

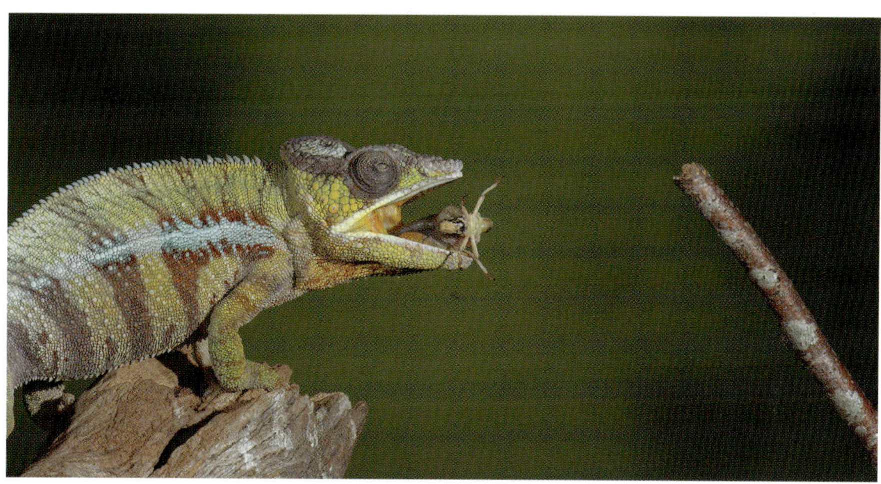

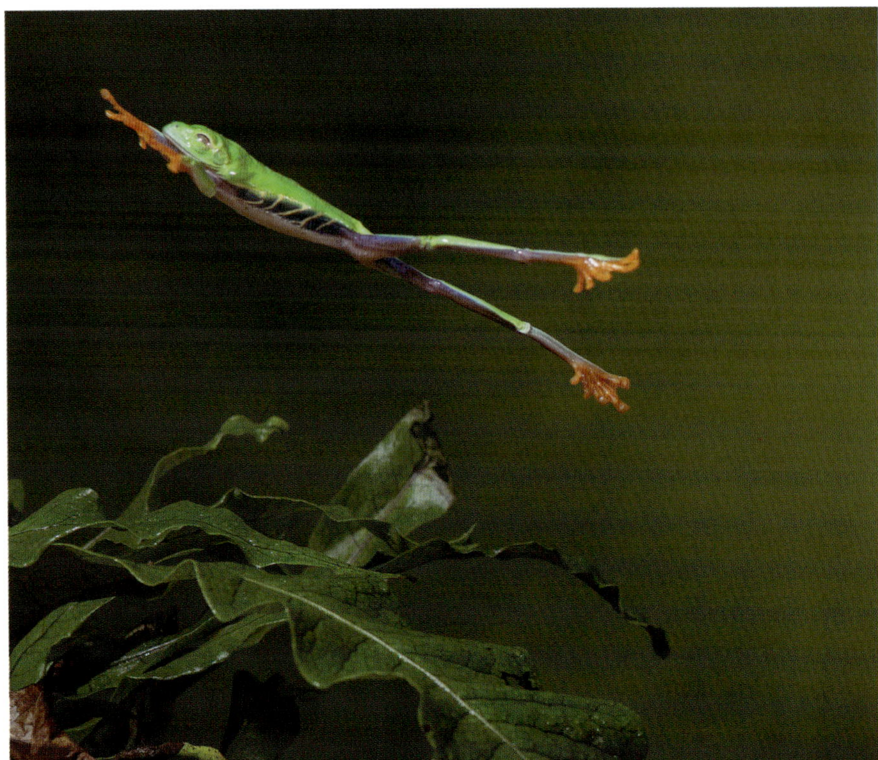

Red-Eyed Treefrog (*Agalychnis callidryas*) jumping.
 Nikon D800 with 105mm and ×1.4 converter. Three Nikon SB-900 flashes, 1/32nd power. 1/160th @ f/16. 400 ISO.

camera was pressed, with the Nikon camera on continuous high-speed mode, firing at five frames per second. Three Nikon SB900 flashguns were used, each set to 1/32nd power, giving an effective shutter speed of around 1/20,000th second. The first flash triggered by the camera was the master that triggered the other two remote units wirelessly. At this low power output, the flashes are able to recycle quickly enough to keep up with the five frames per second shooting mode. This proved highly success-ful and several whole sequences were obtained showing the tongue starting to emerge, catching the prey, through to pulling the prey back into its mouth.

The red-eyed tree frog shown here was far more unpredictable in its jumping, both in terms of direc-tion and height. Again, the specimen was placed on a sturdy rock just out of frame, facing in the direc-tion of the, hoped for, leap. Again, the camera was fired manually without a trigger. After around six jumps just one frame was reasonably sharp.

Snakes

One shot that many photographers wish to get is of a snake with its tongue out, scenting the air. It is, as might be imagined, an unpredictable event, and you may need to shoot multiple exposures to achieve the result. It may well be easiest to do this with a captive snake, handled by an experienced handler. The pit viper shown here, shot in Borneo, was found lying on a branch, and coaxed into a better position by a local guide. After being moving, the snake flicked out its tongue several times, and one exposure, out of around twenty shot, showed the tongue. Although shot at just 1/125th second, the blurring of the end does give the image a sense of dynamism.

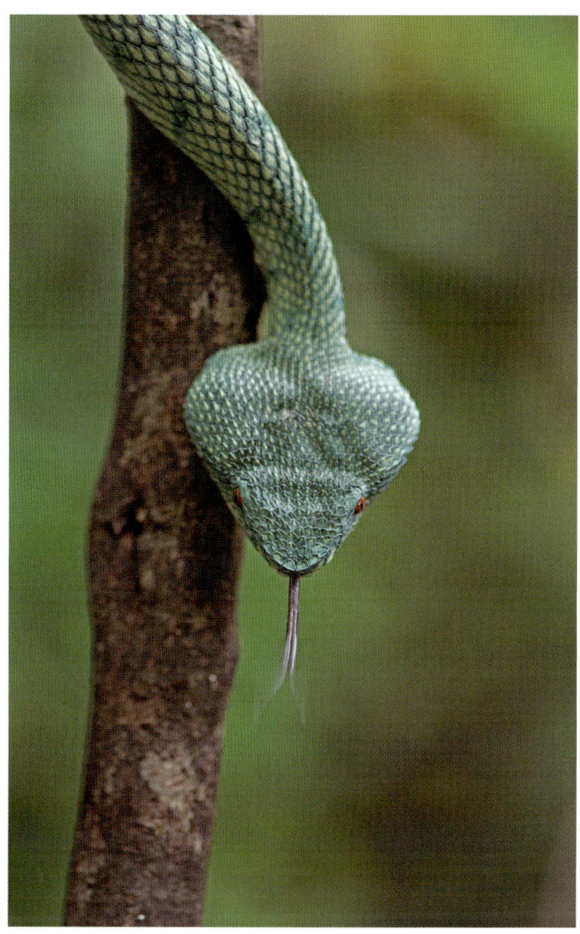

▲ Fig. 6.20
Wagler's Pit Viper (*Tropidolaemus wagleri*). Flicking its tongue. A simple daylight exposure.
   Nikon D800 with 105mm lens with ×1.4 converter. 1/125th second @ f/5.6. 800 ISO.

WELFARE NOTE

When working with any live animal either in the wild, or in a controlled studio environment, it is essential that the welfare of the subject is more important than the image. It is really important that the subject is handled correctly, kept in a room with the correct temperature, and not subjected to prolonged sessions of photography possibly putting stress on it. Handling frogs for example may require keeping your hands moist, possibly wearing disposable gloves to prevent cross infection. Make sure the animal is kept well fed, and not starved before the photography. Chameleons will readily catch live prey (crickets), but perhaps only two or three times before they tire. If the aim is to photograph a frog leaping, make sure there is plenty of space for it to jump into, and not leap off the table onto the floor.

PHOTOGRAPHING LIQUID

Back in 1936 Harold Edgerton photographed drops of milk striking a surface and showed for the first time the beautiful shapes made at the point of impact, including the classic coronet shape. Given the technical difficulties, particularly when working with single sheets of film, his feat was quite remarkable.

Photographing water drops and other liquids with short duration flash can yield some astounding images, both beautiful and also yielding valuable information about fluid dynamics. Several off-the-shelf devices are available, such as the SplashArt 2 system, some of which are highly sophisticated, capable of photographing two drops colliding in mid-air. Other triggering devices using light beam triggering can also be used, with the water drop triggering the flash or camera by falling through a light beam. You will need to use a flash duration of 1/5000th second or shorter to freeze the motion of the liquid.

There are two choices when carrying out this sort of photography – the trigger unit can trigger the camera or trigger the flash. Given the inherent delay in the opening of a mechanical shutter, it may be best for the water drop to trigger the flash. You will need to open the shutter just before the splash, in a darkened room. A shutter speed of one or two seconds in a fairly dark room, at an aperture of f/16 or so should mean that only the flash will expose the image, with little or no ambient light.

Even with highly sophisticated electronic triggering devices, photographing liquid splashes is highly unpredictable. No two drops are the same, and results will vary according to height of drop from the surface, height of drop from the beam, and how much liquid is present on the surface onto which the drop falls. The size of the drop determined by the width of the pipette is also important. It is likely that you will need to expose dozens or hundreds of images in order to achieve the perfect result.

Most triggering devices have a delay setting, allowing images to be triggered at various stages in the cycle of the splash.

It can be tricky lining up the water drop with the beam, and then focusing the camera on to the spot where the drop lands. Meticulous technique and note-taking will be essential for high quality, consistent results.

The Liquid

Good subjects for splash photography are water and milk, both of which can be coloured with food colouring.

However, for achieving those images that show silky smooth plastic like surfaces on the splash it may be a good idea to thicken the liquid, to make it 'gloopier'. As already noted, the whole area is highly unpredictable, and many photographers have developed their own recipes for thickening their liquids. A good substance to thicken water is Xanthan gum, used in cooking as a thickening agent.

Mix a very small quantity of the Xanthan powder (half a teaspoon at most) in a pint of warm water. The powder does not dissolve easily so add it slowly while stirring the water constantly. When dissolved, leave it for a few hours, after that you can add colouring if desired. Food colouring works well, and again, do not be tempted to use too much.

Take care to wash out the solenoid apparatus thoroughly after the photographic session to prevent it getting clogged up.

Safety

Take great care when handling electronic devices such as Flashguns when photographing water and other liquids. Make sure the drops do not splash onto the electrical devices and dry your hands thoroughly before handling flashguns. It may be worth putting transparent plastic bags over the flashguns to protect them.

SplashArt 2 Triggering Device

This is one example of several automated dropping devices currently available, enabling you to shoot single drops, or the collision of two drops in mid air. It uses a sophisticated solenoid and timing circuit to control the size of the drops, delay between the drops, and delay for the camera shutter. The device triggers the camera shutter, so there is no need for a darkened room or high-speed shutter, or to compensate for the delay in the shutter opening. The device can be operated in single drop or double drop mode, when two drops can be captured colliding in mid-air, producing spectacular coronet shaped designs. Adjustments can be made to the size of the drops, and the delay between the two drops being triggered.

Having set up the equipment you will need to line up the camera on the spot where the drop will fall. Try placing a drawing pin into a blob of modelling clay or Blu® Tack, with the pointed end downwards onto a ruler. Place the ruler on top of the container in to which the drop will fall. Move the container around under the dropper until the water drops strike the top of the drawing pin. An aperture of f/16 will help ensure there is sufficient depth of field to cover the depth of the splash.

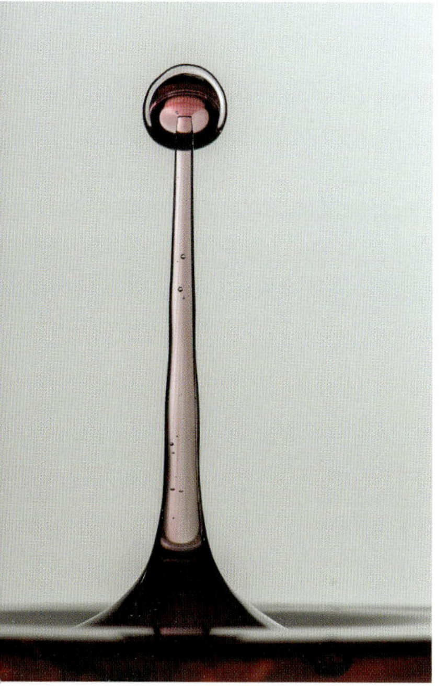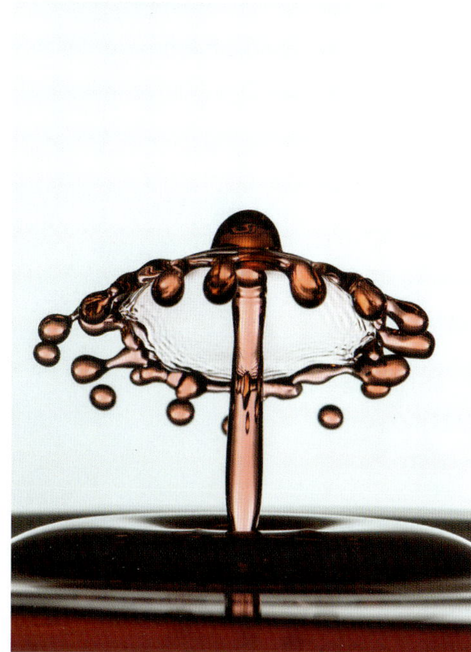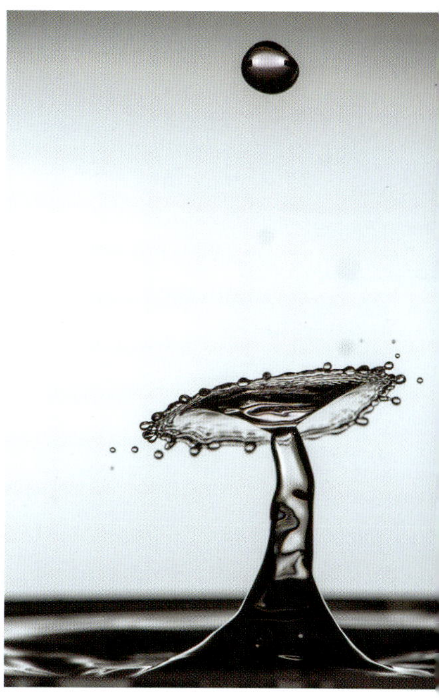

▲ **Fig. 6.21, 6.22, 6.23**
Water drop photography. All shots triggered with SplashArt 2 triggering device, in both single drop mode and two drop mode.
A small quantity of xanthan gum was added to the water, together with food colouring in some instances.
Nikon D810 with 105mm micro NIKKOR lens. Two Nikon SB-900 flashguns at 1/64th power (1/35,000th second).

Basic Lighting

For simple water drops against a white background, a technique for producing silhouettes can be used. Place two flashguns (preferably the same power; using only one will lead to an unevenly lit background) at an equal distance from a clean, bright-white background. Set each to 1/64th or 1/128th power. With the Nikon range of SB Speedlights, they can be linked together by IR, so one becomes the master and the other the remote unit, triggered by the first one, with virtually no delay. The master flash can be fired from the camera by a remote triggering device such as a PocketWizard, or Phottix® trigger. These devices consist of a transmitter and receiver. The transmitter fits on to the hot shoe of the camera, while the receiver fits on to the master flash unit.

Having achieved good black and white images, try filtering the flashguns with coloured gel filters, or try different coloured backgrounds.

MILK DROPLET

The main aim here was to try and replicate Harold Edgerton's famous image of a milk drop at the point of impact, when it formed a coronet shape, taken in 1936. My attempt is shown in Fig. 1.10 in Chapter 1.

A sheet of red Perspex® was placed on a table top, inside a larger metal tray to catch any spilled liquid. The SplashArt device was positioned above it, and lined up using the upturned drawing pin, as outlined above. Two diffused Nikon SB900 flashguns were used at 1/128th power, giving an effective exposure time of 1/38,500th second. These were positioned at around 15cm on either side of the splash area.

The device was filled with milk, and set to single drop mode, with the drop size control set to maximum, and minimal delay on the camera setting. Several dozen images were shot with minor variations to these settings, with around ten showing good coronets.

The depth of liquid into which the drops fell was found to affect the shape of the splash and possible coronet. It was found that no coronet was formed when the milk splashed onto the bare Perspex®, but good shapes were achieved when it splashed onto the milk left by the previous two splashes.

The same shot was attempted with tonic water, using UV modified flashguns to achieve a UV fluorescence version. It was only partially successful, due to the fact, probably, that the fluorescence persisted after the flash had finished, causing a ghost image, similar to the hummingbird shots.

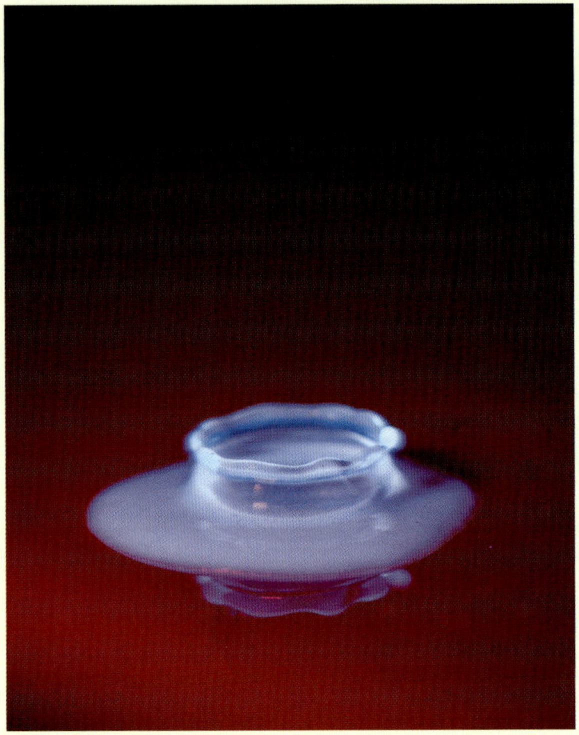

▲ **Fig. 6.24**

A high-speed UV fluorescence shot of tonic water (containing quinine) photographed with the flash filtered with a UV transmitting filter, shot in complete darkness. All of the images shot during the session were slightly soft. This is probably due to the UV fluorescence persisting after the flash had finished, giving a secondary ghost image.

Nikon D810 with 105mm micro NIKKOR lens. Two Mecablitz 45 CT 4 flashguns filtered with Kodak 18A Wood's Glass filter. Flash duration approximately 1/25,000th second.

Drip Tips

Many leaves found in wet tropical rainforests (and other woodlands) have waxy surfaces, and have a pointed tip at the end, with a central rib channelling rain water towards it. This is thought to prevent water sitting on the leaf surface, possibly promoting the growth of other plants and moulds. One way to illustrate this feature is by using high speed photography to freeze the droplets of water as they fall from the leaf.

In the image shown here, a single leaf was held in a clamp in front of a background made from an ink jet print of out of focus vegetation. It was lit from the sides with two Nikon Speedlights set to 1/64th power, giving an approximate duration of 1/35,000th second. Water was slowly sprayed over the leaf until it started to fall from the end. The camera was set to shoot at five frames per second and fired as the water started to fall. No trigger was used.

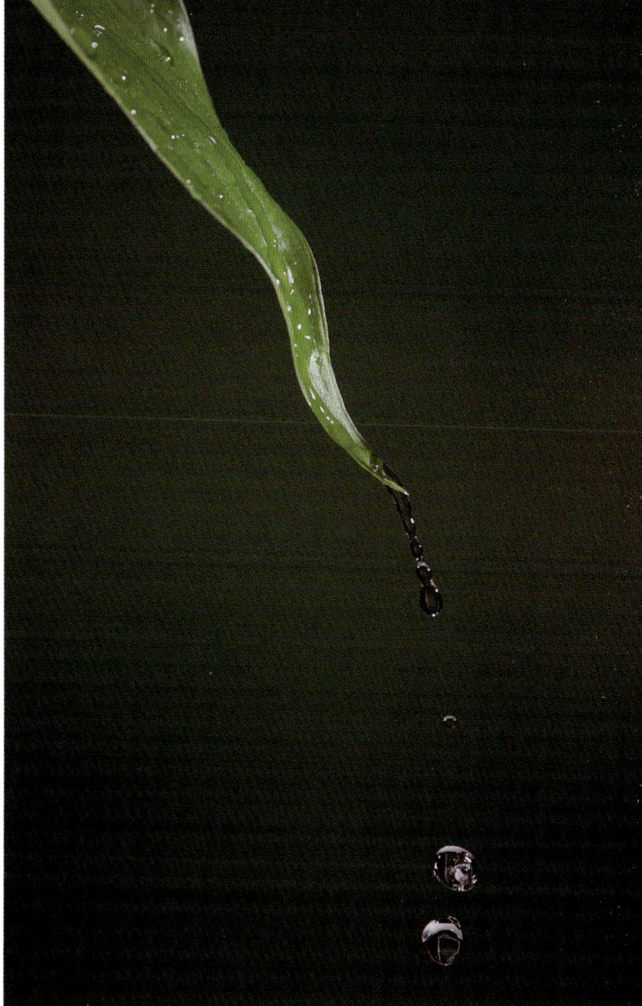

▲ **Fig. 6.25**
Drip tips – many leaves, particularly in wet rainforests have waxy surfaces and pointed leaves with channels allowing water to flow quickly from the leaf surface, allowing it to breathe, and helping prevent other plants and moulds growing on their surface. This image was shot without a trigger.
Nikon D800 with 105mm micro NIKKOR, Two Nikon SB-900 flashguns at 1/64th power. 1/160th second @ f/11.

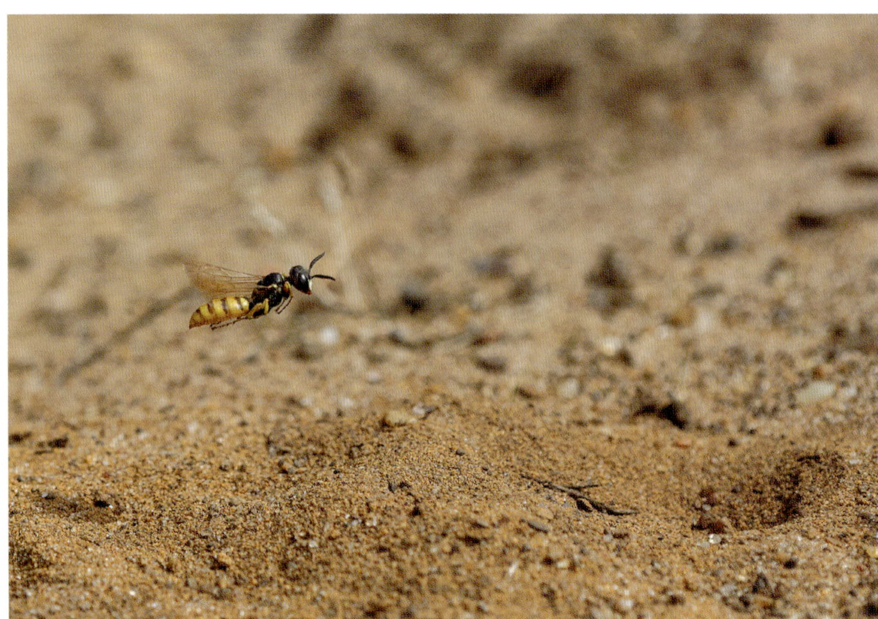

◀ **Fig. 6.26**
Beewolf (*Philanthus triangulum*) are large insects living in sandy heathland, which prey on honeybees and transport them to their burrow by slinging them upside down under their body during flight. In this image, a Beewolf is seen hovering at the entrance to its burrow. Shot with natural daylight. The wings are almost pin sharp at 1/2500th second exposure.
Nikon D800 with 105mm micro-NIKKOR lens, 1/2500th second @ f/6.3, 800 ISO.

INSECTS IN FLIGHT

Free Flight

There are two main approaches to the photography of insects in flight. The first is to photograph them out in the wild, using a fast shutter speed and probably autofocus lenses. Some insects, such as hoverflies, bees and hummingbird hawkmoths will hover in front of flowers and can be reasonably easily photographed in free flight. Others, such as dragonflies often have predictable flight paths, and may too, with practice, be photographed flying. It will probably be necessary to increase the ISO, perhaps to 800 ISO or more, to enable the use of a fast shutter speed. You will probably need to use a medium length telephoto lens such as a 200 or 300mm, with autofocus set.

Several species of dragonfly and damselfly will hover above the water whist laying eggs, either the female dipping her ovipositor into the water, or dropping her eggs into the water.

Light-Beam Trigger System

Insect flight is invariably unpredictable, both in terms of direction and speed. The best way of increasing your chance of achieving sharp images is to use a light-beam trigger system, with a flight tunnel through which the insect flies. This will need to be done indoors where the flashes, background etc can be set up, and will require capturing insects from the wild (or breeding them specifically for the purpose) and encouraging them to fly through the light beam. If the end of the tunnel is dark, most day flying insects will fly towards the light at the other end. When capturing insects, take extreme care not to mishandle them, use a proper butterfly net, and release them back into the wild as soon as possible.

An appropriate background can be placed at the end of the tunnel and would need to be lit separately from the subject.

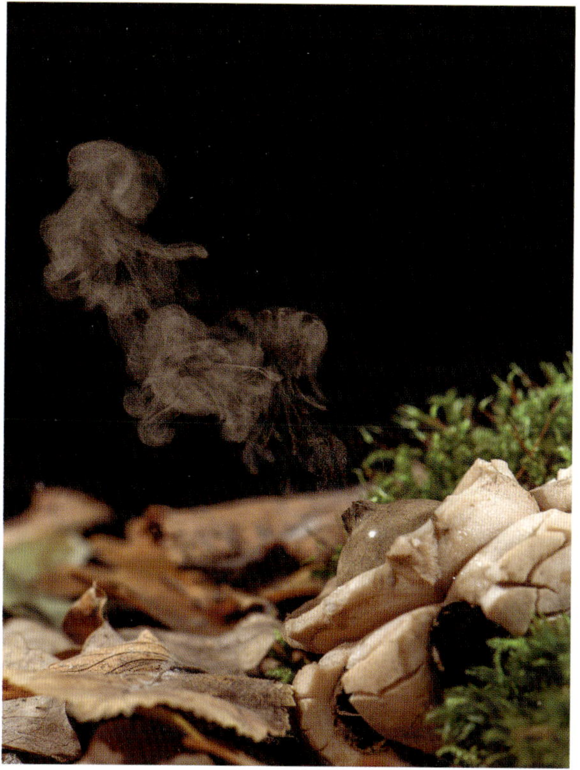

▲ **Fig. 6.27**
The Earthstar (*Geastrum triplex*) is a type of puffball fungus, which discharges spores after being struck by a drop of falling water.
Nikon D800, 105mm micro-NIKKOR lens. 1/160th @ f/16. 200 ISO. Three Nikon SB-R200 flashguns (approximate flash duration 1/600th second).

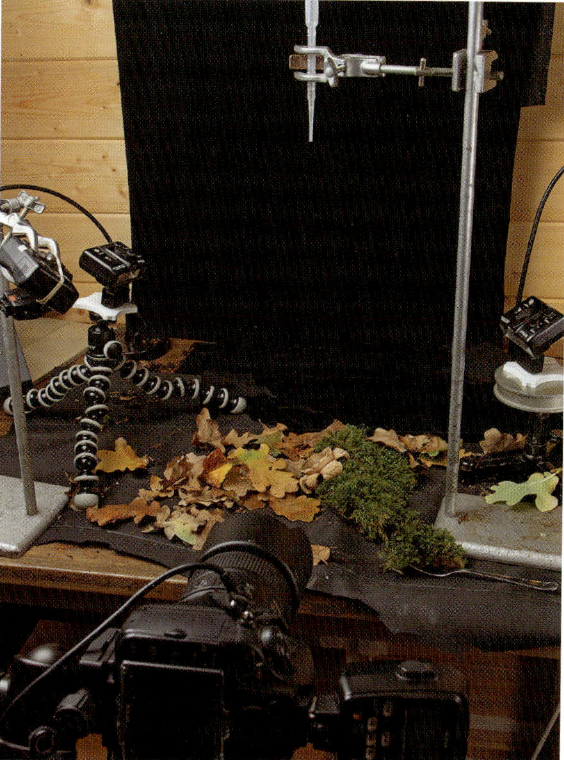

▲ **Fig. 6.28**
Set up for Earthstar spores' image: Note three flashguns, one to the top left of the camera, the other two slightly behind to backlight the spore cloud. A pipette for dropping water is positioned so that the water drop falls slightly behind the aperture of the earthstar.

Plants and Fungi

Although not as active as birds and other animals, many plants also perform some actions that require high speed photographic techniques to capture them. Several fungi, such as puffballs, discharge their spores in an explosive way when stimulated to do so, and the seed pods of some flowering plants such as Himalayan Balsam (the scientific name Impatiens literally translates as impatient!) and Squirting Cucumber literally explode when subjected to heat or touch, scattering their seeds a fair distance. Pollen is blown from catkins such as Hazel, or from tree flowers such as Ash.

To ensure that the pollen or spore cloud can be seen well in the image, a dark background will be most appropriate. Black will provide most contrast, with black velvet or a painted black board being useful. A more interesting and realistic background can be obtained by shooting an out of focus image of an area of a dark woodland or other appropriate scene, for example, and printing it out on an ink jet printer. Make sure to make the print on matt paper that will not give shiny reflections if light hits it.

A major issue is that of logistics – how to get your delicate subject, perhaps catkins with their pollen, from their habitat into your studio. The best way is to very carefully cut the twig on which the catkins are attached, then lay it carefully into the bottom

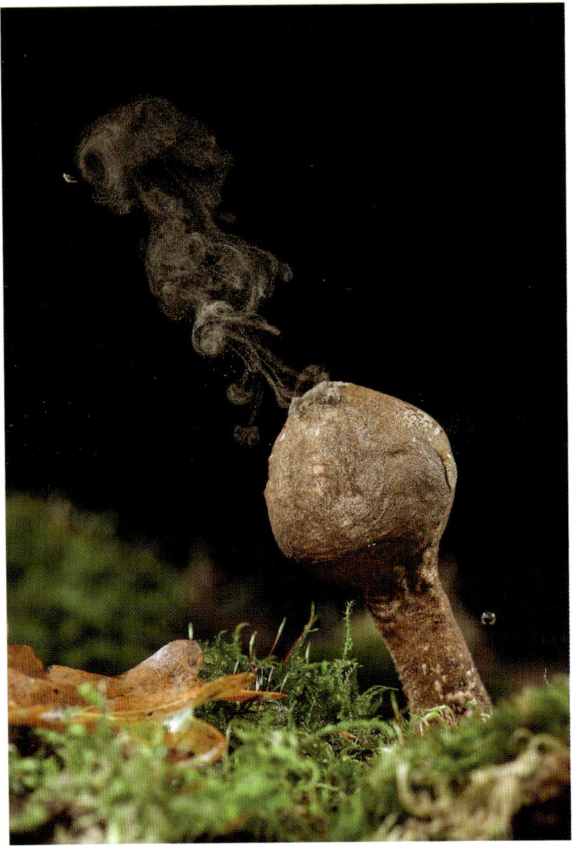

▲ **Fig. 6.29**
Common Puffball (*Lycoperdon perlatum*) discharging spores following
a water strike. Note water drop on right hand side bouncing from
specimen. Using the set-up from Fig. 6.28.

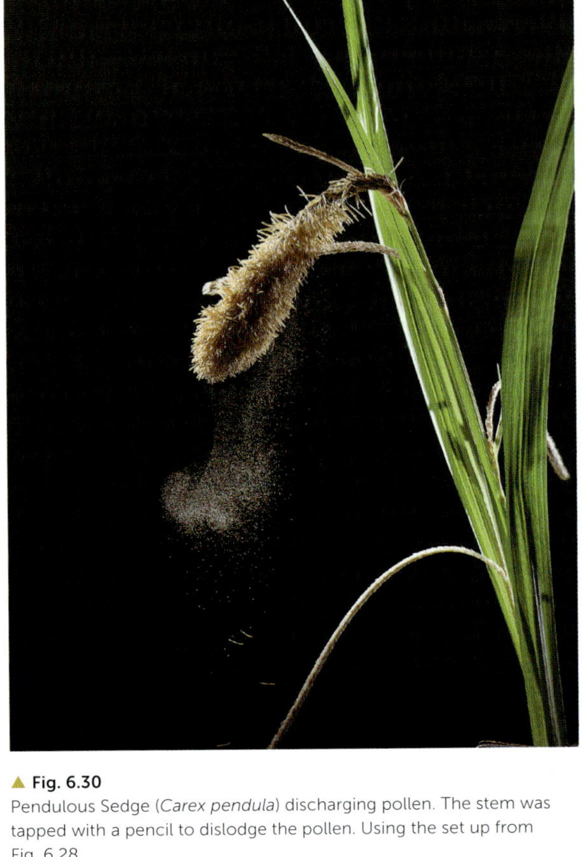

▲ **Fig. 6.30**
Pendulous Sedge (*Carex pendula*) discharging pollen. The stem was
tapped with a pencil to dislodge the pollen. Using the set up from
Fig. 6.28.

of a box for transport home (making sure to get the
permission of the landowner). Explosive fungi such
as puffballs and earthstars can usually be lifted out
of the ground by placing your fingers underneath
and carefully pulling upwards. Do not take too many
specimens, though fungi will almost certainly have
shed some spores by the time you find them.
You will probably want to backlight the pollen or
spore cloud, and possible add a frontal light or
reflector to give detail to the specimen.

With catkins, if you have a good specimen, a
sharp tap with a pencil on the twig should give a
cloud of pollen. With puffballs you will need to drop
water onto the surface of the specimen, near to the
aperture from where the spores will be ejected. This
is best achieved by putting a water filled pipette
in a stand above the specimen. With practice it is
possible to fire the shutter when the spores are being
ejected. You will not need to use the shortest flash
duration – 1/5000th second should be fast enough
to freeze a pollen or spore cloud.

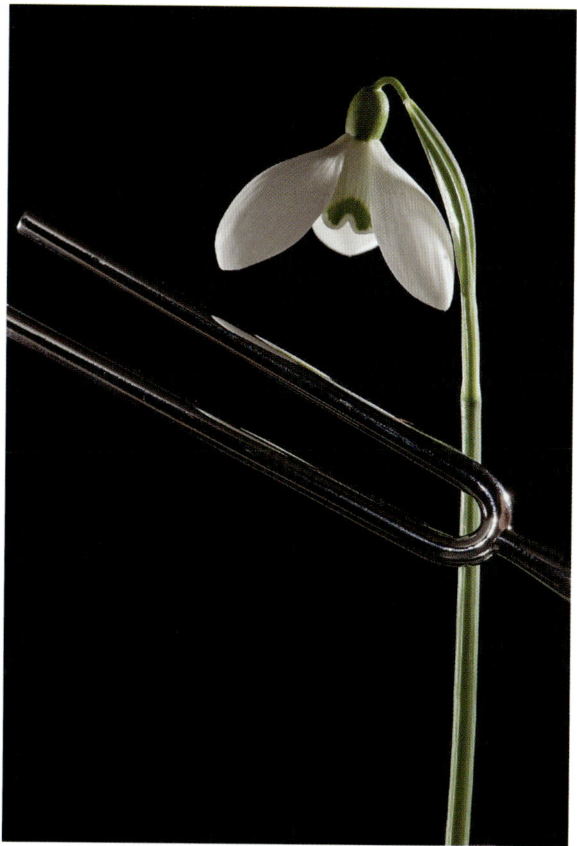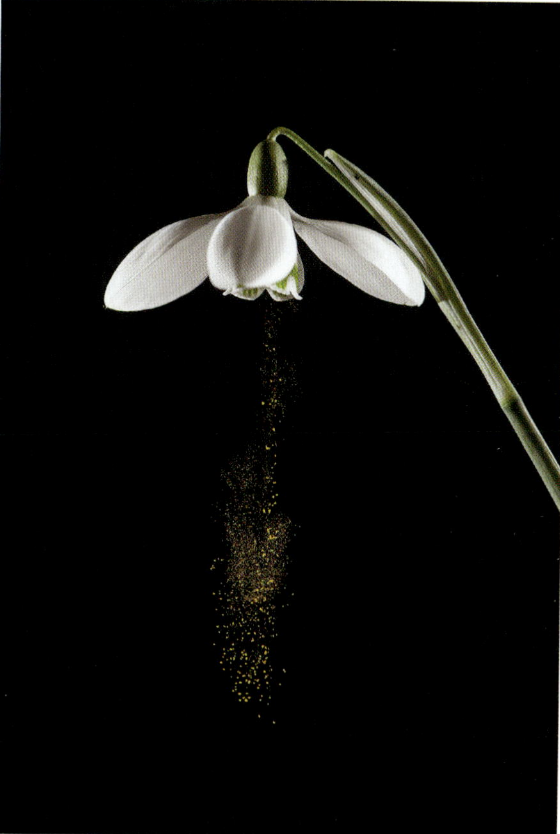

▲ Fig. 6.31, 6.32

A number of flowers including Tomatoes and Snowdrops are pollinated by insects using a process called sonication, or buzz pollination. In order to ensure that only the right insect pollinates the flower pollen is only released when wingbeats of the right frequency stimulate the flower. In this case, the Snowdrop (*Galanthus nivalis*) is pollinated early in the year by bumblebees. To simulate this in the studio a tuning fork was tapped, and placed in contact with the stem, encouraging the discharge of pollen.

Nikon D800, 105mm micro-NIKKOR lens. 1/160th @ f/16. 200 ISO. Three Nikon SB-900 flashguns set to 1/64th power (approximate flash duration 1/35,000th second).

Buzz Pollination

Buzz pollination (or sonication) is where a flower is triggered to release its pollen only when it is visited by an insect with a specific wing beat frequency. Examples include Snowdrops, Tomatoes and Borage – some commercial tomato growers use electric vibration devices to achieve pollination. Here, a Snowdrop is triggered by the use of a tuning fork, simulating the wing beat of a bumblebee.

LIGHTNING

Photographing lightning is always going to be a hit and miss affair, particularly in the UK where it is not common, and highly unpredictable in its appearance. Some photographic trigger systems, such as the Pluto Trigger™ or MIOPS Smart Trigger™, can be used to detect lightning and trigger the camera instantaneously when it occurs.

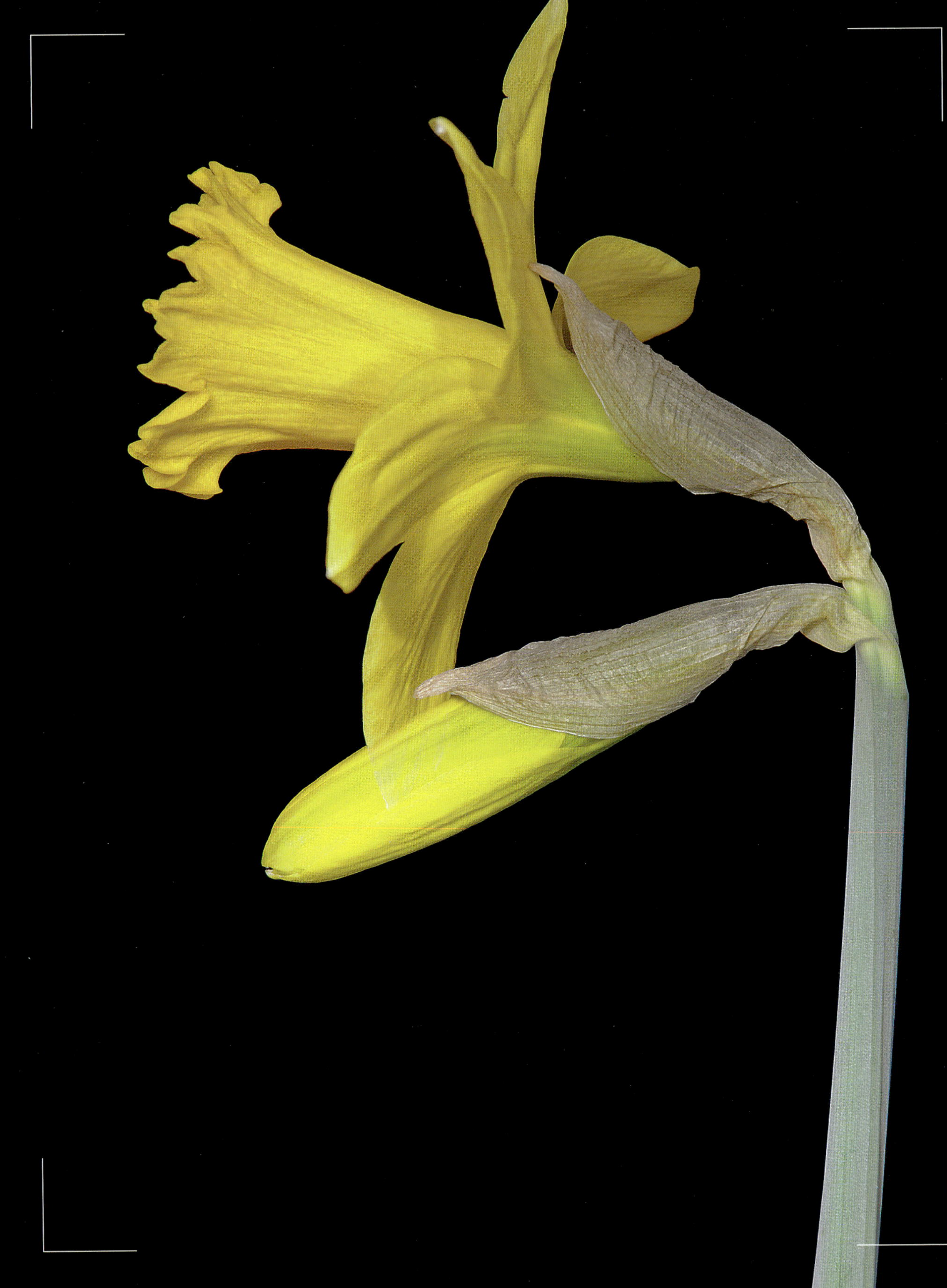

Time Lapse and Other Time Related Imaging

Viewers of natural history documentaries will be familiar with stunning time lapse sequences of plants growing, flowers opening, animal carcases being devoured by maggots, ice forming, clouds moving across the sky or traffic moving through a busy city. Such sequences often develop a narrative all of their own. These video sequences are usually shown at 25 frames per second to give the illusion of continuous movement. Producing such sequences can be a highly complicated process and are outside the scope of this book (they are well covered in the book on time lapse photography in the bibliography at the end of this book). To shoot a time lapse sequence of a plant growing, for example, you might need continuous growing lights (that switch on and off at specific times to simulate natural daylight rhythms), photographic lighting, and perhaps a motorized pan and tilt head or rail (slider) that lets the camera track the plant as it grows upwards. This would be controlled by a programmable stepper motor, capable of extremely fine movement moving the camera by perhaps a fraction of a millimetre for each frame. These items all need to be controlled over, possibly, a long period of time. You may also need an automated watering system, to ensure that the tone of the soil stays the same throughout the sequence for example. Knowledge of the subject is a key factor to success with time-lapse and ideally you will be able to do a dummy run before the main shoot. One famous sequence followed the branch of an apple tree from winter through to autumn, showing flowering and development of fruit during that time. A temporary building was built around the tree to house all of the necessary equipment!

Other uses of time-lapse imaging have included looking at the long-term movement of glaciers over a period of several years, proving conclusively that many are retreating due to global warming.

Perhaps surprisingly, given the technology required, time-lapse imaging has a long history, with Percy Smith in particular, who began filming plant life cycles in 1907. His first studio was his bathroom in his house in north London, with the windows darkened with brown paper. Over the next thirty years or so he filmed plant roots growing, tendrils stretching out looking for an anchor and a host of other subjects, often using microscopes, and increasingly complex devices for tracking his subjects. (A fascinating DVD of some of his early films, called *Secrets of Nature*, is available from the British Film Institute.)

◀ **Fig. 7.1**
Daffodil bud opening. A simple time-lapse pair, showing how the angle of the bud changes as the flower opens.

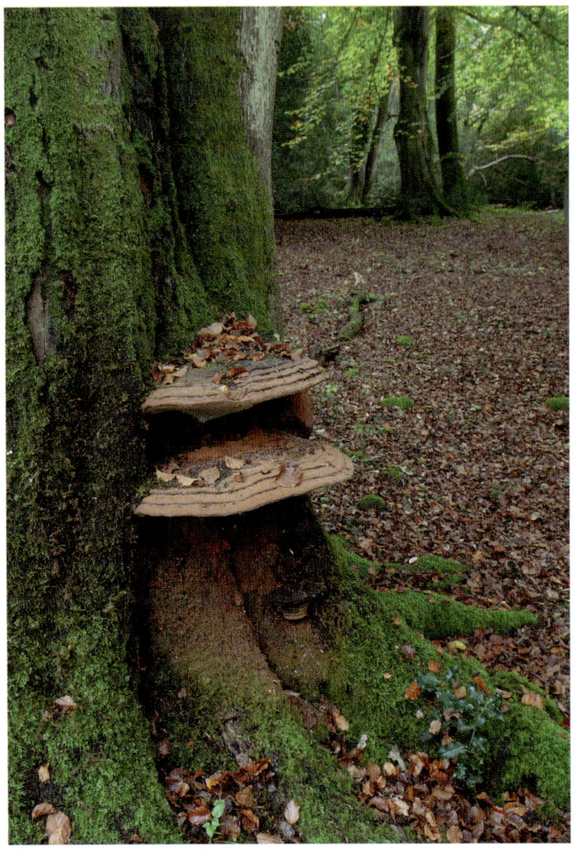

▲ **Fig. 7.2**
The Southern Bracket fungus (*Ganoderma australe*) on a beech tree shot in 2011, in Sussex, UK.

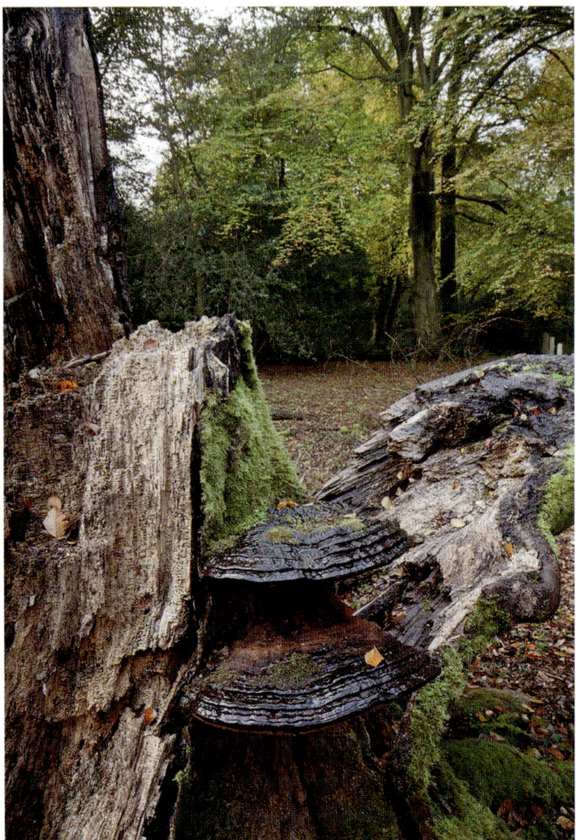

▲ **Fig. 7.3**
The same tree the following year, blown over in a storm. The main break is at the line of the fungus. It was not possible to use exactly the same viewpoint for the second shot.
   Both shots Nikon D300 with 17–55mm lens.

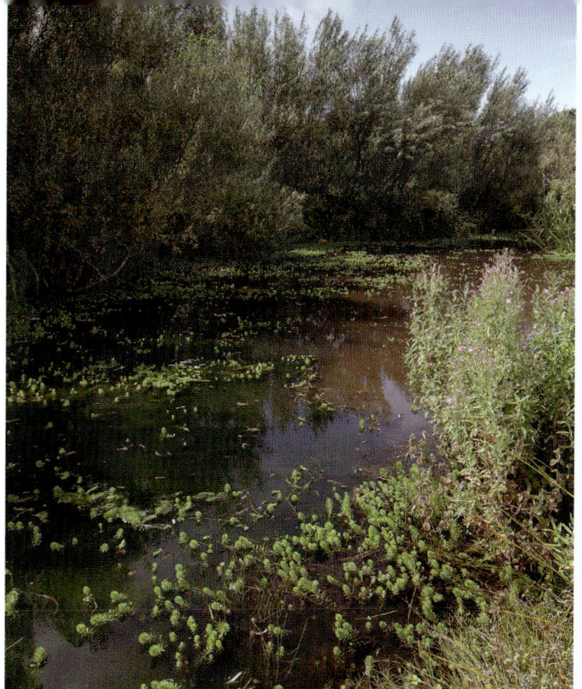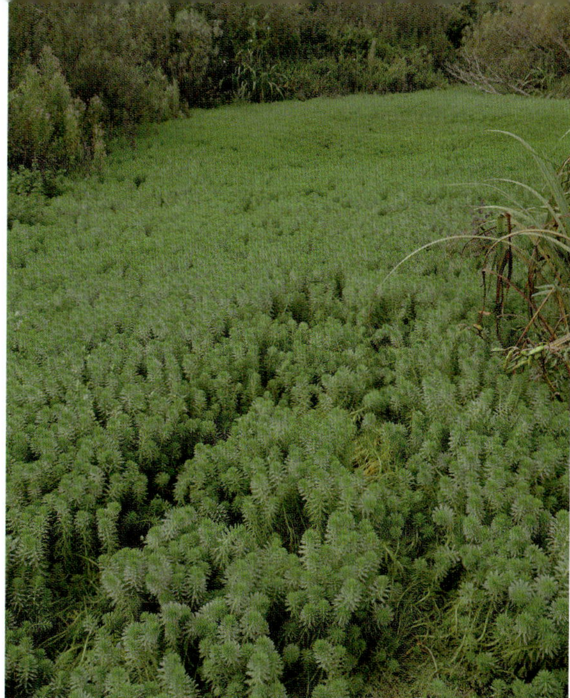

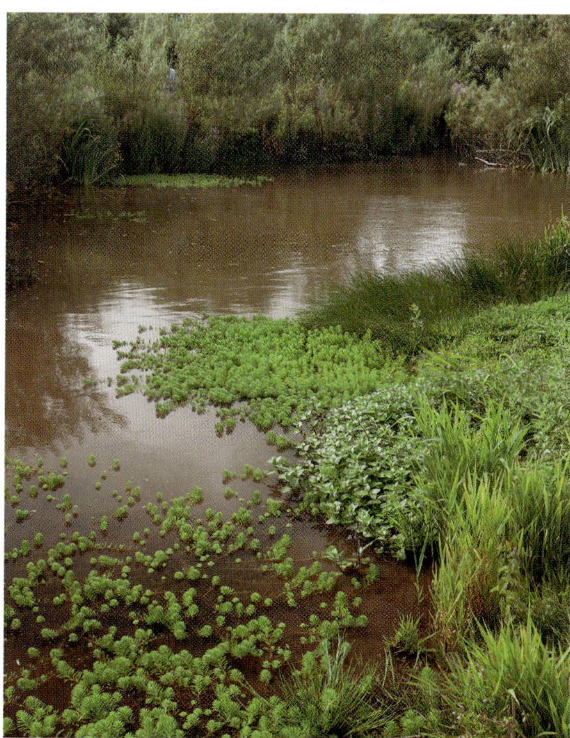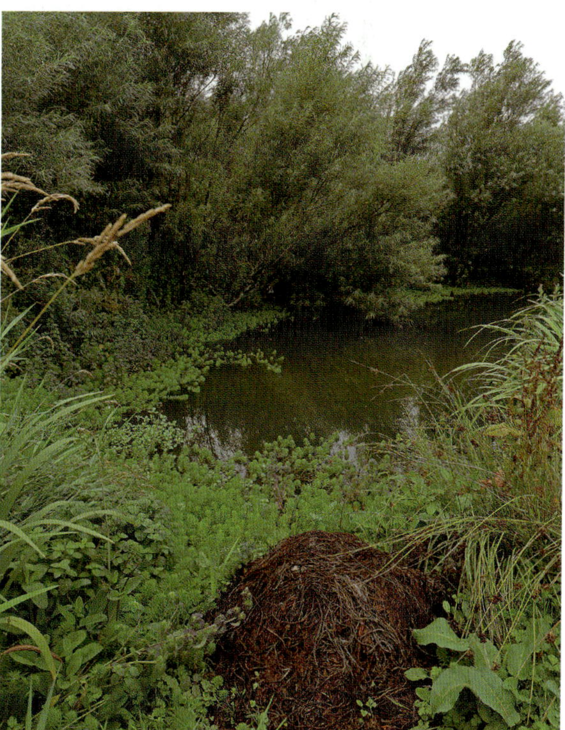

▲ Fig. 7.4, 7.5, 7.6, 7.7

A sequence of four images selected from a number, shot over a period of 15 years, showing the status of an invasive species in a village pond. The images were each shot in the last week of July. The plant, Parrot Feather (*Myriophyllum aquaticum*) has been present in this village pond in East Prawle, South Devon, UK, for well over twenty years. It would have been impossible to shoot the images from a fixed vantage point each year due to the changing management of the pond, but the sequence still shows how invasive the species can be. The plant cannot be removed chemically and instead must be removed manually each year by conservation volunteers. The final image was shot to show part of the mass of plants removed from the pond the previous winter.

Images shot in 2008, 2011, 2016, 2018.

TIME-LAPSE FILMING THEORY

Although outside the scope of this book, the basic theory of shooting time lapse video sequences is included here for reference and may be useful when shooting a series of still images.

The first step in the process is to calculate how many frames are required for your sequence. You will need to know or estimate the length of the event, and for how long the final sequence will be projected. Ideally, you will need to do a rehearsal with your subject, to see how long it takes for a flower bud to open, or for a bean to start sprouting for example, though such things are notoriously unpredictable.

There is a simple calculation to work out the framing rate.

Example:

- The event is predicted to last for sixty minutes.
- The final length of sequence to be shown will be ten seconds (quite a long time in video terms)
- The sequence will be shown at 25 frames per second (fps)

  10 seconds at 25fps =

  $10 \times 25 = 250$ frames required

  60-minute event = 3600 seconds

  3600 seconds divided by 250 =

  14.4 frames per second

Thus, you need to shoot one frame every 14.4 seconds to achieve the ten-second running time. In reality you would probably shoot one frame every fourteen or fifteen seconds.

Many cameras today have time-lapse capabilities built into them, or you can buy external timing units (such as the Nikon MC36a) for controlling the camera. The Nikon D800 series of cameras, for example, has a built in intervalometer where you can programme the interval between frames,

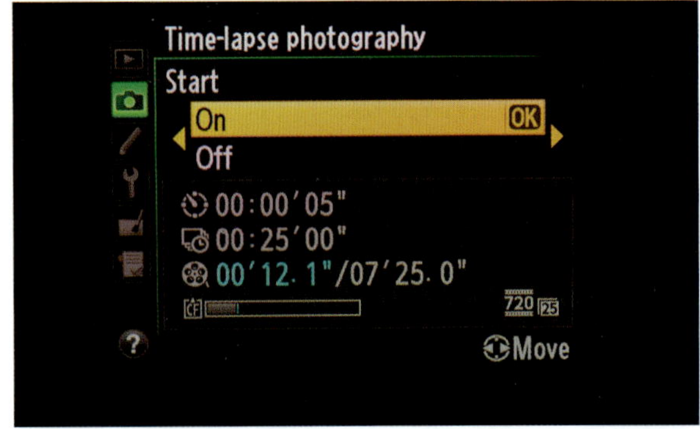

▲ **Fig. 7.8**
Screenshot from Nikon D810 camera showing time-lapse options.

and the shooting length. The final video sequence is compiled in camera, and output as a .MOV file format, compatible with other video sequences and video editing software. If your camera does not compile the sequence itself, and saves the sequence as individual frames, you can output the individual frames into Adobe® Lightroom, for example, where any processing required can be carried out (make sure they all receive the same treatment to ensure consistency within the video). The individual frames can then be output to a program such as QuickTime™ where the video sequence can be compiled.

Make sure, if you are shooting time-lapse sequences that you start with a fully charged set of batteries, and an empty high-capacity memory card. You do not want to risk moving the camera during the shooting sequence by having to change them. Even for a high-definition 4K movie sequence, you will probably only need to use JPEG file format at its minimum setting, when shooting 1920×1080 sized images, so you should be able to get a good number of images on the memory card.

Make sure to cover the viewfinder when shooting, as light can enter the camera through the viewfinder when the shutter is fired and may cause problems with exposure. Many cameras are supplied with a plastic cover for the viewfinder for this purpose, while others have a shutter to cover the viewfinder.

It almost goes without saying that the camera must be mounted on a solid tripod, so that there is no risk of movement while shooting the sequence.

Some specialist time-lapse photographers use old manual focus lenses, where the aperture can be locked for the whole sequence, rather than being stopped down to the taking aperture for each frame, possibly leading to uneven exposures.

Turn off the autofocus setting, and also set the exposure mode to manual. This will ensure that if the scene goes dark (a cloud passing over the sun for example), then the image will darken with it. If the mode is set to shutter priority for example, then the exposure will remain constant, and may look odd. The same goes for white balance – set this to manual, daylight or 5200K if shooting in daylight.

TIME-LAPSE STILLS PHOTOGRAPHY

If you do not wish to shoot video sequences, but instead want to produce a series of still images, it is still possible to make meaningful and interesting time lapse sequences. This can be done either as a series of still images viewed individually, or perhaps several images overlaid on top of each other to give the impression of movement and a sense of narrative.

The simplest form of time-lapse is a simple before and after comparison of a subject. This might be shot over a long length of time, or within seconds of each other if the subject exhibits movement. Try to use the same viewpoint and lens to enable direct comparison.

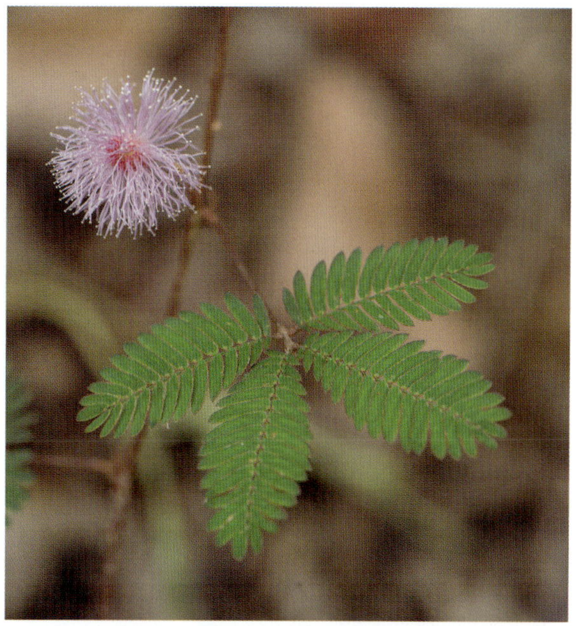

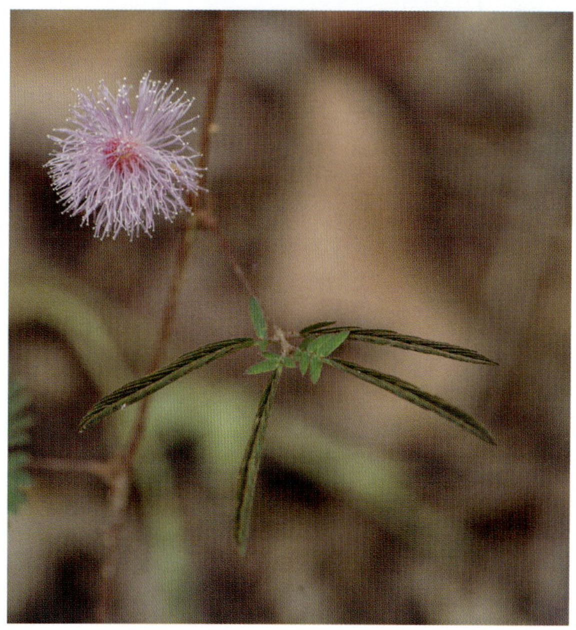

▲ **Fig. 7.9, 7.10**
The Sensitive Plant (*Mimosa pudica*) shot in a rainforest in Borneo, showing before and after touching.
Nikon D800 with 105mm micro-Nkkor lens. 1/60th second @ f/8.

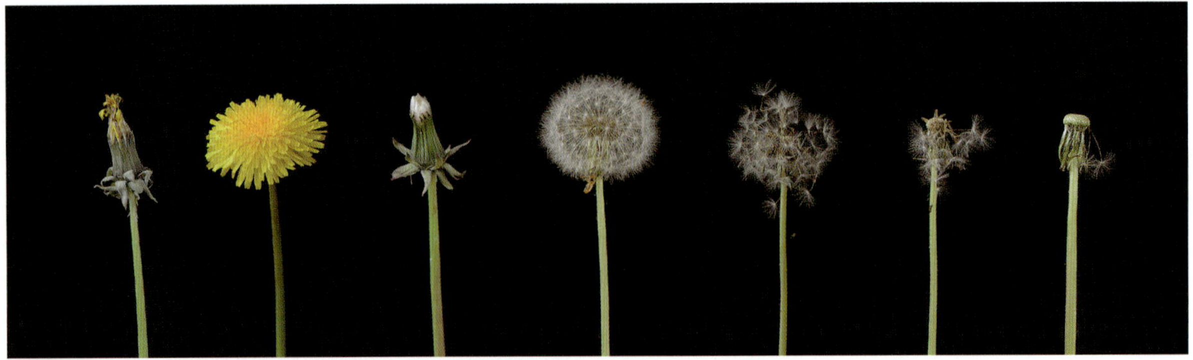

▲ **Fig. 7.11**
This sequence showing the development of a Dandelion (*Taraxacum officinale*) is a composite of images from a number of different specimens, selected specially for the purpose. Each specimen was shot under the same lighting conditions and magnification. A black background was used to enable easy compositing.

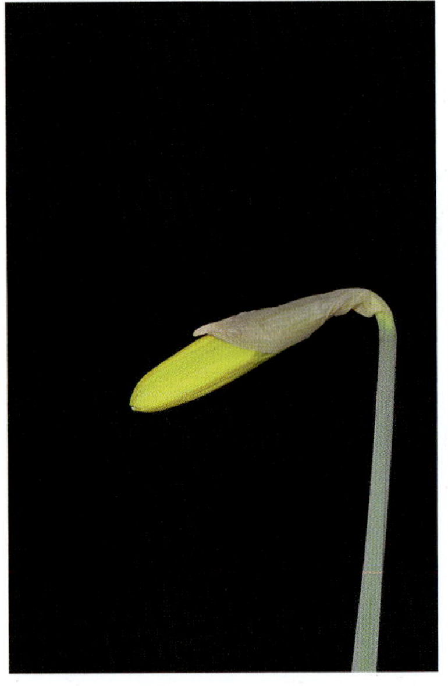
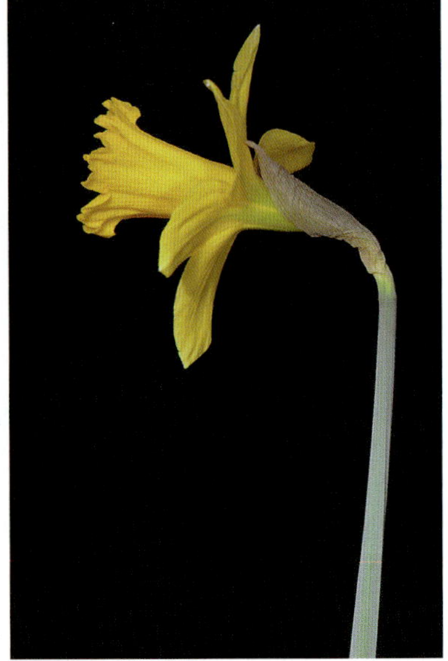
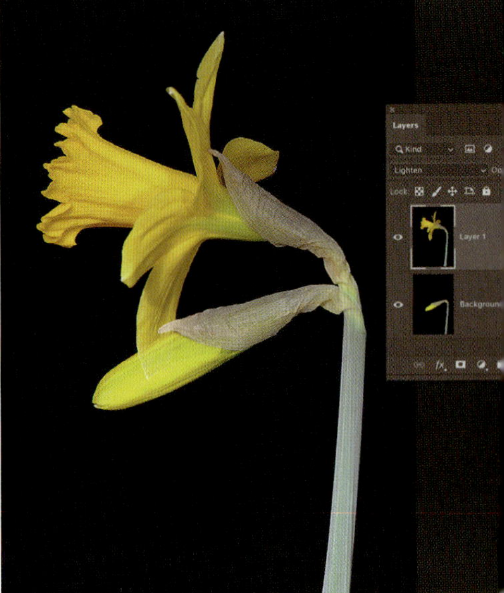

▲ **Fig. 7.12, 7.13, 7.14**
A Daffodil bud opening, the images taken approximately four hours apart. Both images were opened in Photoshop® and blended together using the layers facility shown to produce Fig. 7.1.

FIXED POINT PHOTOGRAPHY OVER TIME

Ecologists and managers of nature reserves make use of fixed point photography to show the growth of vegetation in a particular habitat, for example, and construction sites often have images taken at regular intervals to help monitor progress. This type of photography ideally involves putting a permanent metal marker into the ground onto which a camera can be fitted, to ensure that the same area is photographed on each frame. If this is not possible it may be useful to carry a print showing the previous image to help line up the camera. The same focal

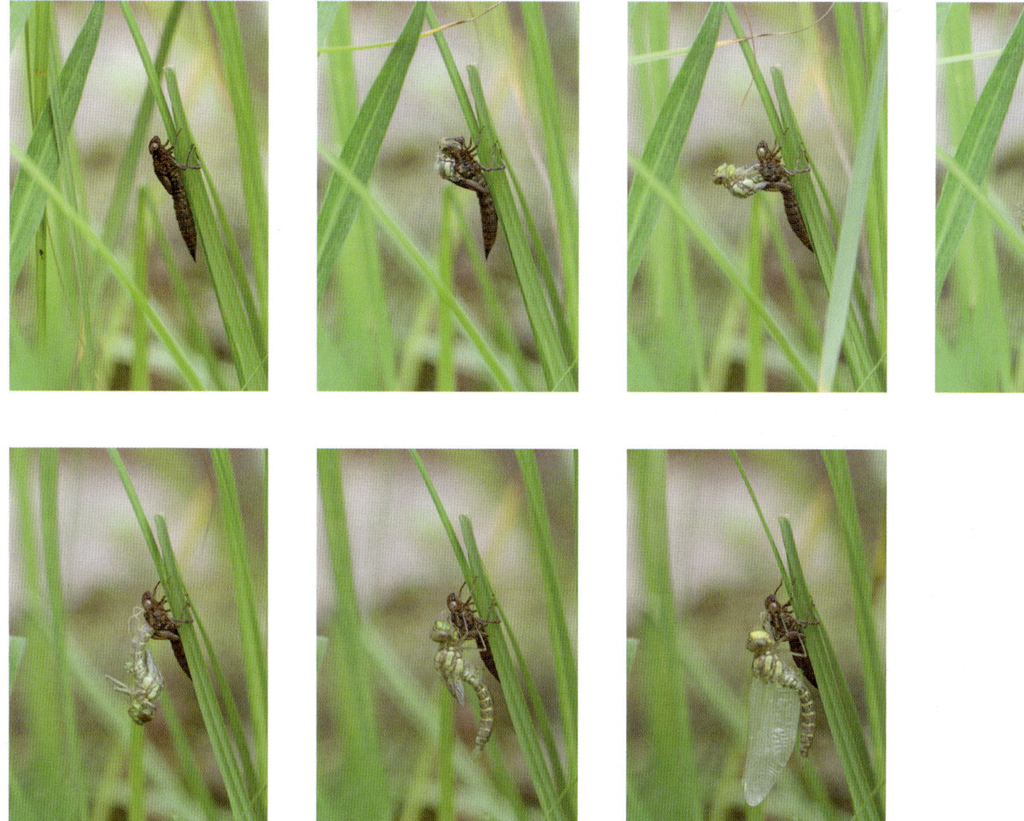

▲ **Fig. 7.15. 7.16, 7.17, 7.18, 7.19, 7.20, 7.21**
Hawker Dragonfly (*Aeshna sp.*) emerging from its larval case. This sequence took around four hours, from the first to last image. The larva was spotted emerging from the pond, and the camera set up on a tripod for the first shot and kept in virtually the same place for each subsequent image, though some of the foliage did move a little. Fortunately, the lighting remained fairly consistent for the whole sequence. The adult dragonfly flew suddenly away before a final portrait could be taken. It is interesting to note the change between images 7.19 and 7.20, which happened extremely quickly.
  Nikon D800 with 200mm micro-NIKKOR lens. 1/60th second @ f/8.

length must be used (a prime lens rather than zoom is preferred to ensure that the focal length of lens is exactly the same in each image). Such sequences may be shot over a period of many years and are an invaluable way for ecologists to monitor management strategies, invasion by alien species or illustrate habitat destruction.

After the simple before and after images, photographing the same subject regularly over a period of time will produce a time lapse sequence. The number of images that are required will depend on whether you want to maximize the information or produce pictorially interesting sequences.

INTERVAL TIMER

As well as having facilities for making time-lapse movie sequences, many modern cameras also have the ability to shoot sequences as a series of still images, using the interval timer setting (this is the Nikon terminology, other cameras might use different terminology). With this facility, you can set a start time, interval between shots, and the number of shots. You have the option to stop the sequence earlier than expected or extend it if the subject does not behave as predicted.

The crucial thing when photographing such sequences is to ensure that the lighting on the subject remains the same throughout to enable the same exposure, and that the magnification remains constant (i.e. subject to camera distance) so that comparison can be made from one image to the next, illustrating growth, for example.

For indoor studio work you will need a room where the subject, camera, lighting and other paraphernalia can remain undisturbed throughout the shoot.

PLANT TROPISMS

A particular feature of botanical subjects are tropisms. A tropism is the way that a plant responds to an environmental stimulus, including light (phototropism), gravity (gravitropism) or touch (thigmotropism – good examples are the Peyote Cactus *Lophophora williamsii*, and Cape Stock Rose: *Sparmannia africana*). Time lapse photography offers a way of visualizing these effects. The way that a plant bends towards a light source for example, or a tendril reaches out looking for a support, can easily be shown with a series of still images.

Producing Composite Images

To place two (or more) images alongside each other in the same frame you will need an imaging program with a layers facility. It is always good to have a simple background such as black or white to enable a seamless composition. To understand the layering concept, think of your image as a background, with a sheet of glass sitting on top of it. The glass may be clear, tinted, have some neutral density, contain text, or contain another image. Altering the layer in some way will not affect the underlying background image.

You will also be making use of the canvas size option available in Photoshop®. By default, an image fully occupies its canvas when opened. But the canvas can be enlarged to provide space around the image, maybe for captioning, or adding another image.

If you want to place two images side by side as one image, open both in Photoshop (for this explanation they should be the same size. If they are not you should alter that first in the Image Size box). Make the left-hand one active by selecting it. Navigate to canvas size (**Image > Canvas Size**). To add extra space to the right-hand side of an image, select the left-hand facing arrow in the anchor box. This will place your image on the left-hand side of the frame. Then, in the width box, change the scale to percent, and type in 200. This doubles the width of the image, with the original on the left-hand side. Now make the second image active by selecting it and go to (**Select > All**). Copy it (**Edit > Copy**), now go back to the first image and paste it (**Edit > Paste**). The second image now becomes a layer floating on top of the image. By using the Move tool, at the top of the toolbar, you can position the second image next to the first one. The two images remain as separate layers. When you are satisfied with the composition you can flatten them using the dropdown menu in the layers dialog box.

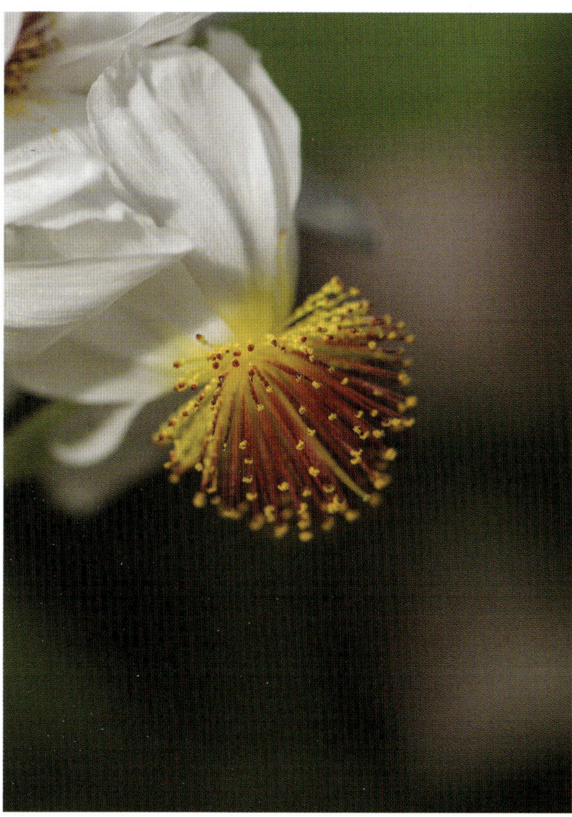

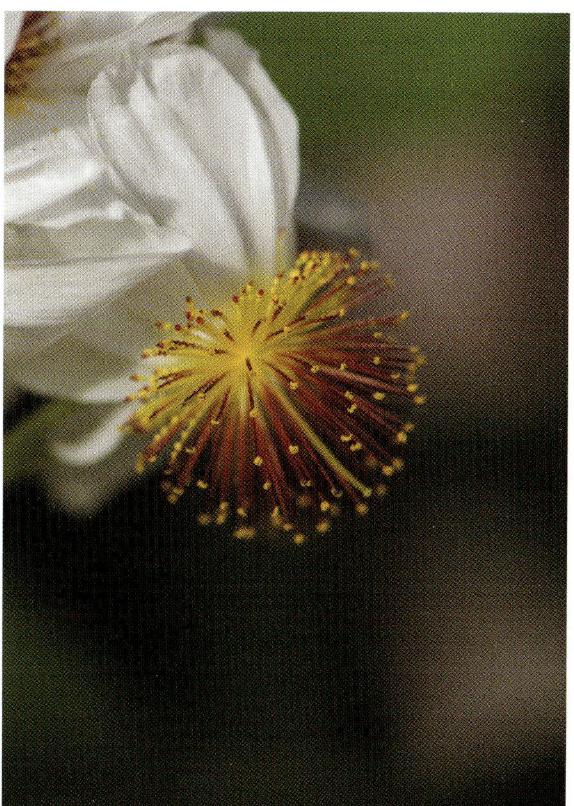

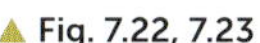 **Fig. 7.22, 7.23**
All plants exhibit gradual movement due to growth, but very few show rapid movement. Examples of this include the Sensitive Plant and Venus Flytrap. The stamen filaments of the Cape Stock Rose, or African Hemp (*Sparmannia africana*) expand rapidly, for a few seconds, when stimulated with a brush, demonstrating thigmotropism. Shot in the glasshouse of a botanic garden on very still day.

Nikon D800 with 105mm micro-NIKKOR lens, 1/200th second @ f/11.

If you want to have a more complex composition with, for example, five images, make the canvas size 500 per cent. You can also add space to the top and bottom of an image for different composition. You may want to reduce the size of your final composite image as doubling the width of an image effectively doubles the file size.

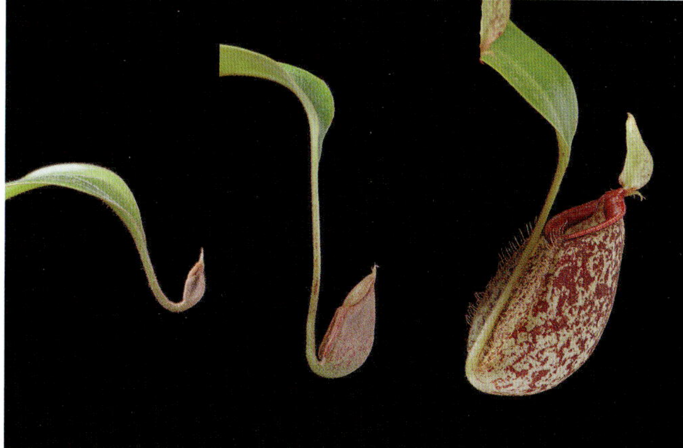

Fig. 7.24
Pitcher Plant (*Nepenthes* × *Hookeriana*). A time-lapse sequence showing development of a pitcher. Images of three separate pitchers shot at same magnification and same lighting, combined into one image in Adobe Photoshop®. Two specimens of the plant were kept in order to provide sufficient pitchers for the photograph.

Nikon D800 with 105mm micro NIKKOR. Two Elinchrom® studio flash heads with soft box diffusers. Each image 1/160th second @ f/16.

Overlaying Images

If the first image and last image of a sequence show significant differences, as shown in Fig. 7.1, it may be worth overlaying one on top of the other to show the difference in one image. The Daffodil image shown here is a good example, where the flower bud is hanging at around 45° downwards, while the final flower is pointing upwards. For the single image to work, there needs to be enough movement for the two original images to be clearly seen. A black or dark background will help to show the differences clearly.

Having shot the sequence with the same exposure and lighting for each image, open the first and last images in a program with a layers facility such as Photoshop®. Select the second image (**Select > All**) and copy it (**Edit > Copy**). Make the first image active and paste the copied image into it (**Edit > Paste**). Open the Layers panel, where you will see both images as thumbnails, the first being the background, the second being Layer 1. Select Lighten mode in the drop-down Blend mode menu, and both images should be shown on the one image. If there is a significant overlap in the two images they will both be seen, perhaps confusingly.

When you are happy with the final image flatten the layers (in the drop-down menu) dialog box. You may need to selectively darken areas common to both images, such as the stem.

ACTION SEQUENCE (OR MULTIPLE EXPOSURE) PHOTOGRAPHY

As we have seen, time-lapse imagery can be used to show growth, development and movement in subjects such as plants, and clouds.

One way to do this is to use Multiple Exposure mode on the camera (this is the Nikon term – other cameras may use a different term). This enables you

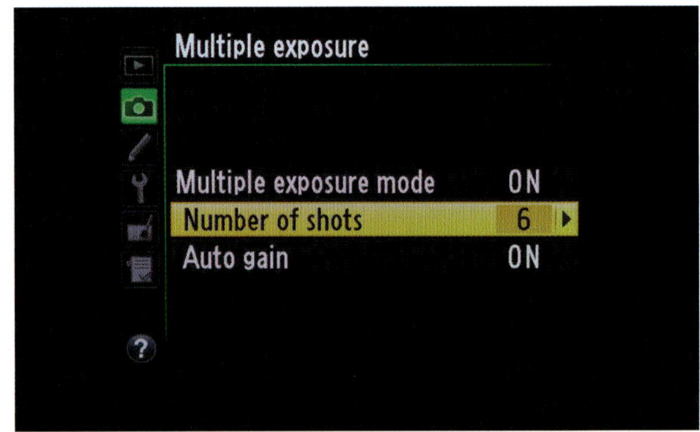

▲ **Fig. 7.25**
The multiple exposure screen on a Nikon D800, showing the ability to pre-programme the number of shots to be taken.

to shoot from two to ten exposures on the same frame. It will have limited application but may be useful for recording stages in the growth of a plant on the same frame for example.

Another method of producing a multiple exposure image, similar to time-lapse, though requiring a very different shooting technique, is that of action sequence photography, where a series of separate images are taken of a high speed event (such as an athlete or horse jumping, bird in flight or caterpillar moving) using the camera's continuous shutter mode, and then the individual images are overlaid onto a constant background to show a sequence of images of the action in the same image. This is one area of imagery only really made possible with the advent of digital photography and digital image processing. Such images can be used by coaches and trainers for analysing the movement of athletes or gait of horses for example.

The basic idea is to shoot a short duration sequence with a fast motor driven camera from exactly the same position, so that you have a number of images of the action in successive frames. Most modern cameras can shoot at 5 frames per second or more, fast enough for example for a horse jumping a fence. Make sure that each frame receives the same exposure by using manual mode.

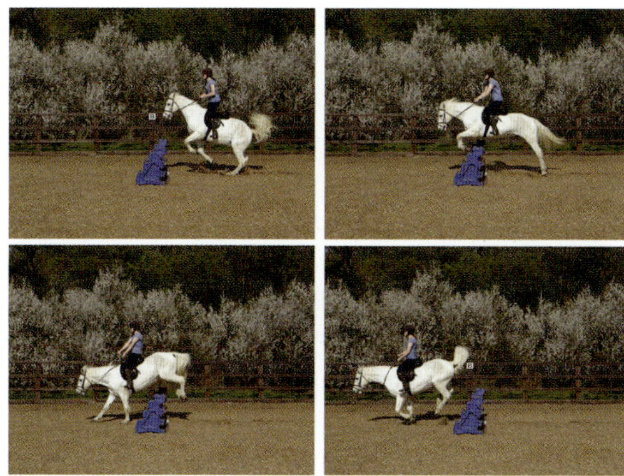

▲ **Fig. 7.26**
Four images from a sequence shot of a horse jumping a barrier.

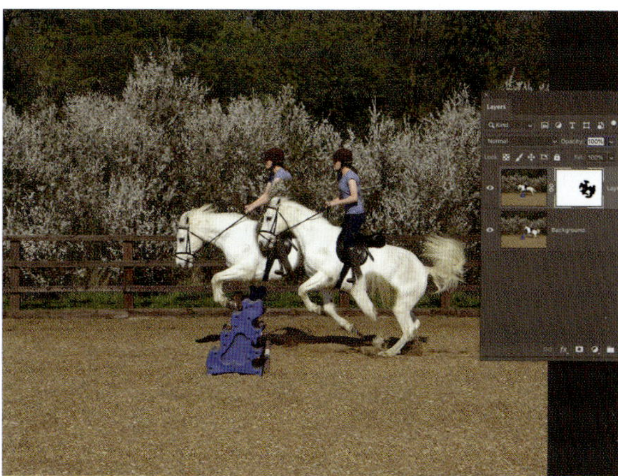

▲ **Fig. 7.27**
Screenshot from Photoshop® showing two of the images opened as layers. Note Layer 1, which has a mask applied to it, this is either used to erase portions of an image or add them back in. See text for details of the procedure. Further images can be added later to extend the sequence.

Having got your image sequence, open the images into Photoshop® (or other imaging program with the facility of layers and masks). The images need to be loaded as a series of layers on top of the first image. The basic idea is that you will select the main moving subject within each of the images, and delete the background around it, so that the final image will consist of the original background, and maybe four or five images on top of it. There are several ways of achieving the effect (there are several YouTube tutorials), and all of the techniques are quite cumbersome and time consuming, but well worth the effort for suitable subjects.

Processing Technique

The method described here uses Adobe Photoshop®, with its ability to work with layers and masks. Make sure the Layers panel is open on the screen (**Window > Layers**).

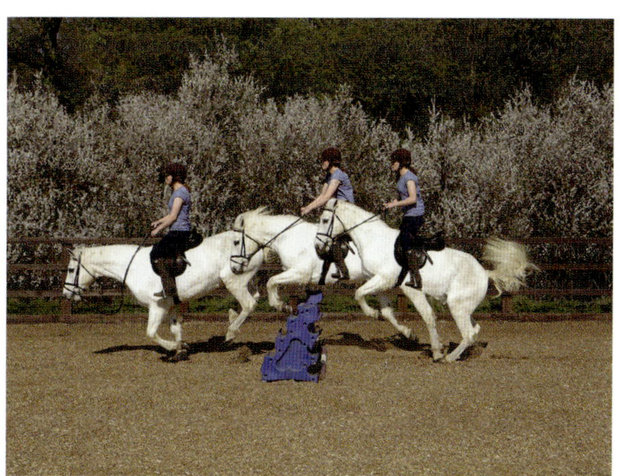

▲ **Fig. 7.28**
The final composite of three images.

1   Open each of the images. Make the first image active by selecting it and going to **File > Save As** and giving it a descriptive name e.g. Horse jump 1.
2   Make the second image active, select it (**Select > All**), and copy it (**Edit > Copy**).

3   Make the first image active again and paste the second image onto it (**Edit > Paste**). It will appear as layer one in the Layers panel.
4   With layer one active, go to the bottom of the Layers panel, and select the layer mask icon (a rectangle with a circle inside it). A blank mask will appear alongside the image of layer 1.

5   You can now start painting away the area not required using a suitably sized paintbrush. The foreground/background colours at the bottom of the toolbox will be black or white. By selecting black you will remove areas of the mask effect-ively making a hole in it. Selecting white for the brush will add areas back to the mask.

6   Brush away all parts of the image not required. If you erase too much, switch the brush to white, and the area removed will reappear. Switch to a small brush when going around the image's edges, (such as the horse's head).

7   Repeat the process with the subsequent images in the sequence.

Don't worry about taking too many images. It is better to take too many and not use one or two rather than not taking enough and having gaps in the sequence. If you think you have too many images in the sequence try turning them on and off in the Layers panel to see which combination of images works best. In the case of the horse shown here, around seven images were taken of the jump, but when all were combined together it the image became very confusing, For the final composite image, three images of the take off, jump and land-ing were used.

When preparing for such a shot, make sure you have a large, fast memory card with plenty of free space, and a fresh set of batteries. There will be a limit to the number of shots that can be recorded before the buffer in the camera fills up, so it will be good to have a practice run first. Depending on the particular subject you will probably need to use a fast shutter speed (1,000th second or shorter) to ensure there is no movement in the individual frames. Apart from anything else, if your subject has blurred edges it can be difficult to select it successfully. Make sure you have left enough room within the frame for the action to fit within it.

You will need a good fast computer with lots of memory too. If your sequence has six images, each of which is 75Mb for example, that means you are dealing with 450Mb of data when processing the sequence.

The composite image of the bats in the frontispiece of this book was created using this technique. The bats were on adjoining frames from a longer sequence.

Long Exposures

A short duration, fast shutter speed is obviously useful for stopping motion, freezing the movement of wings, legs and the like, but sometimes a razor-sharp image of a hummingbird, for example, may appear unnatural. Additional information or images with a more pictorial content can often be achieved with the use of a long shutter speed which can be used to show direction of travel or blurring of wings. Experimentation will be required to see how long the exposure should be to keep a bird sharp, for example, and still show some blurring of the wings. Another technique worth trying is to combine short duration flash with a relatively long shutter speed, so that the movement of the subject is frozen by the flash, but then develops a blurred ghost image while the shutter remains open, as shown in the hummingbird images in Chapter 6. Try using 1/15th or 1/30 second and flash.

One familiar use of long exposures is the photo-graphy of waterfalls, and other images of moving water. A short shutter speed such as 1,000th second or less will freeze the waterfall and show the water as individual droplets. Using a longer shutter speed such as 1/15th second will blur the movement of the water making it appear, depending on the speed used, like a sheet of silk. Landscape photographers make use of the technique, though the effect is not universally liked, and is highly subjective.

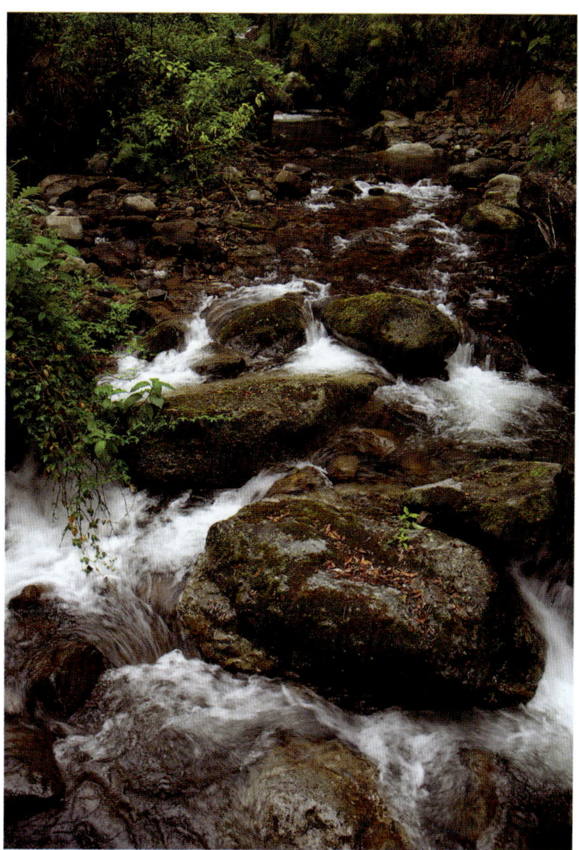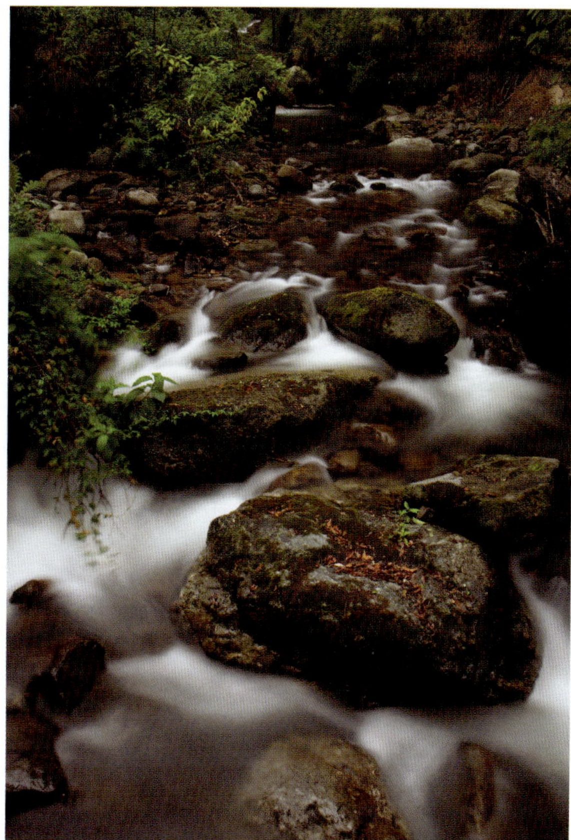

▲ **Fig. 7.29, 7.30**
A Costa Rican river shot at 1/30th second @ f/5.6, and 1/4 second @ f/16. The silky appearance of the water is not universally liked.

When trying to use the technique on a bright day it may not be possible to use a long enough shutter speed, even when the lens is stopped down to its minimum aperture, and the ISO rating set to its minimum setting. In that case you may need to use neutral density (ND) filters to reduce the amount of light entering the lens. An ND filter is a colourless, grey filter with density to reduce the overall amount of light. They can be bought as circular screw in glass filters, or as square filters that fit into special filter holders, made by companies such as Cokin, B+W and Lee Filters. They are available in a range of strengths, and rated in terms of the number of stops absorbed (e.g. one stop, two stop), extra exposure required (e.g. ×2, ×4) or, more usually, by a logarithmic number (e.g. ND 0.3, 0.6, 0.9) where 0.3 absorbs one stop of light, 0.6 absorbs 2 stops and 0.9 absorbs 3 stops.

A number of manufacturers, such as Lee Filters, also make very dense ND filters called Stoppers, which absorb 6, 10 and 15 stops respectively, to allow very long exposures, often in the region of several minutes. They are widely used by landscape photographers for blurring water or cloud movement.

Graduated versions of ND filters are available in the square format, where the filter is dense and/or coloured at the top, and gradually becomes clear towards the bottom. These are used to darken and/or colour skies for example.

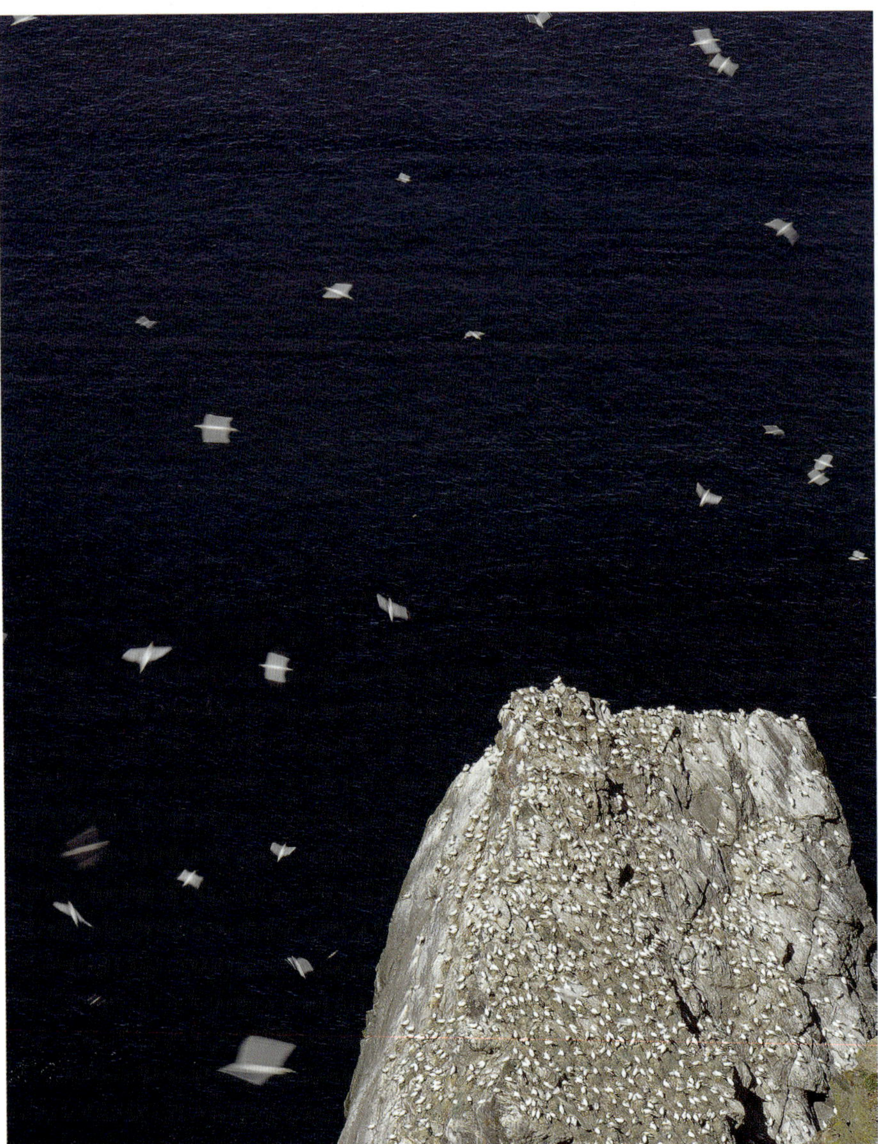

Fig. 7.31
Gannets (*Sula bassana*) photographed in the Shetland Isles, Scotland, with a slow shutter speed (1/20th second) on a tripod mounted camera. Although not yielding any extra information about gannets, the results are very interesting.
  Nikon D800 with 70–300mm lens at 120mm. 1/20th second @ f/32, 100 ISO.

LONG EXPOSURE STREAK

One application of long exposure photography is to produce a streak showing the movement of subjects such as seeds falling from a tree.

  As we have discussed already, much photography of the unseen involves problem solving – how to photographically illustrate unpredictable events, for example. Inevitably, this will sometimes lead to compromise, as in this case. The aim with this image was to photograph a Sycamore (*Acer pseudoplatanus*) seed spiralling down from a tree, with a shot of the seed at the end of the spiral. Several options were explored, but none produced an acceptable result. In the end a combination of exposures was made, then combined together in Adobe Photoshop®.

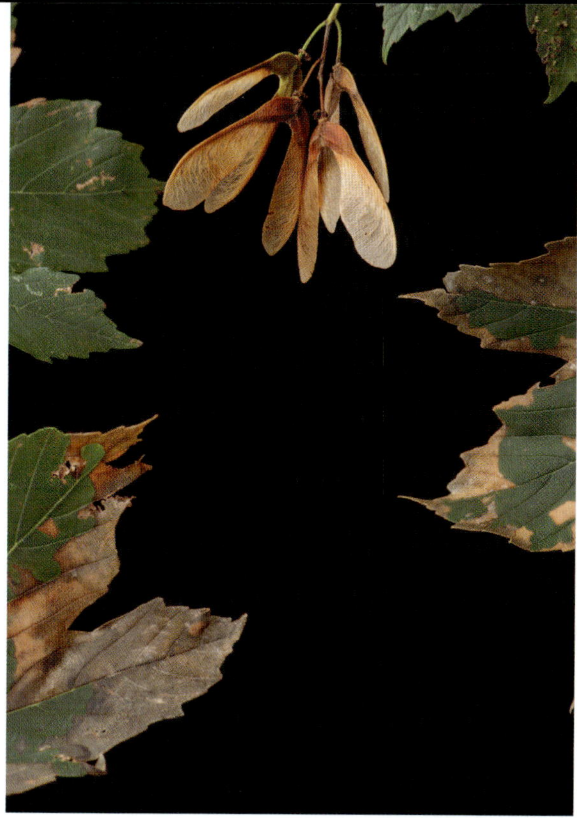

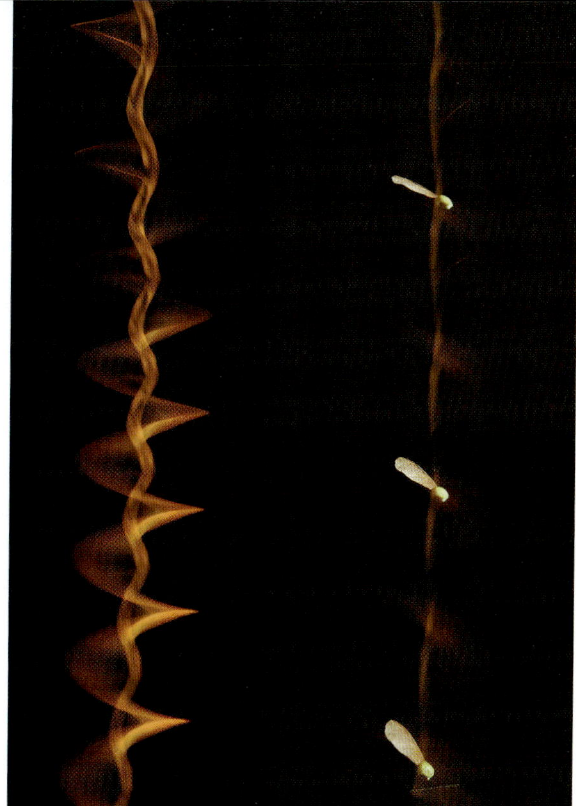

Sycamore seed (*Acer pseudoplatanus*) spiralling down from a tree. This is a Photoshop® composite of three images, the leaves, the spiral of a single seed, and a single seed isolated from a stroboscopic sequence.

PROCEDURE

Stage 1 – Capturing the Images

The leaves and seeds were arranged and photo-graphed in a studio setting, with a black velvet background. They were held in place with the aid of laboratory retort stands and clamps, readily available on eBay and other online sites, and arranged so that a vertical gap was present, to allow space for the seed to fall into.

The spiral was surprisingly difficult to achieve. A colleague dropped seeds from the top of a step ladder in front of a black background. Two LED lights one on either side of the seed were baffled to produce a narrow slit of light through which the seed passed, and prevent light falling on to the back-ground. Many attempts were made to achieve the perfect spiral. In the end, an exposure of 1/2 second @ f/5.6 with 400 ISO was found to give the best

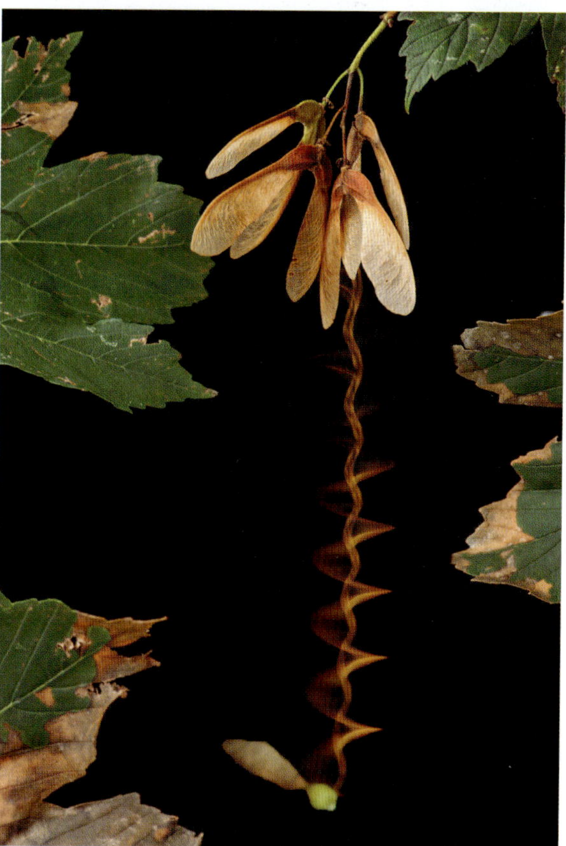

result. One problem was that the contrast between the seed and background was insufficient. This was largely solved by painting the seed with yellow, fluorescent marker pen.

To photograph the seed in mid flight the stroboscopic facility (repeating flash) on a Nikon SB900 was used. This was set to 10 Hz, the seed dropped, and the camera fired. An exposure of 1/2 second ensured that several images of the seed were captured.

Stage 2 – Combining the Images in Photoshop

Step 1: The main image of leaves and seeds was opened, and the seeds selected using the quick selection tool. This selection was inverted **Select > Inverse**, so that most of the image was selected, apart from the seeds.

Step 2: The spiral image was opened and optimized so that it had a good black background and clear spiral. The spiral was selected by drawing a lasso selection close to it. This selection was copied (**Edit > Copy**)

Step 3: The main image was made active again, and the spiral pasted into it using the paste special command (**Edit > Paste special > Paste into**). This ensured that the spiral was pasted into the background, and crucially, behind the seeds of the main image. Using the move tool it was positioned in place. If the scale of the spiral is wrong it can be enlarged or decreased using **Edit > Transform > Scale**.

Step 4: One of the seeds from the stroboscopic image was selected using the lasso tool in Photoshop®, copied and pasted into the image at the bottom of the spiral.

Another way to produce a streak indicating movement of the subject is to use rear-curtain synchronization with flash. This is discussed and illustrated in Chapter 6.

STAR TRAIL PHOTOGRAPHY

Although worthy of a book in its own right, astrophotography, and in particular star trail photography, are other photographic techniques that can be used for visualizing otherwise unseen events. Shooting the Milky Way might involve using special equatorial mounts for the camera, which track the stars over a long exposure so that no blurring is seen in the image. On the other hand however, the way stars move around the night sky can be photographed using long exposure times, yielding star trails.

The key to success with astrophotography is having a dark night sky with no light pollution from towns, cities and streetlamps. This is increasingly difficult in the UK, though certain regions have been designated as Dark Sky Discovery sites, which include Snowdonia in North Wales and many remote areas of Scotland. Other good areas in the UK include Dartmoor, the Dorset coast and areas of the South Downs. A full moon may give too much light as well. Remember to check the weather forecast for clear skies.

Photographing the Milky Way without Trails

Astrophotography in general requires long exposures with high ISO settings and wide maximum aperture.

One rule that astrophotographers use when determining the shutter speed for images of the Milky Way is the 500 rule. Divide 500 by the focal length of the lens you are using for example: 500/50mm = 10.

This means that if you use an exposure time of ten seconds or less, then the stars will appear sharp, rather than blurred due to the rotation of the earth.

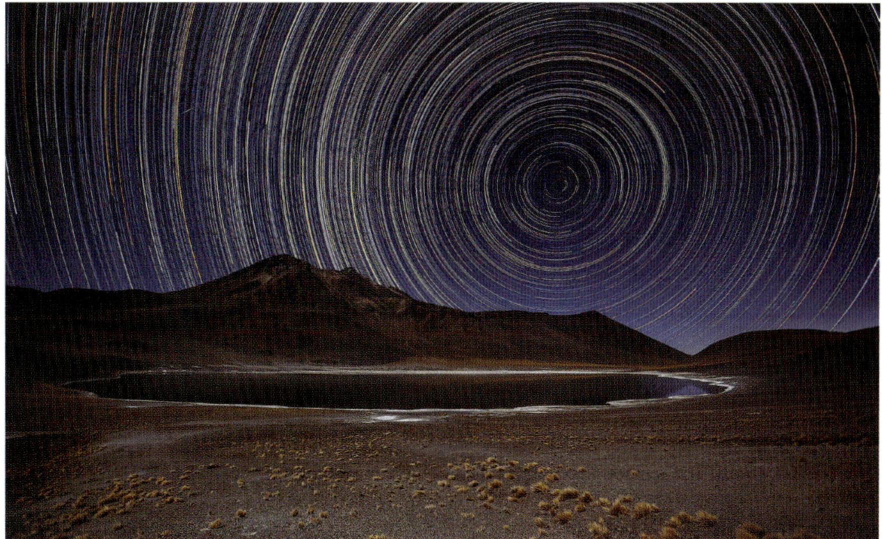

▶ Fig. 7.35
Circular star trail. This image was taken in the Atacama Desert in Chile, by European Southern Observatory Photo Ambassador Adhemar M. Duro Jr. The camera was pointed at the sky's south pole, the point at the centre of all the bright arcs and circles. All the stars in the night sky revolve around this point. Over a period of several hours, this motion creates star trails, with each individual star tracing out a circle on the sky. These trails display the various light levels and colours of each star. Copyright: European Southern Observatory (ESO) This file is licensed under the Creative Commons Attribution 4.0 International licence.

Surprisingly, focusing can be tricky. Don't rely on the infinity setting on the lens, but instead try to focus manually on the stars. A lens with a wide maximum aperture such as f/1.4 or f/2 will be useful here.

Photographing Star Trails

You can choose to photograph star trails tracking their movement as they pass across the sky, or to produce a circular trail.

To achieve a circular star trail (polar aligned) you will need to locate Polaris, the North Star. This is quite easy to locate as you can extend a line from the outer edge of the pan on the Big Dipper (Ursa Major) to the next bright star. Various apps are available to do this including OSR Star Finder and Sky Map. For a polar aligned shot in the northern hemisphere, make sure that Polaris is at, or near, the horizontal centre of the frame to obtain a classic circular star trail.

Preparation

Make sure you have a fully charged battery, and, if working on a cold night, think about having something to keep the camera (and yourself) warm. You will, of course, be working in the dark, so a good torch will be essential to find your way around and make camera adjustments,

A fast, wide aperture lens (f/1.4 or f/2) will be useful for helping focus and compose the scene at night though is by no means essential.

There are two main methods of shooting. The first is to shoot a single long exposure, possibly in excess of an hour. This, depending on the camera model used, may produce a large amount of digital noise, resulting in a grainy image. Many cameras have a noise reduction setting that is well worth using. Problems such as clouds passing over, or airplanes leaving trails during the exposure can occur.

The second method is to shoot a number of images at shorter exposures, which are then stacked in appropriate software, rather like focus stacking in close-up photography. A good piece of software to use is StarStaX, a freeware program for PC and Mac operating systems. Try using a 30-second exposure with a high ISO with the long exposure noise reduction facility turned on. If you use the interval timer you can set the number of exposures that are taken, and over what period of time. Experimentation will be key but try shooting, maybe, 150 exposures over a two-hour period.

As the camera shutter will be either left open for several minutes or even hours, or locked to take several images, make sure your remote release can keep the shutter open during the shoot. Also, ensure the viewfinder eyepiece is covered during the shoot.

You will be photographing at night, when the temperature usually drops significantly from the day time temperature. This may cause condensation to form on the lens, and possibly sensor, which may affect the image. To prevent it you can wrap a couple of re-usable handwarmers around the lens and camera body or you can get small battery powered heating elements or pads, such as the COOWOO® lens heater, which can be wrapped around the lens during the exposure.

To add interest to the image, try to include something in the foreground of the image – a bare tree or rock formation for example. This can be kept as a silhouette, or perhaps light painted with a powerful torch during the exposure.

SMOKE

One possible way to visualize movement is to create smoke, through which the subject moves, creating vortices and other patterns. It is not for everyone, requiring specialist equipment and potentially dangerous chemicals, but is included here for reference. A good example, of a samara-type maple seed spiralling through the air created by scientific photographer Phred Petersen, can be found online. He produced a glass-walled, airtight chamber filled with acetic acid vapour. The tip of the seed was coated with an amine (cyclohexylamine), which simulated white smoke when the two mixed together. It has to be said that the chemicals are very noxious and potentially very dangerous, and this technique must be done in a closed chamber. The chemical vapours need to be safely vented out of the chamber.

PHOTOGRAPHY OF FUNGAL SPORES

These techniques are not strictly photographic, but instead rely on the preparation of the subject, which is then photographed using conventional techniques, but are, nonetheless, ways of imaging the unseen.

One of the ways to help identify a particular fungal species is to take a spore print, where the colour of the spores can be seen. Not only will the colour be revealed, but also an often, beautiful pattern of the gills on the underside of the mushroom.

Remove the stem (stipe) from the cap of the toadstool and place it down onto a piece of card or glass, cover with a bowl and leave undisturbed overnight. If white or pale coloured spores are expected use black card, if dark toned spores are expected use white. In the morning carefully remove the bowl and specimen, and you should be left with a spore print, where the spores have fallen from the gills. The paper or card used should be as black as possible. Black foam board works well, or you may wish to paint something like 6mm MDF board with the Semple Black 3.0 paint, mentioned in Chapter 4. Another interesting subject using the same technique are fern fronds.

A modification to the technique, yielding more interesting images is to place the whole toadstool, vertically, with its stipe intact, onto a black surface. Take a cocktail stick and carefully insert half of it into the stipe, then push the other end into a pre-drilled hole in the background. Cover it with a box and leave overnight. Remember that although the subject may be relatively small the spores may spread over quite a distance so make sure the cover is large enough, maybe a medium sized box. During that period the falling spores will be wafted by the movement of air underneath the cover to reveal a

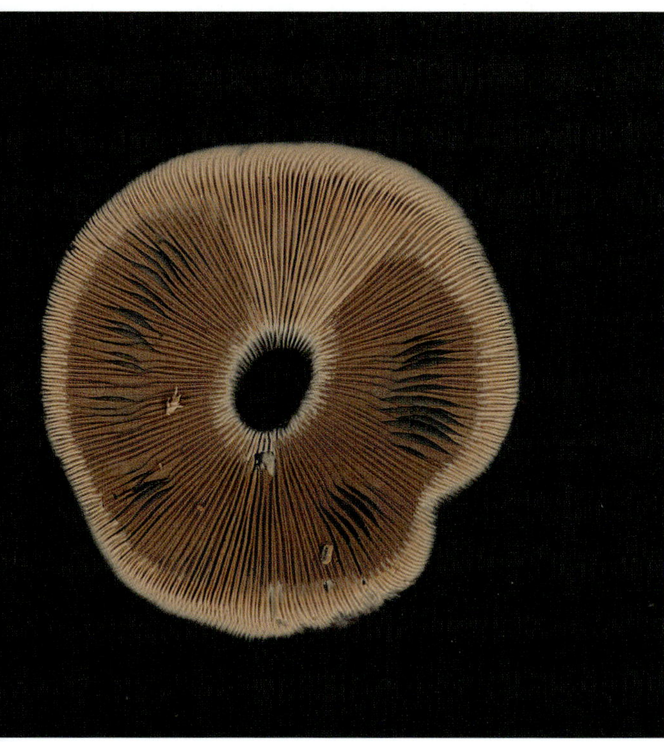

▲ **Fig. 7.36**
Fungal spores shed by a toadstool (*Cortinarius sp.*) overnight, creating a spore print. The colour of the spores is one of the ways of identifying fungi.

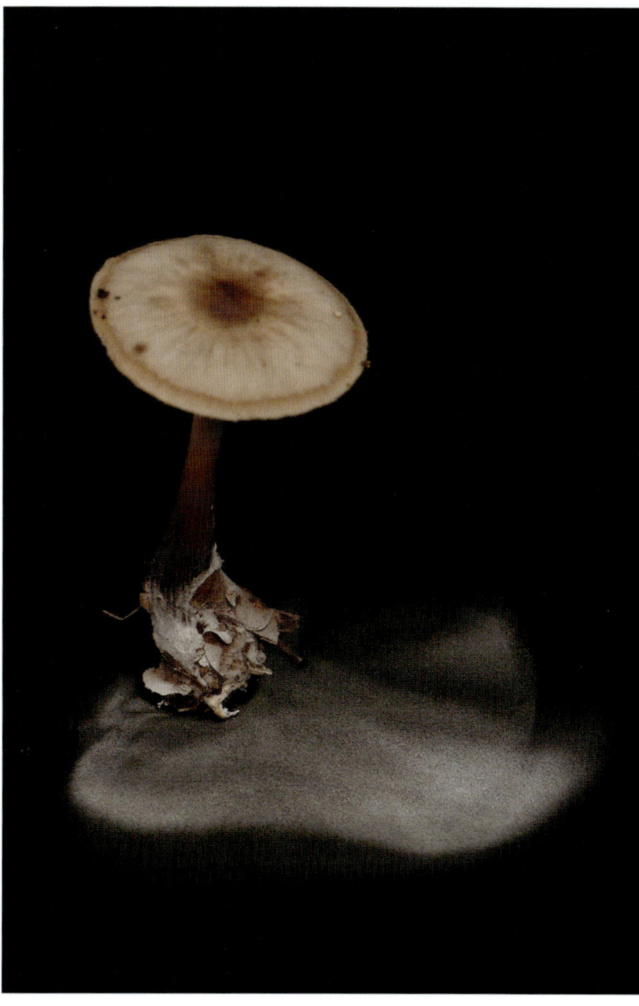

▲ **Fig. 7.37**
The spores of this Butter Cap toadstool (*Collybia butyracea*) created a swirling pattern overnight.

swirling pattern underneath the toadstool. White or pale coloured spores will be best for this technique. You will need a good solid black background for this technique. A piece of MDF board, painted with Semple Black paint works very well. If you have a subject that disperses very dark toned spores then a white background would be more appropriate. Try to photograph the spore pattern as soon as possible and take great care not to touch it or blow on it.

Safety Note

If you have been handling mushrooms and other fungi, make sure you wash your hands thoroughly afterwards. Even ingesting the smallest amount from some species can cause stomach upsets, and some can, in rare cases, be fatal.

THE SENSITIVE PLANT

Even a seemingly simple before and after sequence can be surprisingly complex, requiring careful planning and technical knowledge. The Sensitive Plant (*Mimosa pudica*) is a well-known plant curiosity, exhibiting thigmotropism. When touched lightly the leaflets fold up, remaining closed for several minutes. If the stems are brushed as well, they collapse completely, making the plant look dead. It is thought that the plant has evolved this strategy in the wild to reduce its visibility to grazing animals.

For this image, several seeds were sown, and grown indoors, with six plants being retained for the photography, transferred to separate pots. The final specimens were around 20cm high.

The aim of the final composite image was to show the stem in the process of collapsing using a long exposure. The first image was to be shot with studio flash units, the second image showing the stem movement, to be shot with the modelling lights from the flash units, enabling a relatively long exposure. Tests were made, and an aperture of f/16 was used for both images, giving an exposure time of around one second for the moving image.

Composition of the image was also important – there needed to be blank space for the stem to fall into, ruling out a couple of the specimens. A black background was used to enhance the blur of the moving stem.

Because the images were to be shot with light sources having a different colour temperature (flash and halogen modelling light), a test was made first with the modelling lights including an 18 per cent grey card in the image, to enable white balancing after the shoot.

The first exposure was made with two flash units fitted with diffusers, at 1/160th second at f/16, using Manual mode on the camera.

For the second exposure, the flash synchronization cable was unplugged from the camera, and the exposure mode set to aperture priority, retaining the aperture of f/16.

The plant stem was brushed with a paint brush and when it showed signs of movement, the shutter fired. A remote release was used on the camera to make it easier to reach the plant with the brush.

The reaction of the plant to the brushing was highly inconsistent – some plants did not respond at all, while others operated just once, before taking a day or so to recover. Having a stock of specimens to choose from was very useful.

The two images were composited together in Photoshop. As always there are several ways of doing this. Firstly, the image shot with the modelling lights needs to be white balanced to make it the same colour as the image shot with flash. The image with the grey card and the image without the grey card were opened in Adobe® Camera Raw. The white balance tool was placed on the grey card and clicked to white balance it. The setting from

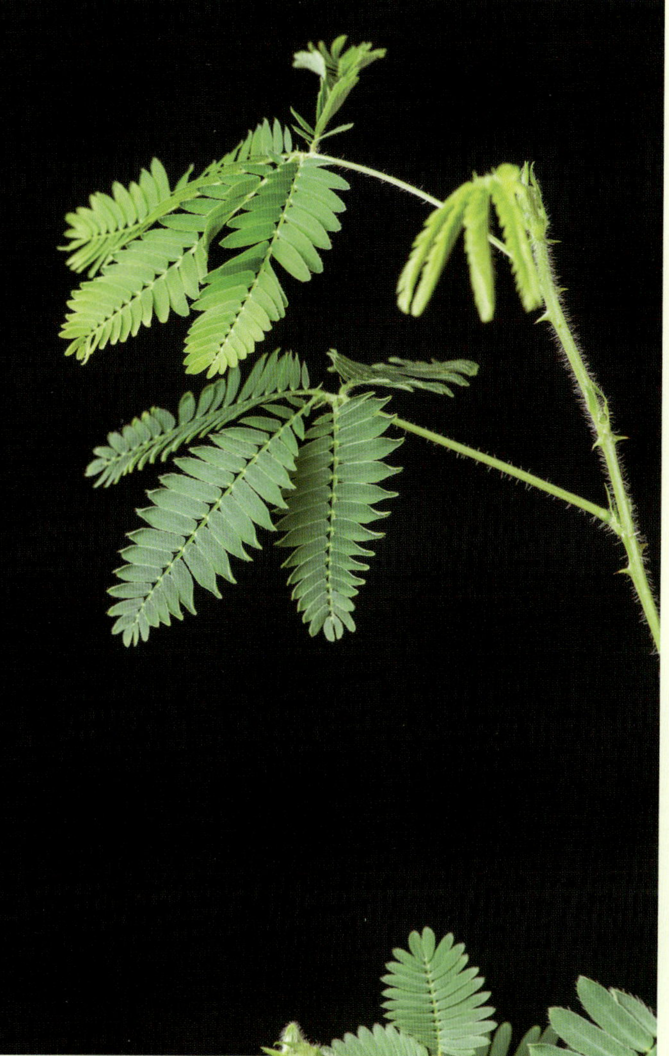
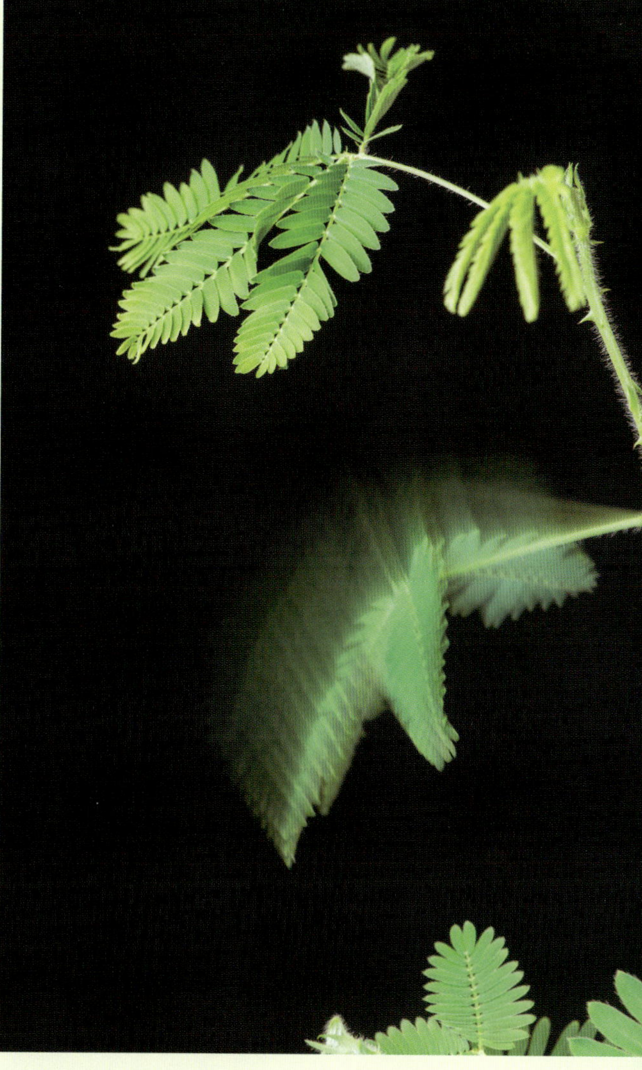

▲ Fig. 7.38, 7.39

The Sensitive Plant *(Mimosa pudica)* is unique in folding the leaflets on its stems when touched. It is not known exactly why it does that, though might be a way of making itself less visible to grazing animals. If the plant is touched more forcibly, the stems themselves collapse, taking only a second or so to do that. This image is an attempt to show the movement of the stem, using a 1/2 second exposure whilst the stem collapsed.

this image was used on the other image (**Select all > Sync setting**). The corrected image was opened in Photoshop®, along with the main image shot with flash. Both images were opened and the image with the blurred stem made active. Using the lasso tool, a selection was drawn around the blurred stem, making sure to include a small piece of the main stem. A feather setting of 5 pixels was used to prevent a hard selection edge. This selection was copied, then pasted into the first image. It was moved into the correct place using the move tool (very precise movements can be made by moving the selection with the keyboard cursor keys).

The final composite image was flattened in the Layers panel and saved as a TIFF file.

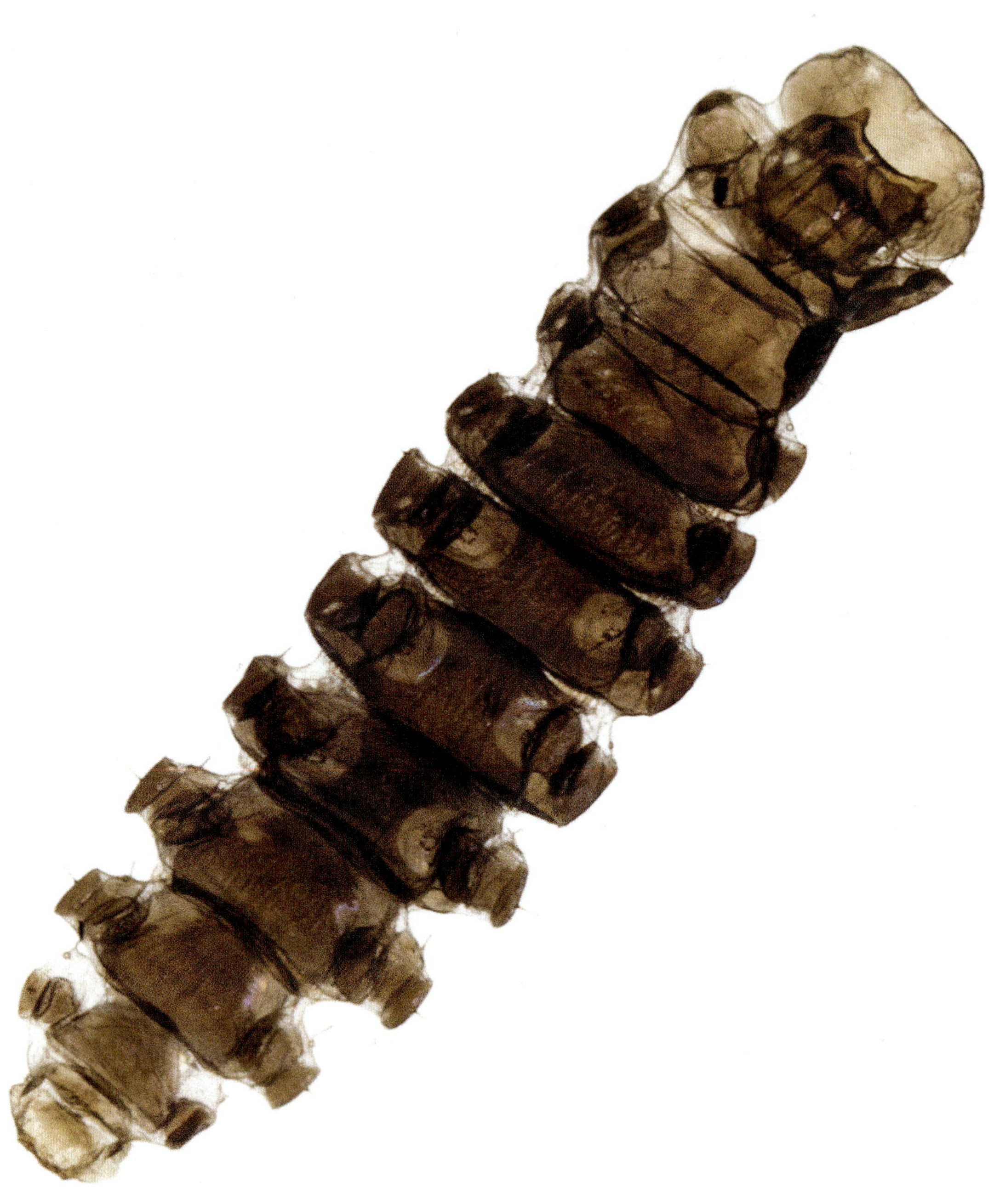

Visualization Through Magnification

From its earliest days, photography has made use of close-up and microscopy techniques to visualize objects and details that we find difficult or are unable to see with the naked eye. Seeing the stamens of a flower or the eye of an insect magnified five times really does open your eyes to a whole new world of photography. There are three main areas of photography associated with close-up and microscopy, which have well established definitions, though they are often confused.

Although close-up photography does not have a universally recognized definition, it is generally reckoned to be the photography of subjects closer than the normal focusing range of a lens. In reality, this will mean different things to different people, but will cover the photography of subjects where the magnification is perhaps from 1/10th to a 1/2 life size in the camera. Macro photography, or photo-macrography, is concerned with the photography of objects where the magnification of the subject, in the camera, is life size or greater. For example, a life size (1:1 or ×1) magnification is where a 25mm subject is seen at a size of 25mm on the imaging sensor. Increasing the magnification becomes increasingly technically difficult, and eventually requires the use of a compound microscope of some kind, when it is referred to as photomicrography. The boundary between macrophotography and photomicrography is not specifically defined but is generally reckoned to be between ten- and twenty-times magnification.

PHOTOMICROGRAPHY VS MICRO-PHOTOGRAPHY

Photomicrography (the photography of subjects with the aid of a microscope) is not the same as micro-photography, which is concerned with the photography of large subjects (such as electrical circuits or documents), and reducing them into a very small area, such as micro-film and micro dots. The traditional scale for micro-photography has been bibles per square inch, i.e. how many complete bibles can be imaged into one square inch of film! As far back as 1926, Emanuel Goldberg, working to archive large amounts of documents, achieved the remarkable feat of recording fifty, using special extra fine-grained film.

DEFINITION: MAGNIFICATION

Magnification is the relationship between the size of the subject, and size of the image. In photography it is a two-step process. There is the magnification of the subject inside the camera, onto the sensor. The image from the sensor will then probably be magnified further when the image is printed, reproduced or projected.

To determine the magnification in camera, you will need to know the size of the sensor in your camera (given in the specifications section of your camera's manual). A full-frame sensor, found in many DSLR and mirrorless cameras, is 24 × 36mm (in reality 35.9 × 24mm). If a 36mm subject exactly fills the width of the frame when looking through

◄ **Fig. 8.1**
Horse Chestnut Leaf Miner Moth (*Cameraria ohridella*). Larva extracted from the leaf shown in Chapter 9. Size approximately 4mm in length.
   Canon 700D with MPE-65mm lens, photographed on light panel Figs 8.2–8.4.

Three images of a swallowtail butterfly (*Papilio machaon*).

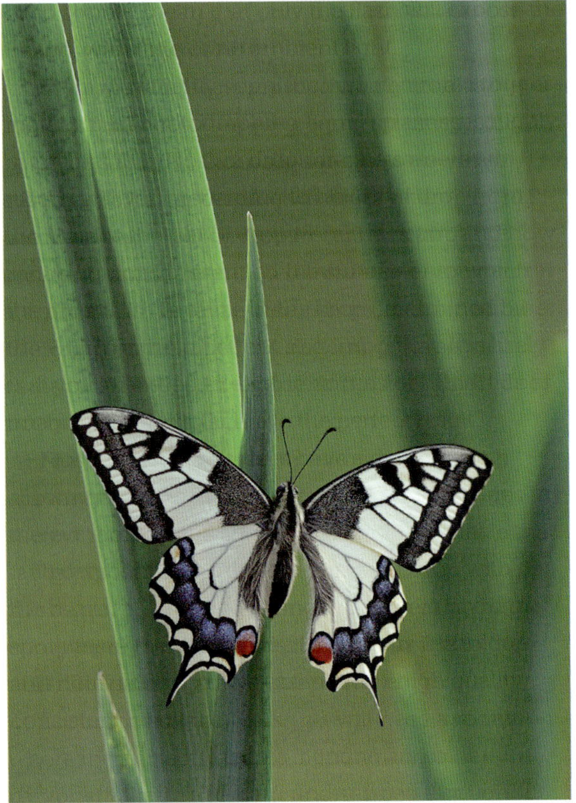

▲ **Fig. 8.2**
Close-up in a field. Nikon D800 with 105mm micro NIKKOR lens and x1.4 converter. 1/100th second @ f/8.

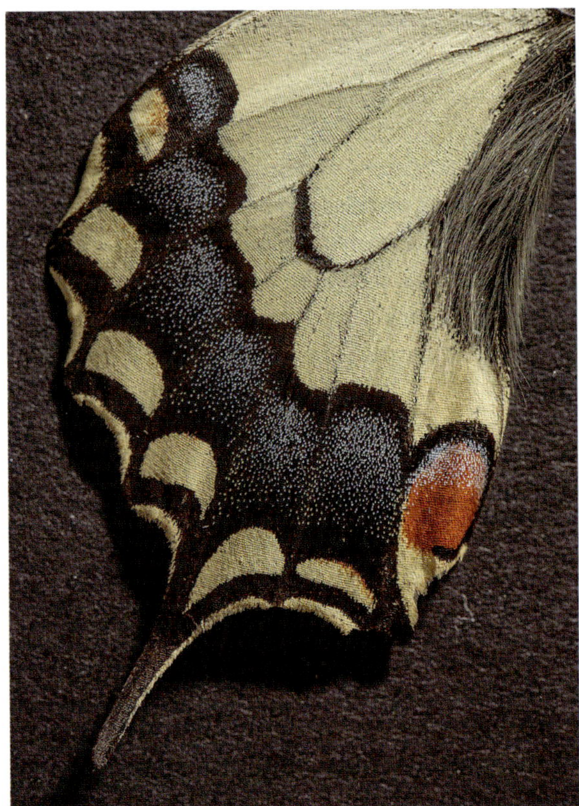

▲ **Fig. 8.3**
Close-up of the wing removed from a dead specimen. Nikon D800, 60mm micro NIKKOR lens, 1/250th second @ f/16 Daylight.

the viewfinder (bearing in mind that very few camera viewfinders show exactly the full frame), the magnification is said to be life size, 1:1 or x1. If a 72mm subject fills the frame, then the magnification will be half life size, 1:2 or x1/2.

This image will then be enlarged, either when it is printed in a book, such as this, printed for exhibition, or included in a website for example.

An easy way of checking the magnification given by a particular lens and camera combination, is to focus on the millimetre scale of a ruler, and then relate the amount of ruler seen to the size of the sensor. It may well be worth including a scale of some sort along the edge of an image so that the final magnification of a subject can be determined when it is printed or reproduced.

CLOSE-UP PHOTOGRAPHY

Basic close-up photography is relatively simple, and many normal lenses nowadays will focus close to a subject, to give magnifications of a quarter or half life size in the camera. The amount of magnification you can achieve with a normal lens can be extended with the addition of close-up lenses screwed onto the front of the lens, or by inserting extension tubes (or bellows) between the lens and camera body.

Close-up lenses are little used nowadays, though Canon do still make a couple specifically for some of their lenses (e.g. the Canon 500D). Unless you

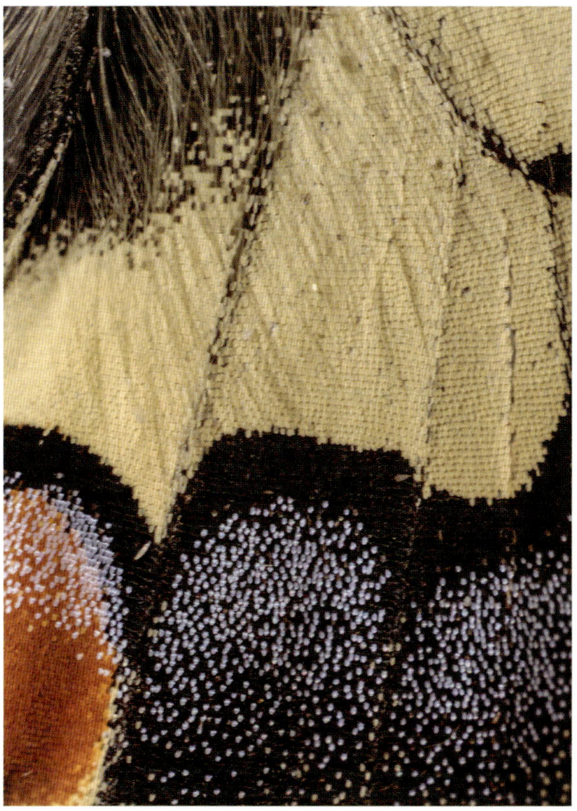

▲ Fig. 8.4
Extreme macro image of wing showing its scales. Note the extremely shallow depth of field. Nikon D810 with an old PB4 bellows unit, and El-NIKKOR 63mm enlarging lens, giving an approximate magnification of ×3. Single LED light source with white reflector. 1/8th second @ f/5.6.

get very high-quality, close-up lenses, equivalent to the quality of the prime lens, then image quality may suffer. If you are just starting with close-up photography they are worth trying though, and some can be found cheaply on internet auction sites. There are different strengths, usually rated in dioptres e.g. +1, +2. The higher the dioptre rating, the greater the magnification that can be obtained.

Extension tubes and bellows are inserted between the camera lens and body – the longer the extension, the greater the magnification that can be achieved.

The amount of extension required can be found from the simple formula:

Lens – sensor distance (V) = Focal length (M + 1)

Where V = lens to sensor distance, and M is the magnification. For example:

To achieve a magnification of ×1, a 100mm lens will require 200mm of extension

$$V = 100 (1 + 1) = 200mm$$

Extension tubes (and bellows) have generally fallen out of use in recent years, in favour of specialist macro lenses, such as the Nikon Micro-NIKKOR 105mm and Canon EF 100mm Macro lenses. These lenses have been designed to give their best performance when used close to the subject, though they can still be used for, and give excellent results, for more distant photography.

Most macro lenses can achieve a life size magnification without the use of further accessories. Sadly, Nikon and Canon no longer make extension bellows units (though they can often be found on online auction sites), though several companies such as NOVOFLEX do still make them. Extension bellows, in particular, can be very cumbersome to use, generally requiring the use of a tripod. They will not have the electrical linkage between the lens and camera body, so the exposure will need to be made in manual mode.

Working Distance

Generally, the longer the focal length, the greater the distance from the camera to subject for the same magnification. If you are photographing a butterfly for example, with a 50mm lens, you may only be 150mm from it. If you double the focal length you double the working distance, and it becomes 300mm with a 100mm lens. Many insect

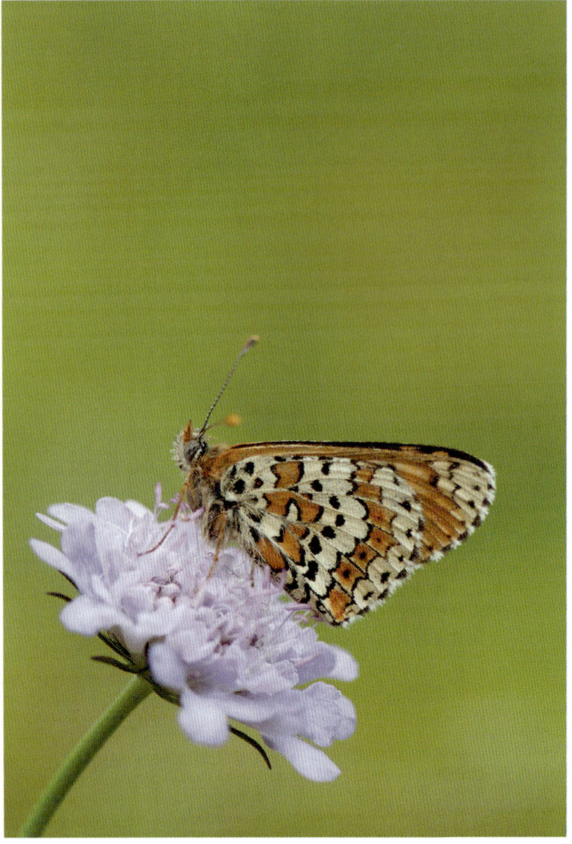

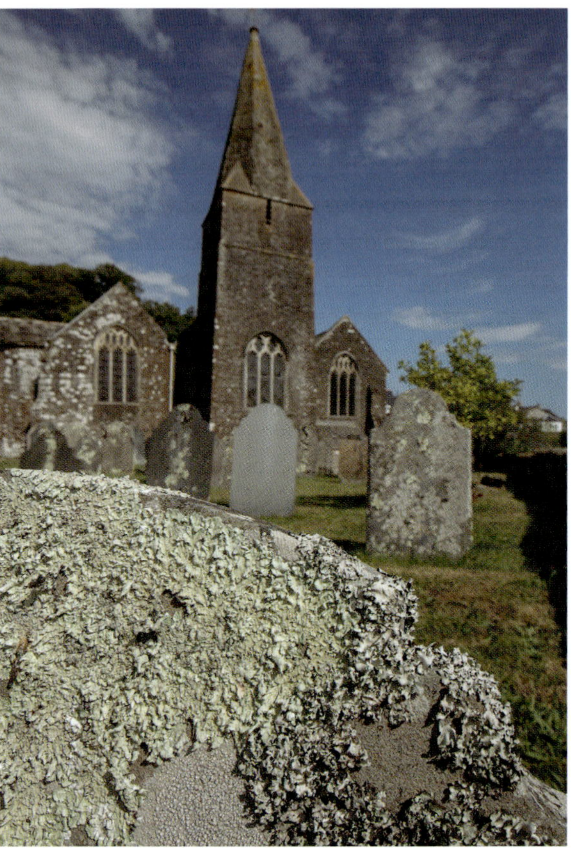

▲ **Fig. 8.5**
Glanville Fritillary (*Melitaea cinxia*) butterfly, Picos de Europa, Spain. A simple close-up using a 105mm micro-NIKKOR lens and ×1.4 teleconverter to maintain a reasonable working distance and throw the background out of focus. The tripod mounted camera was positioned parallel to the plane of the butterfly to achieve maximum depth of field at a low aperture.
  Nikon D800 with 200mm micro-NIKKOR lens, 1/500th second @ f/5, 200 ISO. Tripod.

▲ **Fig. 8.6**
A wide-angle close-up image of lichens growing in a churchyard, taken with a 16mm lens. At least four species are visible including *Ochrolechia parella* and *Parmelia caperata*. The camera was focused on the lichens, and the aperture set to f/5.6 to prevent the church becoming too sharp. Great care was taken to try to keep the walls of the church vertical in the image.
  Nikon D810 with 16–35mm lens. 1/1000th second @ f/5.6.

photographers use 100, 150 or 200mm lenses for their work for this reason. This will also give more room for lighting with flashguns and reflectors, as well as throwing the background out of focus in the right circumstances. One of my favourite combinations is a Nikon 105mm micro-NIKKOR used in conjunction with a ×1.4 teleconverter, giving a final focal length of 147mm with a full frame camera. Again, it is essential to use a high-quality teleconverter in order to maintain high image quality.

In some cases, you may want to use a wide angle short focal length lens to show the subject in its environment or habitat. This will be difficult with insects, but useful for plants for example. A relatively new lens manufacturer, LAOWA, make a 15mm wide-angle lens capable of giving a ×1 magnification.

The use of a tripod is highly recommended, whenever possible, to help hold the camera still during the exposure. All of the close-up and macro images shown here were shot with a tripod mounted camera.

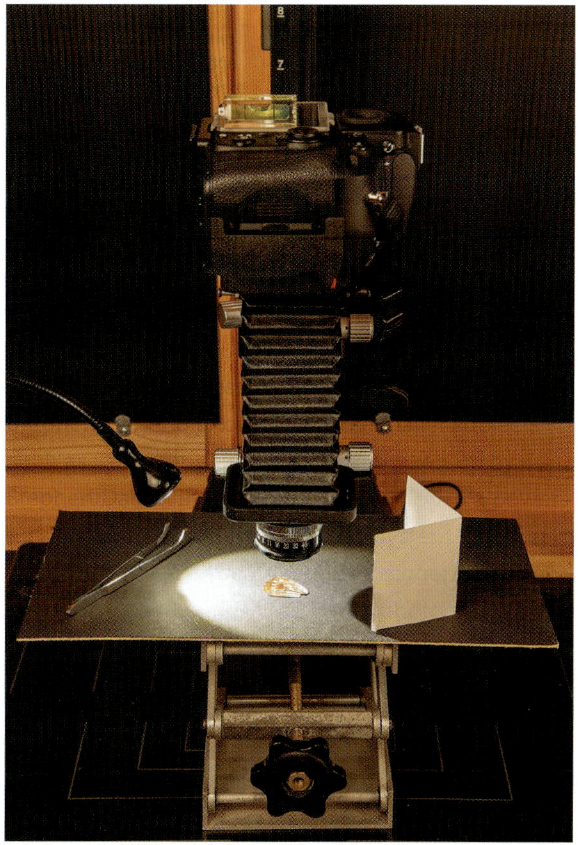

▲ Fig. 8.7
Macro photography with extension bellows unit. A full-frame DSLR on an old Nikon PB4 bellows unit and El-NIKKOR 63mm enlarging lens mounted onto an old copying stand. There is a total magnification of approximately ×4. Note the spirit level on top of the camera and the lighting for the subject provided by an IKEA® LED lamp, with white reflector. The subject, an insect wing, is set on a laboratory scissor jack. Fine focusing is achieved through the controls on the bellows unit.

Macrophotography

Although extension tubes and bellows can be used to achieve magnifications greater than life size there are specialist lenses available, such as the Canon MPE65 that operates at magnifications from ×1 to ×5 and the LAOWA 25mm f/2.8 lens Ultra Macro, which operates from ×2.5–×5 magnification. Neither can be used for standard photography. Other lenses that can be used, and generally give excellent results, in conjunction with extension tubes or bellows, are good quality enlarging lenses, as discussed in Chapter 3.

Another way of achieving high magnifications is to mount, in reverse, a short focal-length lens such as a 28mm or 50mm on to the front of a longer focal length lens such as a 100mm. You will need to use a coupling ring, which has a male filter thread on each side that allows the connection of two lenses via their filter mounts, and commonly available from companies such as SRB in the UK, supplying a host of filter adapters. This combination can give remarkably good results, though the system can become very heavy and cumbersome.

To calculate the final magnification of the combination the following formula can be used:

$$\text{Magnification} = \frac{\text{Focal length of primary lens}}{\text{Focal length of reversed lens}}$$

For example, a 100mm lens with a 28mm reversed lens give an approximate ×4 magnification.

Keep the aperture fully open on the front lens and control the exposure and aperture with the prime lens being used. This may not be possible with some modern lenses, and is a good reason for sourcing old, cheap manual focus lenses, which can give superb results.

Without using specialist lenses or techniques such as these, high-power macro photography is difficult, in particular between the ranges of ×5 and ×20.

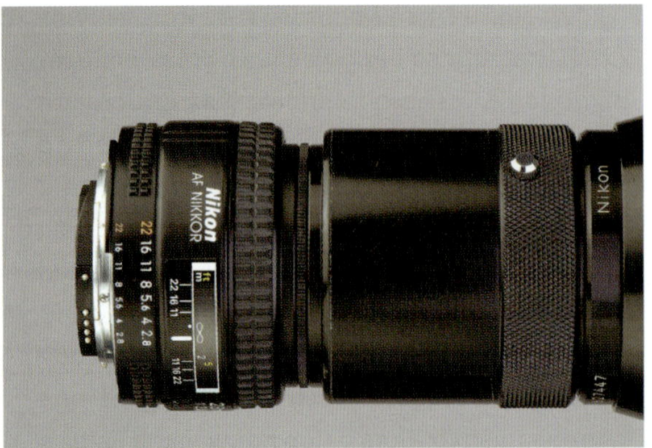

▲ Fig. 8.8
An old manual focus 200mm Nikon lens, with reversed 28mm lens gives an approximate magnification of ×7. It would be worth making some kind of lens hood out of black paper, or use an extension tube, to minimize flare.

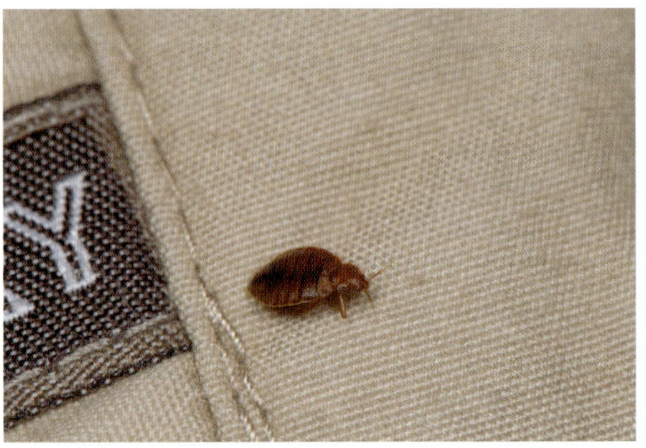

▲ Fig. 8.9
This tiny Bed Bug (*Cimex lectularius*), approximately 3mm in size, was placed on a piece of material to simulate a mattress environment and fenced in with a circular piece of card to prevent it escaping. Canon 700D with MPE-65 lens. Single diffuse flash with reflector. Magnification approximately × 3 to the sensor.

	f/5.6		f/11		f/22	
Magnification	Full frame sensor	APS-C sensor	Full frame sensor	APS-C sensor	Full frame sensor	APS-C sensor
× 1/4	6.5	9.75	13	19.5	27	40.5
× 1/2	1.3	1.95	2.6	3.9	5.2	7.95
× 1	0.44	0.66	0.88	1.32	1.8	2.7
× 2	0.16	0.24	0.33	0.49	0.66	0.99

▲ Depth of Field table
Approximate depth of field, in millimetres, for full-frame and APS-C-sized imaging sensors. The grey shaded boxes indicate where the theoretical diffraction limit has been exceeded, and image quality may be degraded by using this f/stop.

DEPTH OF FIELD

One of the major issues with close-up and macro photography is that of depth of field, or lack of it, and the greater the magnification the smaller the depth of field. At even modest magnification, such as × 1/4, at f/11 the depth of field for a subject can be just a few millimetres or so with a full frame sensor. It is an area where deciding whether to use a full-frame camera or one with a smaller sensor is important – for a given magnification, a smaller sensor will give more depth of field than a larger one. The Depth of Field table gives some examples.

Depth of field can be defined as the area in front of and behind the main point of focus that is acceptably sharp. It is all about how far the nearest and furthest points of a subject are from the camera. If the subject is parallel, or near parallel to the camera, then the need for depth of field will be less than if the subject is at an angle to the camera. This can be a good strategy for subjects such as butterflies but can lead to a series of monotonous images if used extensively. Shallow depth of field can be used to good effect by focusing on the most important part of the subject, and letting other areas go out of focus.

With insects in particular (and any other animal or bird photography), it is always important to

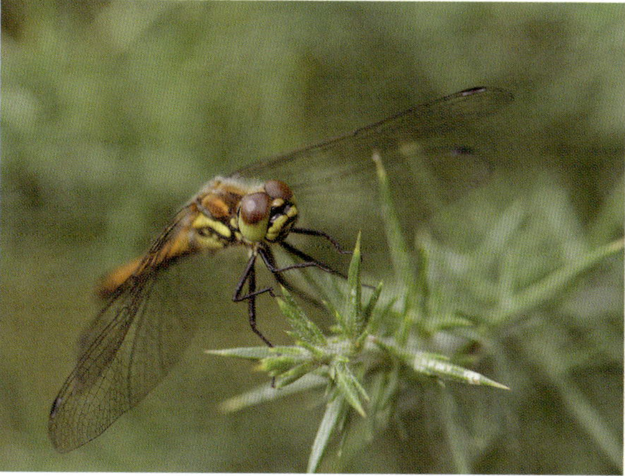

The same specimen from a different angle. Note the extremely shallow depth of field, probably only around 1–2mm. It is important in images such as this to focus on the eyes. I took great care to make sure the ends of both wings were in the frame.
 Nikon D7100 with 105mm micro NIKKOR lens, 1/250th second @ f/7, tripod.

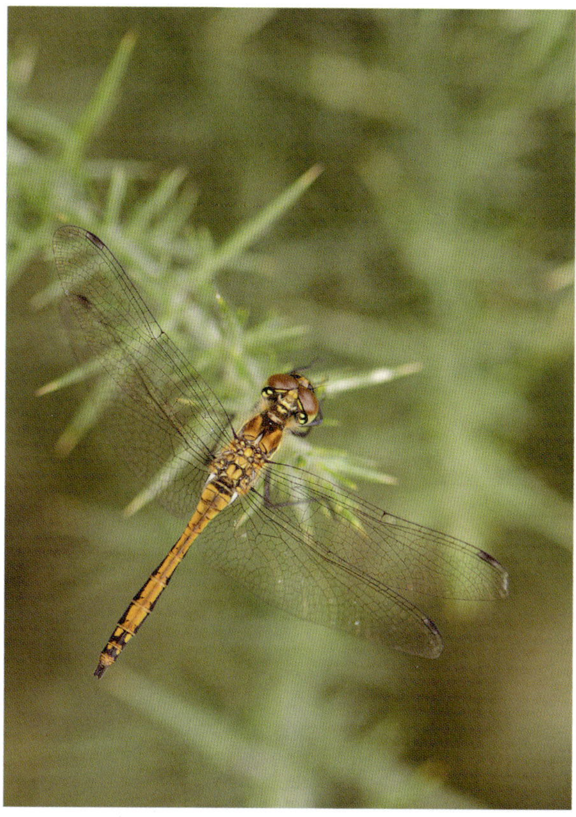

▲ Fig. 8.10
A female Common Darter dragonfly (*Sympetrum striolatum*). In the first image, the dragonfly's body is parallel to the camera and is sharp from head to tail, though the wings are not entirely sharp all over due to the lower ones being in a different plane to the body.
 Nikon D7100 with 105mm micro NIKKOR lens, 1/200th second @ f/5.6, tripod.

focus on the eye of the subject – your eye subconsciously looks straight away at the eye of an animal in an image. If that is sharp, you have a good starting point.

Given that the figures are very small, it might be assumed that a sensible way of working would be to flood the subject with light, so that the smallest possible aperture can be used. However, lens quality is limited by diffraction, where light spills around the edge of the diaphragm, if it is stopped down too far, causing a loss in resolution. This can be seen in the Depth of Field table, in the grey shaded cells. Most lenses give their optimum performance at 2–3 stops down from their maximum aperture, before the

quality starts to fall off. Very often you may need to make a compromise, sacrificing some image sharpness in favour of depth of field, particularly if you will only be using the images for small scale reproduction on a website or small ink jet print for example.

Focus Stacking

A relatively modern technique for combatting depth of field is that of focus stacking, where a number of images are shot of the same subject at different focus points. The resulting images are then merged together in an appropriate software program, which finds and isolates the sharp parts of the image, masking off the rest, resulting in a single image with large depth of field. The technique was originally developed for photomicroscopists, who are always working with incredibly small depth of field values, and also astrophotographers. The techniques require precision, practice and patience.

For the technique to work the camera and subject must not move in relation to each other during the shooting process, with the camera mounted on a solid tripod, and subject possibly clamped in place to

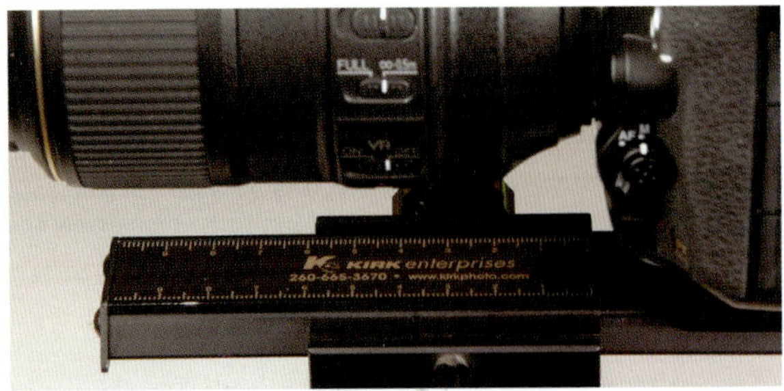

▲ Fig. 8.12
This camera is mounted on a focusing rail, which moves the whole camera backwards and forwards. Note the millimetre scale.

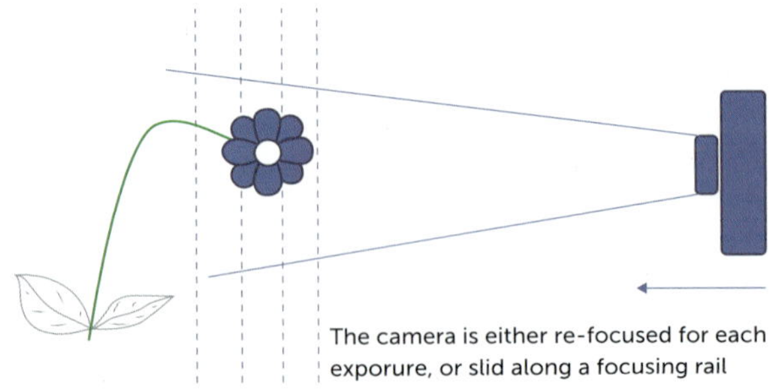

▲ Fig. 8.13
Focus stacking involves shooting images of a subject at different focus points then blending them together in a software program such as Helicon Focus.

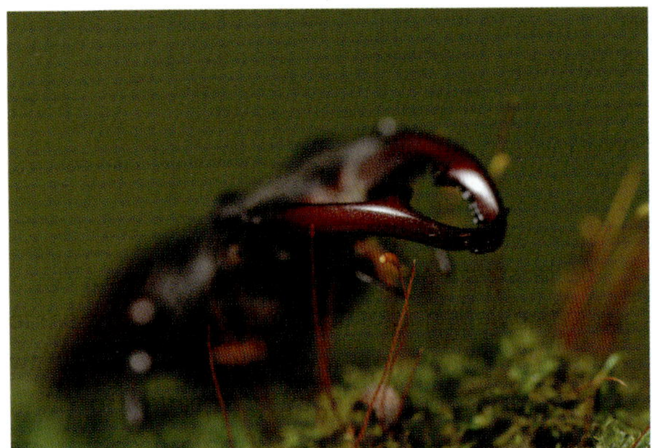

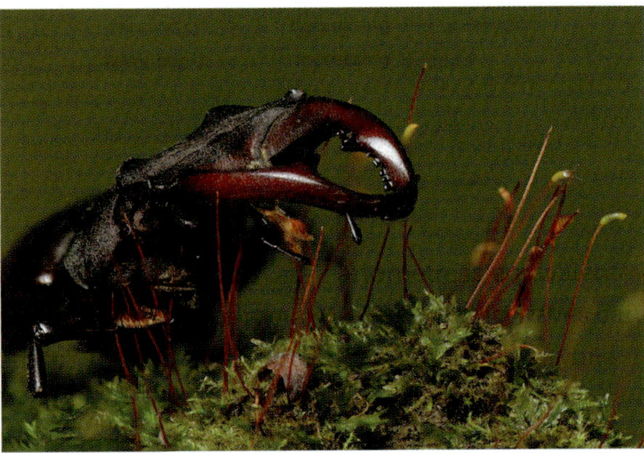

▲ Fig. 8.14, 8.15
Stag beetle (*Lucanus cervus*) museum specimen. Note the extremely shallow depth of field in the first image, shot at f/8. The second image is focus stacked from twelve images shot at f/8. More images would have brought the rear end of the beetle into focus. There are a couple of areas within the image, particularly the stems of the moss, where the focus stacking has not covered the subject and led to areas of soft focus.
Nikon D810 with 105mm micro-NIKKOR lens. Stacked using Photoshop®, from twelve images each at 1/125th second @ f/8.

prevent it moving. The lighting and exposure must also be the same for each exposure. There is no need to shoot at a small aperture – f/5.6 or f/8 should be sufficient, and these figures will be around the optimum apertures for best image sharpness with your lens. They will also ensure that the background is kept out of focus if required. Make sure you have a fully charged set of batteries in your lights and camera, so that they do not need replacing during the shoot, and a memory card with sufficient space for the number of images to be recorded.

The basic idea with focus stacking is that you focus on either the nearest or furthest point within the subject, and re-focus the camera with each successive shot, moving through it rather like a bacon slicer cutting slices of meat, until you reach the other end of the area required. There are two main ways of doing this. Firstly, you can re-focus the lens manually during the sequence, trying to adjust the lens by the same amount each time. As can be imagined, this is tricky, and may lead to uneven coverage of the subject, but works reasonably well with images up to ×1/2 magnification as a rule. The second method is to mount the camera on to a focusing rail, which usually have millimetre scales engraved on them. Then, rather than re-focusing the lens, the whole camera and lens is then moved backwards or forwards for each shot.

It does not matter if you start the sequence at the front or rear of the subject. The number of images that are required will depend on the size of subject, but as a starting point, if you measure the depth of the subject e.g. 20mm, then try shooting twenty images one millimetre apart. Some images, particularly high magnification macro images may require many more than that. Specialist macro photographers may shoot 100 or more images to achieve their results! If you want to keep the background out of focus, use a wide aperture such as f/4 or f/5.6. There is a superb set of focus stacked images of insect specimens by Levon Biss at www.microsculpture.net.

It is possible to buy motorized focusing rails controlled by software, (for example the StackShot, which is capable of moving the camera a fraction of a millimetre at a time) for this purpose if you will be doing lots of this work. Also, there are various apps that work with tablet PCs or smart phones, such as the CamRanger 2, which control the camera and lens from the tablet screen via a wireless network, and then save each image as it goes. Using the CamRanger for example, you touch the furthest part of the image on the tablet screen, and the nearest part of the image that you want in focus, and the software computes the number of images required, and drives the lens to take the appropriate number of shots. Much greater detail on focus stacking techniques is given in the book *Extreme Close-Up Photography* by Julian Cremona (see resources list).

A good tip is to shoot a blank frame at the start and end of the sequence to distinguish it from other images on the same memory card. In Adobe® Bridge or Lightroom it is worth giving each of the images in the sequence a specific coloured label to indicate that they are part of the sequence.

To merge the images together you will need software capable of combining them together as a stack. Adobe Photoshop® can do this, as well as programs designed specifically for the purpose, such as Helicon Focus and Zerene Stacker. This example will use Adobe Photoshop® and Adobe® Bridge.

Using Adobe® Bridge, find the images required for the stack, and select them all by holding down the shift key on your keyboard and selecting them. If the images need any adjustments it may be worth doing that first before starting the sequence. Be sure to process them all with the same adjustments.

Go to **Tools > Photoshop > Load Files** into Photoshop Layers. Each image will be loaded into Photoshop® as a separate layer.

Switch to Photoshop®, and open the Layers panel. Select all of the images in this panel, (**Shift – Select**), then go to **Edit > Auto Align Layers** (this will make any necessary adjustments for any image that moved slightly during the shooting process, possibly when shooting live subjects out of doors). Failure to do this may result in ghost images round the edges of the subject.

Go to **Edit > Auto Blend Layers** then select **Stack Images**.

Note: If your PC or Mac does not have much memory it may be worth purging the memory in between steps 3 and 4 (**Edit > Purge > All**).

The stacking process may take some time, depending on the number and size of the images in the sequence. If you have a sequence containing twenty images, each of which is 103.4Mb (from a 36Mp camera for example), then the computer is having to process over 2Gb of data, a major reason for needing a powerful computer with lots of memory and large hard disc with lots of spare space.

Your final image should be sharp from front to back. Any blurred areas within the subject are usually indicative of having missed out a section during the shooting.

When you are satisfied with the image, go to the Layers panel and flatten it (**Layers > Flatten image**).

Many top of the range DSLR and mirrorless cameras, such as the Nikon D850, Nikon Z6 and Z7 (known as Focus Shift Mode), Panasonic G9 and

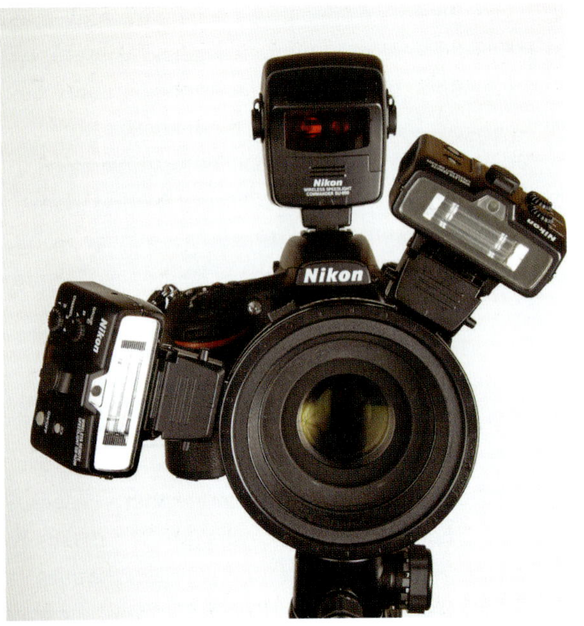

▲ **Fig. 8.16**
The Nikon R1C1 Close-up flash kit, consisting of a camera mounted commander unit and two flashguns attached to the front of the lens. In the case shown here, the unit at the top of the camera is twice as powerful as the lower unit giving a main light and fill-in effect. Because the system is wireless, the flashguns can be held away from the camera if necessary.

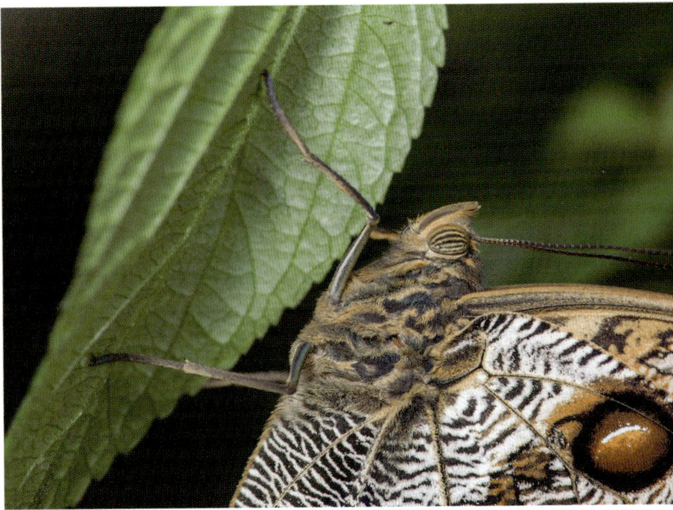

▲ **Fig. 8.17**
Owl butterfly (*Caligo memnon*). Close-up of the remarkable patterned eye of this tropical butterfly. Photographed in a butterfly house with twin flashguns as shown in figure 8.16.
Nikon D800 with 105mm micro-NIKKOR lens with ×1.4 tele converter at 1:1, 1/60th @ f/11, tripod.

Olympus OM-D E-M1 Mark II nowadays have focus stacking capabilities built into them, whereby the camera will shoot a pre-determined number of images. With the Olympus, for example, in focus stacking mode, the camera shoots eight images, varying the focus point for each shot. The images are merged to a final stack and the resulting image is saved, as are the base images. In focus bracketing mode, the user specifies the number of images, (that can be many more than eight), and then has to perform the final stack on a computer.

HAND-HELD FOCUS STACKING

There are several YouTube videos showing how it is possible to shoot focus stack sequences while hand-holding the camera – useful primarily for insects. The technique relies on having a fast frame rate in your camera – six or seven frames per second for example. While shooting a burst of images using the continuous high-speed mode, you move the whole camera through the subject to achieve a set of images that can be focus stacked. The subject will almost certainly move within the frame, which can usually be corrected with the auto-align feature in the stacking software. It is a rather hit and miss technique, but well worth trying.

LIGHTING FOR CLOSE-UP AND MACRO PHOTOGRAPHY

For subjects such as insects and flowers in their natural habitat there is no doubt that natural light is best. The problem of course is that daylight is not predictable, being variable according to time of day, weather and time of year resulting in different contrast and colour. Excessive contrast can be reduced with the use of reflectors or diffusers, but to ensure some sort of consistency you may need to resort to the use of supplementary lighting.

For photographing butterflies and other insects in the field, you may not be using a tripod, but instead hand holding the camera; difficult when shooting large close-ups. When hand-holding, make sure to use the vibration reduction, or image stabilization facility on your camera, if it has one, to help get sharper images. On many cameras you should turn this facility off when mounting the camera on a tripod and you should check your camera manual to see if this is necessary.

Because you are photographing small subjects, you will only require relatively small light sources. Speedlights are ideal, though increasingly photographers are using LED panels in the field, such as the Manfrotto® Lumimuse, particularly for flowers and fungi for example.

Several manufacturers make specialist macro photography lighting units, such as the Nikon Wireless Macro Lighting System R1C1. This consists of a control (commander) unit, together with two or more small flash heads, which can be mounted around the lens on a ring or positioned separately. The flashes can be divided into two or more groups, allowing control of the relative power of the individual flashes, where one flash can be more powerful than the other to act as a main light for example. Because this particular system works using IR communication there are no cables.

PHOTOMICROSCOPY

Photomicroscopy is concerned with shooting images with the aid of a microscope that uses light. Visible light has a limited resolution capable

of producing images at around ×2000 before the effects of diffraction make it useless. Depth of field too is negligible. To obtain high-resolution images at higher magnifications, electrons are used for imaging rather than light, in various types of electron microscope. These are well outside the scope of this book.

The subject of microscopy and photography using microscopes is large, and worthy of a book in its own right, and only a brief discussion is given here.

There are many types of light microscope (sometimes called a compound microscope), all of which have a two-lens system, an objective lens nearest the specimen, and an eyepiece lens. The total magnification of the subject is determined by the combination of the two. A ×10 objective lens used with a ×10 eyepiece will result in a ×100 magnification of the subject. There are usually several different magnification objective lenses on a microscope, mounted on a rotating turret. The magnification for the objectives and eyepieces will usually be engraved on the lens barrel. (It is a convention in microscopy that the magnification of a lens is signified by placing the number before the x, e.g. ×50, while the overall magnification will be shown by placing the × before the number, e.g. ×100.)

Specialist microscopes are available for various specific applications including UV fluorescence, polarizing, metallurgy and incident light work. There are even microscope attachments for smartphones, containing focus and zoom controls, and a built-in LED light source. The quality of these will probably not be as good as a good microscope but may be very useful for field observation.

Microscope slides with very small engraved scales are available, called graticules, which can be placed on to the microscope stage, to help determine the exact magnification of a specimen.

To take photographs through a microscope, a camera (normally without its lens) can be fitted onto the top of the eyepiece via a suitable light tight

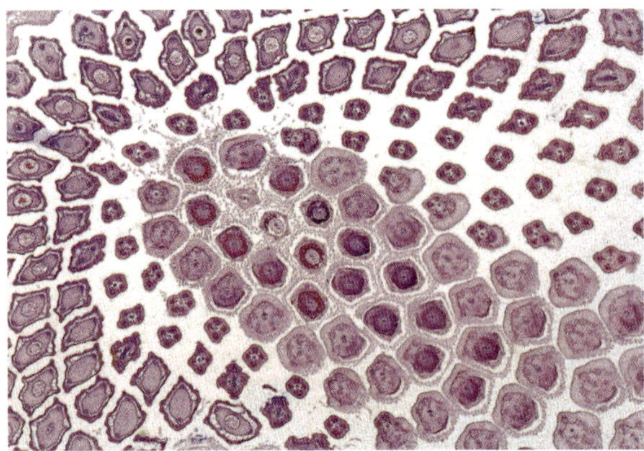

▲ **Fig. 8.18**
Photomicrograph of stained section of a Dandelion (*Taraxacum sp.*) flower, using simple microscope and bright field lighting. Magnification approximately ×20.

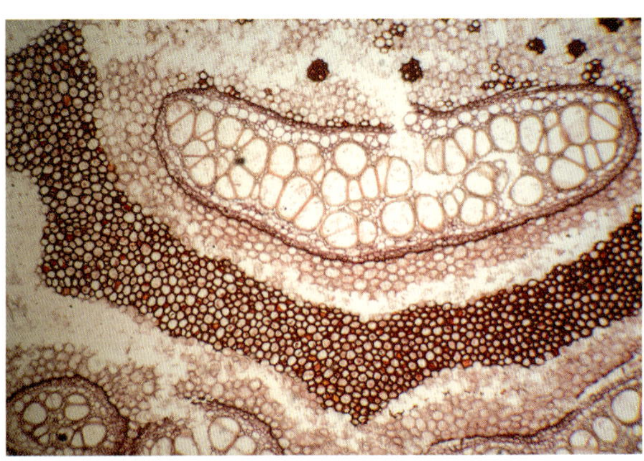

▲ **Fig. 8.19**
Cross section through Bracken (*Pteridium aquilinum*) rhizome. Magnification approximately ×20.

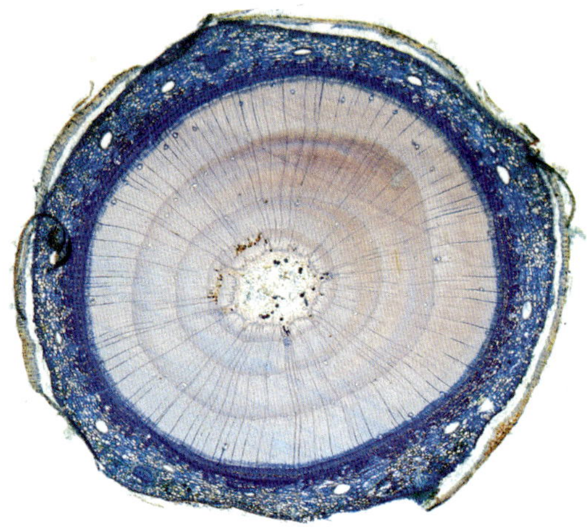

▲ **Fig. 8.20**
Cross section through Fir tree (Abies sp.) twig. Magnification approximately ×40.

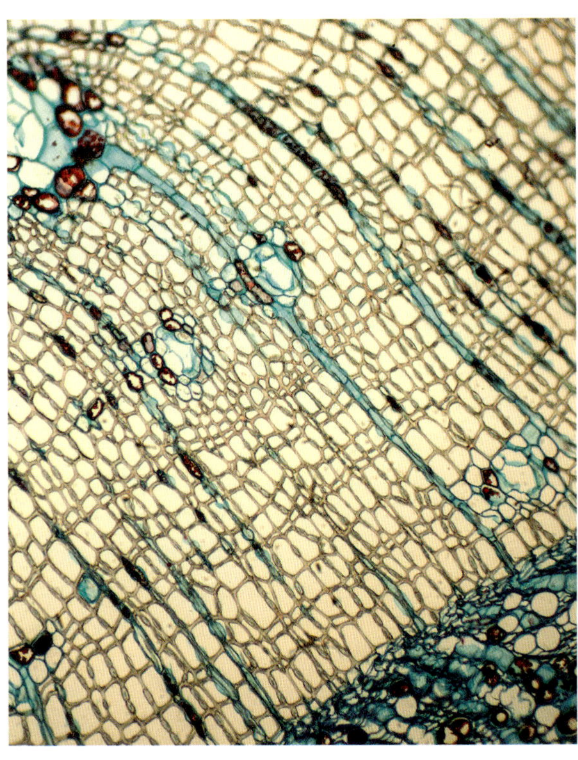

▲ **Fig. 8.21**
Transverse section through root of Spruce (*Picea sp.*). Magnification approximately ×100.

adapter to record the image produced by the microscope lenses. Binocular type microscopes have two eyepieces, while trinocular models have a third port designed to take a camera body. It is possible to place a compact type camera or smartphone on top, but best results will usually be given with a DSLR or mirrorless camera body.

Lighting

Most modern light microscopes have a built-in light source making the critical alignment and set up far easier than the older style microscopes that had a separate light source, though it is still possible to use a separate light source for frontal or grazed reflected lighting if required.

Many modern microscopes have tungsten halogen lamps inside them, though increasingly LEDs are being used. Correct lighting is critical, and just like conventional photography, there are several options, from brightfield and darkfield, to polarized and others.

If you have a tungsten or tungsten halogen light source, you can usually adjust the level of illumination with a variable rheostat. There are usually two settings at the end of the scale, often denoted in red, which are the settings that will give the correct colour temperature for photography (5,500K). Settings lower than that will have a lower colour temperature and will probably give rather orange results. If you shoot raw files, the colour can be easily corrected.

For incident, reflected microscopy, you will need a small light source that can be directed onto the top of the slide, at an angle. One particularly useful type is a fibre optic system. These usually consist of a power supply containing the light source, and one, two or three lengths of flexible fibre optic tubing. These can be directed very precisely where required. Some of these units have a flash tube incorporated as well, used for freezing the movement of minute subjects such as small pond life.

BASIC SET UP

Focusing

Focusing is achieved with two controls, a coarse and a fine focus knob. With some high-power objectives, it is possible to push the lens through the microscope slide, so the best technique is to lower the lens towards the slide while looking at it directly, and then coarsely focus by racking the lens back away from the slide while looking through the eyepiece. Once you have a rough focus, use the fine focus to get the best result. It is a good idea to train yourself to keep both eyes open while using a microscope; one looking through the eyepiece, while the other is used for making sketches or notes, for example.

Because focusing is so critical it is possible to focus in the wrong plane, on the surface of the slide rather than the specimen itself.

The Substage Condenser

The substage condenser moves up and down under the specimen and is used to create a cone of light to illuminate the specimen. It contains an aperture (iris diaphragm) for controlling the light.

Microscope Slides

You can buy pre-prepared microscope slides or make them yourself. Most are of a standard size: 1" × 3" (25.4×76.2mm). For plant and other biological material the specimen will need to be sliced very thinly to allow the light to pass through it. A special machine called a microtome can be used for this, though it is expensive.

Specimens are usually covered with a cover slip, a very thin piece of glass that will protect the specimen. The thickness of the cover slip is important, most are 0.17mm, and the appropriate thickness may be marked on the objective lens. When using high magnifications it is important to make sure slides are scrupulously clean and free from dust particles,

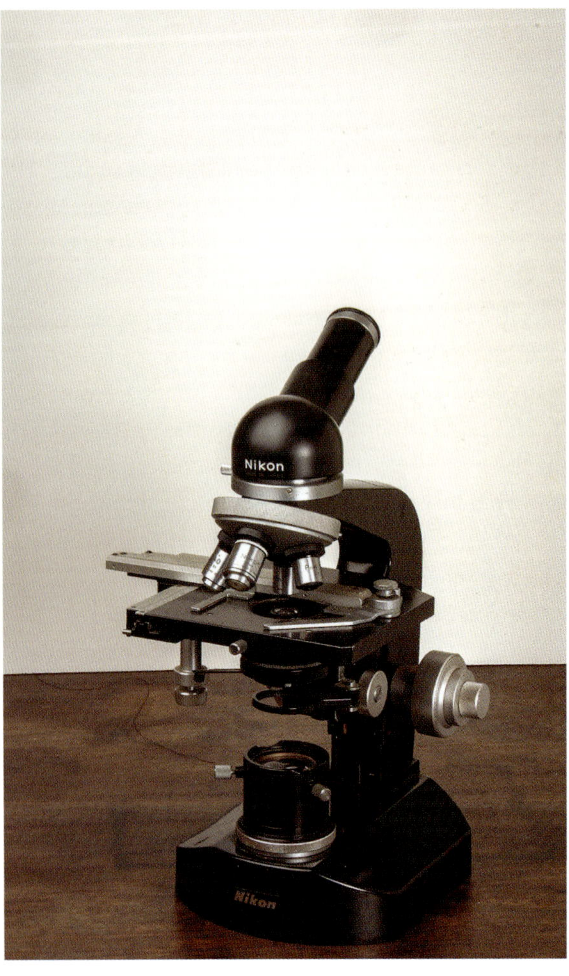

▲ Fig. 8.22
An old Nikon compound microscope with monocular eyepiece. Note the moveable stage, the turret with several objective lenses, and the substage condenser containing an integral light source.

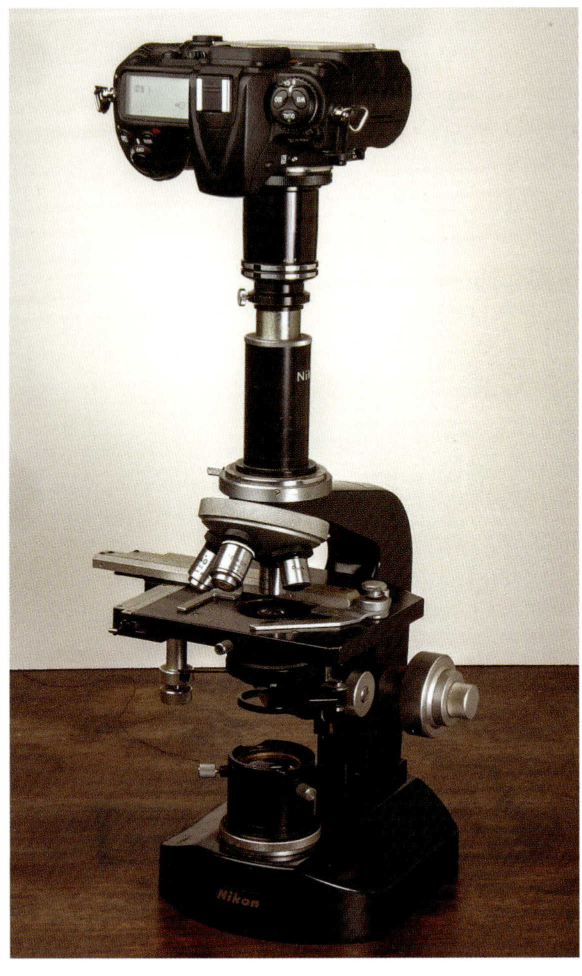

▲ Fig. 8.23
The same microscope with a DSLR camera attached via an adapter. The eyepiece is placed inside the body of the adapter tube. To minimize vibration, use a cable release, mirror lockup, or self-timer mode when releasing the shutter.

which will be magnified by the same amount as the subject itself.

Many specimens are transparent, lacking any colour, making identification of structures within the specimen difficult. Staining techniques are used, primarily for biological subjects, to differentiate different cells. An example is the stain haematoxylin and eosin, used to help show different structures within a brain sample.

You can also get cavity slides that are the same size as conventional slides but have a well or cavity in the centre where you can place a small drop of liquid, when looking at pond life for example. This type is especially prone to movement and vibration.

The microscope slide is mounted onto a stage that usually has controls for moving it in two axes.

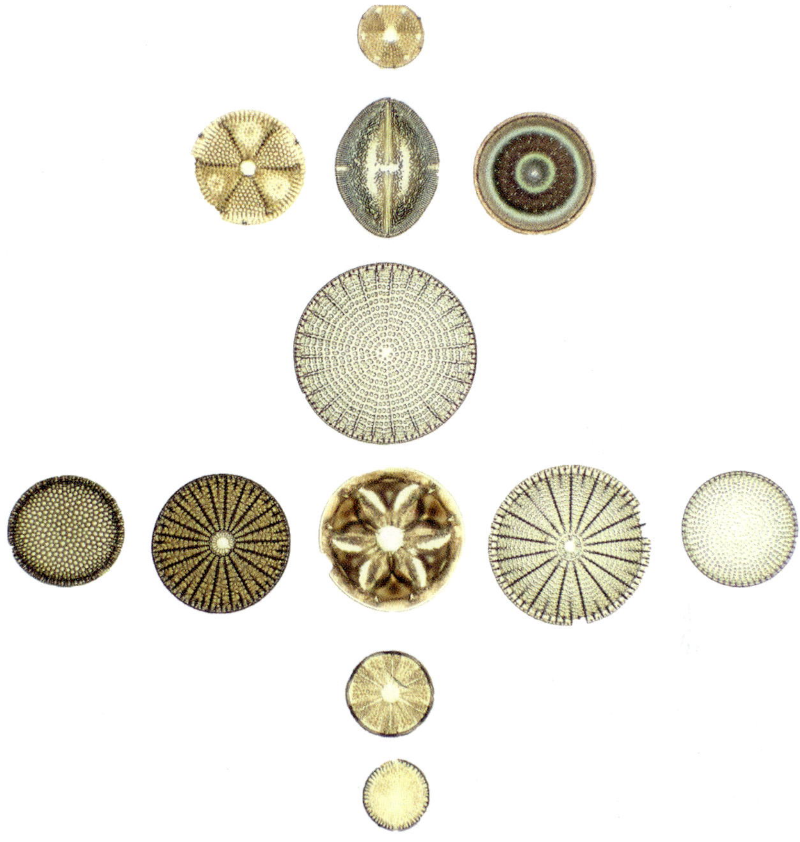

▶ **Fig. 8.24**
Diatoms have been used since Victorian times for testing the resolution of microscopic lenses and for making exquisite image composites. This image is of a slide produced by a Victorian microscopist. Diatoms are single celled algae found living in ponds and because of their intricate nature and fine structure, make good subjects for the testing of equipment. The image shown here was focus stacked from eight images. Magnification approximately ×150.

Photography

With the high magnifications given by the microscope, vibration can become a real issue. If you are photographing a subject at ×100, any movement within the system will be magnified as well. Try to use a solid table for the microscope (some professionals use marble or slate worktops for example), and do not have other equipment on it that may cause vibrations, such as laptops or light sources with internal fans. Use mirror lock-up facility if your camera has one and trigger the camera remotely rather than with a physical release if possible. Some top of the range cameras have an electronic front-curtain shutter facility that can also be used to minimize vibration. Use a low ISO if possible to keep noise to a minimum.

Always focus through the camera, either through the viewfinder or using the Live view facility.

Depth of Field

There is negligible depth of field in microscopy, which is why accurate focusing is so essential. The technique of focus stacking was originally developed for photomicroscopy, using software such as Helicon Focus or Zerene Stacker. Highly sophisticated focusing systems can be found in high-end microscopes, with stepper motors adjusting the focus by minutely small amounts.

It is possible to carry it out manually, moving the fine focus control for each exposure. The image of diatoms was achieved doing that, using a stack of eight images.

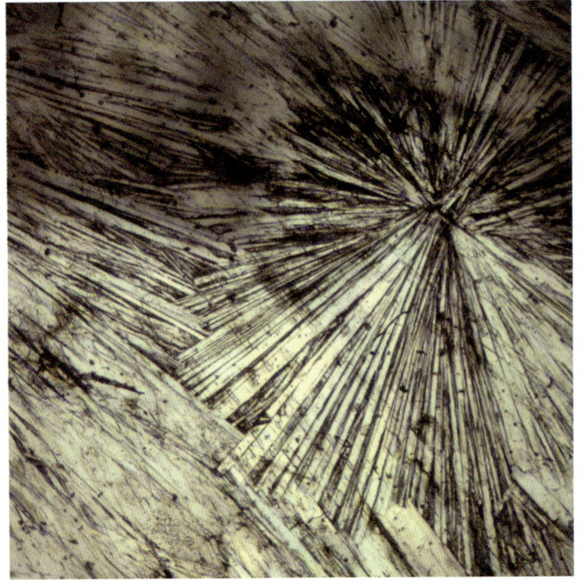

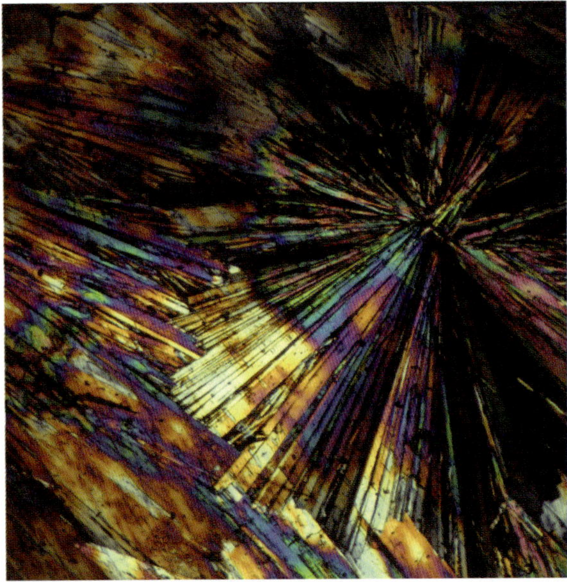

Thiamine (vitamin B1) crystals in normal, brightfield lighting and cross polarized light. Magnification approximately ×20.

Polarized Lighting

As with the polarized light photography discussed Chapter 9, you will need to have a polarizing filter above and underneath the subject. Many microscopes have them built into the system, with a dial-in polarizer in the substage condenser, and another located behind the objective (known as the analyser). Specialist mineralogical microscopes are available where the relative angle of the two filters can be seen, important when identifying minerals.

Other Types of Microscope Lighting

There is a huge variety of other forms of illumination in the field of microscopy, including phase contrast, darkfield, Rheinberg, incident lighting and UV fluorescence. These are used to visualize otherwise invisible features in specimens.

Using a Scanner

One novel way of producing images of relatively large specimens mounted on microscope slides is to scan them, either in a flat bed scanner equipped with a transparency adapter or placing them in a 35mm slide scanner (if physically possible). Use the highest resolution available in the scanner software.

▶ **Fig. 8.27**
Ascorbic acid (vitamin C) crystals in cross polarized light. Magnification approximately ×50.

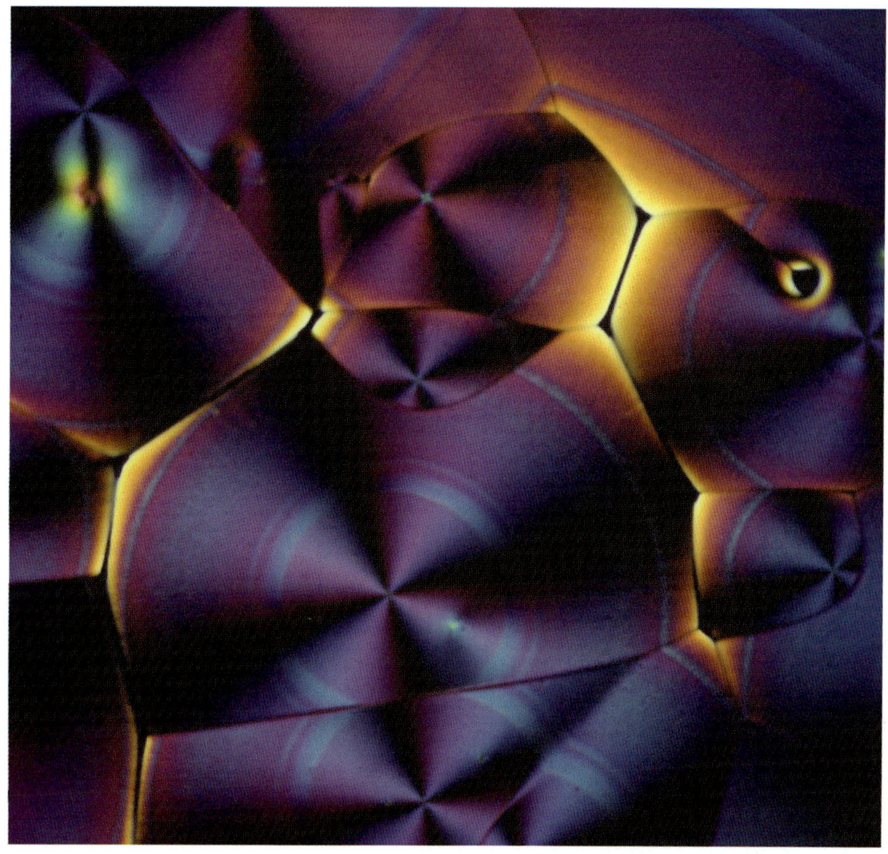

▶ **Fig. 8.28**
A seventy-two hour old chicken embryo scanned on a flatbed scanner fitted with a transparency adapter. The actual specimen is approximately 5mm long.

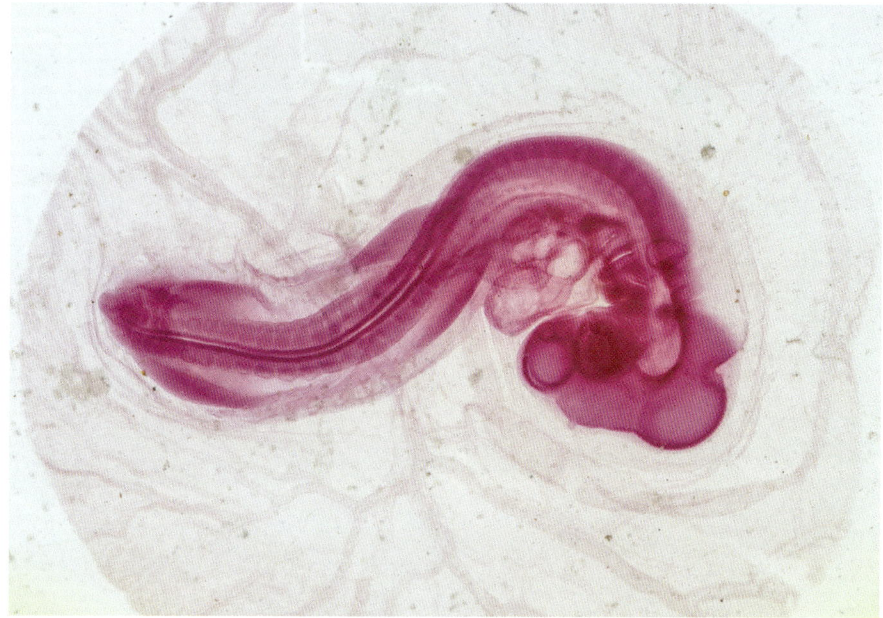

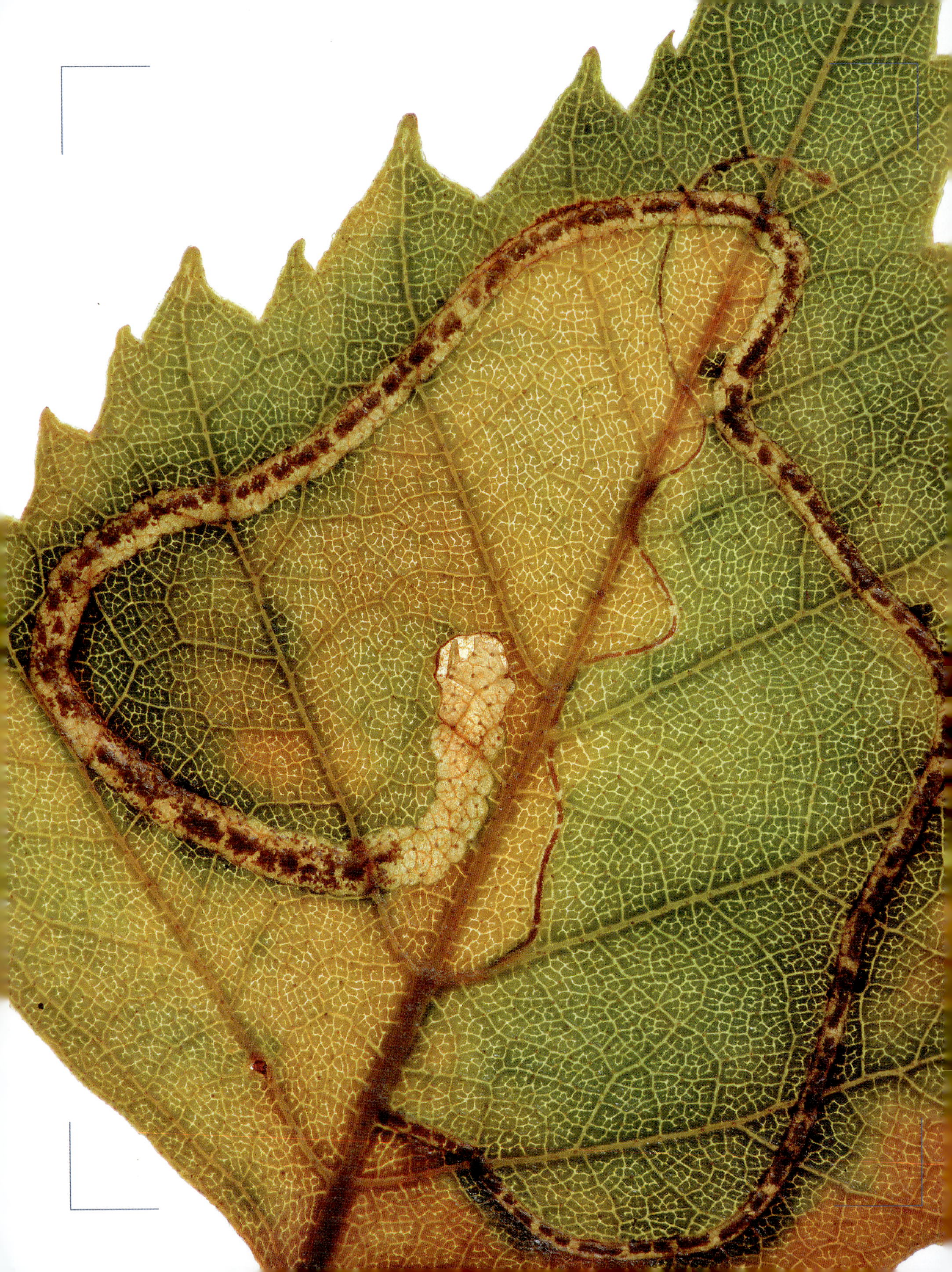

Chapter 9

Polarized Light and Other Visualization Techniques

There are many photographic lighting or filtration techniques that can be used to reveal unseen structures, details or movement, some of which do not fit into neat categories. Many can be used in conjunction with other techniques from the book; for example, dark field lighting can be combined with high speed photography to photograph spore dispersal from puffball fungi. Good lighting is of course key to the success of any image, but here we will look specifically at various techniques for enhancing and revealing otherwise unseen details.

Polarized Light

Many readers will be familiar with the use of polarizing filters in conventional photography. They are used to minimize reflections from shiny surfaces, darken blue skies and increase colour saturation, and as such are used extensively in landscape photography. In the case of minimizing reflections from shiny surfaces, polarizing filters do not work on metallic surfaces, but work well with water, foliage and glass. They are used by technical photographers in museums for photographing artefacts and paintings, and by medical and forensic photographers for recording skin without surface reflections for example. They are especially useful for removing reflections from the surface of lakes, rockpools and other water features for example. Anglers use polarizing glasses to help them see fish underwater.

When light falls on a non-metallic surface such as glass or water, some is absorbed, while the reflected light is said to partly polarized. Some of this polarization can be removed with a polarizing filter. Polarizing filters will only completely remove reflections when used at specific angles to the surface, which will vary according to the substance (technically called Brewster's angle). For glass this angle is 33°, while for water it is 37°. Obviously you will probably not be measuring this precisely when working in the field, but instead viewing the effect through the camera viewfinder, while rotating the filter in front of the lens.

Polarization of Light

Normal visible light is unpolarized – the light rays from the sun vibrate in all directions at right angles to the direction of travel. When unpolarized light passes through a polarizing filter it is restricted to vibrating in one plane. Polarizing filters have a special molecular structure, which restricts the light's rays to one plane, as though passing through parallel railings. The human eye cannot see polarized light (though interestingly some animals can, including many insects and octopuses).

In practice, using a polarizing filter for photography is very easy. They are usually supplied in a rotating mount. Place it on the front of the lens and rotate it, while looking through the viewfinder, until you reach the desired effect. They generally work best at around 90° to the sun. Take care when using them for wide angle landscapes – they can cause a noticeable falloff in light from one side of the image frame to the other, and also can produce rather

◄ Fig. 9.1
Silver Birch leaf with the leaf miner of the Common Birch Pigmy Moth (*Stigmella betulicola)* revealed by backlighting on a light panel.

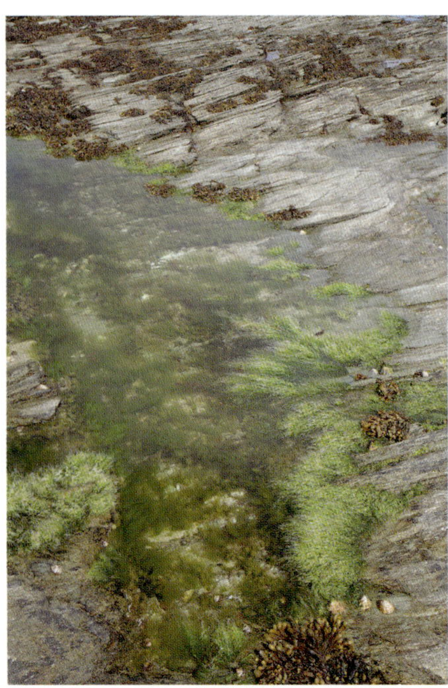
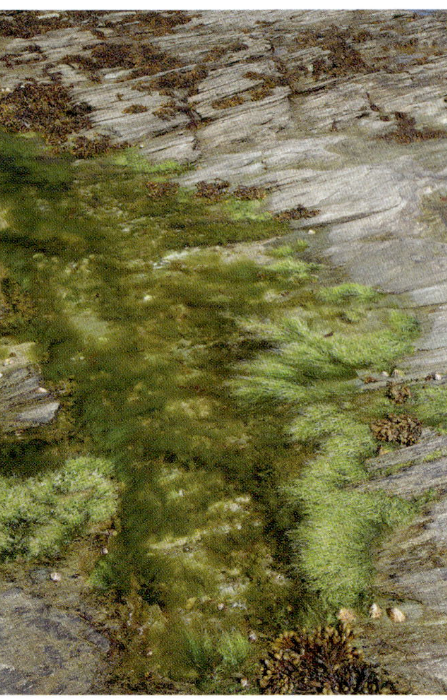

◀ **Fig. 9.2**
Rock pool on a beach with and without a polarizing filter. Note the extra detail visible through the water when the polarizing filter is used, together with an increase in the colour saturation of the seaweed. The angle of the camera to the water was approximately 45°.

Nikon D800 with 16–35mm NIKKOR lens. Left: 1/50th second @ f/11 Right, with polarizing filter: 1/25th second @ f/11.

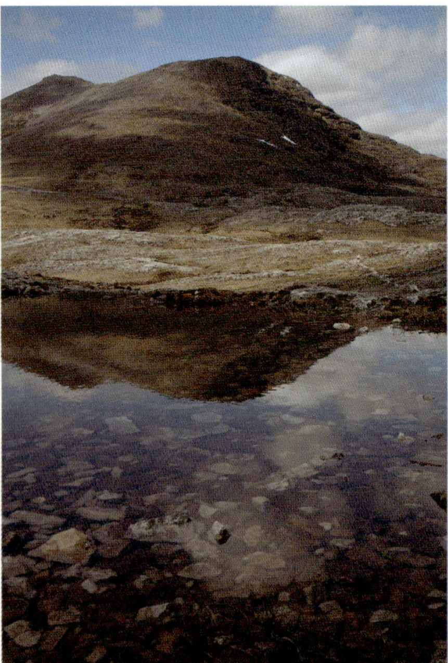
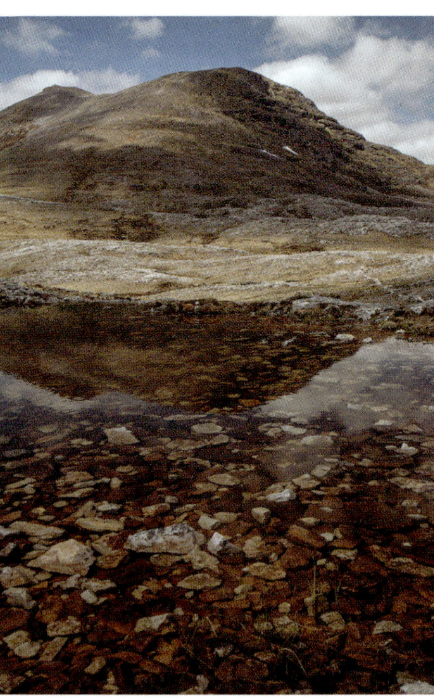

◀ **Fig. 9.3**
View towards Meall a' Ghiubhais, Beinn Eighe National Nature Reserve, Wester Ross, Scotland, with and without a polarizing filter. Note the increased water clarity in the lochan with the polarizing filter, and the darker blue sky.

Nikon D800 with 24–85mm NIKKOR lens. Left: 1/60th second @ f/16. Right, with polarizing filter: 1/30th second @ f/11.

▶ **Fig. 9.4**
Plastic pot in cross polarized light.
   Nikon D800 with 105mm micro-NIKKOR lens, pot placed on polarizing sheet on light panel. 1/8th second @ f/11.

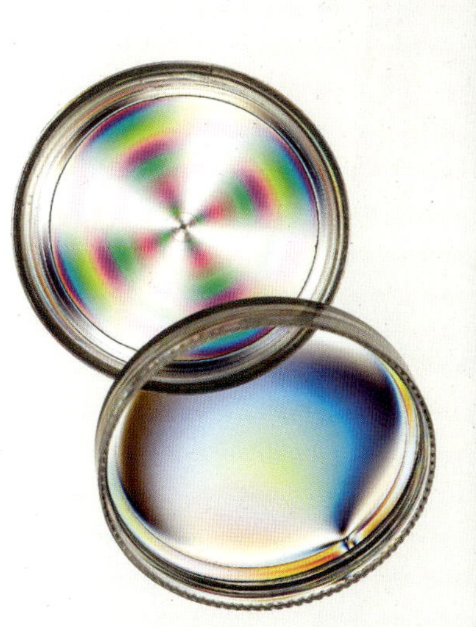
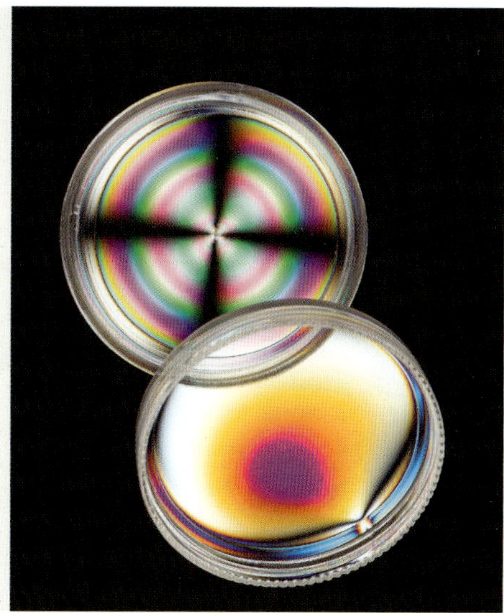

garish blue skies that can make it very apparent that you have used a polarizer. Watch the scene carefully through the viewfinder as you rotate the filter.

Even without the inclusion of areas of sky in the image, polarizing filters can be very effective for saturating colours in foliage for example, by removing reflections from shiny surfaces and thus allowing more colour to come through. Again, use with caution – removing the reflection from a naturally shiny leaf can make it look flat and unnatural.

Circular and Linear Polarizing Filters

There are two types of polarizing filter for cameras, linear and circular. Linear polarizing filters consist of a layer of aligned polymer crystals so that only light waves vibrating in one plane are transmitted, and those at right angles to this plane are absorbed. Older style linear polarizing filters can cause problems with the beam splitter used in the through the lens metering systems in modern cameras, so most polarizers nowadays are of the circular type. Visually, they look the same. Circular polarizing filters are linear filters with a thin layer of suitable material called a quarter-wave plate, which twists the polarized light as the filter transmits it. They do not affect camera metering systems.

Because polarizing filters are removing some of the rays of light entering the camera, they generally require more exposure, in the region of 1–2 stops depending on the orientation of the filter. The Through The Lens (TTL) metering system in the camera should take this into account, but it is always worth checking the image histogram on the rear of the camera to ensure correct exposure.

It is possible to improvise a neutral density filter by using two polarizing filters on the front of a lens and rotating them in relation to each other to absorb varying amounts of light. Theoretically, when they are at right angles to each other, there should be no transmission at all, but polarizing filters are rarely perfect, so will, in all likelihood, transmit some light.

PHOTOGRAPHY OF STRESS PATTERNS

Some transparent substances have the characteristic of being birefringent, in that an incident beam of natural, unpolarized light is split by double refraction into two types of ray, ordinary and extraordinary. The two rays are plane polarized orthogonally to

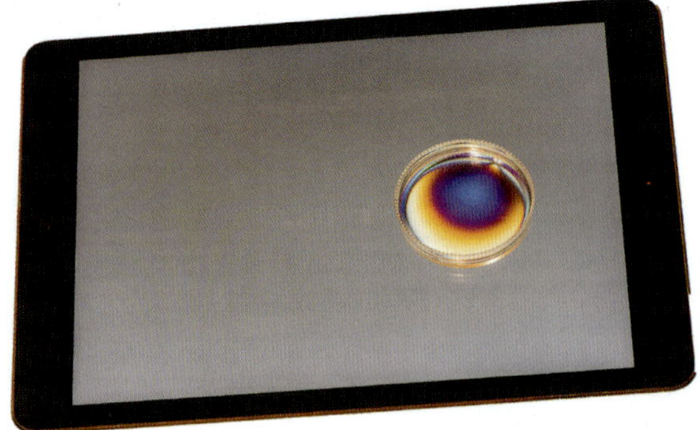

▲ Fig. 9.5
Tablet PC being used as a polarizing filter.

each other. In the right material, the extraordinary and ordinary rays travel at different speed through the crystal. Polarizing filters are made by using crystals orientated in one direction to absorb one ray, while the other emerges plane polarized.

Using polarizing material, polarized light techniques can be used to reveal previously invisible stress patterns in some birefringent plastic materials, minerals, crystals and ice for example. The basic idea is to position the transparent or translucent specimen between two polarizing filters and rotate one of the filters in relation to the other.

You will need a sheet of polarizing material (see resources at the end for sources – a good size is around A4) to go underneath the subject, which is placed on top of a light box or light panel, and then another polarizing filter is placed on the front of the lens. Lightboxes containing fluorescent tubes are largely redundant nowadays and have been largely replaced by LED light panels.

Place the sheet of polarizing film on the lightbox, then a suitable subject. Take care, the delicate polarizing film scratches easily. Good subjects are CD cases, plastic rulers and protractors, transparent plastic cutlery, cellophane wrapping, Sellotape® and also detergent bubbles and ice crystals. Mount the

camera overhead and rotate the polarizing filter on the lens while looking through the viewfinder. If you have a good specimen a whole rainbow of colours should appear, against a dark background. Probably the best colours and patterns are revealed when the filters are at right angles to each other, producing a near black background. In the case of plastic, the stress caused by the manufacturing process is revealed, and the technique was used by engineers for predicting stress in buildings and bridges. Scale model cross sections of bridges for example, were made from suitable plastic materials, weights hung from various points to simulate loading, and photographed between polarizing filters to show potential stress points. The technique was called Photo-Elastic Stress Analysis.

The exposure meter in the camera should give a reasonably accurate reading, but some exposure compensation may be required due to the black background. Use the histogram and highlights flashing facility to check exposure.

Photographing with Light Panels

When photographing subjects on a light panel (either using polarizing techniques or just as a backlight) there is the potential for flare from the bright area of the panel outside the field of view of the lens. This will have the effect of reducing contrast within the image. Lay strips of black card around the subject just out of view of the camera lens or make a window of a suitable size in a piece of black card to place over the specimen so that no extraneous light enters the lens (acting rather like the sun visor in a car).

As an alternative to a light box, try using an electronic flashgun with a sheet of white Perspex® suspended over the front of it. To ensure even coverage position the flashgun around 30cm or so from the Perspex®.

When buying a light panel, most of which are LED-based nowadays, choose one that has a colour temperature of 5,500K, matching average daylight.

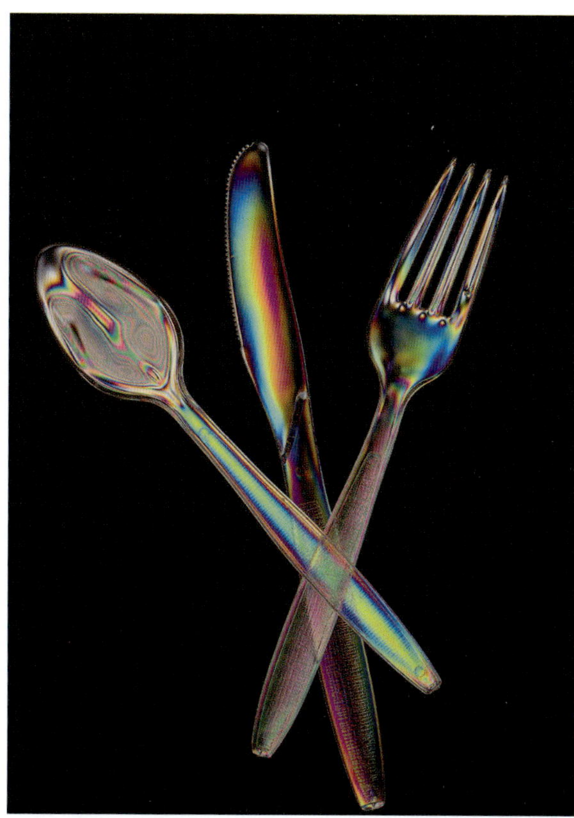

▲ **Fig. 9.6, 9.7, 9.8**
Various plastic objects in cross polarized light: plastic cutlery, plastic
ice cream spoons, plastic syringe.

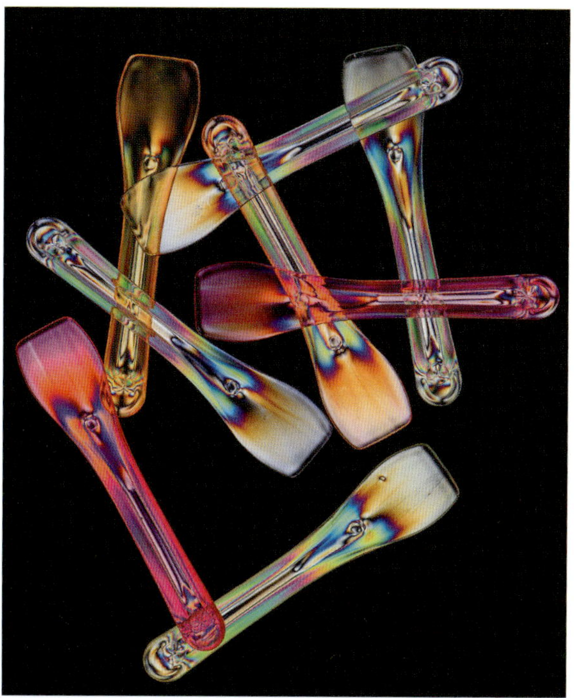

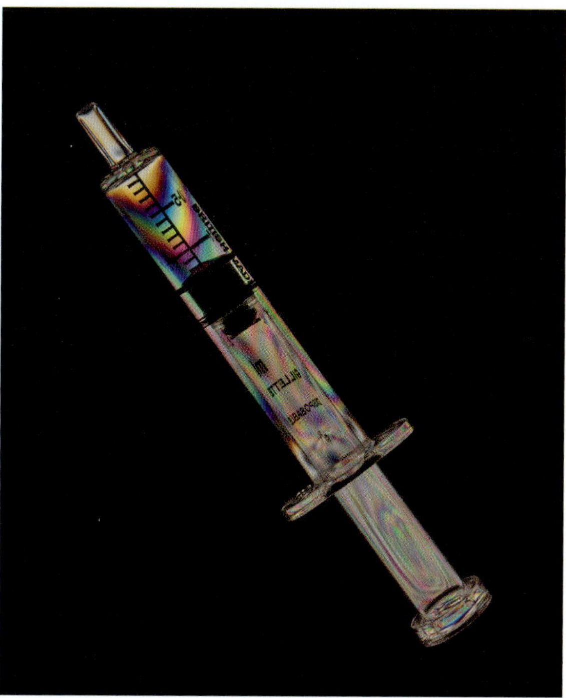

Using a Laptop or Tablet PC Screen

It is also possible to successfully use a laptop screen
or tablet PC screen as an alternative to the light box
and sheet of polarizing material. You will need to
set the screen to a pure white tone. Several apps are
available to do that including the free Color Screen,
available for Mac and PC devices. Alternatively, you
can create a pure white image in Photoshop® or
similar program. In Photoshop® create a new image
(**File > New**) at a size to fill the screen e.g. 1680 × 1050
at 72ppi. This should be a pure white, but to be sure,
fill the new image (**Edit > Fill**) with white. If there is
an adjustment for brightness for the screen, increase
this to maximum for the photography.

Lay the tablet flat or position the laptop screen

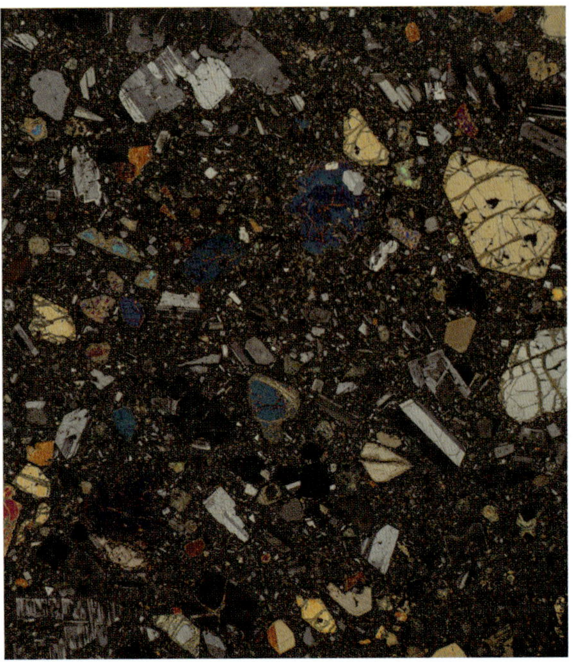

▲ **Fig. 9.9**
Thin section of the rock olivine basalt on a microscope slide.
　Nikon D800 with El-NIKKOR 80mm lens on Nikon bellows unit.
Slide on polarizing sheet on light panel.

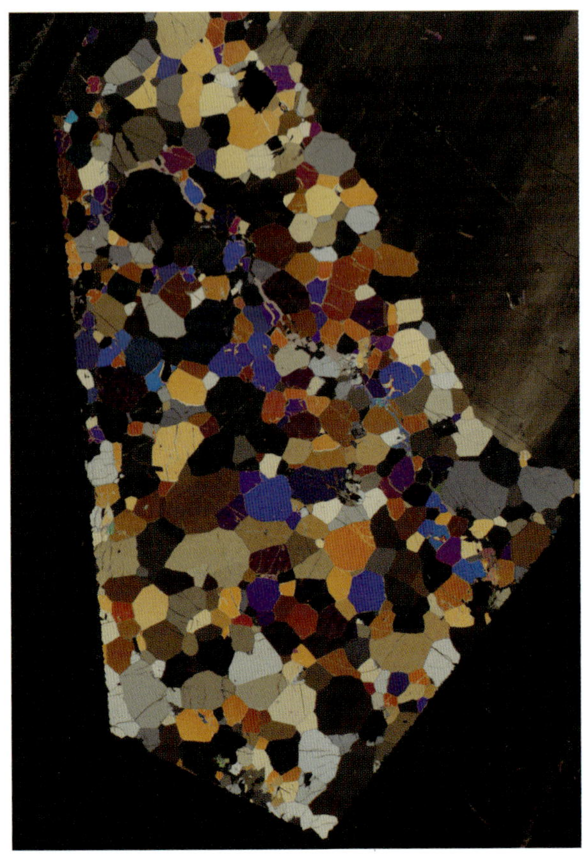

▲ **Fig. 9.10**
Peridotite thin section.
　Nikon D800 with El-NIKKOR 80mm lens on Nikon bellows unit.
Slide on polarizing sheet on light panel.

in a horizontal position. It may be worth placing a sheet of transparent plastic on top of the screen to protect it (and certainly do not place heavy objects on to it), though be careful that this does not interfere with the colours generated by the subject. Position the camera above the screen, with a polarizer over the lens.

The brightness of a tablet screen will probably not be as great as a good laptop screen.

OTHER APPLICATIONS

Cross polarization techniques are also used extensively by microscopists looking at mineral sections and crystals under a microscope, often to aid their identification.

Vitamins, minerals and many other chemicals can work well when seen through cross polarized light, often producing a dazzling array of shapes and colours. Good subjects to try are Vitamin C, Thiamine, Tartaric Acid and Epsom Salts (Magnesium Sulphate: $MgSO_4$). To prepare a suitable specimen of Epsom Salts for example, dissolve some crystals in a small amount of warm water. You are aiming for a saturated solution. If the powder dissolves easily, add more, stirring until this has dissolved. When you get to the point of having a small amount of solid left, add another very small amount of warm water to dissolve the remaining residue. Then, take a microscope slide or piece of thin glass, (a larger one is best e.g. $38 \times 75mm$) and drop a small amount of the liquid onto it.

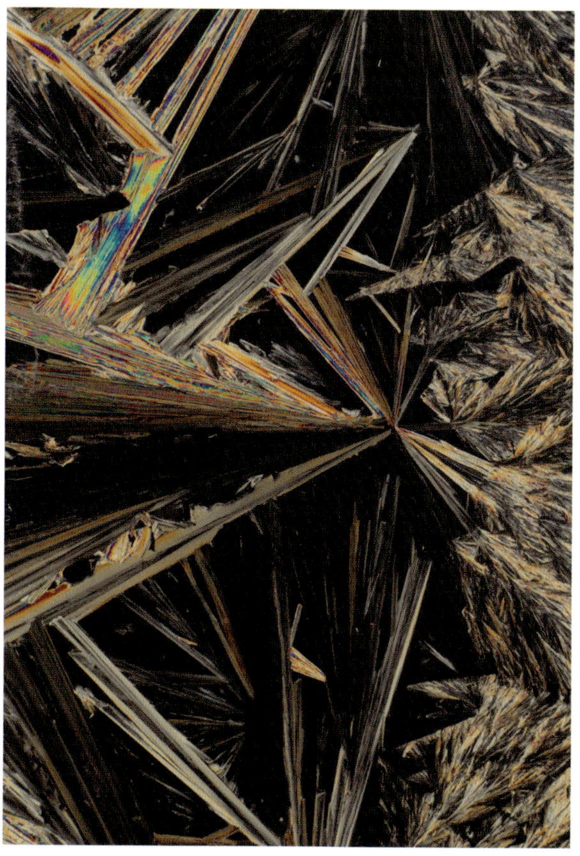

▲ **Fig. 9.11**
Crystals of Epsom Salts.
   Nikon D800 with El-NIKKOR 80mm lens on Nikon bellows unit.
Slide on polarizing sheet on light panel.

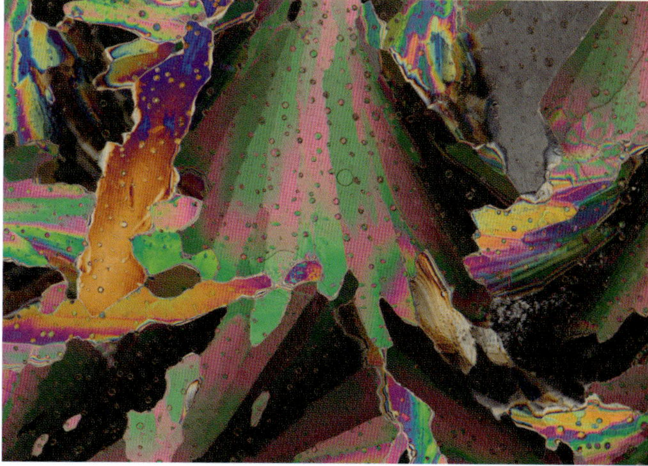

▲ **Fig. 9.12**
Ice crystals seen in polarized light. Water was smeared on a large microscope slide (38 × 75mm) and placed in a freezer overnight. The frozen plate was placed on a sheet of polarizing material on top of a light panel and shot through another polarizing filter on the lens. The lens filter was rotated until the best effect was achieved. The colours changed constantly whilst the polarizing filter was being rotated. A piece of black card with an aperture slightly larger than the specimen was placed on top of it.
   Nikon D800 with 105mm micro NIKKOR lens. 1/10th second @ f/5.6.

You can either place a large drop of liquid on the slide or smear the liquid over the surface of the slide, then leave it in a warm place for the liquid to evaporate. The thickness of the crystal layer does affect the image quality and colours obtained, so it is worthwhile experimenting. Probably too the speed of evaporation will also affect crystal size. When it is completely dry, place it on a sheet of polarizing material, and view it through another polarizing filter, rotating this until you achieve the best visual result. You will need a macro lens, probably at 1:1 or greater to photograph it. Different vitamins and chemicals will have a different crystalline structure.

   For minerals you will need thin sections of rock, cut specially for use under a microscope, though you can use high power macro photography techniques as well, as shown in the examples here. These are available from various microscope suppliers.

ICE

Another good subject for polarization, perhaps surprisingly, are ice crystals. You can smear water over a glass slide and put it in a freezer overnight, or leave a glass slide out in the open on nights when sub zero temperatures are predicted. You will need to work rapidly when photographing the ice crystals as they will melt quickly, particularly when using a relatively warm light panel. The colours and patterns produced by the polarization can be dazzling.

Oil and Water

Another good subject for polarized light techniques is bubbles made by mixing oil and water. Add a drop of washing up liquid to a shallow bowl of water and stir gently. Leave it for ten minutes or so and then add a few drops of cooking oil. A variety of oil droplets should form on the surface of the water. Position the camera directly overhead, parallel to the water surface for maximum depth of field. You may need to use a long exposure with the polarizing filter, so take great care not to disturb the water during the exposure. But you will probably need to use a high ISO to achieve a fast shutter speed. Use a cable or remote release if possible.

OTHER VISUALIZATION TECHNIQUES

Long Exposures

Digital cameras are remarkable nowadays in their ability to photograph in low light situations, often with outstanding clarity. A sturdy tripod and head will be necessary. If the whole scene is dark, then

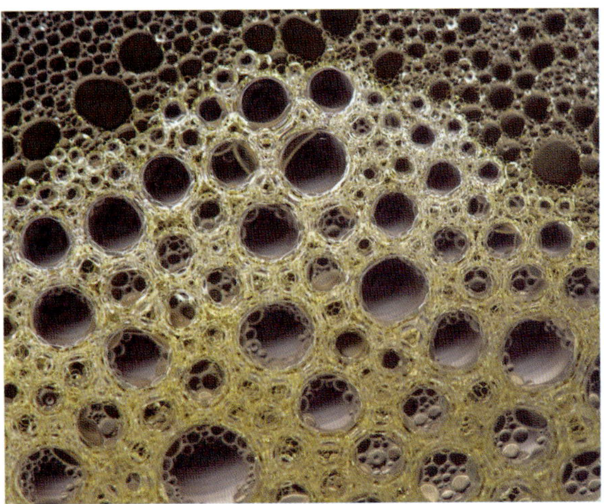

▲ **Fig. 9.13**
Oil and water in cross polarized light.
   Nikon D800 with 105mm micro NIKKOR lens. 1/30th @ f/5.6, 800 ISO.

just giving a long exposure should reveal plenty of detail. In cases such as this cave in Borneo, where the only light came from a circular hole in the ceiling, the subtle use of HDR (as discussed more fully in Chapter 5) has helped reveal detail in all areas of the scene, while retaining the shaft of sunlight. The pile of sticks in the foreground are some of the poles used by local people when harvesting nests from the cave swiftlets for making bird's nest soup.

Adding Light

Just adding light to a subject can reveal previously hidden detail. Many natural subjects, living in dark caves or inside dark holes in tree trunks can only be photographed by the use of extra light, usually electronic flash. The bat shown here was in a very dimly lit room in a wildlife sanctuary, behind glass. No real detail could be seen – the bats could only just be seen as dark shapes. Using the autofocus on the lens and the IR AF Assist illuminator facility on the flash, some surprisingly highly detailed images were obtained of the bats.

It is important not to over-light these subjects, which might give the impression that they were photographed in full daylight. Using one flashgun gives some harsh shadows that maintain the nocturnal, moonlight effect, as well as providing good textural detail on the fur and wings.

Backlighting

Although not strictly an unseen subject, some details on a range of subjects can be greatly enhanced by the use of backlighting (sometimes referred to as contre-jour or rim lighting). Hairs on plant stems, for example, can be improved by shooting against the light, and a dark background. Take care to avoid flare by always using a lens hood and checking that the sun is not shining directly into the lens. Exposure measurement may be tricky, particularly if there is a large area of shadow behind the main subject. If possible, it may be worth taking a spot meter reading

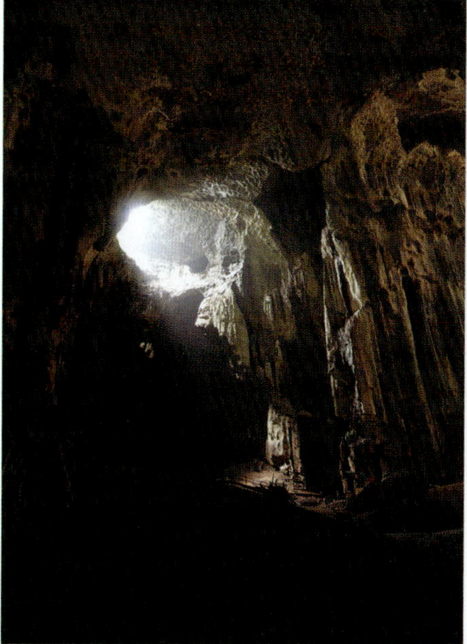
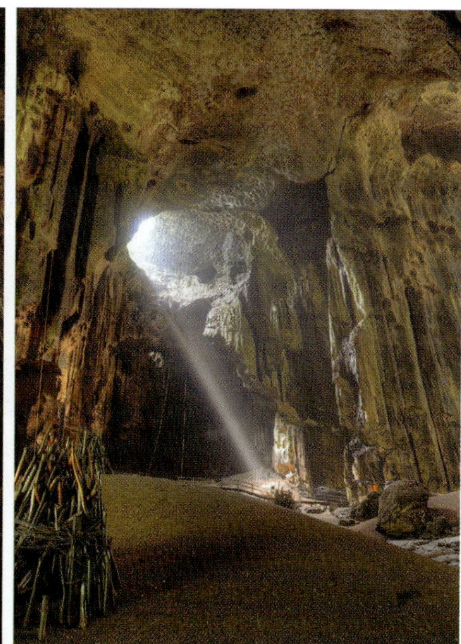

▶ **Fig. 9.14**
The famous Gomantong Cave in Borneo. It is huge, and only lit by a single shaft of light. Three exposures, two stops apart, were blended together using PhotoMatix Pro HDR software to give a much better visualization of the cave interior.

from the light passing through a flower petal, for example. You can also turn away from the subject and take a meter reading from green grass or leaves.

In a studio situation, small flashguns or LED lights can be positioned behind the subject. Try masking them with a cone of black paper to form a snoot to help precise positioning. One particularly useful small LED spotlight is the Jansjo, from IKEA, which is positioned on the end of a flexible gooseneck arm, enabling the precise positioning of the light. The colour temperature of the light emitted from it matches daylight very well.

When using backlighting techniques, it is always worth checking the highlights facility on the rear of the camera, to check that important details in the image are not overexposed. If the main subject is solid, such as a plant stem, it may be worth reflecting some light back into it with a small reflector, small flash or LED light to prevent it becoming black, though sometimes a pure silhouette may be very effective, as shown here.

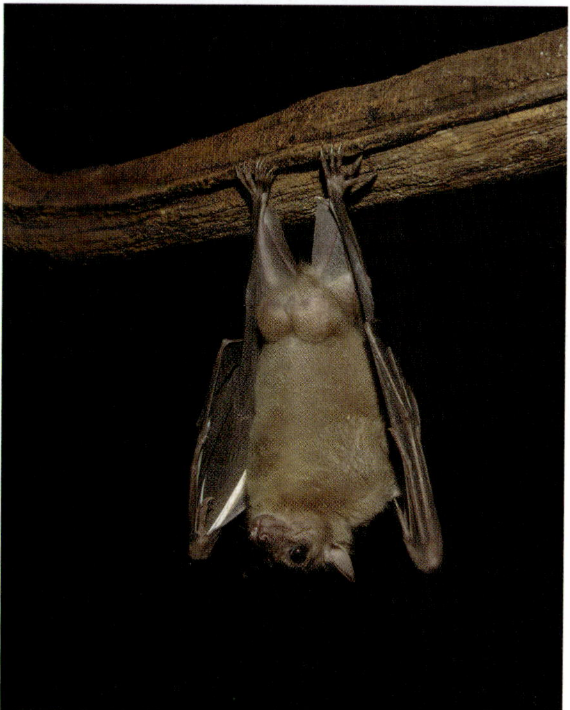

▲ **Fig. 9.15**
This Egyptian Fruit Bat (*Rousettus aegyptiacus*) was housed in a very dark enclosure in a zoo and no detail could be seen. The camera was held close to the glass, set to auto focus, and fitted with a single flash to simulate moonlight.
　　Nikon D810 with 24–210 mm lens at 150mm. SB-900 flash. 800 ISO. 1/125th second @ f/11.

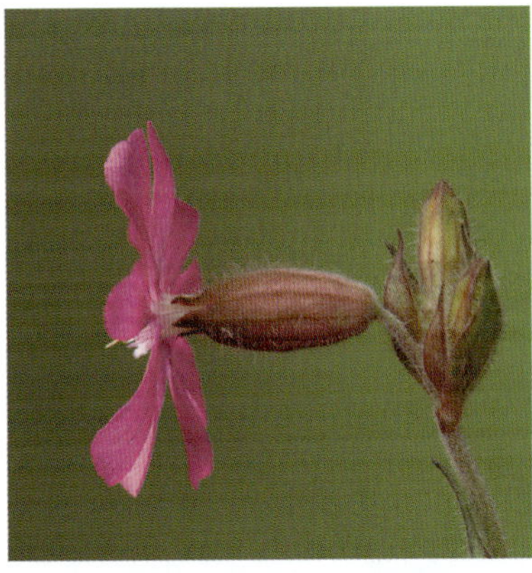

▲ **Fig. 9.16**
Red Campion flower (*Silene dioica*) lit with diffused frontal lighting in front of a pale toned background. Note that the hairs are barely visible.

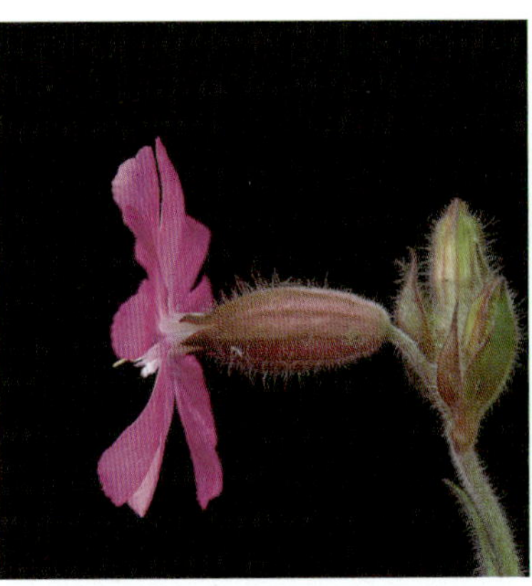

▲ **Fig. 9.17**
The same lighting against a black background.

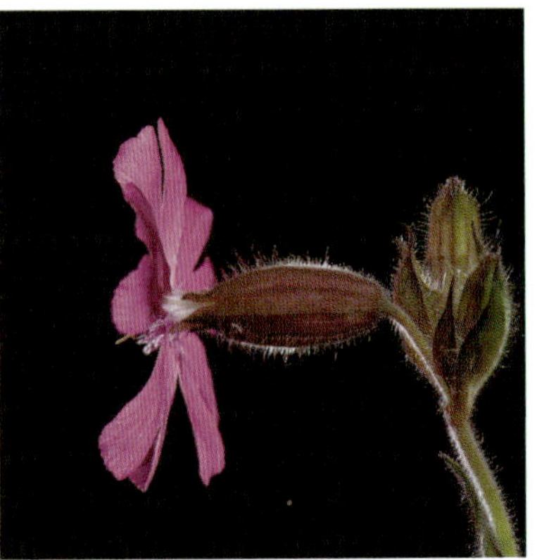

▲ **Fig. 9.18**
Back lighting reveals more of the hairs on the stem and calyx.

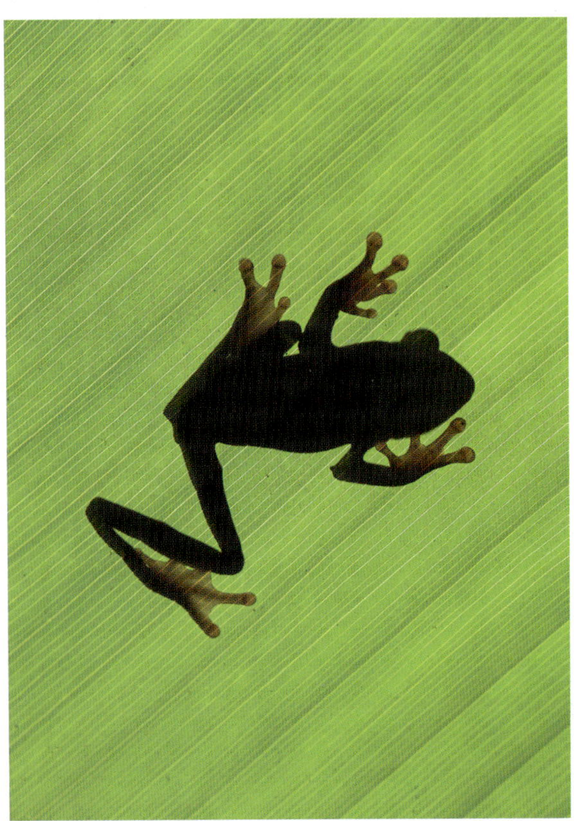

▲ **Fig. 9.19**
Red-Eyed Treefrog (*Agalychnis callidryas*) on the back of a banana leaf in Costa Rica. A single Nikon Speedlight was used to backlight the frog.

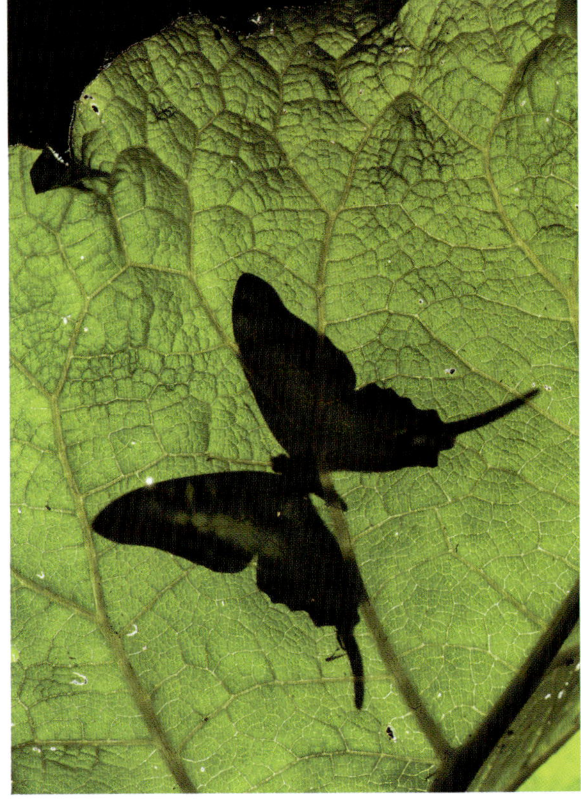

▲ **Fig. 9.20**
A tropical Swallowtail Butterfly (*Graphium polycenes*) silhouetted against a large leaf. The mounted specimen was shot in studio with a single Nikon Speedlight to backlight the leaf.

White Backgrounds

One particular type of backlighting that has become very popular over the last few years is the photography of transparent or translucent subjects against a pure white background. The key to this technique is to achieve a pure white background (that should measure 255, 255, 255 when using the info tool in Photoshop®: **Window > Info**) while retaining detail in the subject. One particular project called *Meet Your Neighbours*, created by Niall Benvie and Clay Bolt, aimed to photograph natural subjects, flowers, insects and the like, against a pure white background in the field. The aim was to '*remove the context, encouraging appreciation of the subject as an individual rather than a species*'.

There are two main methods to achieve the effect. The first is to use a light panel, and place suitable subjects straight on top of it. The second method can be carried out either outdoors in the field, or indoors. The basic idea is to place a sheet of white Perspex® behind the subject that is backlit to achieve a pure white tone. The subject is then lit separately. It is the transparent or translucent subject where previously unseen details can be visualized.

Technique

The technique requires quite a relatively large amount of space, as you need to backlight the Perspex®, and place the subject maybe 25cm in front of it. The lighting from behind must evenly illuminate the Perspex®; this might be achieved with two lights (probably flash) or a single flash with softbox diffuser attached. This can be checked with the highlights facility on the LCD screen on the rear of the camera. The distance from Perspex® to subject will depend on the transparency of the subject and will require some experimentation. Light the subject with soft diffuse light and vary the power of the front lighting to achieve the required effect. Getting the balance of lighting from the white background to the subject will again require some testing.

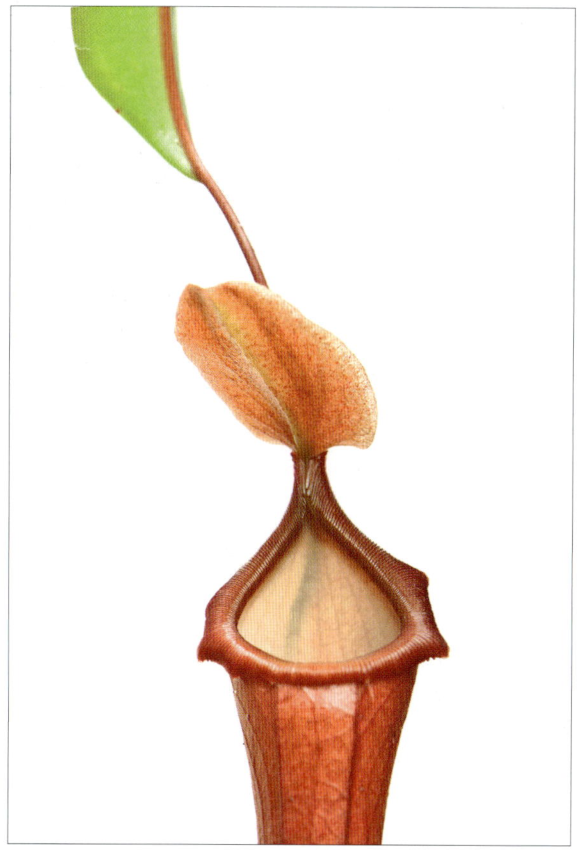

▲ **Fig. 9.21**
The pitcher from a carnivorous plant (*Nepenthes alata*) shot against a pure white background.

Using a Flatbed Scanner

One good way of achieving backlighting of a flat translucent subject such as a leaf is to use a flatbed scanner that has the ability to scan photographic film (sometimes called a transparency adapter). When the scanner is set to transparency mode, light is sent from the lid of the scanner down towards the imaging sensor underneath the subject, passing through it. The subject will need to be flat as the lid of the scanner needs to be closed for this technique. The technique is particularly good for producing images of leaf veins and leaf miners (insect larvae that have burrowed between the top and bottom surfaces of the leaf). Just as with the photography of

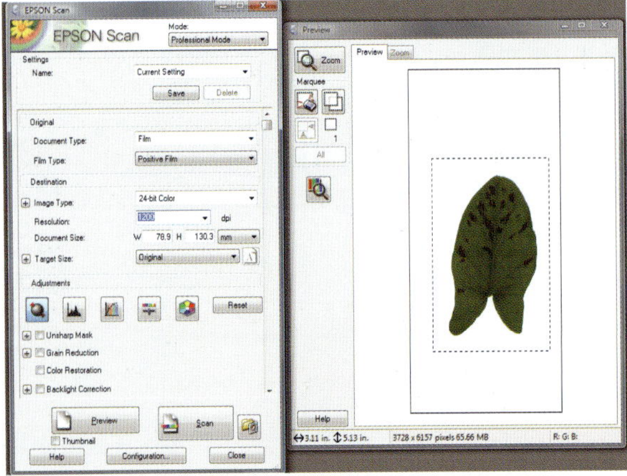

▲ **Fig. 9.22**
Software for Epson Perfection 3200 scanner showing the use of a transparency adapter to backlight flat specimen such as leaves.

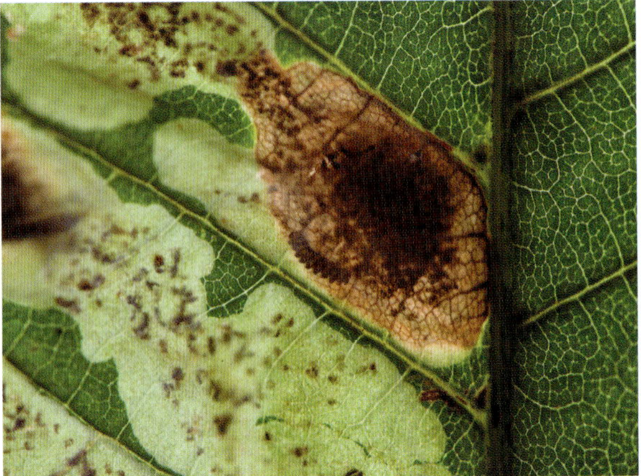

▲ **Fig. 9.23**
A Horse-Chestnut leaf placed in a flatbed scanner with a transparency hood and scanned using transparency mode. Light passes through the translucent leaf, highlighting the mine made by the larva of the horse-chestnut leaf miner moth. One of the larvae can be seen in the image. This was subsequently removed from the leaf and photographed using high power macro techniques and is shown in Chapter 8.

subjects on a light box it is worth masking the area around the subject to prevent glare. Either use strips of black card, or a piece of black card the size of the scanner platen, with a window cut into it just larger than the subject.

Make sure to scan the subject at high resolution, maybe 1200dpi or so, aiming for a file size of around 48Mb, and at 24 bits per channel. Turn off the sharpening facility if the scanner software has it – the image can be sharpened later in an image processing program such as Photoshop®. If the leaf or other subject is naturally curly you may need to tape it to the glass surface to keep it flat for the scan, with non-permanent magic or invisible tape. Take care not to scratch the glass surface.

Window Lighting

Another, simple technique for backlighting translucent subjects such as leaves is to tape the subject to a suitable window and use daylight as the light source. Make sure to clean the window first. You can choose to have the sky as a background (an overcast sky generally works better than a bright blue sky), or out of focus vegetation such as a lawn. Make sure to position the subject at a suitably convenient height that your tripod can reach, enabling you to position the camera parallel to the window surface, ensuring maximum depth of field. Obviously, daylight will vary, both in terms of quality and colour. Like photography of similar subjects on light panels, use a piece of black card with a suitably sized aperture, just slightly larger than the area to be photographed, to minimize flare.

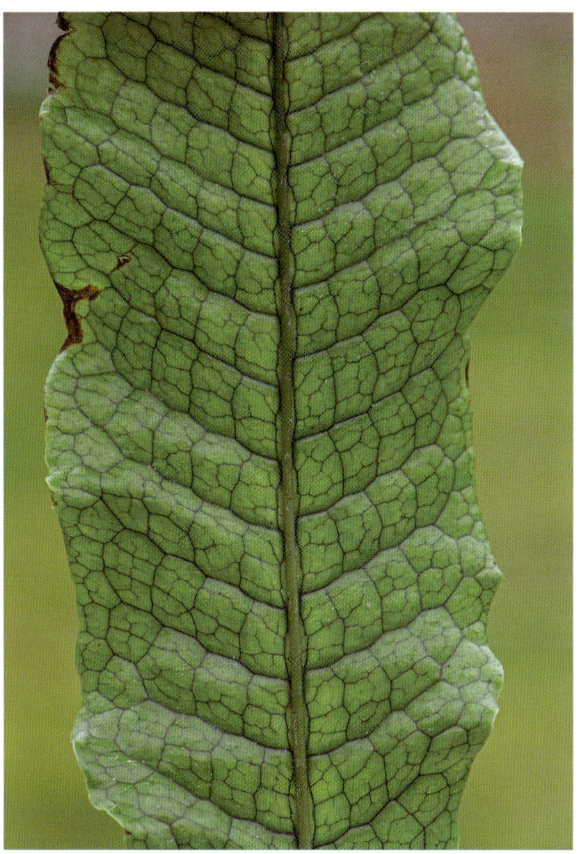

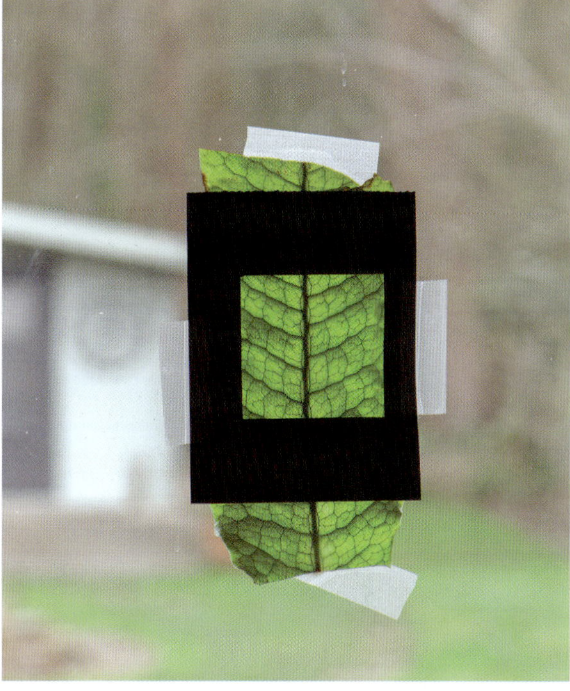

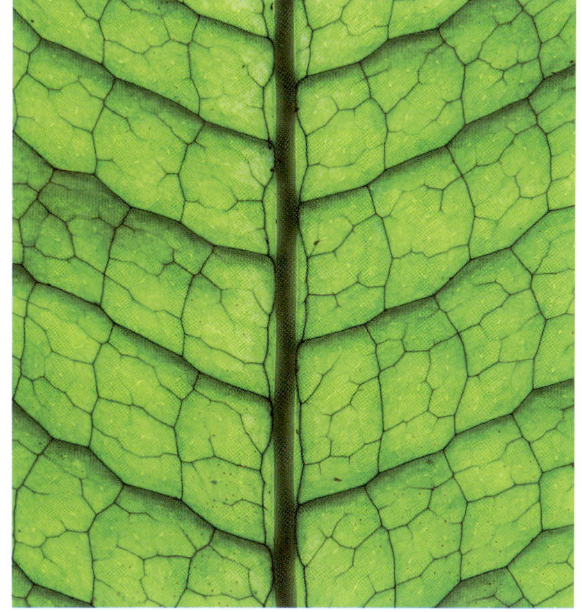

▲▶ Fig. 9.24, 9.25, 9.26
A frond from a Crocodile Fern (*Microsorum musifolium*) photographed in normal daylight. It was then taped to a window and shot using backlighting, revealing the intricate vein structure.

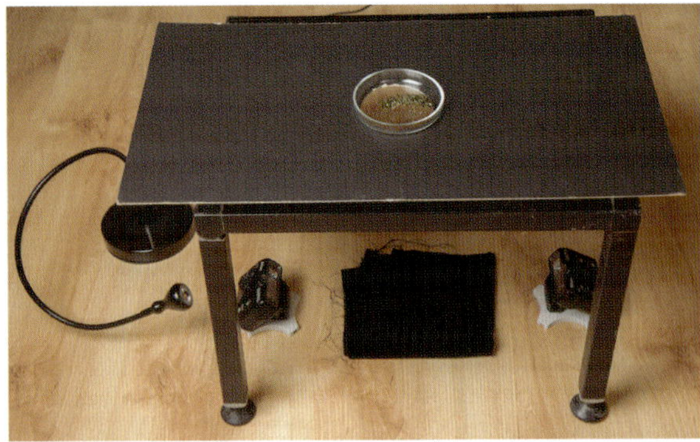

▲ **Fig. 9.27**
A simple setup for darkfield lighting, with two small flashguns underneath the specimen at such an angle that only light refracted by the specimen enters the camera. The IKEA® LED lamp shown is used for focusing. Note the black velvet material underneath the specimen.

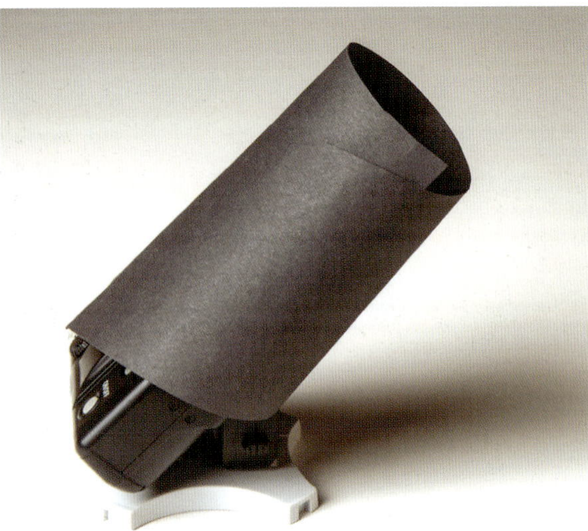

▲ **Fig. 9.28**
A simple snoot constructed for a small flashgun made from thick black paper.

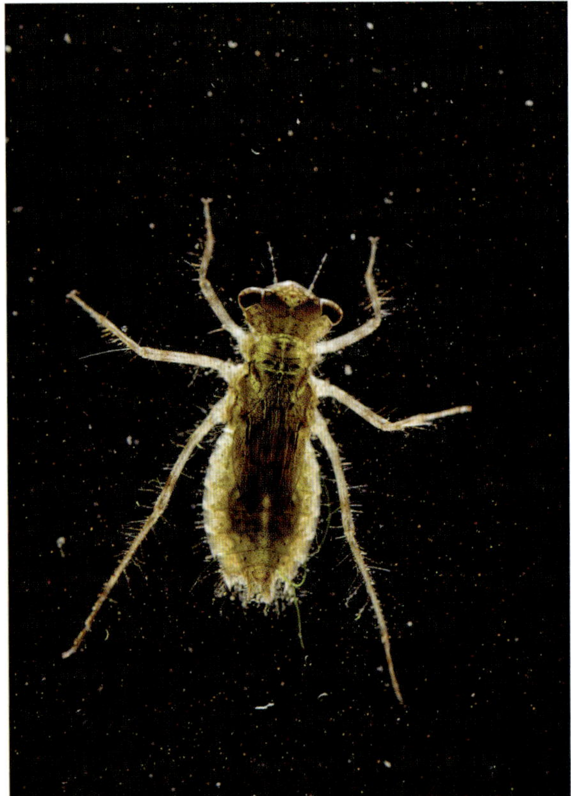

▲ **Fig. 9.29**
Dragonfly larva (*Libellula sp.*) with darkfield lighting. Note the fine hairs made visible but also the debris in the water, which was filtered. This could be retouched in Photoshop® if appropriate.
Nikon D800 with 60mm micro NIKKOR at 1:1 magnification. Two Nikon SB-R200 flashguns from underneath. 1/160th second @ f/16.

Darkfield Lighting

Darkfield lighting is a sophisticated form of back-lighting. It does have certain characteristics though and requires carefully positioned lighting. Darkfield images are characterized by a black background and a transparent or translucent specimen. The resulting image is composed of just the light that has passed through the subject, which appears almost to glow against a pure black background. The technique works well for small aquatic invertebrate creatures such as mayfly and dragonfly larvae, where the internal organs can often be seen, as well as some plants such as the carnivorous Aldrovanda shown here. Shallow glass or plastic petri dishes make good containers for the photography, though check for marks and scratches on the base of the dish. Some will have manufacturing moulding marks, making them unsuitable for the technique.

Welfare Note

When working with small aquatic creatures make sure to keep them in a small tank with water at room temperature before the photographic session to

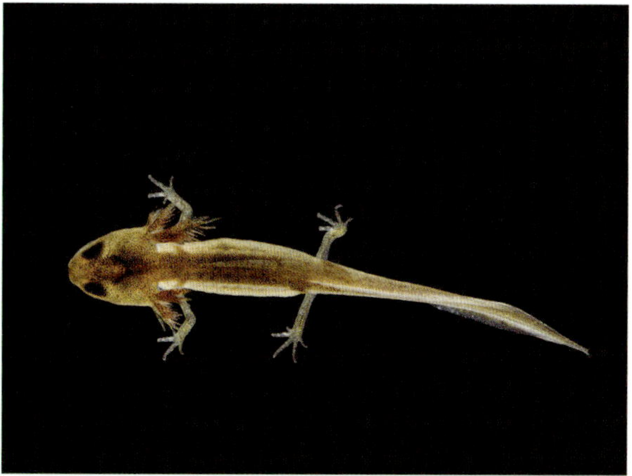

▲ **Fig. 9.30**
An immature Common or Smooth Newt (*Lissotriton vulgaris*) shot with the same set up as Fig. 9.29, with the water debris retouched out using the spot healing brush in Photoshop®. The result is a much starker image. Note the partly translucent body.

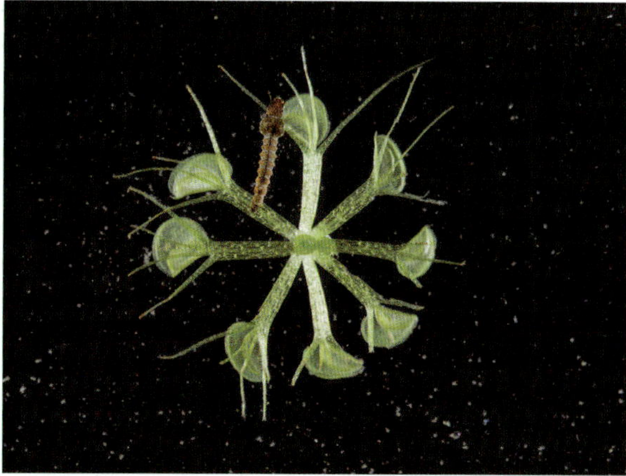

▲ **Fig. 9.31**
An aquatic carnivorous plant (*Aldrovanda vesiculosa*), shot using dark field lighting. The specimen was approximately 25mm in diameter. Set up as for Fig. 9.29.

avoid the stress of sudden temperature change, and take great care when transferring them from the tank to the cell where they will be photographed, possibly using a teaspoon. The temperature of a small quantity of water in a dish will rise quickly, so do not keep the subjects in the dish for too long.

Light is shone through the subject at such an angle (around 45°) that if the subject were not present no light would enter the camera. Only light deflected by the subject is thus seen in the camera viewfinder. It is probably best to use two lights to achieve even lighting, such as two small electronic flashguns. It is a good idea to make cardboard snoots to fit over the flash heads to direct the light onto the subject and prevent light spillage.

The technique does have the disadvantage of picking up the slightest piece of debris in the water, even if you have filtered it. This debris can either be left in the image, giving a semblance of a natural environment, or retouched out.

Some of the images of pollen and spores shown in the chapter on high speed photography were effectively shot with darkfield lighting.

USING A RING FLASH FOR DARKFIELD LIGHTING

Another way of achieving the required setup for darkfield lighting is to use a ring flash (or ring light), placed upside down underneath the subject. A ring flash is a circular electronic flash unit that is usually placed around a lens to provide even lighting of subjects. They were originally designed for medical and dental photographers trying to achieve good, even lighting of body cavities. They have generally fallen out of favour with close-up and macro photographers, but many units are still available (including those using LEDs) cheaply online. Larger units are sometimes used by fashion photographers to achieve totally even lighting of models.

Place the ring flash horizontally, underneath the subject, and place a piece of black card or velvet in the centre of it. You will need to experiment with the height of the unit underneath the subject, and to see if the ring needs to be masked in some way to prevent light spillage.

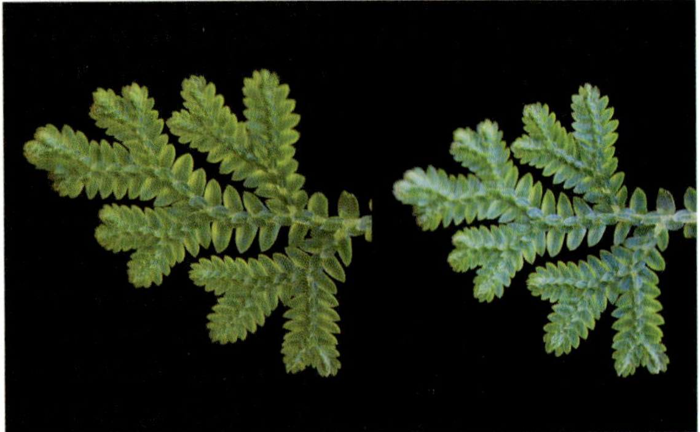

▲ **Fig. 9.32**
Peacock Moss (*Selaginella uncinata*), photographed at two different angles to show iridescence. Shot in diffuse daylight.
 Nikon D800 with 105mm micro NIKKOR lens. 1/60th second @ f/11.

IRIDESCENCE

Iridescence can be defined as a lustrous, rainbow-like display of colour that tends to change with the angle of view. Iridescence is not invisible, and photographing it is not strictly a new technique, but a few words on its photography might be useful. Iridescence is seen in insects such as butterflies and beetles (for example the tropical blue morpho butterfly and Madagascan sunset moth), some plastics, CDs, soap bubbles, an oil and water mix, and various other materials. A few plants also exhibit iridescence, such as the Peacock Mosses (*Selaginella uncinata and S. willdenowii*), some Begonia species and some Blueberries such as Rudraksha (*Elaeocarpus angustifolius*).

Iridescence is where different colours are reflected from a subject when it is placed at different angles to the light source. The colours we see are called structural colours (as opposed to those colours that are produced by chemical pigments such as chlorophyll that makes plants appear green).

The reasons for iridescence are complex but are based around the fact that light travels in waves. If two waves are out of synchronization – that is, the crest of one wave meets the trough of another wave – then they cancel each other out (a

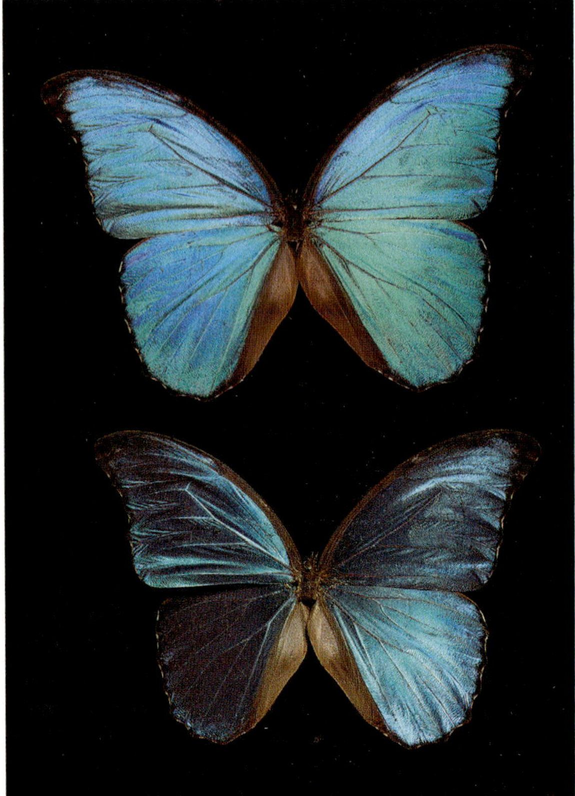

▲ **Fig. 9.33**
A Blue Morpho Butterfly (*Morpho peleides*) photographed at two different angles to illustrate iridescence. The butterfly was a pinned museum specimen, and the pin was mounted in a block of polystyrene through a piece of black velvet, at two different angles for the photography. It was photographed in diffuse daylight on a windless day.
 Nikon D800 with 105mm micro NIKKOR lens. 1/60th second @ f/11.

phenomenon known as destructive interference). But if the crests and troughs of the waves line up (or have the same phase) then they amplify each other. This so-called constructive interference is what causes iridescence.

To understand how light waves interfere with each other, we need to look at the surface of an object on a microscopic level. A soap bubble, for instance, is a very thin sheet of water sandwiched between two layers of soap molecules, which form the outer and inner surfaces. As light passes through the outer surface, some of it is reflected back, while some penetrates to the deeper inner surface where, again, it is reflected back. Depending on the extra distance that the second wave travels before rejoining the first, the two waves will either amplify or cancel each other out. If the extra distance matches a specific wavelength of light then constructive reinforcement can occur. But if the distance is the equivalent of half a wavelength, then destructive cancellation occurs instead. Because white light is made up of all the colours of the rainbow, the reinforcement of some hues and the suppression of others create a rainbow-like optical effect, with different wavelengths of light producing different colours. What's more, the colours change because light strikes the bubble at different points and from different angles, altering the distances between the externally and internally reflected waves.

The interference-based colours seen in a soap bubble are produced by a single thin film. But the surface structures of most biological organisms are typically far more complex. The more surface layers an object has, the more chances there are for the reflections to magnify each other, and the more pronounced the iridescence will be. Such structures are called multilayer reflectors.

Photography is relatively simple, though lighting should be carefully considered – sometimes shooting the subject in diffuse daylight works well.

To illustrate iridescence in a subject, it is worth shooting it from two or more different angles to show the change in colour from the two viewpoints, either by tilting the subject or camera. If you have a mounted butterfly push the mounting pin into a cork or piece of polystyrene at different angles, and sit this underneath a piece of black velvet for example. Make sure to keep the lighting the same for the two images.

Soap Bubbles

One of the most attractive forms of iridescence for photography is that seen in soap bubbles. The surface is a constantly changing kaleidoscope of colour, which makes exciting images. Photography

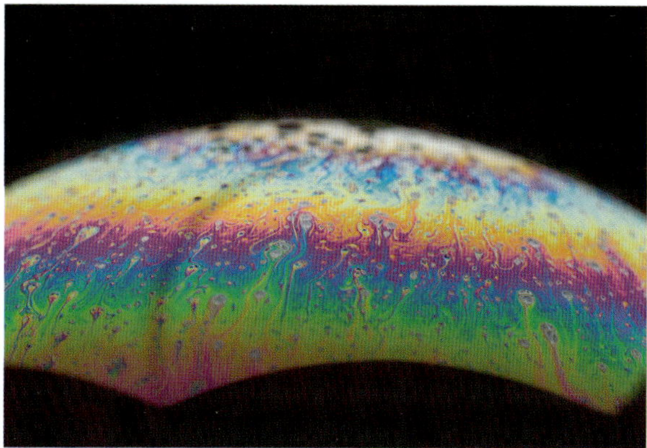

▲ **Fig. 9.34**
Part of a large soap bubble showing beautiful iridescent patterns. Nikon D800 with 105mm micro NIKKOR lens. Single diffused flash, 1/60th second @ f/16.

is relatively simple – probably the most difficult area is creating a large soap bubble that will persist long enough to enable an image to be made.

The internet has a host of recipes and suggestions for creating soap bubbles. For the image shown here, washing up liquid was used, mixed with a small amount of glycerine to give a stronger surface tension to the bubble. As a starter, try a mixture of water and washing liquid in the ratio of 3:1, and then add a teaspoon of glycerine, stirring gently without creating a froth. You may need to experiment in order to get large and persistent bubbles.

Place a small amount of the liquid into a shallow depression, in something like an upturned cup or saucer. Place a straw in the liquid and blow gently until a bubble appears. This may take some practice. If you blow harder, or the straw is partially out of the liquid, a mass of bubbles may be formed, which may also make interesting images. You can also try getting a soap film in a wire loop, and backlighting that through a sheet of white Perspex®.

For the photography, use a black background. A camera with a macro lens will enable you to focus on a small area of the bubble. Lighting can be achieved with a small speedlight, diffused with a softbox, held directly above and close to the bubble to achieve an even light across the bubble.

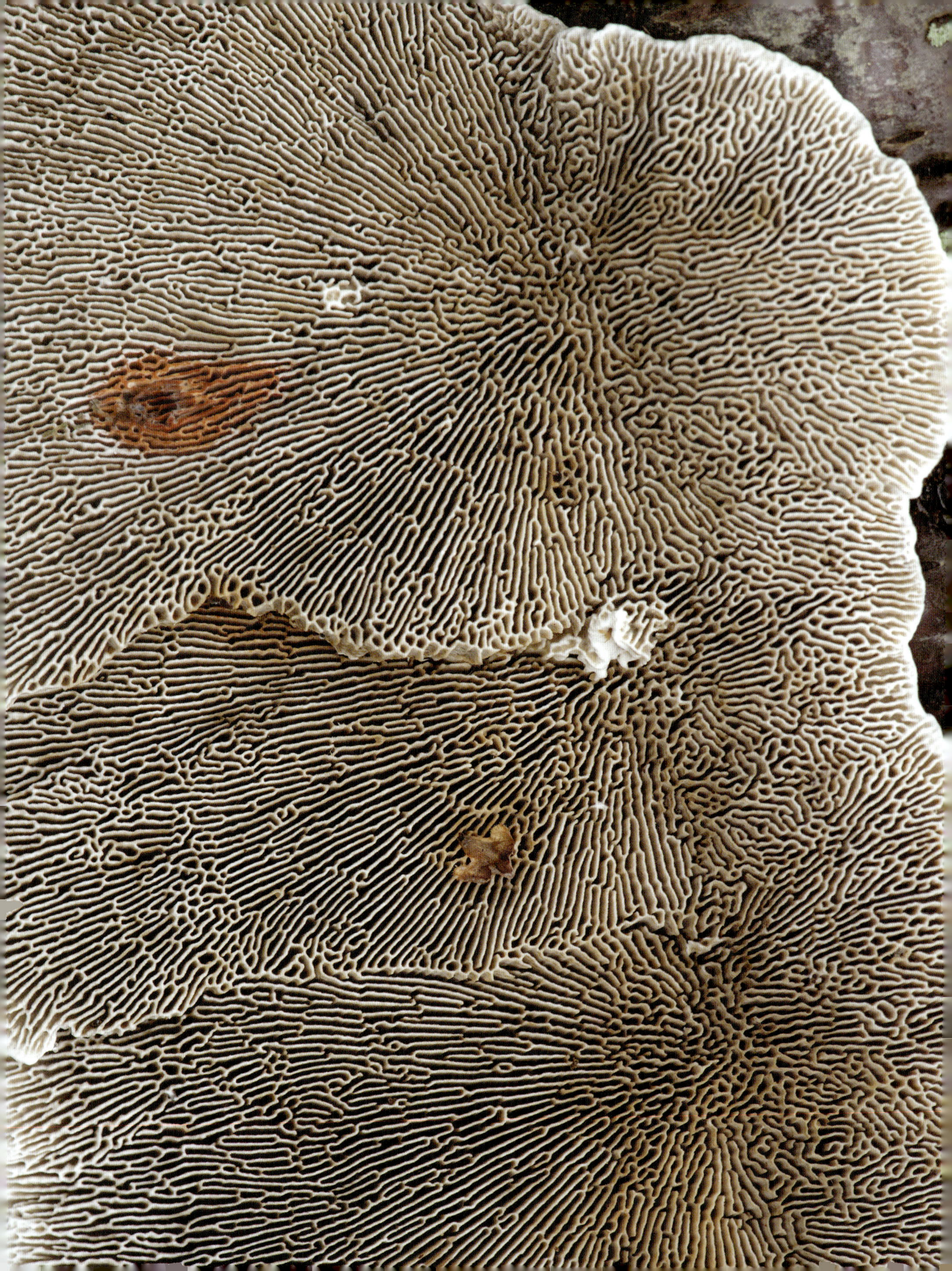

Resources

Chapter 2

Camera conversion companies

Advanced Camera Services (UK) https://advancedcameraservices.co.uk
Life Pixel https://www.lifepixel.com
Kolari Vision https://kolarivision.com
Monochrome Imaging https://www.monochromeimaging.com
Max Max https://MaxMax.com

Chapter 3

A range of filters for UV (and IR) photography including UV transmitting filters is available from UVIROptics.com, including filters for simulating insect vision.

Chapter 6

Triggering systems for high speed flash

Versatrigger
    https://www.versatrigger.co.uk
Cognisys: manufacture triggering systems and a high speed shutter
    https://www.cognisys-inc.com
Plutotrigger.com
The Splash Art triggering system is available from
    www.phototrigger.co.uk

Chapter 9

Sheets of polarizing material are available from Greenweld Optics
    www.greenweld.co.uk

◄ Birch Mazegill Fungus (*Lenzites betulinus*). Close-up shot of underside showing gill pattern. Magnification ×1 in camera. Nikon D810, with 105mm micro Nikkor lens.

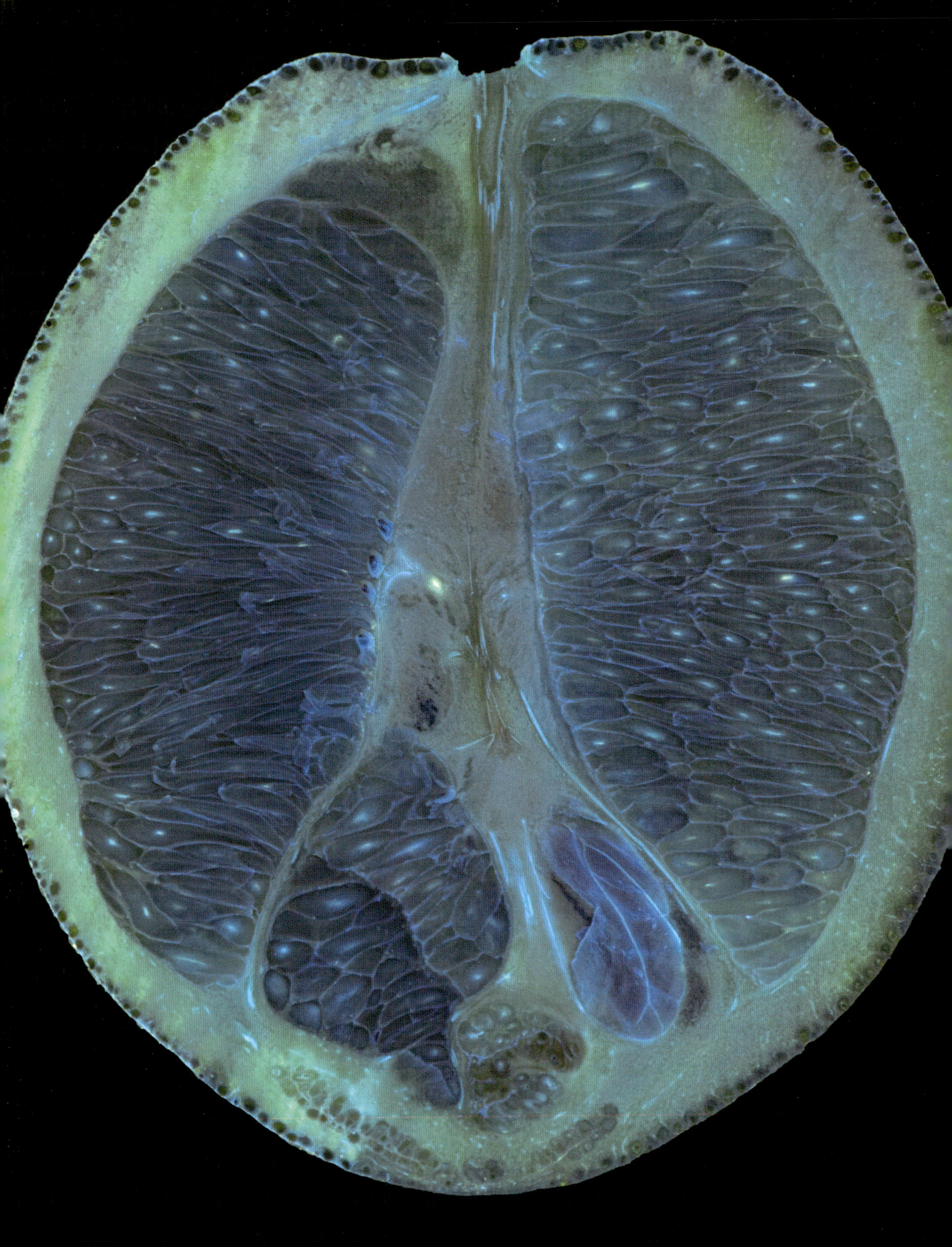

Bibliography

Cremona, Julian *Beyond Extreme Close-Up Photography* (The Crowood Press, 2018)

Cremona, Julian *Extreme Close-Up and Focus Stacking* (The Crowood Press, 2014)

Dalton, Stephen *Borne on the Wind* (Chatto and Windus, 1975). The best collection of images of insects in free flight, shot with film in the 1990s

Dalton, Stephen *Split Second* (J.M Dent, 1983)

Davies, Adrian *Digital Ultraviolet and Infrared Photography* (Focal Press, 2018)

Higgins, Mark *Time-Lapse Photography* (The Crowood Press, 2016)

Interesting websites

A comprehensive gallery of invertebrate species fluorescing in UV light

NickyBay:

https://www.flickr.com/photos/nickadel/sets/72157635395934316/with/13154125093/

High speed insect photography

https://petapixel.com/2010/02/05/photo-grandpa-shoots-with-laser-rigs/

https://www.flickr.com/photos/13084997@N03/sets/72157610450102014/

High speed bat photography

Paul Colley

www.mpcolley.com

UV portraits

Cara Phillips' portfolio of UV portraits can be seen at:

https://www.cara-phillips.com/ultraviolet-beauties/

◀ UV fluorescence image of section through orange. Nikon D850 and 105mm micro Nikkor lens. Approximtely 20 seconds at f/22, light painted with Convoy S2+ UV torch.

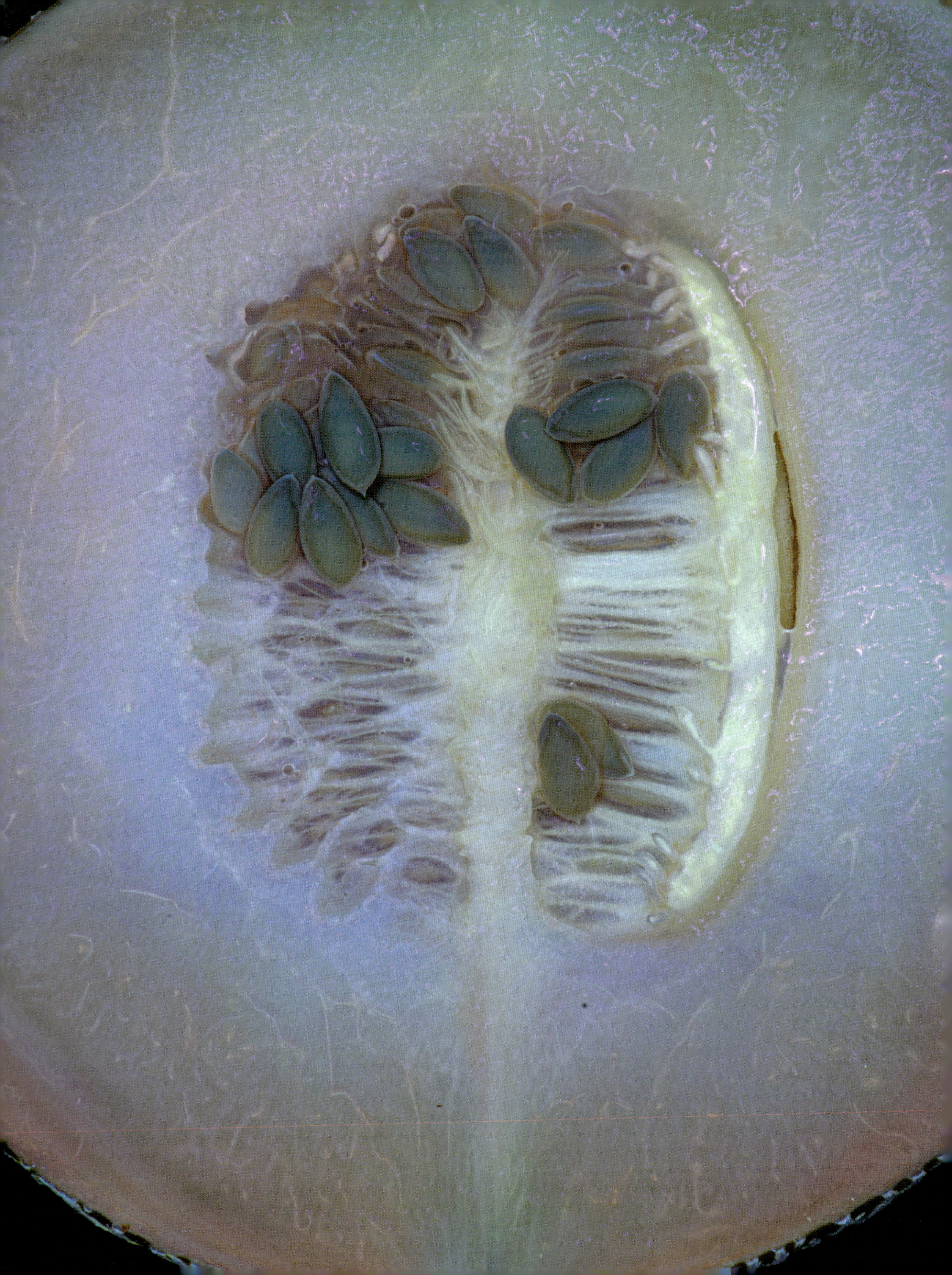

Index

◄ Melon, fluorescing in UV. Nikon D810 and 105mm micro Nikkor lens. Approximately 20 seconds at f/22, light painted with Convoy S2+ UV torch.